D0170536

ALSO BY STEVE NEAL

Rolling on the River: The Best of Steve Neal

Dark Horse: A Biography of Wendell Willkie

McNary of Oregon: A Political Biography

The Eisenhowers: Reluctant Dynasty

Tom McCall: Maverick (with Tom McCall)

They Never Go Back to Pocatello:
Selected Essays of Richard L. Neuberger

ADDITIONAL PRAISE FOR *HARRY AND IKE*

"Like most other Americans, I knew just enough about my grandfather's relationship with Ike to know they didn't like each other. But I never knew why, or whether they had ever really reconciled. With *Harry and Ike*, Steve Neal has opened a new window for me on the lives and relationships of these two revered Americans. And he's done it in a well-researched, beautifully written book that often had me staying up way past my bedtime."

—Clifton Truman Daniel

"Combining the verve of a political journalist and the skills of an accomplished historian, Steve Neal has brought wonderful new insight to a story that Americans thought they knew. In riveting fresh detail, he has untangled a relationship of surprising complexity and shown us twentieth-century giants who were, in spite of pettiness, partisanship, and vanity, above all else admirable men."

—Rudy Abramson, author of *Spanning the Century: The Life of W. Averell Harriman*

"With historical sweep and careful attention to detail, Steve Neal has provided a fascinating examination of the crucial relationship between two of the most important Americans of the twentieth century. . . . This is a book of many virtues. It is balanced and fair and crisply written. While Neal displays a sympathetic understanding of both Harry and Ike, he does not skimp on justified criticism of either man."

—Lou Cannon, author of *President Reagan: The Role of a Lifetime*

"A fair, balanced, and compelling study of two great American presidents. Steve Neal brings both men vividly to life and does justice to his subjects."

—Senator Bob Dole, author of *Great Presidential Wit*

"Steve Neal's *Harry and Ike* is both a fascinating 'inside account' of the postwar relationship of President Harry Truman and General Dwight Eisenhower and a wonderful personal portrayal of these remarkable human beings."

—John Garraty, professor of history, Columbia University, and editor of *American National Biography*

"Writing as a trained historian and an experienced political journalist, Steve Neal splendidly recounts the fascinating story of the tangled relationship between two of this century's most important presidents. . . . This is the best book yet by a talented biographer."

—Alonzo L. Hamby, author of *Man of the People: A Life of Harry S Truman*

"This is a wonderful book about the heart of America. . . . It is a thrill to read about these two men, so ordinary and so extraordinary. Steve Neal makes you proud to be part of their nation."

—Richard Reeves, author of *President Kennedy: Profile of Power* and *President Nixon: Alone in the White House*

"An endlessly fascinating book about two extraordinary figures in American history and the relationship they had with one another during the period both served as president of the United States. Steve Neal sheds new light on that relationship and provides the reader with a deeper understanding of the character and statesmanship of both men. . . . It is an absolute delight."

—Robert V. Remini, National Book Award winner and biographer of Andrew Jackson

"A deeply researched, hugely readable portrait of two very human giants. This is revisionist history at its best."

—Richard Norton Smith, author of *Patriarch: George Washington and the New American Nation*

HARRY AND IKE

THE PARTNERSHIP THAT REMADE THE POSTWAR WORLD

STEVE NEAL

A LISA DREW BOOK

A Touchstone Book
Published by Simon & Schuster
NEW YORK LONDON TORONTO SYDNEY SINGAPORE

Touchstone
Rockefeller Center
1230 Avenue of the Americas
New York, NY 10020

First Touchstone Edition 2002

Touchstone and colophon are registered trademarks of Simon and Schuster, Inc.

For information about special discounts for bulk purchases,
please contact Simon & Schuster Special Sales:
1-800-456-6798 or business@simonandschuster.com

A LISA DREW BOOK is a trademark of Simon & Schuster, Inc.

Design by Colin Joh

Manufactured in the United States of America

3 5 7 9 10 8 6 4 2

The Library of Congress has cataloged the Scribner edition as follows:
Neal, Steve, 1949-
Harry and Ike : the partnership that remade the postwar world / Steve Neal.
p. cm.
Includes bibliographical references and index.
1. Truman, Harry S., 1884–1972. 2. Eisenhower, Dwight D. (Dwight David), 1890–1969. 3. United States—Politics and government—1945–1953. 4. United States—Politics and government—1953–1961. 5. Friendship—United States—Case studies. 6. Presidents—United States—Biography. 7. Generals—United States—Biography. I. Title.
E814 .N43 2001 973.918/092/2 21
2001041108
ISBN 0-684-85355-8
0-7432-2374-8 (Pbk)

For Robert H. Ferrell
and
Elizabeth Safly

Contents

Acknowledgments

As his presidential library neared completion in 1957, Harry S. Truman said that he hoped Dwight D. Eisenhower would "set up a library at Abilene." At this time the erstwhile friends had not spoken in more than four years. But Truman wanted the Midwest to be a center for the study of the presidency and recognized that his successor could be an important ally in this effort.

In giving his papers to the nation, Truman said, "I think this is a precedent for a public servant returning all these things on the theory that, if he had not been President, they would not have been his property." Eisenhower, who shared Truman's commitment to history, followed his predecessor's lead in leaving his papers for posterity. I am most indebted to the subjects of this book for granting public access to their private letters, diaries, and other papers. Without their gifts to the American people, this book could not have been written.

I am appreciative to John S. D. Eisenhower and Clifton Truman Daniel. It was not long after Truman's death when I first interviewed Eisenhower's son. "There was an awful lot of misunderstanding between Dad and Mr. Truman," said John, who was present for their first meeting in June 1945. John told me that much of what had been written about the Ike-Truman feud was less than accurate. I've gotten to know Clifton more recently. A writer of considerable talent who inherited his grandfather's vitality and wry sense of humor, Clifton is the director of public affairs for Harry S. Truman College in Chicago. President Truman once noted that John Eisenhower was a credit to his family. So is Clifton Truman Daniel.

The staffs of the Harry S. Truman Library in Independence, Missouri, and the Dwight D. Eisenhower Library in Abilene, Kansas, were most helpful. I am most indebted to the HST Library's reference librarian Elizabeth Safly, who grew up in Independence and knows more than anyone about the Truman era. She makes the past come alive and provided me with helpful guidance and good company at every phase of this project. The archivists Dennis Bilger and Randy Sowell in Independence and Herbert Pankratz in Abilene shared their vast knowledge of the manuscript collections and made them more accessible to this writer. I want to thank Anita M. Smith of the Truman Library for making available the transcripts of oral history interviews. Susan McNeil-Marshall and Janet Widdel of the Hinsdale Public Library provided much assistance in tracking down books and documents and obtaining oral history transcripts through interlibrary loans. Pauline Testerman at the HST Library and the Eisenhower Library's Kathleen A. Struss provided most of the photographs for this book.

I should like to thank the Harry S. Truman Library Institute, which has generously supported this project. Thanks to Larry Hackman, director of the Truman Library and president of the Truman Library Institute for his encouragement.

This is a better book because of Lisa Drew's deft and judicious editing. Like the author, she is a product of the Truman-Eisenhower era. Her keen understanding of politics and fresh insights into this period have improved this volume. This book is our third collaboration and another is in the works. I enjoy working for her. Jake Klisivitch has also been most helpful. I appreciate the thoughtful copyediting of John Paul Jones.

Several friends have read the manuscript and offered useful suggestions. Robert H. Ferrell, Distinguished Professor of History Emeritus at Indiana University and author of a dozen books about Truman including an acclaimed biography, provided useful advice and thoughtful criticism. Alonzo L. Hamby, Distinguished Professor of History at Ohio University, whose *Man of the People* is a model of political biography, shared his wise counsel and vast knowledge of the Truman era. Both of these Truman biographers and former Senator Paul Simon wrote recommendations in support of my research grant application. Wayne W. Whalen, whose insights and observations were most helpful, and Robert W. Merry, whose biography of the Alsop brothers is among my favorite books, provided invaluable assistance.

My longtime friend Rudy Abramson, W. Averell Harriman's biographer, encouraged me to undertake this project and shared his research files with me. It is through Rudy that I got to know Robert J. Donovan, who sets the standard for the journalist as historian. As a White House correspondent, Donovan covered the subjects of this book and later wrote histories of their administrations. Through my conversations with Abramson and Donovan, I began thinking about *Harry and Ike* as a potential book.

I am grateful to Gerard McCauley, who represented me for twenty-four years and negotiated the contract for this book.

Michael Cooke, editor in chief of the *Chicago Sun-Times*, and John

Cruickshank, vice president of editorial, have encouraged me to do this book. My boss Steve Huntley, the editorial page editor, allowed me to have time when I needed it for this project. Steve also read the manuscript and generously shared his thoughts. Charlotte Ulmanis of the editorial department was most helpful. Thanks also to the *Sun-Times* reference staff of the late Terri Golembiewski, Judith Halper, Ziggy Ulmanis, Herb Ballard, Virginia Davis, Dale McCullough, Ron Theel, and Ted White.

As always, I owe the largest debt to my wife, Susan, and our daughters, Erin and Shannon.

CHAPTER 1

Coming Home

On June 18, 1945, Harry S. Truman led a grateful nation in welcoming home Dwight D. Eisenhower. It would be the first meeting between the new president of the United States and the supreme commander of the Allied forces that defeated Nazi Germany. Truman had sent his presidential aircraft, the Douglas C-54 known as the "Sacred Cow," to pick up General Ike in Bermuda and bring him back to National Airport.[1] As the huge transport plane approached the Midatlantic coast, Eisenhower was met by more than thirty fighters and bombers, which flew in formation and escorted his plane to the runway on the south bank of the Potomac. "I don't think we could do too much to show our appreciation of General Eisenhower," Truman told the White House press corps.

On this Monday in a peacetime June, the first in nearly six years, more than one million men and women greeted Eisenhower as a conquering hero. Truman gave federal workers special permission to attend Ike's homecoming. Despite the oppressive heat and humidity, the crowd that turned out was larger and more enthusiastic than the throngs that had met Charles A. Lindbergh after his 1927 flight to Paris or General John J. Pershing at the end of World War I. "Oh, God, it's swell to be back," Eisenhower declared as he set foot on American soil.[2]

Truman, the first former soldier since Theodore Roosevelt to serve in the presidency, was a keen student of warfare. He had once dreamed of attending West Point but was ineligible because of poor eyesight. Eisenhower, a 1915 graduate of the U.S. Military Academy, had lived Truman's dream. But Truman felt no envy, only admiration for the man who had led history's greatest invasion. "All of us owe to you and your men of many nations a debt beyond appraisal," Truman wrote in his first letter to Eisenhower. "I send also my personal appreciation of the superb leadership shown by you and your commanders in directing the valiant legions to this historic victory."[3]

If Truman had gotten his wish for a military career, he might have been among Ike's lieutenants. In 1940, as a U.S. senator, he approached General George C. Marshall, the army's chief of staff. Following the enactment of the country's first peacetime draft, Truman volunteered to go on active duty. "General, I would very much like to have a chance to work in this war as a field artillery colonel," Truman said. He was then fifty-six years old. "You're too damned old," Marshall replied. "You'd better stay home and work in the Senate."[4]

Truman, who commanded an artillery unit in World War I, knew firsthand the horrors of the battlefield. During the Meuse-Argonne offensive, in which twenty-six thousand Americans died, Truman showed coolness under fire and twice led his battery in destroying enemy artillery units. Eisenhower felt left behind. Despite repeated attempts to get into combat, Eisenhower was kept on the home front as an instructor at training camps. When he finally got orders to lead a tank battalion on the western front, his elation was short-lived. His combat orders were cancelled and he was put in charge of a tank corps training center in Gettysburg. "I was mad, disappointed, and resented the fact that the war had passed me by," he wrote half a century later. Eisenhower was kept home for doing his job too well.[5]

Truman and Eisenhower, who were relatively unknown at the beginning of the 1940s, were elevated to power and prominence by Franklin D. Roosevelt. It was FDR who made the surprise selection of Eisenhower over Marshall in December of 1943 as supreme commander of the Allied Expeditionary Forces. Eight months later, Truman was drafted for the vice presidency when FDR bowed to pressure from party leaders and agreed to dump Henry A. Wallace from the 1944 Democratic ticket. Eisenhower, who had never voted in an election, quietly supported FDR's bid for a fourth term.

Among the reasons that FDR selected Eisenhower and then Truman for their respective roles was that neither acted like men of destiny. Roosevelt was mistrustful of men who were too eager or coveted his job. Truman and Eisenhower were men of intelligence who were ambitious without being threatening. Eisenhower was FDR's favorite field general and Truman was the man that Roosevelt put in place to be a heartbeat away from the presidency. Roosevelt knew their measure. When FDR died on April 12 with the Allies battering Germany, Eisenhower had no idea what to expect from the new commander in chief. "It seemed to us, from the international viewpoint, to be a most critical time to be forced to change national leaders," Eisenhower wrote. "We went to bed depressed and sad."[6]

As Roosevelt's successor, Truman backed Eisenhower's strategy for achieving the quickest military victory in Germany. That meant striking for the center of Germany and leaving Berlin for the Soviet army. Winston Churchill sought to persuade Eisenhower to take Berlin. But the supreme commander did not think it was worth a hundred thousand American casualties. Soviet losses would be three times that. Truman, like Roosevelt, trusted Eisenhower's judgment in the field.

On May 8, Truman's sixty-first birthday, Eisenhower delivered the Allied victory. He would later tell the president it was "especially significant" that V-E Day coincided with his birthday "in view of the firm course you have established for securing the peace toward which our military victory was directed."[7]

Though Eisenhower had made decisions that had changed the course of modern history and was the most popular man in America, he did not confuse public esteem with political power. "My policy-making job ended when the last shot was fired. I am now pro consul for my government in a region where I am going to do what I am told," he told reporters on the eve of his first meeting with Truman.[8]

When General Ike made his way through the House chamber to address a joint session of Congress, he cut short the crowd's roar after two minutes by raising his hand and asking for quiet. "My imagination cannot picture a more dramatic moment than this in the life of an American," he began. "I stand here in the presence of the elected federal lawmakers of our great republic, the very core of our American political life and a symbol of those things that we call the American heritage. . . . I am summoned before you as the representative—the commander of those three million American men and women, to whom you desire to pay America's tribute for military victory. In humble realization that they, who earned your commendation, should properly be here to receive it, I am nevertheless proud and honored to serve as your agent in conveying it to them." He spoke with emotion for the wounded and for the dead, noting that Americans had served with honor and valor on battlefields of Africa and Europe "over which armies have been fighting for two thousand years of recorded history. None of these battlefields has seen a more worthy soldier than the trained American. . . . You have read many reports of his individual exploits, but not one-tenth of them ever has been or ever will be told. Any one of them is sufficient to fill a true American with emotion—with an intense pride of his countrymen."

Eisenhower paid tribute to FDR and Churchill for leading the grand alliance. "Because no word of mine could add anything to your appreciation of the man who, until his tragic death, led America in war," he said of Roosevelt, "I will say nothing other than from his strength and indomitable spirit I drew constant support and confidence in the solution of my own problems."

In looking ahead, Eisenhower said that with Germany defeated, there was still another menace to America's freedom, in the Far East, that remained to be crushed. "Though we dream of return to our loved ones, we are ready, as we have always been, to do our duty to our country, no matter what it may be. In this spirit, we renew our pledge of service to Commander in Chief, President Truman, under whose strong leadership we know that final victory is certain."[9]

That afternoon, on the South Lawn of the White House, Truman pinned an oak leaf cluster on Eisenhower in lieu of his third Distinguished Service Medal. Mamie Eisenhower, wearing a black dress, pearl necklace, and a black hat with flowers, stood proudly at Truman's left as he made the presentation. In congratulating Eisenhower, Truman told him that he would rather have the medal than the presidency.[10]

Truman hosted a stag dinner for Eisenhower that night at the White House. On this night of celebration, there were no speeches. Among those sitting at the table with Truman and Eisenhower were General Marshall, Secretary of War Henry L. Stimson, Chief Justice Harlan Fiske Stone, and Treasury Secretary Henry Morgenthau. "It had been General Ike's first opportunity to visit with the new President, although he had seen him briefly that afternoon," Eisenhower's naval aide Harry C. Butcher wrote in his diary. "What he saw and heard, he liked."[11]

The feeling was mutual. Before his first meeting with Eisenhower, Truman had already placed him on the short list of soldiers that he most admired and contrasted him with the men on horseback that he held in contempt. At their first meeting, Truman was even more impressed with Ike's warmth and humanity. "Eisenhower's party was a grand success. I pinned a medal on him in the afternoon," Truman wrote his wife, Bess, who was back home in Independence, Missouri. "He is a nice fellow and a good man. He's doing a whale of a job. They are running him for president, which is o.k. with me. I'd turn it over to him now if I could."[12]

CHAPTER 2

"From the Very Heart of America"

Truman and Eisenhower, who were destined to change the postwar world, grew up one hundred fifty miles apart in the center of the United States. Their hometowns of Independence, Missouri, and Abilene, Kansas, were rich in history and had contributed significantly to the growth of the Old West. Truman's Independence was the beginning of the frontier, the jumping-off place for the Oregon Trail and the eastern terminus of the Santa Fe Trail. Eisenhower's Abilene was the end of the Chisholm Trail, where more than two million Texas longhorns were driven north between 1867 and 1872 for shipment by rail to Kansas City. It was tough country. Earlier attempts by Texas cattlemen to reach northern markets had met resistance from the settlers of western Missouri and eastern Kansas. It was the land of Wild Bill Hickok and Jesse James.

The journalist Richard Rovere, who covered Truman and Eisenhower, noted that they had more in common with each other than with the seven men who preceded them in the White House. "Their backgrounds are extraordinarily similar. They are products of middle-class families that lived close to the edge of poverty and close to one another," Rovere wrote in *The New Yorker.* "Both are men of simple integrity and personal honor. Both have a kind of standard American personality."[1]

The ascendancy of Truman and Eisenhower did much to end isolationism. Before World War II, a majority of Americans favored a policy of noninvolvement in world affairs. The isolationists were most dominant in the Midwest and Great Plains states. In many ways, the debate over America's role in the world was a conflict between the small businessmen and working people of the Midwest and the Anglo-Saxon elite of the Eastern Establishment. The most bitter critics of internationalism were Main Street conservatives and Western populists who were distrustful of Wall Street and the Council on Foreign Relations. It mattered that Truman and Eisenhower were from the middle of America and yet burned with conviction about the nation's global responsibility.

"This country here, this section, has been called the heart of isolationism," Eisenhower told a Kansas City audience in the hundreds of thousands in June of 1945. "I do not believe it. No intelligent man can be an isolationist, and there is no higher level of education anywhere in the world than in the Midwest. The United States with its great strength and its prosperity is forced, even if unwillingly, into a position of world leadership."

Then Eisenhower noted the importance of Truman's rise to prominence. "Missouri, through its great son, President Truman, has become a factor in world leadership—call it enlightened statesmanship—that will be of the most tremendous importance to the whole world. His background is here; he is one of you; he will carry to his task the qualities of this great Midwest section. I believe he could carry no better equipment."[2]

Eisenhower felt the same way about his midwestern roots. "I am not a native of this land," he told a cheering throng in London after V-E Day. "I come from the very heart of America." On June 22, 1945, he returned to Abilene and was met by a crowd of twenty thousand, which was four times the town's population. "I come here first to thank you," he said, "to say that the proudest thing that I can claim is that I am from Abilene."[3]

The name Abilene, which means "city from the plains," was chosen from the Bible by Sylvia Hersey, the wife of the man who founded the town in 1857 as a stagecoach stop. Jesse Chisholm, a Texas cattleman of Cherokee ancestry, pushed the long trail from San Antonio north and east to the Red River, across Oklahoma to Abilene in 1867. Three generations of the Eisenhower family moved to Abilene in 1878 from Central Pennsylvania with other members of their Mennonite sect, the River Brethren.

Since their emigration from Germany to the United States in November of 1741, most of the Eisenhowers had been farmers. But David, the father of the man who would become supreme Allied commander, wanted a different life and left Abilene to study engineering at Lane University, a school run by the River Brethren in Lecompton, Kansas. In 1885, he married another student, Ida Stover, and returned to Abilene. Jacob Eisenhower, David's father, gave the young couple 160 acres of farmland and three thousand dollars.

With this money and by taking out a mortgage on the farm, David opened a general store in the village of Hope, twenty-eight miles south of Abilene. For a brief time the business did well. But in the fall of 1888, customers who had bought on credit were unable to pay their bills when wheat prices dropped sharply. The Eisenhowers lost everything. Truman's father was also a business failure. In 1901, John Truman invested all his family's assets into wheat futures and lost it all. He was forced to sell the family farm and their home in Independence and to take a job as a night watchman. This financial setback made it impossible for Harry Truman to get a college education.

In an effort to make a fresh start, David moved four hundred miles to Denison, Texas, and took a ten-dollar-a-week job working for the Cotton Belt Railroad. Ida, pregnant with a second child, stayed in Kansas. Their first son, Arthur, was born in 1886; and the second, Edgar, was born in January of 1889. The family was then reunited in Texas.

A third son, David Dwight, was born in Denison on October 14, 1890 in the family's tiny house by the railroad tracks. While growing up he was called Dwight by parents and relatives to avoid confusion with his father. When he applied to the U.S. Military Academy, it was as Dwight David Eisenhower. The Eisenhowers moved back to Abilene in 1891 when David took a job as a mechanic for the Belle Springs creamery, which was organized by the River Brethren. His salary was less than fifty dollars a month.

In 1898, the Eisenhowers moved into a two-story white frame house on South Fourth Street that was on a three-acre lot that provided a family garden. Though it was the largest home that the family lived in, it was crowded. After Dwight, David and Ida had four more sons: Roy born in 1892; Paul born in 1894, who died in infancy; Earl born in 1898; and Milton in 1899. "I don't know how my mother jammed us all in," Dwight recalled years later. By his calculations, his boyhood home had 818 square feet for a household of eight. Eisenhower said that his office in the Pentagon when he was army chief of staff was larger than the family's home in Abilene. Each of the Eisenhower sons grew produce and would sell their vegetables out of a red wagon. They got to keep their earnings. "We were poor but didn't know it," Eisenhower said of his childhood in a 1952 campaign speech.[4]

Like the Eisenhowers, the Trumans were farm people. Both of President Truman's grandfathers were from Kentucky and settled in western Missouri during the 1840s. His maternal grandfather, Solomon Young, became a successful farmer and then led wagon trains to California, Utah, and New Mexico. Anderson Shipp Truman, Harry's other grandfather, bought a two-hundred-acre farm near Westport Landing and also worked four years as director of a one-room schoolhouse. The Youngs and Trumans were devout Baptists with strong moral values.

Harry S. Truman was born on May 8, 1884 in Lamar, Missouri, to John Anderson Truman and the former Martha Ellen Young. John, who traded horses and mules for a living, was so excited about his son's birth that he nailed a mule shoe over the front door. The young Harry strove to please his father, a strict disciplinarian whom he described in a 1963 interview as "the hardest-working man that ever lived." It was from his father that Truman inherited a strong work ethic and the plain-spoken candor. Truman was also greatly influenced by his mother, who got her son to take piano lessons and to become an avid reader. Martha Ellen was largely responsible for her family's move from the farm near Grandview into Independence in the summer of 1890. Her motivation was that Independence had better schools and she believed that nothing was more important for her children than a good education. In an era when it was rare for women to attend college, Martha Ellen Young and Ida Stover were notable exceptions. Martha Ellen had studied music and art at a Baptist college in Lexington, Missouri.[5]

Independence, a town of tree-lined streets, was founded in 1827 as a trading center near a bend of the Missouri River. Settlers built a log cabin that at the time was the westernmost courthouse in the United States. As the departure point for the Santa Fe and Oregon trails, Independence prospered from the expansion of the West. The California gold rush helped the local economy. By 1849, Independence had twenty wagon and blacksmith shops.

Some of the Civil War's bloodiest fighting took place in western Missouri. Neither of Truman's grandfathers fought in the war, but two uncles served in the Confederate cavalry brigade led by General Joseph Orville Shelby. In a 1945 *Life* magazine photo essay, "Harry Truman's Missouri," Alfred Eisenstadt showed that the tallest memorial in Independence was the Confederate monument in Woodlawn Cemetery. Next to this image, Eisenstadt included a photograph of the unmarked graves of fifteen Union soldiers inside the square of an unpainted fence on a farm near Independence.[6]

While growing up, Truman and Eisenhower got to know veterans of the Civil War. The Grand Army of the Republic marched in Abilene during Eisenhower's youth. Eisenhower's grandfather Jacob, a minister in the River Brethren, opposed the war but admired Abraham Lincoln, for whom he named one of his sons. Truman and Eisenhower, like so many of their generation, viewed Lincoln and Lee as heroic figures.[7]

Though Truman later recalled his childhood with nostalgia, it was not without adversity. The second oldest of three children, Harry was five years old when his family settled in Independence. Truman had a brother, John Vivian, and sister, Mary Jane.

Truman in 1890 began wearing thick eyeglasses that made him different from his classmates. In his high school graduation photograph, he was the only member of his class with spectacles. Truman was so fearful of breaking his glasses that he avoided playing sports and restricted other outdoor activities. "He was a quiet, rather shy boy," recalled the class valedictorian, Charles G. Ross. "The mothers of the town knew him for the nice boy that he was. He was never in any scrapes. That he didn't lack any spunk, however, was shown when he braved the jeers of his fellows to go regularly to his music teacher."[8]

Truman and Eisenhower showed resolve in overcoming serious illness during their early years. At the age of ten, Truman had diphtheria and became paralyzed to the extent that he had to be lifted at home and was wheeled by his mother in a baby carriage. Young Harry made a complete recovery. Eisenhower had to take a fifth year of high school because of the time he missed when an infection in one of his legs threatened his life. The family doctor recommended amputation, but the youth said that he would rather die. Like Truman, Eisenhower made a full recovery.[9]

An outstanding athlete, Eisenhower resisted the doctor to save his sports career as well as his leg. Eisenhower first emerged as a leader in his Abilene school days. "He was on the right side of everything and a regular fellow," John "Six" McDonnell said of Eisenhower. "He had all the guts in the world, and the ability to dig things out for himself in his studies."[10]

Truman and Eisenhower, though eight years apart in their high school graduations, shared common interests. Both read widely in history and were most intrigued by studies of warfare. "My first reading love was ancient history. At an early age, I developed an interest in the human record and I became particularly fond of Greek and Roman accounts," Eisenhower wrote more than half a century later. "These subjects were so engrossing that I frequently was guilty of neglecting all others."[11]

Eisenhower's favorite military leader and historical figure was Hannibal. What Ike found noteworthy was that every surviving account of the Carthaginian general was written by his enemies, yet they all acknowledged his strategic brilliance. Truman shared Eisenhower's fascination with the military commander. "I think that the greatest general in all history is Hannibal," Truman said in 1951. "The only records we have of Hannibal have been written by his enemies. There is no Carthaginian history because Carthage was completely destroyed. Everything we know about him is told to us by the Romans. Despite that, he still stands out as the greatest of them all."[12]

While growing up in the heartland, Truman and Eisenhower were inspired to use history to see the far horizons. "The only thing new in the world is the history you don't know," Truman said in 1951. Though he was exaggerating in making the claim to have read every book in the Independence library, there is no doubt that he had a passion for history and that his reading of Plutarch and other ancient scholars did much to help shape his political ideals.[13]

Truman, the career politician, was born into a family with a tradition of political involvement. His father rode a horse in Democratic torchlight parades and flew a flag over the family's house when Grover Cleveland recaptured the White House in 1892. As a sixteen-year-old, Truman got to attend the 1900 Democratic National Convention in Kansas City with his father and both cheered William Jennings Bryan's second nomination for the presidency.[14]

Eisenhower, the career soldier, gave his first political speech more than a dozen years before Truman was first elected to office. In 1909, at the age of nineteen, Eisenhower publicly declared his preference as a Democrat and gained public attention for addressing the annual meeting of the Dickinson County Young Men's Democratic Club.

"The young man just starting in politics is taking a very important step in life and one which to all probability will determine his political standing forever," Eisenhower said. "He will naturally line up with one of the two great parties and the chances are he will remain a life member of that party. . . . For a man, after voting the straight party ticket, seldom changes from one side to the other." Eisenhower noted that the Republican party was split into liberal and conservative factions, "yet they refuse to join any other party, and at the election vote for the Republican candidates. Thus, in reality a man's party becomes a part of him as truly as he becomes a part of it, and he simply will not leave it."

Eisenhower, sounding very much like Truman in his later political career, criticized Republicans as the party of special interests and the power elite. In stark contrast, Eisenhower hailed Democrats as the party of the people, favorably noting their support of low tariffs and popular election of senators. When Eisenhower sought the presidency in 1952, he asserted that twenty years of Democratic administrations was too long. In his 1909 speech, Eisenhower criticized half a century of Republican domination. "The young recruit notices, that because one party has been in power for fifty years, with only two brief interruptions, many evils have sprung up in the machinery of the government, which a change in policy for a time would at least remedy if not blot them out." It would be forty-three years before he delivered his next political speech.[15]

A decade before Eisenhower entered West Point, it was Truman who hoped for a career as an army officer. Truman's ambition was to attend the U.S. Military Academy or the Naval Academy. Margaret Phelps, Truman's history teacher, helped him prepare for the service academy exams. But Truman recalled that he "failed physically on account of my short sight" at the army recruiting station in Kansas City. He memorized the visual chart and joined the National Guard in 1905.[16]

After graduation from high school in 1909, he became interested in a possible naval career. Edward "Swede" Hazlett, a high school classmate, had been nominated for Annapolis and proposed that Ike join him. Eisenhower wrote Senator Joseph L. Bristow in August of 1910: "I would very much like to enter the school at Annapolis or the one at West Point. In order to do this, I must have an appointment to one of these places and so I am writing you in order to secure the same."[17]

Eisenhower scored first among Annapolis applicants and second among West Points candidates in the competitive examinations held in Topeka. When the applicant who placed first at West Point was unable to accept Bristow's appointment, Eisenhower was selected by Bristow for West Point. Though Annapolis had been his first choice, he was grateful to have this opportunity for a free education and military career. The young man from Abilene would be stationed on four continents in the next two decades.

CHAPTER 3

Parallel Lives

Harry S. Truman and Dwight D. Eisenhower grew up in an age of optimism when the United States was coming into its own as an industrial giant and great power. Yet neither Truman nor Eisenhower could have imagined in their wildest dreams what large roles they were destined to play in the American century. Compared with FDR, who was a vice-presidential nominee at thirty-eight or JFK who was a senator at thirty-five and president of the United States at forty-three, Truman and Ike were late bloomers. Both endured adversities that might have left them frustrated but in their cases made them more determined to succeed.

Truman's first job out of high school was as the timekeeper for a contractor building a new double track for the Santa Fe Railroad. He found more steady employment at a leading Kansas City bank, where he began as a clerk and was promoted to bookkeeper. In three years his salary went from $35 to $125 a month and he seemed headed for a successful banking career. He lived for a while in the same boarding house as Ike's brother Arthur, who also worked for a bank. Truman recalled that Arthur did not know how to turn on a gas jet when he first came to the boardinghouse.[1]

In the middle of 1906, at twenty-two, Truman was summoned by his father to give up his job and help out on the family farm in Grandview. "It was always my job to plant the corn, sow the wheat and run the binder to cut the wheat and the oats," Truman recalled. "I usually pitched hay to my father on the stack also. My father hated a crooked corn row or a skipped place in a wheat field." After his father's death in 1914, he managed the six-hundred-acre farm. This work made him unique among American presidents. Lincoln and Grant had briefly worked on farms but their respective occupations were lawyer/politician and soldier. Truman was a working farmer and never forgot it. His mother once noted, "It was on the farm that Harry got his common sense. He didn't get it in town."[2]

If Truman was of the farm, Eisenhower was molded by West Point. His class of 1915, which produced fifty-nine generals, would become known as "the class the stars fell on." It was as a football halfback that he first achieved distinction. *The New York Times* described him as "one of the more promising backs in Eastern football" after Eisenhower led Army to a 19-0 win over Rutgers. But his sports career was cut short by a knee injury. Eisenhower's academic record was undistinguished. He graduated sixty-first in a class of 104 and stood ninety-fifth in conduct. The future president of the United States later attributed his long list of demerits to "a lack of motivation in almost everything other than athletics." But he learned much about his profession and made lifelong friendships in his four years at the U.S. Military Academy.[3]

Eisenhower's first assignment was to the Nineteenth Infantry regiment at Fort Sam Houston, Texas. It was there that he met Mamie Geneva Doud, an attractive, dark-haired young woman whose parents wintered in San Antonio. Eisenhower had an engagement ring made for her that was a duplicate of his West Point class ring. As the daughter of a packing house owner, she came from a background of wealth and comfort. When he asked her father for permission to marry, John Sheldon Doud told him not to expect a sudden advance in income. Eisenhower was advised that Mamie would be on her own. Eisenhower noted that he would soon be transferring into the aviation section of the army and that his income would be doubled. Doud vowed to block the marriage if he became a fighter pilot. Ike turned down the transfer and chose marriage over flight wings. He married Mamie in Denver on July 1, 1916.[4]

Not unlike Eisenhower, Truman married a woman from a more prosperous background. Truman met Bess Wallace when they were in grammar school and courted her from 1910 until their marriage in June of 1919. Like the Eisenhowers, the Trumans would celebrate half a century of marriage and have an additional three years together.

If Truman and Eisenhower had much in common, so did their wives. Like Mamie Doud, Bess Wallace grew up in a family that had financial security and social status. Her grandfather had owned a milling company that produced Queen of the Pantry flour, which sold briskly in the Midwest and South. Both women attended finishing schools for girls instead of college. As young women, Bess and Mamie coped with tragedies. More than a decade before her marriage, Bess Wallace's world shattered when her father shot and killed himself. Margaret Truman said that her mother never fully recovered from this painful loss. For Ike and Mamie, the death of their first son, three-year-old David Dwight to scarlet fever in 1921, was a tragedy that they could never forget. For the rest of his life, he would send flowers to Mamie on their son's birthday. A second son, John Sheldon Doud, was born in 1922. The Trumans had only one child, Margaret, born in 1924. The children would be young adults by the time their fathers had gained national prominence.[5]

Truman and Eisenhower were young officers called to play different roles in World War I. Only half of the four million soldiers in the U.S. Army made it to Europe and only half of these troops were in combat. Truman and Eisenhower both wanted to be in the thick of the fighting. As fate would have it, Truman the citizen soldier got to the western front as Eisenhower the professional soldier trained others on the home front. When the United States went to war in 1917, Eisenhower was an instructor at an officer training camp in Georgia. Later that year he was transferred to Fort Leavenworth. From there he went to Camp Meade and organized the Sixty-fifth Engineer Battalion. Ike trained tank units for combat and in the winter of 1917–1918 was elated at receiving orders that he would be going to France as commander of a tank battalion. Much to his disappointment, his orders were changed and he was placed in command of the Tank Training Center at Camp Colt near Gettysburg. He had ten thousand men under his command but not a single tank. Eisenhower improvised with flatbed trucks during maneuvers until he finally obtained three small French tanks. Under his leadership, he transformed the camp into the army's training center for the new mobile warfare. He was promoted to the wartime rank of major in June and to lieutenant colonel on October 14, his twenty-eighth birthday. That fall he finally got his wish and was ordered to command a tank unit in France. But the Armistice was signed before he was scheduled to depart.

"I suppose we'll spend the rest of our lives explaining why we didn't get into this war," he lamented to another officer. "From now on, I am cutting myself a swath and will make up for this."[6]

Truman, who acknowledged that he had been "afraid of a gun and would rather run than fight," would show courage under fire and would first realize his potential for leadership as an artillery captain in what was then history's greatest war. It is doubtful that Truman would have ever been president of the United States if he had missed this experience. "My whole political career is based upon my war service and war associates," he said years later.

When America went to war in April of 1917, Truman promptly joined the army. "I was stirred in heart and soul by the war messages of Woodrow Wilson," he recalled, "and I thought I ought to go."

Truman, who would have been content with the rank of sergeant, was elected as a first lieutenant after he had helped to organize several batteries into what became the 129th Field Artillery Regiment of the Thirty-fifth Division. In September of 1917 the regiment was assigned to Camp Doniphan at Fort Sill, Oklahoma. "My duties really piled up after we arrived at camp," he recalled. "Not only was it expected of me to do regular duty as a first lieutenant in Battery F but the colonel made me regimental canteen officer." Truman had barbers assigned to the canteen and even set up a tailor shop. In April of 1918, as he departed for Europe from New York, he learned of his promotion to captain by reading it in *The New York Times.* "There we were watching New York's skyline diminish, and wondering if we'd be heroes or corpses," he wrote years later. "Most of us got by without being either."

That summer, he took command of Battery D, a group of German-American and Irish-American Catholics from Kansas City that had gained a reputation as the most unruly battery in the regiment. The hard-boiled men of Truman's battery had broken four previous commanders. In his first comments to his unit, he stated that it was their responsibility to get along with him, not the other way around. "You boys get along with me and I'll bring you all back," he declared.

Truman's men fought in the battle of the Meuse-Argonne. More than fifty thousand Americans were killed on the western front. None of those casualties was from Battery D. Truman stood up for his men. When one of his sergeants twisted his ankle, Truman let him ride on his horse. The colonel scolded Truman, for only officers were supposed to be on horseback. He ignored the order to remove the sergeant from the horse. This incident was among the reasons that Truman's men held him in such esteem and would remember him with warmth as Captain Harry.[7]

At the outbreak of the war, Truman had been a Missouri farmer who had never ventured beyond the Midwest but for an excursion to Texas. He had shown courage and leadership on the battlefield and fired his artillery until the war ended. "The great drive has taken place and I had a part in it, a very small one, but nevertheless a part," Harry wrote Bess during the Meuse-Argonne offensive. " I shot out a German battery, shot his big observation post, and ruined another Battery when it was moving down the road. . . . I brought my battery forward and never lost a horse nor a man."[8]

Across the street from Hotel Crillon in Paris, Truman was among a group of American soldiers that watched President Wilson on his arrival for the peace conference. This would be the only encounter between the American leaders who presided over the Allied victories in World War I and World War II. Truman was discharged two days before his thirty-fifth birthday. Eisenhower, who was twenty-eight and a lieutenant colonel when the war ended, reverted to the rank of captain in June of 1920 but was promoted a month later to major. He would hold this rank for sixteen years.

For Truman and Eisenhower, the 1920s were the crucial decade in their respective paths to power. Eisenhower became known during these years as one of the army's rising stars. Truman began his political career and turned out to be an effective administrator and one of the Kansas City area's strongest vote-getters.

Eisenhower kept on learning about warfare. In 1922 he went to Panama as an assistant to General Fox Conner, commander of the Twentieth Infantry Brigade and one of the brightest American strategists of the Great War. Conner told him that another world war would be inevitable because the Allied leaders had been harsh in their treatment of Germany. Eisenhower said that his three years with Conner were "sort of a graduate school in military affairs and the humanities." In a 1962 oral history interview, he said of Conner: "I would think that more than any other one—outside of my parents—no one influenced me as much. Probably because he made the study of military things, both history and the current, he made them fun. He didn't insist that you just handle things as a matter of rote."[9]

It was on Conner's recommendation that he was selected in 1925 for the Command and General Staff School at Fort Leavenworth. Conner assured Ike that he would be better prepared than any other student. Eisenhower graduated first in the class of 275. He was assigned by General John J. Pershing to the Battle Monuments Commission. Pershing, at Conner's urging, tapped Eisenhower to help with the official guidebook to the American battlefields of World War I. He assisted in the production of a readable and insightful reference work that met with Pershing's approval. "What he has done was accomplished only by the exercise of unusual intelligence and constant devotion to duty," Pershing wrote in a letter of commendation.[10]

Eisenhower was then chosen for the Army War College. For the second time, he graduated first in his class. On his return to the Battle Monuments Commission, he spent the next year in Europe visiting battlefields and working on a revised edition of the guidebook. In November of 1929, just a month after the Great Crash, he reported for duty as staff officer for the assistant secretary of war. For the next six years, he worked in the nation's capital and would become a keen student of politics. "I have been in politics, the most active sort of politics, most of my adult life," Eisenhower told the journalist Merriman Smith in 1962. "There's no more active political organization in the world than the armed services of the United States. As a matter of fact, I think I am a better politician than most so-called politicians."[11]

Truman got into politics by accident. Following the war, Truman and one of the regimental sergeants, Edward Jacobson, opened a men's clothing store in Kansas City across from the Muehlebach Hotel. Their business did quite well in its first year but the value of their inventory dropped by two-thirds in the recession of 1920 to 1921 and they were forced to close their doors. Jacobson declared bankruptcy. Truman assumed all of their debts and would spend the next two decades paying off their creditors. "I spent twenty years of my life with a heavy debt hanging over my head," he recalled in 1950. "Every year I paid $1,000 on the debt when my clothing store went under. It wasn't all paid until the next year I was nominated for vice-president [1944]."[12]

Had Truman been more successful in business, it is doubtful that he would have entered politics. Jim Pendergast, who had served with Truman in the 129th Field Artillery, was the son of Mike Pendergast, brother of Kansas City's emerging Democratic boss, Thomas J. Pendergast. The younger Pendergast liked Truman and had been a frequent customer at the haberdashery. When Truman lost his business, the Pendergasts suggested that he think about running for judge of the Jackson County court.

The title was misleading, for the three elected Jackson County judges were the equivalent of county commissioners. A presiding judge was elected countywide and served as the county's chief executive officer. Another judge was elected from Kansas City and Truman was recruited to run for the eastern district that included Independence. Truman narrowly won the primary in 1922 but got voted out of office two years later because of a split between factions of the Democratic organization. Following this loss, the only one of his long career, he sold memberships in the Automobile Club of Kansas City, engaged in insurance and savings and loan ventures, and began plotting a comeback.

Truman wanted the Democratic party's endorsement for county collector, a job that paid as much as $25,000 a year in fees. "I figured I could make a record collecting back taxes and could also pay off my accumulated debts and maybe go back to the farm at the end of eight years and enjoy life," he remembered. Tom Pendergast, though, promised the collector's slot to one of his friends. In 1926 Truman was slated for presiding judge of the Jackson County court and won by a decisive margin. He handily won reelection in 1930.[13]

In eight years as presiding judge of Jackson County, Truman showed considerable vision and leadership. He proposed and built public support for a modern highway system that would gain national attention. Truman also persuaded voters to approve the construction of a new art deco courthouse in Kansas City and renovation of the old Georgian courthouse in Independence. He shared patronage with the Pendergast machine but contracts were awarded to the lowest bidders. Truman named Republican and Democratic engineering firms as the consultants for his highway plan. As the presiding judge, he was hard-working, honest, fair, and a skillful coalition-builder. When he assumed the presidency of the United States a decade after leaving the courthouse, he wrote to his wife: "It won't be long until I can sit back and study the whole picture and tell 'em what is to be done in each department. When things come to that stage, there'll be no more to this job that there was to running Jackson County and not any more worry."[14]

Truman had become a political man. From his return to the county court in 1926 until he left the White House in January of 1953, he had held elective office longer than any twentieth-century chief executive. He explored a possible run in 1932 for the Missouri governorship but lacked the statewide support. He then sought the collectorship and a seat in the U.S. House. When Pendergast offered to back him for the Senate, Truman told him that it was improbable that voters would choose a county judge for that office. Two congressmen, John Cochran of St. Louis and Jacob Milligan of Richmond, were already seeking the Democratic nomination and had substantial support. But Truman took up Pendergast on his offer. "I have come to the place where all men strive to be at my age," Truman wrote on the eve of his announcement, "and I thought two weeks ago that retirement on a virtual pension in some minor county office was all that was in store for me."[15]

Nobody worked harder than Truman in the 1934 Democratic primary for the U.S. Senate. He waged the most intensive campaign of his public career, delivering up to sixteen speeches a day. Truman campaigned on populist themes, pledging to support a pension for the elderly and bonus for World War veterans. More than any Democratic contender, Truman aligned himself with Franklin D. Roosevelt and the New Deal. Truman won the primary by a plurality of forty thousand votes and trounced Republican incumbent Roscoe Patterson in the general election.

Like Truman, Eisenhower had faith in Roosevelt's leadership. An assistant to the army chief of staff when Roosevelt took office, Eisenhower welcomed the change in administrations. "While I have no definite leanings toward any political party I believe it is a good thing the Democrats won—

and particularly that one party will have such overwhelming superiority in Congress," he wrote in his diary.[16] He also liked FDR's activism and his efforts to strengthen the presidency. "President Roosevelt's power is of tremendous extent—greater by far than is realized by the average citizen," he wrote in his diary in the first autumn of FDR's presidency. "We must conform to the President's program."[17]

In the Senate, Truman did just that, becoming one of Roosevelt's more reliable allies. He voted for the Social Security Act, the Wagner Labor Relations Act, and the Works Progress Administration. He even supported FDR's controversial attempt to pack the Supreme Court. But Truman showed independence of the White House in backing Senator Pat Harrison of Mississippi for majority leader in 1937 over FDR's choice of Kentucky Senator Alben W. Barkley.

Truman seldom spoke on the Senate floor but proved himself with colleagues in committee work. As a freshman he was appointed to the Appropriations and Interstate Commerce committees. He developed and passed important legislation, including the Civil Aeronautics Act and the Transportation Act of 1940. When he first arrived in the Senate, he was glad just to be there. Many of his colleagues were pretentious and self-important. At least a dozen were once or future presidential contenders. Truman said that Democratic Whip J. Hamilton Lewis of Illinois helped him to put it in perspective. "Don't start out with an inferiority complex," Lewis told Truman. "For the first six months, you'll wonder how you got here, and after that, you'll wonder how the rest of us got here."[18]

Truman described himself as a workhorse and had minimum regard for showhorses. "Several so-called people's friends in the Senate would be in a hell of a fix if there were not some good old workhorses here who really cause the Senate to function," he wrote Bess, who was back home in Missouri. "There isn't a so-called progressive who does anything but talk."[19]

Like Truman, Eisenhower found that the more he worked in the nation's capital, the less he was awed by its elite. "There are no 'great men' as we understood that expression when we were shavers," Eisenhower wrote in his diary. "The man whose brain is so all-embracing in its grasp of events, so infallible in its logic and so swift in formulation of perfect decisions, is only a figment of the imagination. Yet as kids we were taught to believe in the shibboleth of the 'super-man' possibly because it is easier to exaggerate than not."[20]

As assistant to Chief of Staff Douglas MacArthur, Eisenhower spent much time on Capitol Hill and had extensive dealings with legislators in both parties. Much to the frustration of Eisenhower and MacArthur, military spending was cut sharply by the Roosevelt administration. Truman was among the few Democratic senators who were persistent in calling for a stronger national defense. Eisenhower was responsible for drafting the army's annual report, helping MacArthur with his speeches, and developing strategies for national security. "This is the best officer in the Army," MacArthur wrote of Eisenhower in a fitness report. "When the next war comes, he should go right to the top."[21]

Eisenhower, who had not been promoted in more than a decade, lamented to his son that he might not become a full colonel until 1950 when at sixty years of age he would be close to retirement. In 1935 he came close to resigning from the army when a national newspaper chain's Washington, D.C., bureau tried to hire him as its military editor. Eisenhower was then making $3,000 a year and the newspaper job would have paid five times his army salary. But if another war was coming, he wanted to be part of it, which is why he remained in the army.

In the fall of 1935, MacArthur became military adviser to the Philippine government, then preparing for independence. Eisenhower went to Manila as MacArthur's executive assistant and took his family with him. Working with MacArthur, he helped in the organization of the Philippine Army and in modernizing plans of response to an invasion. The defense plan, developed under Theodore Roosevelt, included a retreat to the Bataan peninsula and a last stand on the island of Corregidor, which would become reality sooner than either Eisenhower or MacArthur could have known.

Eisenhower was at long last promoted to lieutenant colonel in July of 1936, which was two months before his forty-sixth birthday. He became a friend and confidant of Philippine President Manuel Quezon. But with the outbreak of the European war when Germany invaded Poland on September 1, 1939, Eisenhower felt a sense of isolation and wanted to be back where the decisions would be made about the next war. He also was anxious to get away from MacArthur, with whom he had clashed.

On his return in January of 1940, Eisenhower was at first assigned to temporary duty at the Presidio in San Francisco and then became executive officer of the Fifteenth Infantry at Fort Ord. In March he transferred up the coast with the Fifteenth Infantry to Fort Lewis, Washington, and directed combat training in the rugged terrain of the Pacific Northwest. "I've been with this regiment for about five months and am having the time of my life," he wrote West Point classmate Omar Bradley in July of 1940. "Like everyone else in the Army, we're up to our neck in problems big and little. But this work is fun!"[22]

Eisenhower wanted a tank command and Colonel George S. Patton of the Second Armored Brigade wanted him. "I am flattered by your suggestion that I come to your outfit. It would be great to be in the tanks once more and even better to be associated with you again," Eisenhower wrote in September of 1940. But he specified that he wanted the responsibility of command. "It's not only that like yourself I like to work with soldiers, but I'm weary of desk duty. I suppose it's too much to hope that I could have a regiment in your division, because I'm still almost three years away from my colonelcy. But I think I could do a damn good job of commanding a regiment." That fall Eisenhower wrote Mark Clark in the War Department and asked that the chief of infantry allow him to join Patton when that opportunity came.[23]

In 1940, while Eisenhower was vying for a better position in the army, Truman was fighting for his political life. Federal prosecutors had smashed the Pendergast machine and sent the boss to prison for nonpayment of taxes. Governor Lloyd C. Stark, who had been elected with the help of Truman and Pendergast, challenged Truman in the Democratic senatorial primary of 1940 and had Roosevelt's tacit support. Maurice Milligan, the U.S. attorney who had brought down Pendergast, also took on Truman. But Truman, though an underdog as he sought renomination, had a lot going for him. His legislative accomplishments were substantial for a first-term senator. He was also very well-liked in the Senate and several of his colleagues, including Missouri's Bennett Champ Clark, made campaign appearances for him. Stark and Milligan split the opposition vote and enabled Truman to maximize his political base. Blacks and organized labor provided Truman with his margin of victory. He prevailed by 7,976 votes over Stark in the August 1940 primary, out of 656,501 cast.

From his earliest days in the Senate, Truman had promoted a buildup of the armed services and the development of modern weapons. At a time when isolationism was a dominant force in the Midwest, he alerted his constituents to Nazi Germany's threat to Western democracy. "We are facing a bunch of thugs," he wrote in 1941, "and the only theory a thug understands is a gun and a bayonet." The Missouri senator worried that the national defense had been seriously compromised as a result of spending cuts, "but I still think we can defeat our enemies, and I am going to devote the rest of my life in trying to do it."[24]

Eisenhower's rise was nothing less than meteoric. In the summer of 1941, as chief of staff for the Third Army, he went to Louisiana and directed the strategy that defeated the Second Army in the largest peacetime maneuver in American history. Soon afterward, at fifty, Ike got his first star, promotion to brigadier general. In the wake of Pearl Harbor, Marshall put him in charge of the War Plans Division. Within two months, he had overall responsibility for war planning. This is where he first proposed a cross-channel invasion to launch an offensive against Nazi Germany. By June of 1942, Eisenhower was in London as U.S. commander of the European theater of operations. He would lead the Allied invasion of North Africa that achieved victory in six months and then directed the successful invasion of Sicily and began the Italian campaign.

Truman's fortunes were on the rise. Even before Pearl Harbor he had been troubled by reports of waste and inefficiency in defense production. On March 1, 1941, he became chairman of the Special Committee to Investigate the National Defense Program. "I went to see the President and told him what I wanted to do," he recalled. "I explained to him that I wanted to help him win the war, that I would keep him informed of what I found, and that if he could remedy the situation, he'd hear no more from me. I also went to see General Marshall and told him the same thing."

Between 1941 and 1944, the Truman committee produced thirty-two reports that led to reforms in defense production and saved ten billion dollars in public funds and countless lives. "We had to investigate crooked contractors on camp construction, airplane engine manufacturers who made faulty ones, steel-plate factories which cheated and hundreds of other such sordid and unpatriotic ventures," he recalled. "We investigated procurement, labor hoarding, Army and Navy waste in food and other supplies. But when we were coming to our conclusions, we all decided that by and large the greatest production and war preparation job in history had been done."[25]

There were eventually nine members of Truman's special committee and he managed this panel with remarkable skill. Truman took much pride in the consensus that he built and noted that a minority report was never issued by a member of his committee. An investigation into the construction of army camps, which began when Truman received reports of waste at Fort Leonard Wood near St. Louis, led to major changes and saved the government hundreds of millions in defense dollars. The committee documented shortages of raw materials and prodded the Roosevelt administration to build synthetic rubber plants. "There's only one thing that worries me more than the present state of the war effort," a Washington official told *Time* magazine in March of 1943. "That's to think what it would be like now without Truman." The historian Bruce Catton, who served as spokesman for the War Production Board, recalled that the Truman committee "enjoyed more prestige than all other congressional committees put together and earned it by being eminently fair, intelligent, and aggressive."[26]

It had long been assumed that Marshall would be Roosevelt's choice as supreme allied commander to lead the invasion of Western Europe. Eisenhower was regarded as Marshall's likely successor as chief of staff, though he would have preferred a field command. Near the end of the Cairo conference in December of 1943, Roosevelt selected Eisenhower as commander of Operation Overlord. Roosevelt liked Ike and said that he would sleep better with Marshall directing strategy as chief of staff.

On June 6, 1944, five thousand ships and twelve hundred planes headed for Nazi-occupied France in history's greatest amphibious assault. "The hopes and prayers of liberty-loving people everywhere march with you," Eisenhower told Allied troops on their departure. "In company with our brave allies and brothers-in-arms on other fronts, you will bring about the destruction of the German war machine. Your task will not be an easy one. Your enemy is well-trained, well-equipped and battle hardened. He will fight savagely." But Eisenhower said that the tide had turned and predicted that the Allies would prevail.[27]

That night, June 5, Eisenhower wrote another message that was to be made public only if the invasion was thwarted. "My decision to attack at this time and place was based upon the best information available," it read. "If any blame or fault attaches to the attempt it is mine alone."[28]

But the invasion of Fortress Europe would be the greatest Allied triumph of World War II. Within two months, Eisenhower's armies had broken out of Normandy and were heading for Paris. In less than a year, Hitler and his Thousand-Year Reich were gone from the face of the earth. Eisenhower would be long remembered as the man who beat Hitler.

The summer of 1944 changed Truman's life. Roosevelt was up for reelection to a history-making fourth term and was in frail health. There was a growing consensus among the Democratic party's leadership that Vice President Henry A. Wallace should be dropped from the ticket because of the real possibility that Roosevelt would not live out his term. Wallace was a good and decent man devoid of political skills and naive in foreign policy. FDR played it coy and encouraged Wallace and James F. Byrnes, the former senator and U.S. Supreme Court justice, who was then his chief White House assistant, to seek the nomination. Truman, who had been told by Byrnes, the "assistant president," that he was FDR's choice, agreed to give the nominating speech for Byrnes and went to the Chicago convention as his ally. Byrnes, though, had even more enemies than Wallace, including leaders of organized labor and African Americans.

While Eisenhower's armies were still on the battlefields of Normandy, the Democratic National Convention was choosing the next president on Chicago's West Side. Truman emerged as the president's choice. He was a party loyalist and when FDR made known his preference, it was an offer that he couldn't refuse. "You tell him that if he wants to break up the Democratic party in the middle of a war," Roosevelt said of Truman in a telephone conversation with party chairman Robert Hannegan, "that's his responsibility."[29] Truman took that as an order from the commander in chief.

Truman's nomination was a tangled affair. The phone conversation so quoted had been worked out in advance by Roosevelt and Democratic National Chairman Hannegan. Truman himself had wanted the nomination, well knowing what it meant, but had to be careful not to solicit it directly because FDR would not have liked that. Another reason that the Missouri senator could not openly seek the vice presidency is that his wife Bess did not want him to do it. She valued their privacy and may have been concerned about how the national spotlight might affect their daughter, Margaret. FDR, in his increasing illness, which had sapped his vitality, almost fumbled the vice-presidential nomination at Chicago, having allowed both Wallace and Byrnes to attend the convention and promote their candidacies. But once Roosevelt made known his preference, Truman was the convention's choice.

FDR won his fourth term with Truman as his running mate. He would serve only eighty-two days in the vice presidency. Roosevelt's death on April 12, 1945 stunned the world. In winning the war and securing the peace, Truman and Eisenhower would carry on his work.

CHAPTER 4

Potsdam

The meeting at Potsdam in the summer of 1945 would be the first and last summit conference of Harry Truman's presidency. Churchill had called for the meeting; Stalin chose the site. "I have a briefcase full of 'agenda' and minutes of Yalta, Teheran, Casablanca, Quebec, San Francisco, and numerous notes by Byrnes, Hopkins, Davies," Truman wrote Bess on the eve of his departure. "I hate to go." As much as he dreaded the pomp and ceremony, Truman knew that it was also unavoidable. "I have to take my Negro preacher coat and striped pants, tails, tux, winter clothes, and spring ones, high hat, soft hat and derby. It'll be a circus sure enough. But we will get it done I hope."[1]

Eisenhower was Truman's advance man for the summit. Soviet leader Joseph Stalin had decided to hold the meeting of the Big Three in the Russian-occupied zone of Germany, in Potsdam, just outside of Berlin. The old Prussian capital and royal village of the Hohenzollerns had been founded by Frederick William I and is where Frederick the Great was buried in the garrison church. It was in this same church that Hitler convened the first Reichstag of the Third Reich on the sixty-second anniversary of Otto von Bismarck's Second Reich.

Truman's official party included the newly appointed Secretary of State James F. Byrnes, special envoy Averell Harriman, Joseph E. Davies, General George C. Marshall, and Admiral William D. Leahy. Instead of flying to Europe, Truman departed from Norfolk on the heavy cruiser USS *Augusta* on July 7. "Talked to Bess last night and the night before. She wasn't happy about my going to see Mr. Russia, and Mr. Great Britain—neither am I," Truman wrote in his diary aboard the *Augusta*. "How I hate this trip! But I have to make it—win, lose or draw—and we must win. I'm not working for any interest but the Republic of the United States. I (am) giving nothing away except to save starving people and even then I hope we can only help them to help themselves."[2]

When the *Augusta* arrived in Antwerp on July 13, Eisenhower went onboard to greet Truman and Byrnes. Eisenhower briefed them on what to expect at Potsdam and went over the housing arrangements and logistics. Charles Sawyer, the U.S. ambassador to Belgium, who sat in on these discussions, said that Eisenhower "was very gracious and aware of protocol."

Eisenhower, who in two days would be assuming a different role as commander of the United States Occupation Zone in Germany and U.S. representative on the Allied Control Council, took this opportunity to talk about Germany's future and the war in the Pacific. "I urged that civilian authority take over military government of our portion of Germany at the earliest possible date. I pointed out to the President and the Secretary that, while the Army would obviously have to stay in control until order was assured, the government of individuals in their normal daily lives was not a part of military responsibility. I felt that no matter how efficiently and devotedly the Army might apply itself to this task, misunderstandings would certainly arise. In the long run American concepts and traditions would be best served by the State Department's assuming over-all responsibility in Germany, using the American Army there merely as an adjunct and supporter of civil authority and policy." Even though Truman and Byrnes agreed with Eisenhower in principle, they were noncommittal about when this transition could be made. That fall, Byrnes concluded that he did not want the responsibility of managing another country, though Eisenhower tried on several occasions to change his mind.

Truman was elated that Stalin was preparing to join the Allies in the war against Japan. Eisenhower advised the president that the Russian intervention wasn't necessary to achieve victory. "I foresaw certain difficulties arising out of such participation and suggested that, at the very least, we ought not to put ourselves in the position of requesting or begging for Soviet aid," Eisenhower wrote in his memoirs. "It was my personal opinion that no power on earth could keep the Red Army out of that war unless victory came before they could get in."[3]

Neither Eisenhower nor Truman anticipated the long ideological struggle that would dominate international affairs for the next forty years. "I merely feared serious administrative complications, and possible revival of old Russian claims and purposes in the Far East that might prove very embarrassing to our country," Eisenhower said. The supreme commander spoke from recent experience in dealing with the Soviets. When Truman told Eisenhower that Potsdam would be the site for the Allied summit, the Russians had exclusive control of Berlin. "We had to make preparations in a city where our authority existed only on paper, a city one hundred miles distant from the American and British zones," recalled Eisenhower's political aide Robert Murphy.[4]

It took a direct appeal to Stalin for Eisenhower's advance team to gain access to Berlin. U.S. military government offices were finally opened just before the conference. Eisenhower and Ambassador Sawyer rode with Truman from Antwerp to the Miller Oak Airport north of Brussels. A military band and four hundred American soldiers performed an honor ceremony. Truman then boarded his plane, nicknamed the "Sacred Cow," for the flight to Berlin's Gattow Airport.

Truman would never forget the "unbelievable devastation." In the First World War he had seen villages in ruins, but nothing like the mass destruction that he witnessed on this trip. Berlin's famous buildings and landmarks were reduced to rubble, including the Reichstag, and the Berlin opera house. Less than half of the prewar population of 4.2 million were still living in the bombed-out wasteland.[5]

On July 17, the last wartime summit opened in the Cecilienhof, the 176-room summer residence of former Crown Prince Wilhelm. The American, British, and Soviet flags blew in the summer wind in front of the palace. At Stalin's suggestion, Truman presided over the conference as the only Allied leader who was also head of state. "I told Stalin I am not a diplomat but usually said 'yes' and 'no' to questions after hearing all the arguments. It pleased him," Truman wrote in his diary on the first day of the conference. "He'll be in the Jap War on August 15th. Fini Japs when that comes about." As Stalin repeated this pledge at the first plenary session, Truman felt that his journey was already a success. "Could go home now," he confided to Byrnes.[6]

Truman, though, had news from Secretary of War Henry L. Stimson that made it doubtful that the Red Army would be needed in Japan. The president had delayed the start of the Potsdam conference from July 1 until the middle of the month, when there would be news from New Mexico about the test of a new weapon that would make world war obsolete in the second half of the century. It was the atomic bomb and its blast was reported as "brighter than a thousand suns." On July 16, Stimson received this message announcing the test results: "Operated on this morning. Diagnosis not yet complete but results seem satisfactory and already exceeds expectations." Truman was relieved that the Americans and not their enemies would have this awesome power. "We have discovered the most terrible bomb in the history of the world," he wrote in his diary. "It may be the fire destruction prophesized in the Euphrates Valley Era after Noah and his fabulous ark."[7]

Eisenhower was greatly troubled by the prospect of nuclear weapons. Stimson informed him that the test was a success and asked for his reaction. "I voiced to him my grave misgivings, first on the basis of my belief that Japan was already defeated and that dropping the bomb was completely unnecessary, and secondly because I thought our country should avoid shocking world opinion by the use of a weapon whose employment was, I thought, no longer mandatory as a measure to save American lives."

That wasn't what the courtly Stimson wanted to hear. "The Secretary was deeply perturbed by my attitude, almost angrily refuting the reasons I have for my quick conclusions," Eisenhower recalled.[8] Soon afterward, he shared his doubts with his son John. "Secretary Stimson told me something today. He says that they've now developed a new bomb, based on splitting the atom, that'll be so powerful that it exceeds the imagination of man. They're thinking very seriously about using this against the Japanese. This is, of course, highly secret." John S. D. Eisenhower recalled three decades later that his father's reaction "was obviously one of depression."[9]

Truman had learned about the development of the bomb just two weeks into his presidency. On the voyage to Europe, he had anxiously awaited news from the desert. Now that the test had been successful and the bomb would soon be ready, he faced a decision that had implications far beyond World War II. "I went into immediate consultation with Byrnes, Stimson, Admiral Leahy, General Marshall, General [Henry H.] Arnold, General Eisenhower, and Admiral [Ernest J.] King. I asked for their opinions whether the bomb should be used," Truman recalled. "The consensus of opinion was that the bomb should be used."[10]

Eisenhower and General Omar Bradley lunched with Truman on July 20 at his "Little White House," a three-story mansion in a grove of trees overlooking Griebnitz Lake. As they sat around the table, Truman discussed strategy in the war against Japan, including the possible use of the bomb. "Ike was not asked his opinion, but he volunteered it that day," Bradley recalled. "Curiously, Ike, almost alone among senior military men, opposed using the bomb." Bradley, who did not volunteer his opinion, agreed with the president's decision to use the bomb.[11]

So did Marshall, who regarded the bomb as a weapon that might shock the Japanese into surrendering. Marshall noted that the Japanese had fought to the finish at Iwo Jima and Okinawa. The armed services were set to invade Japan by late fall with 762,000 men. Marshall told Truman in

Potsdam "that if the bomb worked we would save a quarter of a million American lives and probably save millions of Japanese."[12]

Truman would not have taken Eisenhower's advice lightly. But he agreed with Stimson that using the bomb against Japan was "the least abhorrent alternative." It was Truman's conclusion that the Japanese should be warned and given an Allied ultimatum to surrender. "We call upon the government of Japan to proclaim now the unconditional surrender of all Japanese armed forces and to provide proper and adequate assurances of their good faith in such activity," Truman, and British leader Clement R. Attlee, declared in their statement issued with China's Generalissimo Chiang Kai-shek. "The alternative for Japan is prompt and utter destruction."[13]

When Truman in veiled language told Stalin about the development of a new weapon, the Soviet leader responded that he hoped the American president would make good use of it against the Japanese. "It was not an easy decision to make. I did not like the weapon," Truman said. "But I had no qualms if in the long run, millions of lives could be saved."[14]

Churchill agreed with Truman's decision. "Up to this moment we had shaped our ideas toward an assault upon the homeland of Japan by terrific air bombing and by the invasion of very large armies," Churchill wrote in *Triumph and Tragedy*. "We had contemplated the desperate resistance of the Japanese fighting to the death with Samurai devotion. Now this nightmare picture had vanished. In its place was the vision—fair and bright—indeed it seemed—of the end of the whole war in one or two violent shocks."[15]

In the middle of the Potsdam Conference, Churchill and Labour opposition leader Clement R. Attlee returned to London for the results of the parliamentary election. Churchill and the Conservatives were soundly defeated. "Sent Churchill a note of consolation, telling him we regretted his failure to return and wishing him a long and happy life," Truman wrote in his diary.[16]

If the Potsdam Conference would be remembered as Churchill's last hurrah, it represented a different milestone in the public career of another World War II leader. Eisenhower had never had political ambitions. "You've been standing in the sun too long," he told a war correspondent in 1943 who had suggested that Eisenhower would be a presidential contender. But while in Potsdam, Truman had several long visits with Eisenhower and sensed that he had extraordinary potential in another arena. While Truman rode in a car with Bradley and Eisenhower from Babelsberg to Berlin, the president began discussing the postwar options of World War II's military commanders. "I told him that I had no ambition except to retire to a quiet home," Eisenhower recalled in *Crusade in Europe*, "and from there do what little I could to help our people understand some of the great changes the war had brought to the world and the inescapable responsibilities that would devolve upon us all as a result of those changes."

Truman's response would come as a jolt to Eisenhower. "General," he replied, "there is nothing that you may want that I won't try to help you get. That definitely and specifically includes the Presidency in 1948." In a televised interview with Edward R. Murrow in 1958, Truman said that he had never made such an offer. But Murrow interviewed the former president at a time when his relationship with Eisenhower had soured. Truman acknowledged during the 1952 campaign that he had viewed Eisenhower as a potential successor. He also told Murrow that he could see how his comments might have been construed as an offer. Bradley, who remained on good terms with Truman, confirmed in *A General's Life* that Truman had indeed offered the presidency to Eisenhower. "I kept a poker face wondering how Ike would reply to that," he recalled.[17]

"I doubt that any soldier of our country was ever so suddenly struck in his emotional vitals by a President with such an apparently sincere and certainly astounding proposition as this," Eisenhower wrote later. "Now and then in conversations with friends, jocular suggestions had previously been made to me about a possible political career. My reaction was always instant repudiation, but to have the President suddenly throw his broadside into me left no recourse except to treat it a very splendid joke, which I hoped it was."

Eisenhower grinned, laughed, and responded: "Mr. President, I don't know who will be your opponent for the presidency, but it will not be I." The general thanked Truman for his generous comments but insisted that he had no interest in running for any political office. "I added that I would never in my lifetime experience a moment of more intense personal satisfaction than that which saw the surrender of Hitler's remaining forces at Reims, France. I was very proud of the Allies and their performance, and of the great victory they had achieved."[18]

Truman and Eisenhower arrived in Berlin for the official raising of the American flag over the headquarters of the U.S. occupation zone. Flanked by troops on both sides of the cobbled street, Truman walked down the entrance drive with Eisenhower, Bradley, and General George S. Patton. As the flag was raised, a military band played the national anthem. With eloquence, Truman made brief remarks that defined the meaning of the Allied victory:

> General Eisenhower, officers and men:
>
> This is an historic occasion. We have conclusively proven that a free people can successfully look after the affairs of the world.
>
> We are here today to raise the flag of victory over the capital of our greatest adversary. In doing that, we must remember that in raising that flag we are raising the name of the people of the United States, who are looking forward to a better world, a peaceful world, a world in which all the people will have an opportunity to enjoy the good things of life, and not just a few at the top.
>
> Let us not forget that we are fighting for peace, and for the welfare of mankind. We are not fighting for conquest. There is not one piece of territory, or one thing of a monetary nature that we want out of this war. We want peace and prosperity for the world as a whole. We want to see the time come when we can do the things in peace that we have been able to do in war.
>
> If we can put this tremendous machine of ours, which has made this victory possible, to work for peace we can look forward to the greatest age in the history of mankind. That is what we propose to do."[19]

General Lucius D. Clay, who was then Eisenhower's deputy, called Truman "a lasting inspiration to all of us." Bradley, Eisenhower's close friend, also thought that Truman more than rose to the occasion. "I liked what I saw. He was direct, unpretentious, clear-thinking and forceful," Bradley wrote of his impressions of the new commander in chief. "His knowledge of American history, particularly U.S. military history, was astonishing. I found him to be extremely well-informed about the battles we had fought in Sicily, Italy, and on the continent."[20]

Eisenhower, who was just getting to know Truman, "found him sincere, earnest, and a most pleasant person with whom to deal." When the Allied leaders took a break in the second week of their summit, Truman flew to Frankfurt to review American troops and pay a visit to Eisenhower's headquarters. Ike arranged for Truman to inspect the Eighty-fourth Division, in which the president's cousin, L. W. Truman, served as chief of staff.[21]

In Eisenhower's office, Truman became fascinated with the large globe that the supreme commander had used throughout the war in planning strategy and monitoring the progress of the grand alliance. Eisenhower would surprise Truman by shipping the globe to him as a gift with a brass strip engraved: "Presented to President Harry S. Truman by General of the Army Dwight D. Eisenhower, who personally used this globe throughout the campaign of 1942–1945."

At the end of the Potsdam Conference, Truman wrote Eisenhower: "It was certainly a very great privilege and a pleasure for me to have a chance to associate with you while I was over here, and to get your viewpoint on the German situation. It was very helpful in the Big Three conference. I think we have outlined a program for the government of Germany which will be practical and effective.

"I also want to thank you most sincerely for the pleasant day spent in the inspection of the Third Armored Division and in the 84th division. As I told you, that was the most pleasant day I spent in Germany."

Eisenhower proposed a reply to Truman in a letter to White House Press Secretary Charlie Ross: "Won't you please tell him how honored we were to have him."[22]

CHAPTER 5

Fortunes of War

Truman and Eisenhower were in agreement that occupied Germany should be held accountable for Hitler's crimes against humanity. "We have a stern duty to teach the German people the hard lesson that they must change their ways before they can be received back into the family of peaceful civilized nations," Truman wrote General Evangeline Booth of the Salvation Army in May 1945. Twice in twenty-five years Germany had launched wars of aggression and mass destruction. The Allies were determined to break up the German war machine and thwart the possibility of another Hitler. "The German people must not be allowed to escape a personal sense of guilt," Eisenhower told Treasury Secretary Morgenthau in August 1944. "Germany's war making power should be eliminated."[1]

Neither Truman nor Eisenhower drew the boundaries for the zones of occupation. Roosevelt and Churchill had agreed at the 1943 Quebec Conference that the Americans would occupy southwestern Germany and the British would rule the northwest, including the industrial center of the Ruhr valley. It had already been decided that the Soviet Union would have control of the eastern half of Germany, including Prussia. As early as 1943, Eisenhower had recommended a single West German zone occupied by the Americans, British, and French on a unified basis. "My plan was considered politically inexpedient," he wrote in *Crusade in Europe*, "although I urged that, since occupation would be a residual task of the war and would require armies of the Western Allies for its accomplishment, there could be no reasonable objection to the maintenance in western Germany, of the same Allied organization that had attained victory. The question was, however, clearly a political one, and our governmental leaders believed that my plan would be subject to unfortunate misinterpretation by the Soviet Union."[2]

As Truman's military governor, Eisenhower had responsibility for a region of more than sixty-six thousand square miles that included the states of Bavaria, Hesse, and Baden-Württemberg, a population of more than seventeen million Germans and millions of refugees. Eisenhower's headquarters in Frankfurt was the former headquarters of the I. G. Farben chemical empire and his massive and regal office was the former boardroom. Truman and Eisenhower were in charge of the part of Germany that had given rise to National Socialism. The American zone included Munich, which was named by Hitler as the "Capital of the Movement"; Hitler's house at Berchetesgaden in the Bavarian Alps that was reduced to rubble by American bombers of the Eighth Air Force; and Nuremberg, the site of Hitler's most dramatic rallies where the führer made his descent from the sky in Leni Riefenstahl's *Triumph of the Will*.

In Truman's first month as president, he approved a policy directive to Eisenhower: Joint Chiefs of Staff Memorandum No. 1067. Eisenhower was advised that "you are, by virtue of your position, clothed with supreme legislative, executive, and judicial authority in the areas occupied by the forces under your command." He was instructed to bring "home to the Germans that Germany's ruthless warfare and the fanatical Nazi resistance have destroyed the German economy and made chaos and suffering inevitable and that the Germans cannot escape responsibility for what they have brought upon themselves." Eisenhower was told to arrest Nazi leaders and other war criminals and was further advised that "all members of the Nazi Party who have been more than nominal participants in its activities, all active supporters of Naziism or militarism and all other persons hostile to Allied purposes will be removed and excluded from public office and other positions of importance in quasi-public and private enterprises."[3]

Even though the German economy was in ruins and its factories destroyed, he was told that nothing should be done by the American occupying forces to rebuild the economy: "No action will be taken in execution of the reparations program or otherwise which would tend to support basic living conditions in Germany or in your zone on a higher level than in any of the neighboring United Nations."

Truman and Eisenhower believed that Germany deserved harsh treatment. "Eisenhower found it easy to obey this instruction meticulously," his diplomatic aide Robert Murphy recalled of JCS 1067. "In fact, during his brief period as military governor, he usually managed to avoid even official contacts with Germans by delegating almost all negotiations to members of his staff. Eisenhower and President Truman, in their aloof and distrustful attitude toward Germans, typified the sentiments of millions of Americans. During Truman's eighteen days at Potsdam, while he was charting Germany's future, he did not ask to meet any anti-Nazi German statesmen, publicly or privately, and almost everyone in the President's entourage followed his example."[4]

Eisenhower was so outraged by Nazi atrocities that he shunned the ceremony when Germany formally surrendered. "Dad hated the Nazis so much that he didn't want anything to do with them. He never forgot the horrors of the concentration camps," John S. D. Eisenhower recalled in a 1976 interview.[5]

Not everyone in the American zone understood that Truman's military governor meant what he said about the treatment of Nazis. Eisenhower was embarrassed by press reports after the Allied victory that an American general had warmly greeted Hermann Goering and shared a chicken dinner with the Nazi. "The press of the United States has reacted bitterly and justifiably against what is alleged to be the friendly and hospitable treatment that certain high Nazi and other German officers have received upon capture. If such instances have occurred, they have been against my express orders," Eisenhower wrote in a message to his commanders. "Any such incident in the future will be summarily dealt with: after the successful conclusion of this campaign I am not going to have the whole public effect ruined in America by such ill-advised actions on the part of any officer."[6]

Eisenhower's resolve on this issue was tested by General Patton, commander of the Third Army and military governor of Bavaria. One of Eisenhower's oldest friends in the army, Patton disagreed with the official policy of bringing Nazi officials to justice and removing all Nazis from local government and industry. In an August 11, 1945 letter to Eisenhower, Patton contended that "a great many inexperienced or inefficient people" were in local government because of the "so-called de-Nazification program." Patton went on: "It is no more possible for a man to be a civil servant in Germany and not have paid lip service to Nazism than it is possible for a man to be a postmaster in America and not have paid at least lip service to the Democratic party, or to the Republican party when it is in power." Eisenhower responded that the Joint Chiefs of Staff had specifically given instructions that no former Nazis should be retained because of administrative necessity or expediency. "Such sweeping provisions seem to me to be required," Eisenhower told Patton, "in order to carry out one of our major war aims, namely the obliteration of the Nazi party."[7]

A defiant Patton ignored Eisenhower's directive, and at a press briefing on September 22, went public with what he had privately written Eisenhower, suggesting that "... To get things done in Bavaria, after the complete disorganization and disruption of four years of war, we had to compromise with the devil a little."[8]

Despite warnings, Patton kept up his belligerent insubordination. "George Patton has broken into print again in a big way," Eisenhower wrote Mamie. "He misses more good opportunities to keep his mouth shut than almost anyone I ever knew."[9] Eisenhower summoned Patton to Frankfurt. Eisenhower's aide, Kay Summersby, sensed that Patton was suddenly expendable: "When General Patton came in ... the office door closed. But I heard one of the stormiest sessions ever staged in our headquarters. It was the first time I ever heard General Eisenhower raise his voice."[10]

At this meeting, Patton was relieved as military governor of Bavaria and from command of the Third Army. Transferred to the Fifteenth Army, Patton died three months later from injuries he received in an automobile accident in the German village of Kafertal. He was buried in an American military cemetery near Luxembourg City.

Eisenhower, who lived on an estate in Bad Homburg during his tenure as military governor, sought permission to have Mamie join him in Germany. It had been more than three years since they had been together for more than a brief interlude. "I must confess that my own conviction is somewhat colored by personal desire," he wrote General Marshall. "It involves the possibility of enunciating some policy whereby certain personnel in the occupation forces could bring their wives to this country." Eisenhower proposed that any officer or enlisted man of the first three grades who volunteered to extend their service in the occupation forces could apply to bring their wives.

> In any event, so far as my own personal case is concerned, I will admit that the last six weeks have been my hardest of the war. I presume that aside from disappointment in being unable to solve in clean-cut fashion some of the nagging problems that seem to be always with us, part of my trouble is that I just plain miss my family.
>
> My youngster is with the First Division and I can get to see him about once a month, but it is not the same thing as being able to reestablish, after three years, something of a home. Moreover, the strain of the past three years has also been very considerable so far as my wife is concerned, and because of the fact that she has had trouble with her general nervous system for many years I would feel far more comfortable about her if she could be with me.

> In the event that no policy of any kind could be approved by the War Department at this time, the personal question would become whether this whole Command, or public opinion, would resent my arranging to bring my own wife here. This is something that of course I cannot fully determine, but my real feeling is that most people would understand that after three years continued separation at my age, and with no opportunity to engage, except on extraordinary occasions, in normal social activities, they would be sympathetic about the matter.
>
> I should like very much to have your frank reaction beause while I am perfectly willing to carry on in this assignment as long as the War Department may decide I should do so, I really would like to make it a bit easier on myself from the personal viewpoint.[11]

Eisenhower told Mamie about his appeal to Marshall, "asking about an approved 'policy' on the matter, but have told him that even if general policy cannot be made, I'd be willing to risk the cry of 'favoritism' to have you here. It is undoubtedly asking a lot of you to come into a country where the 'non-fratenization' [sic] rules apply—but I have a nice house that you'd love. While you might be lonesome during the day I could even, occasionally, get home for lunch and the nights I'd be away would be few. Your protection is perfect—guards everywhere."[12]

Marshall replied that the War Department had not yet decided on allowing wives in the European theater but that his own "superficial thought" was that "the time has not yet come for such a procedure and I am rather dubious about ever restricting it to a select group if authorized." As for Eisenhower's own wishes, Marshall wrote that he was "highly in favor of doing anything to help you in a rather impossible situation" but could not change policy at that time.[13]

Eisenhower, though disappointed, appreciated Marshall's candor. "I understand the difficulty raised in my letter," Eisenhower wrote back. "I am really sorry that I ever mentioned any personal considerations to you because from every standpoint of logic and public relations I know that the thing is impossible, at least for the time being."

After Truman's death, the novelist Merle Miller made the dubious claim in his book *Plain Speaking* that Truman had made harsh comments about Eisenhower's relationship with Kay Summersby. During the war years through the occupation, Eisenhower's close association with Summersby was the subject of gossip and Mrs. Eisenhower was aware of the rumors. David Eisenhower wrote in his 1986 biography of his grandfather that the truth of the Eisenhower–Summersby relationship was "known only by them and both are gone." Another Eisenhower biographer, Stephen E. Ambrose, concluded that Summersby was in love with Eisenhower but could not determine whether Eisenhower reciprocated, "although obviously he had strong feelings about her. In fact, she was the third most important woman in his life, behind only his mother and his wife."[14]

Mamie's letters to her husband occasionally put him on the defensive. He assured her that she had nothing to be concerned about. "Of course, we've changed," he wrote in 1944. "How could two people go through what we have, each in his own way, and without seeing each other except once in more than two years, and still believe they could be exactly as they were. The rule of nature is constant change. But it seems to me the thing to do is to retain our sense of humor, and try to make an interesting game of getting acquainted again. After all, there is no 'problem' separating us—it is merely distance, and that can some day be eliminated."[15]

Marshall did go to Truman, after Eisenhower's request to send for Mamie, and discussed the possibility of bringing wives overseas. But Truman "expressed opposition to sending families of soldiers overseas."

Eisenhower wrote Mamie of his unsuccessful effort: "It's an uphill fight because of the millions of Americans still here—our location in a hostile country—and the necessity of carefully avoiding 'favored' treatment for Generals. It will undoubtedly take some time. If it appears that my stay here is to be indefinite in length and that establishment here of my family life will be delayed several months, Johnny has promised to come live with me and to give up his insistence on going to the Pacific. . . . You cannot be any more tired than I of this long separation, particularly at my age."

Truman and Eisenhower were hopeful about maintaining a positive relationship with the Soviet Union. Eisenhower believed that the success of the occupation was linked to overcoming Russian suspicions about the Anglo-American alliance. At a press conference in Paris just a month after V-E Day, he was asked for his response to speculation about a future war between the Soviets and Americans. A hush came over the room as a correspondent for *The New York Times* made reference to these rumors of war and asked: "There is nothing in your experience with the Russians that leads you to feel we can't cooperate with them perfectly?"

"On my level, none," Eisenhower answered. "I have found the individual Russian one of the friendliest persons in the world. He likes to talk with us, laugh with us. He loves to laugh, and I have talked to many British officers and they find him the same way. He likes to see the humor of life, and I am sure they like the allies and were darn glad to see us. In an atmosphere of this kind, it has effects. The peace lies, when you get down to it, with all the peoples of the world, not just for the moment with some political leader who is trying to direct the destiny of a country along a certain line. If all the peoples are friendly, we are going to have peace."[16]

During the Potsdam Conference, Truman instructed Eisenhower that he should accept an invitation from Stalin to visit Moscow. His host for the trip was the Soviet Marshal Georgi K. Zhukov, one of the more accomplished field commanders and Eisenhower's friend. During Eisenhower's visit, Stalin showed his admiration for the supreme allied commander by asking him to stand next to the Soviet leader on the reviewing stand above Lenin's tomb. No other foreigner had ever stood in this place of honor. "General Eisenhower is a very great man," Stalin told the U.S. Ambassador W. Averell Harriman, "not only because of his military accomplishments, but because of his human, friendly, kind, and frank nature."

Eisenhower told Harriman he was optimistic about the future of U.S.-Soviet relations and predicted that Zhukov would be Stalin's successor. "I told Ike that when the war was behind us, the Soviet military brass would seldom be seen in Moscow," Harriman recalled. "He was not persuaded and when, at a Kremlin banquet in his honor, Marshal Zhukov entered the reception room at Stalin's side, Ike pointed this out to me as evidence that he was right. I explained that Zhukov's appearance beside Stalin was a courtesy to him, that if the Secretary of State had been the guest of honor, it would have been Molotov who stood at Stalin's side."[17]

Harriman said later that Marshall and Eisenhower "were among the last to agree that we couldn't get along with Stalin. . . . The reason for it was that Stalin kept his military commitments, and neither Marshall nor Eisenhower were involved in the political phase. Stalin attacked the Germans after the Normandy landing, and if the Russians hadn't attacked at that time we would have been in real trouble. . . . This made a deep impression on Marshall and Eisenhower. They were convinced that since Stalin kept his word on vital military commitments he'd keep his word on the political matters."[18]

Eisenhower would always remember the meeting of American and Soviet soldiers on the banks of the Elbe and Mulde rivers. But the joint occupation of Germany made it inevitable that the relationship between the Western Allies and Soviet Union would be strained. Under the Potsdam declaration, the Soviets were to receive industrial equipment from the western zones in exchange for food from the eastern zone. But there were conflicts from the start. The Americans and British alleged that the Soviets had stripped heavy equipment and cultural treasures from Berlin's western zones. Stalin caught Truman by surprise during the Potsdam conference with a report from Zhukov that listed equipment and property removed from Germany by American troops. "I want to make it clear that not only the Russians have sinned," Stalin said in response to Western charges that the Soviets were cheating on reparations. Truman answered that he would have Eisenhower investigate the allegations.

"With minor exceptions, I believe it may be granted that the Russian report is correct," Eisenhower wrote Truman on August 8. "Actually, equipment, documents and personnel exceeding the claims made were evacuated for various reasons in accordance with competent directives of the Combined and Joint Chiefs of Staff and under directives from myself as Supreme Commander." More than eleven thousand railroad cars had been removed from Germany by the Western Allies in the closing weeks of the war. Eisenhower told Truman that any German equipment claimed by the Allies was to help in the war effort.[19]

Berlin, which was to be occupied by the Western Allies and the Soviets, would become the site of the first major battle of the cold war. In the fall of 1945, the Soviets grounded an American plane that had been making regular flights to Poland and announced that U.S. planes would no longer be permitted to fly over Soviet territory. When Eisenhower conferred with Zhukov about this incident, he was assured that it was an error and that Moscow would punish the official who gave the order. "I disclaimed any desire to see anyone punished. I merely insisted that if both of us should issue general orders to protect the reasonable rights and privileges of either side," he wrote in a memorandum, "we would not only have less trouble of this kind, but would be doing much to promote mutual confidence between the Armies and the countries."[20]

General Lucius D. Clay, who was known as the army's "prize troubleshooter," would be the most influential figure not just in the American zone but in the development of West Germany's political system and its economic revival. The son of a three-term U.S. senator from Georgia and a descendant of Henry Clay, he possessed formidable political skills. An organizational genius and natural leader, Clay graduated near the top of West Point's class of 1918 and began his career in the Engineers Corp. He helped FDR launch the Works Progress Administration and presided over the construction of massive earth-filled dams and hundreds of airports. He contributed mightily to the Allied invasion of Europe when he took charge of Eisenhower's supply bases in Normandy. Supplies and material were quickly doubled and then tripled. Secretary of State James F. Byrnes, a longtime friend and fellow southerner, recruited Clay as his chief assistant in the Office of War Mobilization and Reconversion. When Roosevelt offered to name Byrnes as high commissioner for occupied Germany, Byrnes instead recommended Clay as Eisenhower's deputy military governor.

In looking to the future, Truman rejected the so-called Morgenthau Plan that would have reduced Germany to an agrarian economy. "Such a program could starve Germany to death. That would have been an act of revenge, and too many peace treaties had been based on that spirit," Truman wrote in *Year of Decisions.* Clay, like Truman, wanted to keep many of the factories and rebuild Germany as a western democracy. Eisenhower, who had initially been receptive to the Morgenthau Plan, soon became an advocate for Germany's economic recovery.[21]

"Clay and I were convinced that the rehabilitation of the Ruhr was vital to our best interests," Eisenhower recalled. "Nowhere else in Europe were there coal deposits equal in quality and so easily workable. And already it was apparent that coal would be the key to successful administration of Occupied Germany. Without coal, transportation could not be restored and without transportation the whole country would remain paralyzed."[22]

Truman wanted Germany's resources tapped for the benefit of other nations. On learning that northwestern Europe faced a coal shortage, Truman instructed Eisenhower to make available twenty-five million tons of West German coal for export over the next ten months. "Coal for western Europe in adequate quantities cannot, as a practical matter, be obtained from any source other than Germany."

Of all the problems facing Truman and Eisenhower, none compelled more immediate attention than millions of refugees, the survivors of the Holocaust and others who had fled the Axis forces. In the summer of 1945, Truman sent a team headed by Earl Harrison, the dean of the University of Pennsylvania Law School and former U.S. Immigration commissioner, to investigate the conditions under which refugees were living. After inspecting centers for displaced persons, Harrison reported back. Less than three months after V-E Day, Harrison noted that two-thirds of the six million refugees had been relocated to their own countries, which he termed "a phenomenal performance" by Allied military units. But he was appalled that between fifty thousand and a hundred thousand Jewish survivors of the Holocaust were still behind barbed wire. "As matters now stand, we appear to be treating the Jews as the Nazis treated them except that we do not exterminate them. They are in concentration camps in large numbers under our military guard instead of S.S. troops," Harrison reported to the president.[24]

Truman wanted action and directed Eisenhower to give immediate priority at getting refugees "out of camps and into decent houses until they can be repatriated or evacuated." The murders of six million Jews during the Holocaust had nearly wiped out the Jewish population of Europe and

Truman told Eisenhower that the Germans "cannot escape responsibility for what they have brought on themselves." The president said that Eisenhower should requisition houses from the German population for the refugees. Truman also advised Eisenhower that he had urged the British government "to have the doors of Palestine opened to such of these displaced persons as wish to go there."[25]

Eisenhower promised to do everything within his power to help survivors of death camps. "It is possible as you say, that some of my subordinates in the field are not carrying out my policies," he reported to Truman, "and any instances found will be promptly corrected. . . . I will give you a detailed report after we complete our current inspections, but in the meantime you can be sure that in the United States zone in Germany no possible effort is being spared to give these people every consideration toward better living conditions, better morale, and a visible goal."[26]

On September 17, Eisenhower inspected the displaced persons camp and its new synagogue at Feldafing in Bavaria. Eisenhower told residents that he was representing President Truman. "We can assure you," he said, "that everything will be done to secure for you a fine future as you deserve after all your suffering."

A day later, Eisenhower reported to Truman that he had inspected five camps, of which two were villages taken from the Germans and two were suburbs taken over and occupied by displaced persons. "In one camp, which was Jewish, I found conditions less than satisfactory, but found also that the camp and local authorities were taking over additional houses in the immediate vicinity, throwing the Germans out of these houses in order to provide more and better accommodations . . . problems of feeding, distribution and medical care for this completely helpless group make it imperative that they be sufficiently concentrated in order that these services can be performed."

Eisenhower wrote Truman: "A very large percentage of the persons from the Baltic states, as well as from Poland and Romania, definitely do not want to return to their own countries at this time. Although such a return represents the height of their ultimate ambitions, they constantly state, 'We cannot go back until there is a change in the political situation—otherwise we will all be killed.' " The individuals with whom Eisenhower talked did not want to return to their homelands under Soviet domination. The Truman administration supported the rights of citizens from Estonia, Latvia, and Lithuania to refuse repatriation to the eastern zone because the American government did not consider them Soviet citizens. But nearly two million Soviet citizens found in the U.S. zone were repatriated.

"With respect to the Jews, I found that most want to go to Palestine,"

Eisenhower wrote. "I note in your letter that you have already instituted action in the hope of making this possible."[27]

On October 6, the International Military Tribunal, then established in Nuremberg, handed down indictments against former leaders of the Third Reich, including Goering, Rudolf Hess, Albert Speer, and Martin Bormann, who remained a fugitive. Truman believed that the "barbaric practices" of the Nazis compelled the war crimes trials. Eisenhower also favored the allied tribunals but said years later that the leading Nazi offenders should have been summarily executed by the victors. Truman thought that the trials were important in establishing "the legal culpability of war-makers." Clay, whose goal was to bring democracy to Germany, regarded the Nuremberg trials as critical to this purpose: "The mass of evidence, which exposed not only the relentless cruelty of the Nazi regime but also the grasping rapacity of its leaders, was convincing to the German people. They may have known something of the crimes committed by their own leaders, but they did not know the full extent of the mass extermination of helpless human lives, or the ruthless cruelty of the concentration camp. The trials completed the destruction of Nazism in Germany."[28]

Two days after the Nuremberg indictments, Eisenhower updated Truman on the Holocaust survivors: "This is my full report on matters pertaining to the care and welfare of the Jewish victims of Nazi persecution within the United States Zone of Germany. . . . Since Mr. Harrison's visit in July many changes have taken place with respect to the condition of Jewish and other displaced persons. Except for temporarily crowded conditions, the result of shifts between established centers and an influx of persons into centers as winter approaches, housing is on a reasonable basis. Nevertheless, efforts to improve their condition continue unabated. Subordinate commanders are under orders to requisition German houses, grounds, and other facilities without hesitation for this purpose."

Eisenhower disputed Harrison's more controversial findings:

> At the time of Mr. Harrison's report there were perhaps 1,000 Jews still in their former concentration camps. These were too sick to be moved at that time. No Jewish or other displaced persons have been housed in these places longer than was absolutely necessary for medical quarantine and recovery from acute illness. It has always been our practice, not just our policy, to remove these victims with the utmost speed from concentration camps.
>
> The assertion that our military guards are now substituting for SS troops is definitely misleading. One reason for limiting the numbers permitted to leave our assembly centers was depredation and ban-

> ditry by the displaced persons themselves. Despite all precautions, more than two thousand of them died from drinking methylated alcohol and other types of poisonous liquor. Many others died by violence or were injured while circulating outside our assembly areas. Perhaps we were overzealous in our surveillance.

In the wake of the Harrison report, Eisenhower told subordinate commanders that guards at the centers should be displaced persons and unarmed. Eisenhower reported to Truman that the new American policy at the centers was: "Military supervisors may be employed, but will not be used as sentries except in emergency. Everything should be done to encourage displaced persons to understand that they have been freed from tyranny."

Eisenhower concluded: "Perfection will never be attained, Mr. President, but real and honest efforts are being made to provide suitable living conditions for these persecuted people until they can be permanently resettled in other areas.

"Mr. Harrison's report gives little regard to the problems faced, the real success attained in saving the lives of thousands of Jewish and other concentration camp victims and repatriating those who could and wished to be repatriated, and the progress made in two months to bring these unfortunates who remained under our jurisdiction from the depths of physical degeneration to a condition of health and essential comfort. I have personally been witness to the expressed gratitude of many of these people for these things."[29]

Eisenhower, who wanted to go home after more than three years in Europe, was urged by prominent American visitors to stay on the job. "The great error these people make is in magnifying the accomplishments possible to the American representative," Eisenhower wrote Marshall. "No matter how skillful a man here might be in convincing, on a personal basis, his colleagues of the soundness of a particular proposition, all the others operate under very rigid charters from their government. This definitely lessens the opportunities of the American representative to achieve what the uninformed seem to believe can be done. Actually Clay is the only 'indispensable' man in the whole business."[30]

Ending the military's political role in Germany was Eisenhower's goal. It frustrated him that there had been little progress in making the transition from military to civilian rule. In his view, soldiers shouldn't be running a government. Eisenhower became visibly irritated at a press conference when asked about newspaper commentaries that the army would never give up its control of Germany. "The Army does not want to stay one minute more than necessary," he responded with uncharacteristic terseness.[31]

With Marshall's approval, Eisenhower wrote Truman and made his case: "You will recall that, when you were in Frankfurt, you and I agreed upon the desirability of so organizing the Army's current functions in Europe as to facilitate turning U.S. participation in the government of Germany over to civil authority at the earliest possible moment. It is my understanding that the War Department completely supports this view. Every organizational step we have taken has been accomplished in such a way as to facilitate eventual transfer. Nevertheless I am quite sure that there is a very widespread lack of realization as to the governing intent along this line, basing this statement upon the frequency with which visitors express astonishment that this purpose exists as a guiding policy."

Eisenhower added: "The true function of the Army in this region is to provide for the United States that reserve of force and power than can insure within our zone the prompt enforcement of all laws and regulations prescribed by the Group Council, or in the absence of such law and regulation, the policies laid down by our own Government for the United States zone.

"As you pointed out when here, separation of occupational and governmental responsibility is sound just as soon as there is no longer any military or security reason for holding them together, if for no other reason than because of its conformity to the American principle of keeping the Army as such out of the civil government field." Eisenhower recommended a deadline of no later than June of 1946 for making this transition.[32]

Truman was on his side. In opening his October 31 press conference, the president read Eisenhower's letter and had it distributed to the White House press corps. "I am in agreement with what the General has said. We discussed it while he was in Frankfurt, and eventually it will be carried out," Truman said.[33]

It would be nearly four years before Truman named John J. McCloy as the first high commissioner of Germany. But Eisenhower would be military governor for only three more weeks. When he left Frankfurt on November 10 for Paris, then to the United States, he expected to be gone for only a few days. Eisenhower testified about the U.S. occupation of Germany before the House Foreign Affairs Committee. He was an honored guest at the National Press Club's dinner for Truman. "Once again, my personal crystal ball was cracked," Eisenhower recalled. "President Truman had plans for me."

On November 20, Truman announced Marshall's resignation as chief of staff and sent Eisenhower's nomination to the Senate. Eisenhower told Truman that he would prefer retirement. "Mr. President, I just don't want the job. I want to get out," he told the president. Truman then asked Eisenhower for his recommendation. "Omar Bradley. Bradley's the only man who should take it," Eisenhower said. Truman, who held Bradley in high regard, said that he would be a fine chief of staff. But Truman had just appointed Bradley to head the Veterans Administration and said that he couldn't afford to move him.

"Will you take the job until he can get out?" Truman asked.

"Could you fix a limit?" Eisenhower replied.

"I think I can get him out in two years," Truman said.

"All right," answered Eisenhower. "I'll just postpone retirement."[34]

CHAPTER 6

"What Can I Do to Help?"

At the beginning of 1946, Truman spoke to the American people about the challenges of the postwar era. "This year we shall have to make the decisions which will determine whether or not we gain that great future at home and abroad which we fought so valiantly to achieve. I wish could say to you that everything is in perfect order—that we are on the way to eternal prosperity. I cannot," the president declared.

"The months ahead will be difficult. We are well along the road toward our goal, but at every turn, we run the risk of coming upon a barrier which can stop us," Truman said. He spoke with characteristic bluntness: "Unless we can so meet the need of obtaining full production and full employment at home, we shall face serious consequences." In announcing an extension of price and rent controls, he warned that inflation was a real threat to postwar recovery: "The inflationary pressures now at work can bring an inflation and a crash that will be much more serious than 1920. This is why it so important to get a high volume of production and a large supply of marketable goods right away. Production is the greatest weapon against inflation."[1]

Eisenhower thought that his commander in chief had risen to the occasion. "I hope you don't mind me congratulating you on that speech last night," Eisenhower told him, according to the transcript of a telephone conversation taped by the chief of staff's office.

"That swells me up like a pizened pup," Truman replied.

"I listened to every word of it, Mr. President."

"Well, I'm glad you liked it."

"And I think that I'm due to see you tomorrow evening, possibly."

"Well, that's fine," Truman said. "I want some time to sit down with you and talk about a lot of policy and one thing and another that I'm very much interested in locally here."

"As a matter of fact there's one or two things on universal training I want to discuss with you very carefully, sir, because we've got to know where we're going and where we're drifting," Eisenhower said.[2]

Eisenhower served as chief of staff of the army from November 1945 until February 1948 and would help Truman with national defense policy and in reorganizing the armed services. The position of chief of staff had been created in 1903 by an act of Congress on the recommendation of Secretary of War Elihu Root, replacing the old rank of commanding general of the army. "In this country," Eisenhower wrote a British comrade from World War II, "the position of Chief of Staff of the Army is looked upon as a part of the Government. In spite of all the War Department can say, I am regarded, and my actions are closely scrutinized, as an individual whose office carries a great deal of weight in national policymaking as opposed to the executive functions for which we are actually set up."[3]

If Eisenhower hadn't made history in World War II, the chief of staff's job would have been the pinnacle of his career. But to move into the Pentagon so soon after achieving victory in Europe was a letdown. "The job I am taking now represents nothing but straight duty," he wrote one of his oldest friends. "Naturally I will do it as well as I know how."

"This job [chief of staff] is as bad as I always thought it would be," Eisenhower wrote in his diary in his first month on the job.

> I came home from Europe on temporary duty to testify before a congressional committee, expecting to return to wind up my affairs over there, preparatory to coming home for this job. Got sick, couldn't go back, and wound up taking over here on the first.
>
> I'm astounded and appalled at the size and scope of plans the staff sees as necessary to maintain our security position now and in the future.
>
> The cost is terrific. We'll be merely tilting at windmills unless we can develop something more in line with financial possibilities. Of course the number one problem is demobilization, and due to a bundle of misunderstandings, I'll soon have to go before Congress personally and give them the facts of life. They won't like it, but I can't help it. Selective service must be continued for the year, otherwise the thing is chaos. The extension should be indefinite, but no one has the courage to support me in that.
>
> If we can get through one year together we can go to volunteer system. At that time UMT [universal military training] should be

> ordered, but it will cost one billion a year and, aside from prejudice against it, the cost will hurt.[4]

Eisenhower's most frustrating problem as chief of staff was demobilization as the instant downsizing of the army was then known. "We know that many of our troubles in the theaters and here at home," he told a staff conference, "arise from the fact that great groups of officers, nearly all of them citizen soldiers are just as anxious to get home as is the GI. In many instances they have just quit. Our own efforts, directed through commanders of all sorts, ought to be shaped so as to restore the sense of responsibility and the morale of these officers. . . . It's a perfectly normal and human feeling as an aftermath of war; but if we can restore morale and responsibility among that group, I think it will greatly lessen the troubles we are having in the enlisted group."[5]

Truman, after consultation with Marshall and Eisenhower, was committed to the largest peacetime army in the nation's history. In May of 1945, the army had more than 8.3 million officers and men on active duty. They would be released as individuals rather than whole units on the basis of a point system that gave credit for overseas duty, combat, length of service, and fatherhood. Marshall announced in September that seven hundred thousand soldiers would be getting out monthly and by the following winter all men with two years of service would be reunited with their families. By the end of the year, more than five million of these soldiers were home.

But the army was coming apart. The draft and enlistments weren't producing enough soldiers for the nation to maintain its credibility as a military force or to uphold its overseas commitments. Truman and Eisenhower agreed that the demobilization rate should slow to three hundred thousand and the War Department made this surprise announcement on January 4, 1946. There was no reference to Marshall's plan for discharging soldiers with two years of service by late winter. Truman and Eisenhower needed them, at least for a while.

Angered and disappointed by the unwelcome news from the Pentagon, about twenty thousand U.S. servicemen in the Philippines demonstrated and jeered when a general tried to explain the new demobilization timetable. When Secretary of War Robert Patterson, on an inspection tour in the Pacific, arrived in Guam, he was heckled by American soldiers and later burned in effigy. There were mass demonstrations in occupied Japan and Germany, and in Britain and France. Wives organized "Bring Daddy Home" demonstrations in the nation's capital and sent baby shoes to congressional offices. At one point, Eisenhower was confronted by wives and mothers in the Capitol and sternly questioned for a half hour. Eisenhower said later that this encounter left him "emotionally upset."[6]

Two days after the first protest by soldiers, Truman sought to explain the importance of their mission and the reason for the demobilization slowdown: "The armed forces have been reduced as fast as possible. For many reasons, it is impossible for every member of the armed forces to be discharged promptly. First, there is the enormous size of the task involved. Second, there is the fact that our nation must assume its full share of the responsibility for keeping the peace and destroying the war-making potential of hostile nations that were bent on keeping the world in a state of warfare. . . . The future of our country is as much at stake as it was in the days of the war."[7]

Then it was Eisenhower's turn. In mid-January the chief of staff went before congressmen gathered in the Library of Congress auditorium and explained why it was necessary to slow demobilization. "I have come here this morning because a very human desire to get soldiers home in a hurry has clashed with the Army's manpower needs to do the job which has been assigned us by the Government," he began. "It is a big job. Even with the fighting over it takes a great many men to carry out our mission."

More than five million men had already been discharged, he noted. But if the demobilization had continued at that rate, "we would literally have 'run out of Army.' That is the reason for the slowdown." He expressed regret that it wasn't possible to have all soldiers with two years of service out by March as Marshall had hoped. "General Marshall based his statement on the best forecast that could be made at the time. Factors governing the entire demobilization picture have changed frequently in the five intervening months, all but once resulting in an acceleration of the rate of return," Eisenhower said. It would be nothing less than "catastrophic" if all two-year men were sent home by the end of March, according to the new chief of staff. "We simply cannot do it."

By July of 1946 Eisenhower estimated that another two and a half million men would be home. Only a half million V-E Day veterans would still be in uniform fourteen months after the German surrender. "All the rest will be recruits. It is with this relatively untrained Army in the throes of reconversion that we must undertake the grave tasks still ahead. . . . I consider our July 1 figure to be almost without a safety factor. It is a risk which, under any other circumstances than the vastly appealing one of reuniting men with their families, I should be unwilling to take."[8]

It was a masterful performance by the soldier of democracy. As a result of Eisenhower's speech, a great many Americans were persuaded that the demobilization slowdown was justified. Political critics were suddenly muted. Representative Andrew J. May (D-Kentucky), chairman of the Military Affairs Committee, said that his colleagues should be as candid with their constituents as Eisenhower had been with them and warned "that we can still lose the peace unless we act with discretion." May urged Congress to "pull together for the good of our common country."[9]

Appearing before a Senate subcommittee the next day, Eisenhower was taken aback when several members of the panel suggested that the demobilization timetable was unfair to the GIs. "If there is anyone in this world who has an undying interest in the enlisted men, it is I," he shot back. "Those fellows are my friends. I have commanded more American soldiers than anyone in history. You cannot possibly have a greater interest in them than me."[10]

Truman was moved by Eisenhower's speech. In a handwritten letter to the army chief of staff, Truman wrote from the perspective of an old soldier:

> Dear General Eisenhower:
>
> I have been thinking about the situation about which you addressed the Congress.
>
> In the 1st World War it was my duty to command a battery of field artillery in a National Guard division and after the war to take part in the training of National Guard and Reserve Officers.
>
> As a result of my limited experience I came to the conclusion that if the top command, that is Supreme and Army commanders, are able and efficient and company and battalion commanders have the confidence of the men whom they command, the in-between officer material is not of much consequence so far as discipline and control are concerned.
>
> I wonder if the Lieutenants, Captains and Majors of our present home and overseas forces haven't gotten too far away from their commands.
>
> As you know a real leader who is a unit commander at the company level knows exactly what his men are thinking. He knows how to keep them busy in a constructive way—even if there is apparently nothing to do. He feeds them, sleeps them, and his whole life should be in their welfare. He stands between the next higher commander and his men. I know you've lost your best and that the untrained and the inefficient are what we have left now.
>
> But can't we start over—from the squad up, rebuild that pride and

morale which are the backbone of any organization? What can I do to help?

Sincerely,
Harry S. Truman[11]

Eisenhower responded:

I have used your recent note as the basis for a number of conferences with senior commanders and staff officers. All are quite alive to the need for making a concerted drive on the morale and efficiency of our junior officers. As you have so clearly indicated, the tone of the entire Army depends on the leadership, ingenuity and diligence of the company grade officer.

Because of the drastic demobilization program, there is not a unit in the entire Army which does not suffer from the demoralization of losing its experienced veterans. We are in almost the same state as we were while forming new divisions in the early months of the war, and without the incentive of preparing for battle. We need time to inculcate the new men with sound principles of discipline. It follows that, to some extent, the problem is a temporary one. As the units are shaken down, the able leadership of division, regimental and battalion commanders overseas will begin to reassert itself to produce high-grade junior officers.

As you say, most of our best young leaders have already returned to civilian life. The efficiency of those officers remaining with troops is seriously affected by their own desire to be separated from the service. Business opportunities are beckoning and the authorized increase in the Regular Army of only 9,000 officers is but a first step toward offering our temporary officers a permanent career in the Army. We will have to ask for an additional authorization and I hope to have such a proposal for your consideration shortly.

From the day I came back from Europe, the leadership and morale of our junior officers have been of the utmost concern to me and I have previously sent out instructions emphasizing the importance of this matter. I will insure that all commanders continue to stress the points you mentioned.

I deeply appreciate your timely interest in this vital subject, and thank you sincerely for taking the time to write me about it.[12]

From Eisenhower's perspective, Truman was already doing a great deal to help rebuild the armed services and to provide more benefits for World

War II veterans than for the soldiers who had returned from any other war.

Truman made their dreams come true. Nearly half of the sixteen million veterans would attend college on government grants under the GI Bill of Rights administered by the former high school graduate. More than any legislation of the war years, the GI Bill would change America by making higher education accessible to millions of first-generation college students. Speaking in a college town in 1948, Truman took enormous pride in noting that more than half of the students at the local school were there because of the GI Bill. "You know, education is one thing that can't be taken from you," declared the veterans' president. Truman made low-interest mortgages and unemployment benefits available to veterans. At one point, 20 percent of the federal budget was pegged to benefits for returning veterans.[13]

Eisenhower supported Truman's proposal for unification of the armed forces under a single cabinet secretary and with the creation of Air Force as an equal of the other services. "One of the lessons which have most clearly come from the costly and dangerous experience of this war is that there must be unified direction of land, sea and air forces at home as well in other parts of the world where our armed forces are serving," Truman said in a message to Congress. ". . . Whether we like it or not, we must all recognize that the victory which we have won has placed upon the American people the continuous burden of responsibility for world leadership. . . . We would be taking a grave risk with the national security if we did not move now to overcome permanently the present imperfections in our defense organization."[14]

Eisenhower welcomed Truman's proposal for unification. When his navy friend Swede Hazlett grumbled that unification was counterproductive, Eisenhower defended Truman's idea: "The American public should understand that war has become a triphibious affair, and unless one laboriously picks out special circumstances, land, sea and air in varying ratio are employed in every operation of war. The closest possible kind of association among the individuals of these three forces throughout their Service careers is mandatory. You must remember that for three and a half years I have not been an infantryman! I have not even been a ground commander. I have had land, sea, and air, and naval and as much air as it has been ground."

Whatever reservations his friend might have about Truman's plan, Eisenhower pointed out that the alternative would be wasteful and expensive: "Each of the Services will consider itself individually responsible for the safety of the nation and, if you are truly security minded, you will wind up with numbers of duplications which in the long run you cannot afford."[15]

Although Eisenhower would be losing the army's air force as part of his command, he was a team player and, like Marshall, recognized that it was in the national interest to make the U.S. Air Force an equal partner. Partly because of the navy's bitter resistance to unification, there would be months of debate before Congress finally approved Truman's plan.

In pushing for universal military training, Truman was seeking to promote the "moral and spiritual welfare of our young people" and strengthen the nation's defenses. Truman, who believed in citizen soldiers, was appalled that the selective service had a rejection rate of 30 percent during the war and felt that his proposal could make the nation's youth more physically fit and more literate. "All men should be included in the training, whether physically qualified for combat service or not," Truman told a joint session of Congress. "There should be a place into which every young American can fit in the service of our country." He said that the backbone of the nation's armed forces "should be the trained citizen who is first and foremost a civilian, and who becomes a soldier or sailor only in time of danger—and only when Congress considers it necessary."[16]

Eisenhower felt the same way. "I share the conviction of General Marshall that this plan must be the keystone in the arch of our national security and international responsibility," he wrote Bernard Baruch. "If we are to retain any semblance of military power, we can only do so by establishing a ready reserve of trained manpower to support our regular military establishments."[17]

There was much support for Truman's proposal. According to a Gallup poll not long after Truman called for universal training, 70 percent of Americans favored it, including three out of four young men, and 60 percent of parents.[18] But building political support for universal training was difficult. In an unusual alliance, conservative Republicans Robert A. Taft and Joseph W. Martin aligned with organized labor in opposing Truman's call for national service. Truman and Eisenhower made a strong case for universal training but could never get it enacted.

Truman announced in late March that he was making permanent appointments of Marshall, MacArthur, Eisenhower, and Arnold as generals of the army and that of Admirals Leahy, King, Nimitz, and Halsey as five-star admirals. "It creates for the President an elder statesmen organization for national defense," he told reporters. "These men will not, under that [salary] increase, have to go into any advertising business, or go to work for any airplane companies, or anything else for their support.

That—for once, a Republic, I think, has been fair to the people who have taken it through one of the greatest emergencies in the history of the world."[19]

Before embarking on a journey to the Pacific for meetings with General Marshall in China and MacArthur in Japan, Eisenhower conferred with Truman aboard the presidential yacht *Williamsburg*, docked at Quantico. It was reported in news accounts of this meeting that Truman had discussed the extension of selective service with Eisenhower. But that wasn't all they talked about. "At my conference yesterday with the President, he did not mention unification except most casually and he definitely inferred that he was not weakening in the slightest degree in his stand on the matter," Eisenhower reported to Secretary of War Patterson. "He did ask me to recommend an officer to take over the intelligence job now held by Admiral Souers in the State Department. . . . Aside from this my conversation with The President was mainly taken up with questions involving the Philippines and General MacArthur."[20]

Truman and Eisenhower talked about something else. It was on the fantail of the *Williamsburg* that the president told the army chief of staff of his intention to replace Byrnes later in the year as secretary of state. Truman had liked and admired Byrnes, with whom he had served in the Senate and planned to support for the vice presidency in 1944. When Truman was instead nominated and after Roosevelt's death became president, Byrnes was his first major appointment. But in the State Department, Byrnes began making foreign-policy pronouncements without bothering to consult Truman. He would never regain Truman's confidence. Then came a bombshell.

"There's only two men I would have for Secretary of State, that's you and General Marshall," Truman told Eisenhower.

"Well, I knew I didn't want any part of that," Eisenhower would recall, "and I said, 'Mr. President, it just happens that I'm going out to the Far East. I'll see General Marshall and carry your message to him right away.' And that was the last word. . . . So I told him I'd take this message."

In his memoirs, written when he was no longer friendly toward Eisenhower, Truman said that Marshall was the only person he considered for secretary of state but confirms that Eisenhower was his intermediary. It is probable that Truman sounded out Eisenhower about whether he would be available but that Marshall was his first choice.[21]

Marshall had been summoned out of retirement by Truman for an impossible mission: securing a truce in China's civil war and bringing together a coalition government. In less than a month Marshall brought about a cease-fire and he would show extraordinary patience and diplomatic skills in months of talks between the Communists and Nationalists. At the time of Eisenhower's visit to Marshall, Chiang Kai-shek's corrupt government was in trouble and Mao Tse-tung's Communist opposition was gaining strength. Though both sides listened to Marshall, neither Chiang nor Mao showed interest in compromise. For Marshall, the year in China was the longest of his military and later diplomatic career.

Eisenhower delivered Truman's message. "Great goodness, Eisenhower," Marshall replied. "I'd take any job in the world to get out of this one!"

"That's the nearest I ever heard him express any opinion about the policies and orders under which he was working anywhere, because he was absolutely selfless and subordinate," Eisenhower recalled two decades later.[22]

In a code message, Eisenhower wired Marshall that "Courier [Truman] was more than pleased to have my report." He elaborated in a letter to Marshall: "This morning I reported to The President to give him a short account of my visit to the Far East. I took advantage of the opportunity to tell him about the results of our conversations, explaining your position in detail. He expressed great satisfaction, saying 'This gives me a wonderful ace in the hole because I have been terribly worried.' "[23]

From China, Eisenhower went on to Japan and was reunited with MacArthur for the first time in seven years. As the supreme commander of the Allied Occupation Forces in Japan, MacArthur had instituted land reform and dismantled its military machine. Though Eisenhower was a decade younger than his former boss, he held the five-star rank and was now MacArthur's superior. In his memoirs MacArthur recalled a "pleasant visit" with his former aide and wrote: "I have always felt for him something akin to the affection of an older man for a younger brother. His amazingly successful career has filled me with pride and admiration." In truth MacArthur, for all of his fame, resented that Eisenhower's popularity rivaled his own.[24]

As chief of staff, Eisenhower was often irritated when MacArthur would issue pronouncements without bothering to check with the War Department. During the controversy over demobilization, MacArthur asserted that the occupational forces in Japan could be reduced to two hundred thousand men, but in his private communications with the Pentagon he indicated that he needed twice that number. When asked repeatedly by Eisenhower to make public comments in support of unification and the extension of selective service, MacArthur demurred.[25]

At his palatial residence that had formerly been the American embassy, MacArthur hosted Eisenhower for a dinner with thirty guests. Following the dinner, MacArthur took Eisenhower into his study where they talked into the wee hours. Even though Truman had just given him the permanent rank and salary of a five-star general, MacArthur asked Eisenhower if it was true that five-star admirals were now getting more perquisites than generals of comparable rank. Eisenhower replied that he didn't care and said that all officers from brigadier general up were entitled to the same salute and that special honors ought to be abolished. "That's all right, Ike," MacArthur said. "Just so long as those navy sons of bitches don't get ahead of us. I don't care."

Then MacArthur talked politics. In a Gallup poll that had been published several months previously, MacArthur and Eisenhower were favored by half of all respondents when voters were asked this question: "It is often said that many people who have not held public office would make good presidents. Can you think of anyone in this state or nation who you think might make a good president?"

MacArthur told Eisenhower that one of them would almost certainly be the next president of the United States. He suggested that Eisenhower ought to run. "When I suggested that he was the one to be a candidate, he merely dismissed the notion with the remark that he was too old for the job," Eisenhower years later told MacArthur's biographer D. Clayton James. MacArthur was then sixty-six years old, but had not abandoned his dream of winning the presidency.

When MacArthur persisted in encouraging Truman's chief of staff to run against his commander in chief, Eisenhower became uncomfortable and told his former boss that military men had no business in politics. Eisenhower said that he had already received more than enough honors for a lifetime.[26]

MacArthur condescendingly patted Eisenhower on the knee and told him: "That's all right, Ike. You go on like that and you'll get it sure."

Eisenhower told Truman about this conversation and predicted that MacArthur would be coming home to make a run for the White House. Though MacArthur was in Tokyo in 1948, he allowed his name to be entered in the Republican primaries with this declaration: "In this hour of momentous importance I can say, and with due humility, that I would be recreant to all my concepts of good citizenship were I to shirk . . . accepting any public duty to which I might be called by the American people." The call never came. MacArthur would be defeated in Wisconsin by former Minnesota Governor Harold E. Stassen, a navy veteran of the Pacific War.[27]

Truman and the nation were plagued by labor troubles in early 1946 as workers sought to regain the sacrifices they had made during the war years. In the year following the Japanese surrender, five million workers went on strike, including such major unions as the United Auto Workers, the United Steelworkers of America, and the United Mine Workers. Coal was still America's major source of energy and the strike of four hundred thousand miners had a huge impact throughout the country. At Truman's direction the government took over the mines and railroads when those industries were hit by strikes. Two-thirds of the American public supported Truman's proposal that employers and workers should be compelled to run strike-bound industries that the government had taken over.[28]

The nation's railroads, the dominant form of nonautomobile transportation in the 1940s, were stopped when the Brotherhood of Locomotive Engineers and the Brotherhood of Railway Trainmen turned down a contract that had been approved by the other eighteen railroad unions. The engineers and trainmen went on strike in defiance of the administration's efforts at a settlement. Truman asked for congressional authority to draft the striking workers. More than half of the country approved of Truman's idea. Secretary of War Patterson told Truman that the army could run the trains because it was a strike against the government.[29]

In a radio address on the railroad crisis, Truman said that the emergency had been "caused by a group of men within our own country who place their private interests above the welfare of the nation." If the workers didn't return to their jobs, Truman said that the U.S. Army would operate the trains and "furnish protection to every man who heeds the call of his country in this hour of need."[30]

Truman was counting on Eisenhower. "I was recalled hastily from a trip," Eisenhower wrote in his diary, "because of a feeling that if the government had to go through with its threat of confiscating, or taking over, the railways, I was the one to explain the matter over the radio to the public and to appeal to strikers to stay on the job. Everybody had the jitters, but, in my humble opinion, they worry too much about surface manifestations of something that is of life and death importance instead of about the thing itself."[31]

As Truman spoke before a joint session of Congress on May 25, he asked for authorization "to draft into the Armed Forces of the United States all workers who are on strike against their government." At that point in Truman's remarks, he was given a message by the secretary of the Senate. He then announced, "Word has just been received that the railroad strike has been settled, on terms proposed by the President."[32]

After his break with Truman in 1952, Eisenhower made public reference to the railroad crisis of '46, recalling that he had been directed to return to Washington, D.C., from Georgia and assume command of the railroad strikers. More than six years later, Eisenhower claimed that he had refused these orders with a protest. Sources at Eisenhower's campaign headquarters told reporters that Eisenhower told Truman that he would resign as chief of staff rather than break the strike. But he did return to the nation's capital as directed and his diary gives no hint that he disagreed with Truman's directive or was on the verge of resignation.[33]

"No such conversation took place," Truman said when reporters asked him if Eisenhower had protested drafting the railroad workers. "No such conversation took place, and I know that the Chief of Staff of the United States Army would not tell the Commander in Chief that he would not obey an order. That just isn't done."[34]

For a year after V-J Day, many Americans were uncertain about their future. Polls showed that 60 percent of the voters were fearful that there would be another depression within the decade. Strikes and labor problems were listed by four out of ten voters as their main concern. In the summer of 1946, a coalition of Republicans and conservative Democrats passed legislation on price controls that diminished the authority of the Office of Price Administration. Truman vetoed the legislation on grounds that it was too weak. As a result of this veto, price controls were terminated and prices on all goods increased by more than 25 percent. When Congress responded by enacting a price-control measure acceptable to Truman, stockmen held back their cattle to sell at black market prices and meat vanished from neighborhood butcher shops. Blamed by angry consumers for the shortages, Truman lifted the controls on meat and prices surged. Within a month of his veto, he signed an extension of price controls, though he was unhappy with the legislation.[35]

At the start of 1946, Truman was riding high with an approval rating of 63 percent in the Gallup poll. After the strikes and the price-control fiasco, only 32 percent of the public liked him. "You've deserted your President for a mess of pottage, a piece of beef—a side of bacon," Truman remarked in a speech that he wrote venting his frustration but never intended to deliver. "My fellow citizens, you are the government. This is a government of, by and for the people. If you the people insist on following Mammon instead of Almighty God—your President can't stop you all by himself. He can only lead you to peace and happiness with your consent and your willing cooperation.

"You've decided that the Office of Price Administration should be a whipping boy. You've decided not to support price control although price control has saved your bonds, your insurance policies, your rent—in fact has kept our economic structure sound and solvent."[36]

Truman felt a sense of betrayal at the wave of strikes. "Mr. Lewis wanted to be sure that the President would be in the most embarrassing position possible for a congressional election," Truman wrote in his diary when the president of the United Mine Workers called a strike in the fall of 1946.[37]

"Had enough?" Republicans asked in the '46 midterm election. In a low turnout, the GOP won majorities in both the Senate and House for the first time in eighteen years. But Truman was philosophical about his party's loss. "It couldn't be much worse than it was last winter," he wrote Eleanor Roosevelt. "In fact, I think we will be in a position to get more things done for the welfare of the country, or at least to make a record of things recommended for the welfare of the country, than we would have had we been responsible for a Congress which was not loyal to the party."[38]

CHAPTER 7

America's Mission

In the summer of 1946, the Soviet Union made its move for dominance of the oil-rich Middle East. Stalin demanded control of the Turkish Straits and proposed a puppet government in Ankara that would allow him air and naval bases. The Dardanelles, thirty-seven miles long and an average width of three to four miles, leads through the Aegean Sea and joins it with the landlocked Sea of Marmara. From the ancient world into the modern age, great powers have battled for control of the passage that separates Europe from Asia.

Truman was briefed about the Soviet threat by Undersecretary of State Dean Acheson, who recommended holding the line against any Soviet takeover and sending a naval force, including the newly commissioned supercarrier *Franklin D. Roosevelt* and the battleship *Missouri* into the eastern Mediterranean. Truman listened, asked a few questions, and then said, "I approve. Go ahead."

Eisenhower, sitting beside Acheson, whispered his concern that Truman might be acting too quickly. "Do you think the President really understands what's really going on?" he asked Acheson.

"General Eisenhower asked me in a whisper whether I had made it sufficiently clear that the course we had recommended could lead to war," Acheson recalled. "Before I could answer, the President asked whether the General had anything to add. I repeated his question to me. The President took from a drawer of his desk a large map of the Middle East and Eastern Mediterranean and asked us to gather around him."

Truman talked about the historic and strategic importance of the Dardanelles and the Bosporous, the strait that joins the Black Sea to the Sea of Marmara. Truman had studied how Alexander the Great led his army over a bridge of boats across the Dardanelles and into Asia. As Truman unfolded his map that was made in sections and covered with plastic, he talked about what it would mean if Stalin gained control of these waterways and delivered a masterful lecture on the strategic importance of the area.

Ending this presentation, Truman grinned and asked Eisenhower if he had been responsive to his question. Eisenhower, who was duly impressed, laughed and acknowledged that he was satisfied with the president's answer. "When he finished," Acheson said of Truman's response to Eisenhower, "none of us doubted that he understood fully all the implications of our recommendations."[1]

"There were things about Harry S. Truman that never ceased to amaze even his closest associates—the wealth of his knowledge derived from wide reading, the deeply held historical and philosophical pegs on which he hung his thinking, his common-sense judgment that mixed idealism and practicality in workable proportions, and above all his courage in the face of politics and other risks when he knew or thought that he was right," recalled Joseph M. Jones, a senior official in the State Department during the Truman years.[2]

On Truman's instruction, Acheson gave the Soviets this message: "It is the firm opinion of this government that Turkey should continue to be primarily responsible for the defense of the Straits. Should the straits become the object of attack or threat of an attack by an aggressor, the resulting situation would constitute a threat to international security and could clearly be a matter for action on the part of the Security Council of the United Nations." After the *Franklin D. Roosevelt* and other units of the American fleet arrived in the eastern Mediterranean, the Truman administration announced that the navy would be a permanent presence. The Soviets, at least for the moment, dropped their demands for the Turkish straits.[3]

In the early months of his presidency, Truman had an open mind about the Soviet Union. But his attitude began to change after Stalin broke his pledge at Yalta to hold free elections in the liberated countries of Eastern Europe. Winston Churchill, who had alerted the world to the danger of Hitler in the 1930s, alleged that Stalin was the new menace. "From Stettin in the Baltic to Trieste in the Adriatic," the former prime minister declared on March 5, 1946, "an iron curtain has descended across the continent." In this speech, which America's favorite Englishman delivered at Truman's invitation in his home state of Missouri with the president sitting on the platform, Marlborough's descendant said that the Soviets didn't necessarily want another war. "What they desire is the fruits of war," said Churchill, "and the indefinite expansion of their power and doctrines."[4]

Truman's first showdown with Stalin was over Iran in March 1946.

Under a wartime agreement, Britain and the Soviet Union had pledged to withdraw their troops from Iran within six months after World War II. Stalin sent in more troops and two hundred tanks. The Soviets established a government in northwestern Iran. "Iran was our ally in the war. Iran was Russia's ally in the war," Truman wrote Byrnes. "Iran agreed to the free passage of arms, ammunition and other supplies running into the millions of tons across her territory from the Persian Gulf to the Caspian Sea. Without these supplies furnished by the United States, Russia would have been ignominiously defeated. Yet now Russia stirs up rebellion and keeps troops on the soil of her friend and ally—Iran.

"There isn't a doubt in my mind that Russia intends an invasion of Turkey and the seizure of the Black Sea Straits to the Mediterranean," Truman went on. "Unless Russia is faced with an iron first and strong language another war is in the making. Only one language do they understand—'how many divisions have you?' "[5]

At the beginning of the cold war, Stalin had far more divisions than Truman. In Central Europe, the Soviet Union had thirty, three times the combined strength of the Americans, British, and French in the same region. Stalin was emboldened by the downsizing of America's military strength. Two years after World War II, Stalin had two hundred divisions and four and a half million soldiers. Eisenhower's army had shrunk to twelve divisions and a million men. "The worst mistake we made," Truman told journalist Arthur Krock in 1948, "was to demobilize and I helped make it." Harriman agreed: "We had the greatest military power that had ever been brought together in 1945 and we destroyed it ourselves. No one has ever destroyed their own military strength as rapidly as we did and nobody can question that."[6]

But Truman led a nation that thoroughly dominated the world's economy. In contrast with the other great powers, the United States had not been ravaged by war. More than half of the world's goods were produced by American workers and the United States had three-fourths of the earth's gold bullion. Truman, who had used the atomic bomb to end the war, still held a monopoly on the most destructive weapon in the history of mankind. Under Truman's leadership, the United States would bring democracy to West Germany and Japan. As if to symbolize America's new role on the world stage, the United Nations complex was under construction in New York on land donated by John D. Rockefeller, Jr.

Truman used America's influence at the United Nations to protest Soviet occupation of northwestern Iran. Andrei Gromyko, the Soviet ambassador to the UN, defiantly walked out of the Security Council in the face of this criticism. In May of 1946, the Soviets withdrew from Iran and four months later their northwestern provincial government collapsed.

Clark M. Clifford, Truman's White House counsel, prepared an analysis of the Soviets in the fall of 1946 that would help shape Truman's foreign policy.

> The Near East is an area of great strategic interest to the Soviet Union because of the shift of Soviet industry to southeastern Russia, within range of air attack from much of the near East and because of the resources of the area. The Soviet Union is interested in obtaining the withdrawal of British troops from Greece and the establishment of a "friendly" government there. It hopes to make Turkey a puppet state that could serve as a springboard for the domination of the eastern Mediterranean. It is trying by diplomatic means to establish itself in the Dodecanese and Tripolitiana, and it already has a foothold in the Mediterreanean through its close alliances with Albania and Yugoslavia.
>
> . . . The language of military power is the only language the disciples of power politics understand. The United States must use that language in order that the Soviet leaders will realize that our government is determined to uphold the interests of its citizens and the rights of small nations. Compromise and concessions are considered by the Soviets to be evidences of weaknesses and they are encouraged by our "retreats" to make new and greater demands.
>
> In addition to maintaining our own strength, the United States should support and assist all democratic countries that are in any way menaced or endangered by the USSR. Providing military support in case of attack is a last resort: a more effective barrier to communism is strong economic support. . . . The United States can do much to insure that economic opportunities, personal freedom, and social equality are made possible in countries outside the Soviet sphere by generous financial assistance.[7]

George F. Kennan of the State Department had done two stints in Moscow as the secretary and minister-counselor. In the winter of 1946, Kennan wrote his celebrated "long telegram" advocating what would become known as the "containment" policy. "Soviet power, unlike that of Hitlerite Germany," wrote Kennan, "is neither schematic nor adventuristic. It does not work by fixed plans. It does not take unnecessary risks. Impervious to logic of reason, it can easily withdraw—and usually does—when strong resistance is encountered at any point. Thus, if the adversary has sufficient force and makes clear his readiness to use it, he rarely has to do so. If situations are properly handled, there need be no prestige engaging showdowns."[8]

In the winter of 1946–47, Truman was presented with just such a challenge. The British government informed the State Department on February 24 that Her Majesty's Government could no longer afford the financial and military burden of aiding Greece and Turkey. The British economy had been weakened by six years of war and a coal shortage had made this winter even more devastating. Prime Minister Clement R. Attlee couldn't provide military and economic aid to Greece and Turkey when his own countrymen lacked enough fuel to heat their homes. But Attlee was deeply concerned about the future of the Mediterranean. Unless the Americans intervened, the Soviet Union was all but certain to extend its sphere of influence. Attlee and Foreign Secretary Ernest Bevin were counting on Truman to prevent Stalin from getting his way.

The situations were different. The Greek government was under siege from Communist guerrillas with support from the Soviet satellites of Albania, Bulgaria, and Yugoslavia. During more than three years of Nazi occupation, the Communists had led the Greek resistance. A conservative government had been elected in March 1946, but leftist forces were threatening its ouster. In Turkey the government was more secure, but the Soviets were renewing their claim on the Dardanelles. "Not since Athens and Sparta, not since Rome and Carthage have we had such a polarization of power," Acheson said at a meeting with Truman and Secretary of State Marshall. "It is thus not a question of pulling British chestnuts out of the fire. It is a question of the security of the United States. It is a question of whether two-thirds of the area of the world and three-fourths of the world's territory is to be controlled by Communists."[9]

At a cabinet meeting on March 7, Truman said that he was "faced with a decision more serious than had ever confronted any President."[10]

Five days later, Truman went before a joint session of Congress and sought $400 million in military and economic aid for Greece and Turkey in what would be the most influential foreign-policy message by an American president since James Monroe set forth his doctrine in December of 1823. Monroe had written in his speech that the western hemisphere was no longer open for colonization and that any future intrusion by the European empires would be considered "dangerous to our peace and safety" and "the manifestation of an unfriendly disposition toward the United States." Instead of asking Congress for more foreign aid, he declared that the United States had a special mission in the global struggle for democracy.

"At the present moment in world history," he said, "nearly every nation must choose between alternative ways of life. The choice is too often not a free one. One way of life is based upon the will of the majority, and is distinguished by free institutions, representative government, free elections, guarantees of individual liberty, freedom of speech and religion, and freedom from political oppression. The second way of life is based upon the will of a minority forcibly imposed upon the majority. It relies upon terror and oppression, a controlled press and radio, fixed elections, and the suppression of personal freedoms.

"I believe that it must be the policy of the United States to support free peoples who are resisting attempted subjugation by armed minorities or by outside pressures," he said in what would become known as the Truman Doctrine. ". . . The free peoples of the world look to us for support in maintaining their freedoms. If we falter in our leadership, we may endanger the peace of the world—and we shall surely endanger the welfare of our own Nation."[11]

The Truman Doctrine sparked much debate. Walter Lippmann of the *New York Herald Tribune* warned that a pledge to come to the defense of "free peoples everywhere" would lead to less justified interventions in other foreign lands. "Instead of such a large promise," Lippmann wrote, ". . . it would be better, much less dangerous, and far more effective to announce, not a global policy, but an American Middle Eastern policy." Lippmann's rival Arthur Krock of *The New York Times* observed: "For better or for worse, the global anti-Communist policy . . . is the 'Truman Doctrine' far more than a famous predecessor's was the 'Monroe Doctrine.'. . . But both are founded on the fear that our freedom is threatened by ambitious European powers, and both were precipitated by Russian policy."[12]

The public rallied behind Truman. By nearly two to one, Democrats and Republicans favored Truman's program, according to a Gallup poll. A few New Deal liberals voiced their doubts because of the reactionary Greek government and some Republican isolationists were against all foreign aid. But large congressional majorities approved Truman's emergency support for Greece and Turkey.[13]

The Soviet Union was not mentioned by Truman in his March 12 speech. But on the day after Truman's appearance before Congress, Eisenhower submitted a report on behalf of the Joint Chiefs of Staff that outlined the potential Soviet threat and made a compelling argument for the Truman Doctrine:

> The projected discontinuance of British economic and financial aid to Greece strikes directly at vital Turkish security interests. An

> extension of Soviet power into Greece, which might well eventually result were all aid to the present Greek government to be abandoned, would place that power on a flank particularly dangerous to the Turks in that it would strengthen Soviet ability to cut off allied supply and assistance in event of war.
>
> Implications to Turkish security, if Greece is not made secure from the control of a Communist minority, will not be lost upon the Turks. Despite the vigor with which they upheld Turkish independence and the detestation in which they hold the USSR, fear of ultimate and unavoidable Soviet domination might induce the Turks to compromise with the Soviets. The amount and extent . . . of assistance, which would be required on the part of the United States and Britain to prevent such an occurrence would be far greater than if Greece were held secure from Communist domination.
>
> . . . Should Russia dominate Turkey in peace time we consider it highly probable that all the Middle East countries would then come rapidly under similar Soviet domination. If Russia can absorb Turkey in peace our ability to defend the Middle East in war will be virtually destroyed.

But Eisenhower knew that Russia had paid such a heavy price in World War II that Stalin was not ready for another global conflict. "It is believed," he reported, "that the Soviet Union currently possesses neither the desire nor the resources to conduct a major war. Further, the Soviet Union must now have a clear appreciation that open aggression...might inevitably result in war with the Western powers, which, alone for the present, possess atomic bombs."[14]

Truman's military and economic aid deterred the Soviets in Turkey. But Communist guerrillas seized the momentum in the Greek civil war in late 1947. Two months after the Truman Doctrine was announced, an investigation for the Security Council reported that Albania, Bulgaria, and Yugoslavia were in violation of the United Nations charter by aiding the insurgency in Greece. There were discussions in late 1947 within the Truman administration of providing combat forces to help the Greek army. U.S. officers and men had advisory roles in training Greek soldiers. Truman's economic and military aid and Tito's defiance of Stalin and abandonment of the guerrillas enabled the Greek army to regain the initiative. In October of 1949 the Athens government announced that the civil war was over. Churchill wrote about the U.S. intervention in Greece in the final volume of his World War II memoirs: "It is odd, looking back on these events, now that some years have passed, to see how completely the policy for which I and my colleagues fought so stubbornly has been justified by events. Myself, I never had any doubts about it, for I saw quite plainly that Communism would be the peril civilization would have to face after the defeat of Nazism and Fascism. It did not fall to us to end the task in Greece. I little thought, however, at the end of 1944 that the State Department, supported by overwhelming American public opinion, would in a little more than two years not only adopt and carry on the course we had opened, but would make vehement and costly exertions, even of a military character, to bring it to fruition."

The Soviet Union denounced the Truman Doctrine as an act of aggression and introduced a resolution at the United Nations in the fall of 1947 condemning the United States, Greece, and Turkey for waging "a new war . . . against the peace-loving democratic countries."[15]

Eisenhower viewed this bluster as weakness. Walter Bedell Smith, Truman's ambassador to the Soviet Union and Eisenhower's former deputy, told Eisenhower that the Kremlin leadership was "fully alive to the powerful influence exerted by the threat of another war."[16]

Even before Truman proposed the aid package for Greece and Turkey, Eisenhower was working within the administration on behalf of aid for other beleaguered nations. Eisenhower failed in an effort to get other countries included in the Truman Doctrine appropriations bill. But he did not give up the cause. "It would be wrong to assume that no substantial threats to U.S. security exist except in an ideological war," Eisenhower wrote in a May 10 memorandum to the Joint Chiefs of Staff. "In peacetime, during the period extending from the present until the assumed ideological war begins, there are requirements for U.S. aid which must be met in order to oppose expansionist efforts which would otherwise progressively impair U.S. security. For some countries, such as Greece and Turkey, it may be that this end can be attained only through the provision of 'emergency aid.' Wherever possible, however, *preventive* action should be taken in advance of the development of a crisis. In the long run, the U.S. must depend upon forehanded action in its foreign policy because of the high price of a continuous series of crises, and because the failure to prevent them will contribute to the continuation of international instability and expansionism."[17]

From the closing days of the war through his months in occupied Germany, Eisenhower felt that the United States had a special responsibility to help in the rebuilding of Europe. "Many cities have been devastated beyond imagination and are a shambles of roofless walls and rubble. Transportation systems have been disrupted," he testified before the House Foreign Affairs Committee in November of 1945. "Destroyed bridges still block the waterways of Europe. Railroad travel is a rare and cumbersome operation."

On Marshall's return in April 1947 from a foreign ministers conference in Moscow, he reported in a national radio address: "The recovery of Europe has been far slower than had been expected. Disintegrating forces are becoming evident. The patient is sinking whilst the doctors deliberate." On April 29 he asked the State Department's policy planning staff headed by George F. Kennan to develop a program for European recovery.[18]

Eisenhower had the same idea. "Abroad there are so many nations needing our help that the whole job seems appalling, even though it is clear that help to some of them is definitely in our own interest," he wrote in his diary on May 15, 1947. "Great Britain, France, Italy, Greece, and Turkey are possibly foremost, although Germany and Austria likewise present situations that can grow most serious if we do not take positive and intelligent action. I personally believe that the best thing we could now do would be to post 5 billion to the credit of the secretary of state and tell him to use it to support democratic movements wherever our vital interests indicate. Money should be used to promote possibilities of self-sustaining economies, not merely to prevent immediate starvation."[19]

In a commencement speech at Harvard University on June 5, 1947, Marshall said that America would help Europe help itself. "The truth of the matter is that Europe's requirements for the next three or four years of foreign foods and other essential products—principally from America—are so much greater than her present ability to pay that she must have substantial additional help or face economic, social, and political deterioration of a very grave character.

"Aside from the demoralizing effect on the world at large and the possibilities of disturbances arising as a result of the desperation of the people concerned, the consequences to the economy of the United States should be apparent to all. It is logical," Marshall declared, "that the United States should do whatever it is able to do to assist in the return of normal economic health in the world, without which there can be no political stability and no assured peace. Our policy is directed not against any country or doctrine but against hunger, poverty, desperation, and chaos." At Truman's insistence, the European recovery program was named the Marshall Plan for the man he viewed as "the greatest living American."[20]

Eisenhower hesitated to think of Europe's fate without the Marshall Plan. "Unless broken economies are restored they will almost certainly fall prey to communism, and if the progress of this disease is not checked," he wrote in his diary, "we will find ourselves an isolated democracy in a world elsewhere controlled by enemies. The result is clear. We must restore these broken economies and give freedom a chance to live. We must be strong, morally, industrially, financially, militarily. Most of all in our common understanding of basic issues and common determination to do those things we need to do to insure the health of American democracy. Unity is more necessary now than it was in [Operation] Overlord."[21]

Churchill referred to the Marshall Plan as "the least sordid act in history." The British and French governments were the first to sign up. In the summer of 1947, a Committee on European Economic Cooperation was organized with sixteen member nations: Austria, Belgium, Denmark, France, Greece, Iceland, Ireland, Italy, Luxembourg, the Netherlands, Norway, Portugal, Sweden, Switzerland, Turkey, and the United Kingdom. West Germany, not yet organized, would later become part of this group. The Soviet Union and its satellites were invited to participate in the Marshall Plan. Vyacheslav M. Molotov, Stalin's foreign minister, attended the first meetings in Paris but pulled out of the talks when the Kremlin became suspicious of Western motives. "Our withdrawal was correct," Molotov insisted in his memoirs. "At first I agreed to participate and, among other things, proposed to the Central Committee that not only we but the Czechs and the Poles, too, take part in the conference. Then I came to my senses and sent a second memorandum: let's refuse. . . . The imperialists were drawing us into their company, but as subordinates. We would have been absolutely dependent on them without getting anything useful in return."[22]

The Marshall Plan was among Truman's greatest accomplishments. The United States provided $13.3 billion for European recovery, which would be the equivalent of $180 billion in today's money. The largest share of this aid was targeted to Britain, France, and West Germany. When the Marshall Plan ended, European productivity was more than a third higher than prewar levels. The British writer Barbara Ward summed up the Marshall Plan's significance: "It found a continent shattered by war, divided between warring parties, fearful, uncertain, lacking the thread of hope and faith that all men need to guide them out of the labyrinth. Within two years it had created, if not a continent without problems, at least a community with a sense of promise and purpose."[23]

CHAPTER 8

Common Cause

Truman and Eisenhower would become outspoken advocates for unification of the armed forces. As the chairman of the Senate committee investigating defense expenditures, Truman was appalled by the duplication of army and navy operations. While in the Senate, Truman had urged the consolidation of the army and navy. On moving up to the presidency, Truman made unification a priority. "It was my opinion that the Commander in Chief ought to have a co-ordinated and co-operative defense department that would work in peace and war," he recalled.[1]

Truman believed that this lack of coordination by the army and navy was among the reasons the United States was surprised at Pearl Harbor. Testifying in support of Truman's unification plan before the Senate Military Affairs Committee, Eisenhower said that "unity of command" had been critical to the Allied victory in World War II. In acknowledgment of the bitter debate over unification, Eisenhower said that he could "not perceive the logic behind the objections which are voiced against the proposal before you."[2]

In a December 1945 special message to Congress, Truman proposed merging the War and Navy departments into a Department of Defense headed by a civilian with cabinet rank. A military chief of staff would preside over the armed services. It was probable that Eisenhower would be Truman's choice to fill this role as the new chief of staff. Truman advocated a limited term rotated among the services.

"Unification of the services must be looked upon as a long-term job," recommended Truman. "We all recognize that there will be many complications and difficulties. . . . But I am certain that when the task is accomplished, we shall have a military establishment far better adapted to carrying out its share of our national program for achieving peace and security."[3]

Truman sensed but did not know how difficult it would be to accomplish the most sweeping reorganization of the military in the nation's history. The navy and its allies in Congress were adamant in opposition. From Benjamin Stoddert in 1798 through James V. Forrestal in the Truman administration, the navy had been represented in the presidential cabinet by its own secretary. Theodore Roosevelt and his cousin Franklin D. Roosevelt had served as assistant secretaries of the navy. But under Truman's proposal, the secretaryship of the navy would be eliminated and downgraded to assistant secretary of defense.

That was not all that bothered Forrestal. The navy worried that the marines might be transferred to the army or phased out. These fears were not unfounded. Truman and Eisenhower regarded the marines as a small army within the navy. "The conduct of land warfare is a responsibility of the Army," Eisenhower wrote in a confidential memorandum to the Joint Chiefs of Staff. "Operationally, the Navy does not belong on the land, it belongs on the sea." Truman would write a congressman: "The Marine corps is the Navy's police force and as long as I am President that is what it will remain. They have a propaganda machine that is almost the equal to Stalin."[4]

Another dispute was over the future of navy aviation. Forrestal didn't want the Air Force taking over his planes and aircraft carriers. Led by Forrestal and Admiral Chester W. Nimitz, the chief of Naval Operations, the navy would seek to preserve their influence by coming up with its own plan for unification.

Truman and Eisenhower were up against formidable opposition. The Senate and House each had a "naval" and "military" affairs committee, and Carl Vinson, chairman of the House Naval Affairs Committee, was the most skillful legislative technician of his time. Sixty-three years old in 1946, Vinson had been a congressman for more than half of his life. As the chairman of the Naval Affairs Committee, he had written the legislation that had made it possible to build the world's most powerful fleet. The father of the modern navy, Vinson was fiercely protective of the service's independence.[5]

Forrestal, the son of Irish immigrants, former boxer, and navy lieutenant, was among the more articulate political figures of the 1940s. The tough and aggressive Forrestal gained prominence as a Wall Street financier but never lost his competitive drive. Roosevelt recruited him as a presidential assistant in 1940 but soon named Forrestal to the newly created position of undersecretary of the navy. In this position, Forrestal played a critical role in the expansion of the navy's fleet to fight the two-ocean war. When U.S. Navy Secretary Frank Knox died in 1944, Forrestal was named by FDR as his successor. Forrestal and his admirals determined to block what they viewed as a takeover by the army.

It was on the suggestion of Massachusetts Senator David Walsh, chairman of the Senate's Committee on Naval Affairs, that Forrestal enlisted his longtime associate Ferdinand Eberstadt to draft an alternative to Truman's unification plan. Eberstadt responded with a proposal that kept the War and Navy departments and added a new department of the Air Force. All three would be headed by civilian secretaries with cabinet rank. Eberstadt also proposed the creation of a National Security Council, whose members would include the president, the secretary of state, and the secretaries of the War, Navy, and Air Force departments. The plan also called for the establishment of a Central Intelligence Agency.

Walsh and Vinson publicly came out against Truman's proposal and vowed that it would never be approved by Congress. The Senate and House chairmen objected most to the idea of a single chief of staff and a consolidated military department in place of the Navy and War departments.[6]

In the middle of May 1946, Truman summoned his military and national security advisers to the White House in an effort to work out a unification compromise that could win congressional approval. Eisenhower was in Japan on his Pacific inspection tour and General Thomas Handy, Eisenhower's deputy chief of staff, attended the meeting in his place. During the meeting, Truman sought the advice of Admiral William D. Leahy, who held a comparable position as the president's chief of staff. Leahy told Truman that a compromise could probably be worked out if the legislation eliminated an overall chief of staff. If the nation "could always count on having someone like Admiral Leahy" as chief of staff, Truman said that he would have no problem with a single chief of staff. But Truman said that he now worried about the possibility of a "man on horseback" and had decided against one chief of staff for the entire armed forces. Truman had such doubts about MacArthur but at this time he had none about Eisenhower. It is probable that Truman made these comments to soften the navy's opposition to unification. When Truman asked the War secretary for his views, Patterson replied that it would be more efficient to have a single chief of staff.[7]

Always the team player, Eisenhower put military unification above his own personal interests and supported Truman's attempt to build consensus. On his return, Truman summoned him to the White House for a meeting with Patterson, Forrestal, and Nimitz. "Both Patterson and Eisenhower went to great pains to emphasize that no matter what the President's decision was to be, they would accept it cheerfully and loyally and do their best to support it," Forrestal wrote in his diary. ". . . I realized that Patterson's and Eisenhower's remarks flowed from the realization that the President was already pretty much on the Army's side of the case and they had nothing to risk in volunteering such a statement."[8]

Truman and Eisenhower, though, did make a major concession in abandoning the proposal for a single, all-powerful chief of staff. Forrestal had also gained Truman and Eisenhower's support for much of Eberstadt's reorganization plan including the National Security Council, Central Intelligence Agency, and the National Security Resources Board. "It was gratifying to have both of you and General Eisenhower and Admiral Nimitz assure me that you would give your wholehearted support to a plan of unification no matter what the decision would be on those points upon which you did not fully agree," Truman wrote Patterson and Forrestal.

Truman then outlined his position on issues that were still unsettled: There should be a single Department of National Defense. Each of the services would be headed by a civilian with the title of secretary but they would not be members of the presidential cabinet. Each of the services would have autonomy "subject of course to the authority and overall control by the Secretary of National Defense." The Marine Corps would remain under the jurisdiction of the navy. As for air power, the newly created air force "shall have the responsibility for the development, procurement, maintenance and operation of the military air resources of the United States." Truman said that the navy would still have responsibility for ship, carrier and water-based aircraft, air transport over routes of sole interest to naval forces, and marine aircraft. But Truman also wanted the navy to give out some of its air responsibilities: "Land-based planes for Naval reconnaissance, anti-submarine warfare and protection of shipping can and should be manned by Air Force personnel. If the three services are to work as a team there must be close cooperation, with interchange of personnel and special training for specific duties."[9]

When Forrestal played it coy, Truman reached him by telephone at San Francisco's naval air station and delivered a stern message. Forrestal told his naval aide: "That was the President and he told me in no uncertain terms that, if I wouldn't go along with a single secretary and a single department of defense, he would transfer naval aviation to the Air Force and the Marine Corps to the Army."[10]

On September 10, Truman convened another meeting at the White

House with Eisenhower, Nimitz, Leahy, Forrestal, Patterson, and Clifford. He noted that the army and navy had agreed on eight out of twelve points from their previous meeting and said that Clifford and Leahy would be drafting legislation. "Eisenhower repeated what he had said at earlier meetings," Forrestal wrote in his diary, "that the broad principle of a Secretary of Common Defense should be accepted with the details left to be worked out afterward. He said he could not conceive that the Navy need fear any actions following such legislation would impair its ability to perform its mission. I was again constrained to say that the Navy did have deep apprehensions as to what would happen under such a plan as the War Department has proposed."[11]

Truman knew that Eisenhower meant what he said. Clifford had already sounded him out on the possibility of compromise. Shortly before this meeting, the Eisenhowers and Cliffords had been dinner guests at Assistant War Secretary Stuart Symington's apartment in the Shoreham Hotel. Following dinner, the men retreated into Symington's library to talk about the unification struggle while their wives visited in the living room. Until after midnight, Truman's men chatted with Eisenhower. "Ike said he believed in military unification with all his heart," Clifford recalled. "He agreed with President Truman that it would be unconscionable to fight another war organized the way we had been in World War II, but, recognizing the Navy's power and determination, he said he was willing to accept substantially less than the Army position in order to get the reform process started." The navy would get most of what it wanted in the final version of Truman's unification legislation that would become known as the National Security Act.[12]

Truman needed Eisenhower to win congressional approval for his plan. During testimony before congressmen, Eisenhower was asked to explain why he had given up on the idea of a military chief of staff. "In order to get this thing done," he responded.[13]

In the final version of Truman's legislation, the navy retained its air power including land-based planes and the marines got long-term security. Eisenhower was privately angered by the navy's tactics. "Some services were apparently so unsure of their value to the country that they insisted upon writing into law a complete set of rules and specifications for their future organizations and duties," Eisenhower wrote in his diary. "Such freezing of detail in an age that is witnessing the most rapid and significant scientific advances of all history is silly, even vicious. The writers of such provisions would probably have done the same with respect to horse cavalry, old-fashioned coast defense artillery, and towed field guns."[14]

Eisenhower's public comments were more conciliatory. "The President has signed the National Security Act of 1947 and unification of the armed forces will soon be an established fact," he said in a message to troops under his command. "It is incumbent upon all ranks to accept and practice unification in spirit and in action as a patriotic duty. We of the Army must do our full part to insure the success of this legislation and demonstrate that it results in greater unification as opposed to separation."[15]

The National Security Act of 1947, which was signed into law by Truman on July 26, created the Department of Defense, Central Intelligence Agency, National Security Council, and made permanent the Joint Chiefs of Staff, which had been established during World War II by executive order. Truman may have gotten less than he wanted but his reorganization greatly improved the coordination of the nation's foreign policy and defense institutions. Neither Truman nor Eisenhower envisioned that the National Security Council would be playing a larger foreign policy role than the State Department by the 1960s. In one of the ironies of the struggle for unification, Forrestal was chosen by Truman as the first secretary of defense. Eisenhower may have had misgivings about Truman's choice. But Eisenhower would later describe Forrestal and Truman in his diary as the men in the federal government that he most admired. "We'll make it work," Eisenhower wrote of military unification in his diary, "and as changes are needed possibly even the supporters of special interests will be made to see the necessity."[16]

CHAPTER 9

Jacob's Ladder

When Truman assumed the presidency in 1945, African Americans weren't much closer to racial equality than they had been at the turn of the century. Under an 1896 ruling of the U.S. Supreme Court (*Plessy* v. *Fergeson*), segregation was the law of the land. From Delaware to Texas, blacks were treated as second-class citizens under statutes known as Jim Crow laws. Blacks were denied access to white public schools and relegated to overcrowded, substandard classrooms. In the nation's capital city, African Americans traveling by train from north to south were required to change to segregated trains. An international symbol of democracy, Washington, D.C., had an official policy of racial segregation. Local hospitals refused to admit black patients. In the downtown area, African Americans weren't allowed to eat in restaurants, attend theaters, or register in hotels. Of the 435 members of the U.S. House of Representatives, only two were African Americans, though about 10 percent of the nation's population was black.

More than one million African Americans served in the armed forces during World War II and another two million worked on the home front in war-related jobs. In going to war against the proponents of the master race, black servicemen were fighting for freedom and democracy. But African-American soldiers did not have the benefits of those ideals at home. In his 1944 study, *An American Dilemma: The Negro Problem and Modern Democracy*, the Swedish social scientist Gunnar Myrdal noted the disparity between America's democratic promise and the reality of racial injustice. "Now America is again in a life and death struggle for liberty and equality," Myrdal wrote, "and the American Negro is again watching for signs of what war and victory will mean in terms of opportunity and rights for him in his native land."[1]

On their return, black veterans were subjected to brutal acts of violence that shocked the world. Isaac Woodard, an army veteran of the Pacific war, boarded a Greyhound bus in Georgia after his discharge and was headed for home in North Carolina. After Woodard got into a minor dispute with the bus driver, he was taken into custody by police in Batesburg, South Carolina. Woodard was then beaten into a bloody pulp and left permanently blinded. The cops had gouged one of his eyes with nightsticks. In the summer of 1946, World War II veteran Maceo Snipes became the first African American registered to vote in Butler, Georgia, and was promptly killed. An army corporal, John C. Jones, was hacked up with a meat cleaver and then tortured with a blowtorch by a mob in Webster Parish, Louisiana, and two deputy sheriffs were among the killers. In late July in a spot near Monroe, Georgia, white terrorists lined up and shot army veteran George Dorsey, his wife Mae, and another African-American couple. One of the bodies was shot 180 times.[2]

Walter F. White, executive director of the National Association for the Advancement of Colored People, and five other human rights activists conferred with Truman in the Oval Office on September 19, 1946. "I was asked to be spokesman," White later recalled. "The President sat quietly, elbows resting on the arms of his chair and his fingers interlocked against his stomach as he listened with a grim face to the story of the lynchings in Georgia and Louisiana . . . and of the blinding of Isaac Woodard."

Truman was horrified. "My God! I had no idea it was as terrible as that! We've got to do something."

White had been dealing with presidents since Coolidge and was accustomed to getting lip service from the White House and not much else. "Everybody seems to believe that the President by himself can do anything he wishes on matters such as this," Truman lamented. "But the President is helpless unless he is backed by public opinion."

David K. Niles, Truman's assistant for minority affairs, suggested that Truman could name a task force to investigate the southern lynchings and other abuses of civil liberties. Niles told Truman and White's delegation that this panel would recommend corrective action. Truman thought this would be a good starting point.[3]

White was skeptical. Though Truman seemed well intentioned, the NAACP leader had no reason to believe that he would follow through on his commitments.

But he would soon learn that Truman was different.

On the day after his meeting with White, Truman wrote Attorney General Tom Clark:

> I had as callers yesterday some members of the National Association for the Advancement of Colored People and they told me about an incident which happened in South Carolina where a Negro Sergeant, who had been discharged from the Army just three hours, was taken off the bus and not only seriously beaten but his eyes deliberately put out, and that the Mayor of the town had bragged about committing this outrage.
>
> I have been very much alarmed at the increased racial feeling all over the country and I am wondering if it wouldn't be well to appoint a commission to analyze the situation and have a remedy to present to the next Congress—something similar to the Wickersham Commission on Prohibition.
>
> I know you have been looking into the Tennessee and Georgia lynchings, and also been investigating the one in Louisiana, but I think it is going to take something more than the handling of each individual case after it happens—it is going to require the inauguration of some sort of policy to prevent such happenings.

White had warned Truman that the House Rules Committee, which was then dominated by southern racial conservatives and old-guard Republicans, would block the creation of a federal commission. So Truman established the President's Committee on Civil Rights by executive order on December 5, 1946. The committee's work would be subsidized out of Truman's presidential contingency fund. Charles E. Wilson, president of the General Electric Company, was named by Truman as the committee's chairman.

"Freedom from Fear is more fully realized in our country than in any other on the face of the earth," Truman told members of the panel. "Yet all parts of our population are not equally free from fear. And from time to time, and in some places, this freedom has been gravely threatened. It was so after the last war when organized groups fanned hatred and intolerance, until, at times, mob actions struck fear into the hearts of men and women because of their racial origin or religious beliefs. Today, Freedom from Fear, and the democratic institutions which sustain it, are again under attack. In some places, from time to time, the local enforcement of law and order has broken down, and individuals—sometimes ex-servicemen, even women—have been killed, maimed, or intimidated.

"The preservation of civil liberties is a duty of every government—

state, federal, and local. Wherever the law enforcement measures . . . are inadequate to discharge this primary function of government, these measures and this authority should be strengthened and improved," Truman said. ". . . We must provide the Department of Justice with the tools to do the job."[4]

By reaching out to all Americans, Truman was showing more leadership on civil rights than any of his predecessors since Lincoln. He told members of his civil rights panel that he wanted the Bill of Rights "implemented in fact." There was no doubt about his commitment. On no other issue would Truman and Eisenhower be so clearly identified with different viewpoints.[5]

In foreign policy and national defense, the president and his army chief of staff were in general agreement. But in the struggle for racial equality, Truman advocated change while Eisenhower defended the status quo. Truman favored the use of federal authority to provide civil rights for all Americans. Eisenhower believed that responsibility should be held by individual states. When black veterans fell victim to mob violence, Truman spoke out against injustice. As army chief of staff and later as president, Eisenhower was appalled by such violence but said nothing. Eisenhower, the most admired American of his time, was unwilling to spend any of that popularity on this divisive and emotional issue. Truman, who was politically vulnerable, would put his presidency at risk.

Truman and Eisenhower grew up in families that were aligned with different sides in the Civil War, so it wasn't unexpected that they parted company on racial issues. What is surprising is that both men broke with their heritage at the racial divide. Truman was the product of a border state and a family that owned slaves, supported the South in the Civil War, and hated Lincoln. Two of Truman's uncles served in the Confederate cavalry. Eisenhower's grandfather, Jacob, a Mennonite clergyman, used his pulpit to speak out against slavery and named one of his children after Lincoln. Some of the Eisenhowers fought for the Union. Eisenhower grew up in Kansas three decades after it was admitted to the Union as a free state. A keen student of the Civil War, he would purchase his only house at Gettysburg near the hallowed ground where Union forces achieved their most critical victory.

Neither Truman nor Eisenhower saw themselves as prejudiced. But as products of the late nineteenth century, they used racial slurs well into adulthood. In a 1939 letter to his wife, Truman, then in the Senate, made a reference to "nigger picnic day." That same year, in another letter to Bess, he repeated a colleague's racial joke: ". . . and finally the nigger said 'Hole still little fish. I just wants to gut you.' " In the winter of 1943, Eisenhower wrote his son from North Africa that "a group of darkies" were taking "gorgeous care of me" as servants in a comfortable house. Such language was not uncommon among white men of Truman and Eisenhower's generation.[6]

Truman, as the moderate alternative to the liberal Wallace, won the 1944 vice-presidential nomination with substantial support from southern segregationists. From his earliest days in the Senate, Truman had close relationships with southern colleagues, including Byrnes of South Carolina and Pat Harrison of Mississippi.

Despite a solid voting record on civil rights, Truman was regarded by southern colleagues as a border-state politician who was really one of them. They were slow to realize that he was genuine in his advocacy of civil rights. As presiding judge of Jackson County, he had saved a home for African-American youth that some whites sought to close. In his first Senate term, he joined forces with the NAACP in their unsuccessful quest for an antilynching law. Black voters in Missouri took notice. Truman's support among African Americans provided his margin of victory in the 1940 Democratic primary for the U.S. Senate. In opening his bid for renomination at Sedalia, he struck the theme of fairness to all Americans:

> When we speak of man and his labor, at least in this country and, more particularly in this locality, we must consider the problem of our Negro population and bend our every effort that, at least under law, they may claim their heritage of our Bill of Rights to "life, liberty, and the pursuit of happiness." Their social life, will, naturally remain their own, but as freemen they must have their equality before law.
>
> The relations of colored and white people in this community and this state is one that should be given our interest and attention. We all desire to see proper and helpful relations exist between all classes of people. . . . In all matters of progress and welfare, of economic opportunity and equal rights before law, Negroes deserve every aid and protection.
>
> I believe in the brotherhood of man; not merely the brotherhood of white men, but the brotherhood of all men before law. I believe in the Constitution and the Declaration of Independence. In giving to the Negroes the rights that are theirs we are only acting in our accord with our ideals of a true democracy. If any race or class can be permanently set apart from, or pushed down below, the rest in polit-

> ical and civil rights, so may any other class or race when it shall incur the displeasure of its more powerful associates, and we may say farewell to the principles on which we count our safety.[7]

In July of 1940, Truman went even further in his advocacy of civil rights. "If white men wish to do better for themselves, it would be well for them to give more definite attention to the education of the Negro," he told the National Colored Democratic Association. "By this I mean not merely more and better buildings and equipment but very careful attention to what is taught in these buildings. We exert no little care to see what white children are taught in our public schools but seem to have little or no concern about what the Negro child is taught. . . . Some say the Negro is not capable of assimilating cultural study. I have always denied this and have studied the problem sufficiently to know that given an equal opportunity with white students the Negro can more than hold his own." The Truman of 1940, though, wasn't calling for an end to segregation: "I wish to make it clear that I am not appealing for social equality of the Negro. The Negro himself knows better than that, and the highest types of Negro leaders say quite frankly that they prefer the society of their own people. Negroes want justice, not social relations."[8]

In his presidential memoirs, Eisenhower wrote that since youth he had believed in equality under the law regardless of race or creed. According to his biographer Stephen Ambrose, Eisenhower took a more enlightened view of race relations than other members of his high school football team. On one occasion, an opposing team had an African American playing center. Eisenhower normally played end for Abilene High. But when Abilene's interior linemen refused to play across the line from the African American, Eisenhower took their place. "Rest of the team was a bit ashamed," Eisenhower told a friend years later.[9]

Eisenhower's racial conservatism was forged in the army, which had segregated white and black units since 1863. As chief of staff during World War II, General Marshall opposed changing this policy because that "would be tantamount to solving a social problem which has perplexed the American people throughout the history of this nation. The Army cannot accomplish such a solution and should not be charged with the undertaking. The settlement of vexing racial problems cannot be permitted to complicate the tremendous task of the War Department and thereby jeopardize discipline and morale."[10]

Holding similar views, Eisenhower told war correspondents on background that his policy would be equality of treatment but segregation. During the Battle of the Bulge, he was prepared to make an exception to the rule. Facing a troop shortage, he made an appeal for African-American service troops to volunteer for infantry training and an opportunity to serve as individual replacements in white combat units. "It is planned to assign you without regard to color or race to the units where assistance is most needed," read the circular approved by Eisenhower, "and give you the opportunity of fighting shoulder to shoulder to bring about victory."

On reading this circular, Eisenhower's deputy Walter Bedell Smith warned Eisenhower that he was undercutting the War Department's policy. Eisenhower revised his appeal for reinforcements, eliminating the special call for African-American troops, and the promise of integrated units. Thousands of blacks volunteered and fought with distinction in all-black platoons.[11]

After V-E Day, he was asked for comment about the role of African Americans in the European war: "To start with, I would like to say this: that I do not differentiate among soldiers. I do not say white soldiers or Negro soldiers and I do not say American or British soldiers. To my mind I have had a task in this war that makes me look upon soldiers as soldiers. Now I have seen Negro soldiers in this war and I have many reports on their work where they have rendered very valuable contributions and some of them with the greatest enthusiasm."[12]

Throughout his two years as army chief of staff, he confronted the racial question. In the same week that Truman nominated him as Marshall's successor, the War Department completed a task-force report about the role of African Americans in the postwar army. Assistant Secretary of War John J. McCloy and civilian aide Truman K. Gibson were the dominant influences in shaping the report in consultation with the panel's chairman Lieutenant General Alvan C. Gillem. The Gillem Board concluded that African Americans had a constitutional right to serve in combat roles and that the army had an obligation to make the most effective use of all soldiers. Blacks had been discriminated against by the army. More than three hundred thousand eligible African Americans were passed over for service in World War II. The Gillem Board recommended that the level of black troops in the army should reflect "the proportion of Negro to white manpower as exists in the civil population."[13]

The Senate's most outspoken racist, Theodore Bilbo of Mississippi, called on Eisenhower to repudiate the Gillem Board's recommendations. Bilbo ranted in a letter to Eisenhower that the proposed "mongrelization has been quickened by the persistence of the negro intelligentsia, white quislings, and politicians who play up to the negro for his vote." Bilbo urged Eisenhower to retain the army's policy of segregation.

Responding to Bilbo, he said that he had not yet seen the report.

"When the recommendations on this subject come to me, I will certainly study them most carefully, for unquestionably this is, as you say, a very important matter," he told the segregationist senator.[14]

On reading the report, Eisenhower thought it had merit. When Gillem told the new chief of staff that the black quota should be 9.5 percent, Eisenhower suggested making it "an even 10 percent." The Gillem Board stated in January 1946 that the War Department's "ultimate objective" in the event of another war should be "the effective use of all manpower . . . without regard to antecedents or race."

The chief of staff endorsed the report "subject to such adjustment as experience shows is necessary." Doubtful that Eisenhower truly accepted the findings of the Gillem Board, Gibson advised a senior official in the War Department that the Gillem reforms would make a positive difference "only if they are effectively carried out."

But Eisenhower needed more soldiers. With the army reduced to a shell of its World War II strength, he lifted all restrictions on enlistment of African Americans. Blacks would continue to be drafted by the selective service based on a rate of 10 percent of overall troop strength. But Eisenhower eliminated quotas for black enlisted men. In the spring of 1947, he allowed African-American companies to be integrated into white National Guard units. But blacks couldn't serve in white companies or platoons.[15]

"I know from first hand observation no element in U.S. Army suffers more from caste and racial discrimination than the Negro," the NAACP's White told Eisenhower. "From our conversations I am certain you agree that no really democratic Army will ever be achieved as long as such racial demarcations resulting in discrimination and segregation continue."[16]

As thousands of African Americans responded to the call, Eisenhower and the army worried about the social consequences. Blacks would make up 16 percent of the army in July of 1946 and it was projected that this total could reach 24 percent within a year. On July 17, 1946, the War Department suspended enlistments of African Americans. Three months later, the army discriminated against blacks by making it more difficult for them to pass the general classification test. Whites enlisting in the army only had to score 70 points on the test. African Americans had to score 100. The army also allowed whites to have a choice of assignment but denied this opportunity to African Americans. These harsh measures did what the army wanted. By June of 1947, the percentage of African Americans fell to 7.91 percent

The army's policies were clearly discriminatory. Yet Eisenhower tried to have it both ways. "Both as Chief of Staff and as an American citizen I opposed any discrimination in the rights and privileges awarded American soldiers based on color or race," he wrote a prominent black historian in 1947. "A soldier's worth to the service and the country can be measured only by his ability and his will to give the best within him."[17]

But during his tenure as chief of staff those soldiers would give their best in segregated units. Later in the Truman administration, he told a friend that it was not the role of the army to spearhead social reform.[18]

In April of 1948, two months after stepping down as chief of staff, he told the Senate Armed Services Committee that he favored continuing segregation in the army: "I do not mean to say that I have any final answer to the problem, and I believe that the human race may finally grow up to the point where it [race relations] will not be a problem. It [the race problem] will disappear through education, through mutual respect, and so on. But I do believe that if we attempt merely by passing a lot of laws to force someone to like someone else. we are just going to get into trouble. On the other hand, I do not by any means hold out for this extreme segregation as I said when I first joined the Army 38 years ago."

During this testimony, Eisenhower questioned whether African Americans would benefit from desegregation. "In general," he said, "the Negro is less well educated . . . and if you make a complete amalgamation, what you are going to have is in every company the Negro is going to be relegated to the minor jobs, and he is never going to get his promotion to such grades as technical sergeant, master sergeant, and so on, because the competition is too tough. If, on the other hand, he is in smaller units of his own, he can go up to that rate, and I believe he is entitled to the chance to show his own wares."[19]

E. Frederic Morrow, who later worked for Eisenhower as the first African American on the senior White House staff, said that Eisenhower's testimony before the Armed Services Committee was "one of the great crosses I had to bear as the black pioneer in the White House." In 1952, Morrow asked Eisenhower why he testified against desegregation of the armed forces. "Well he got very red," Morrow recalled years later. "He hesitated for a minute. He looked at me and he said, 'Son, your father's a minister, isn't he?' I said 'Yes, sir. That's right.' 'Did your father ever teach you anything about forgiveness?' Eisenhower asked. 'Yes he did,' I replied. 'Well, that's where I am now,' Eisenhower said. 'When I was called back to the United States to testify on that problem, I sent for all my field commanders to let me have their viewpoints. Their viewpoints were negative. I never, never questioned them. I just thought that here, a man commanding these men, and they had a responsibility, they ought to know. So the bulk of my testimony came from the reports from these field commanders. I want to confess to you that it has only been in the last few months that it dawned on me that most of these men had a southern exposure and this, in itself, would color their decision.' "[20]

Yet Truman came out of a similar background and would have the opposite viewpoint. In June of 1947 he became the first president of the United States to address the NAACP. Speaking from the steps of the Lincoln Memorial, Truman embraced the civil rights cause. "It is my deep conviction that we have reached a turning point in the long history of our country's efforts to guarantee freedom and equality to all our citizens," Truman declared. "Recent events in the United States and abroad have made us realize that it is more important today than ever before to insure that all American enjoy these rights. When I say all Americans I mean all Americans. . . . We cannot be content with a civil liberties program which emphasizes only the need of protection against the possibility of tyranny by the Government. . . . We must keep moving forward, with new concepts of civil rights to safeguard our heritage. The extension of civil rights today means, not protection of the people *against* the Government, but protection of people *by* the Government."[21]

As Truman sat down, he asked the NAACP's White for his reaction. White assured Truman that his speech couldn't have been better. "I said what I did," Truman replied, "because I mean every word of it—and I am going to prove that I do mean it."[22]

Four months later, Truman's committee on civil rights issued its report, *To Secure These Rights*, which would set the civil rights agenda for the next two decades. It would take that long for Truman's bold program to be carried out. Before this historic report, racial issues were commonly referred to as "the Negro problem." After Truman's report, the phrase "civil rights" would replace such paternalistic terms. *To Secure These Rights* noted that the federal government's failure to guarantee equal rights had resulted in "a kind of moral dry rot which eats away at the emotional and rational bases of democratic beliefs."

The President's Committee on Civil Rights made thirty-five specific recommendations including "the elimination of segregation, based on race, color, creed, or national origin from American life." It called for the elimination of the poll tax and other restrictions on voting; a federal anti-lynching law; the establishment a civil rights division in the Justice Department; the establishment of a federal commission on civil rights and a fair employment practices commission; the elimination of segregation and discrimination in schools, housing, transportation, and employment; equal access to places of public accommodation; a law that would deny federal funding to public or private agencies that discriminated; and the desegregation of the armed services.

Truman knew that it would be years before many of these goals could be accomplished and that public opinion would be against him. Yet he also believed that the committee's report could be the prologue for a new era of civil rights. Truman endorsed *To Secure These Rights* and used it as the basis for his February 1948 special message to Congress on civil rights. "We shall not achieve the ideals for which this nation was founded so long as any American suffers discrimination as a result of his race, or religion, or color," he stated. ". . . If we wish to inspire the peoples of the world whose freedom is in jeopardy, if we wish to restore hope to those who have already lost their civil liberties, if we wish to fulfill the promise that is ours, we must correct the remaining imperfections in our practice of democracy."[23]

In his message, he made no reference to the elimination of segregation in society at large but outlined an ambitious agenda. He asked Congress for an antilynching law, voting-rights laws, the elimination of Jim Crow practices in interstate transportation, and the creation of a civil rights division in the Justice Department. Near the end of his speech, he said that he had asked the secretary of defense to end discrimination in the armed services. Even though he had avoided the emotional and divisive issue of segregation, his civil rights program was bold for its time. Only 6 percent of the American public thought that Congress should approve his civil rights proposals, according to the Gallup poll. Fifty-six percent of the poll's respondents were opposed to Truman's program. Only 21 percent of whites outside of the South endorsed Truman's civil rights proposals. More than half of white southerners felt that Truman had dealt unfairly with their part of the country. Even Ralph McGill of the *Atlanta Constitution*, a civil rights progressive, felt that Truman had gone too far. Franklin D. Roosevelt and the Democratic party had carried every southern and border state in the previous four national elections. But after his advocacy of civil rights, Truman could no longer count on a Solid South. A bloc of fifty-two southern congressmen denounced Truman's message and vowed to work against his reelection.

Following Truman's lead, the Justice Department filed briefs supporting the plaintiffs in *Shelley* v. *Kramer*, which culminated in the Supreme Court decision outlawing restrictive housing covenants.

Ending segregation in Washington, D.C., was among the goals of Truman's civil rights commission. *To Secure These Rights* documented the racial divide in the nation's capital. "The President can't get things done in the District of Columbia simply by waving a wand," Truman lamented. But his administration began breaking down barriers with the integration of public swimming pools and recreation areas in Washington, D.C. As a result of the Supreme Court decision in *Shelley* v. *Kramer*, more than 450 residential blocks were opened to African Americans in less than two years. Beginning with Truman's civil rights initiatives of 1948, there would be gradual progress in the integration of restaurants, theaters, and private schools. It was symbolic of the times that a theater that closed in 1948 rather than admit African Americans would open its doors to everyone under new management in the final year of Truman's presidency.

A World War I army friend, Ernie Roberts, urged Truman to reconsider his civil rights position and "let the South be the South." Roberts appealed to Truman as a southerner.

Truman's response indicated the depth of his commitment: "The main difficulty with the South is that they are living eighty years behind the times and the sooner they come out of it the better it will be for the country and themselves. I am not asking for social equality because no such thing exists, but . . . when a Mayor and City Marshal can take a Negro sergeant off a bus in South Carolina, beat him up and put out one of his eyes, and nothing is done about it by the State authorities, something is radically wrong with the system."

Listing other abuses against African Americans, Truman concluded, ". . . as long as I am here, as I told you before, I am going to try to remedy it and if that ends up in my failure to be re-elected, that failure will be in a good cause."[25]

Southern state's rights Democrats walked out of the 1948 Democratic convention in protest of Truman's civil rights policies and in July nominated South Carolina Governor J. Strom Thurmond for the presidency. In contrast with FDR, Truman risked his presidency by splitting the Democratic party's historic southern base. Thurmond would carry four states of the Deep South in the 1948 general election.

Truman was under pressure from the African-American community. The labor leader A. Philip Randolph called on blacks to refuse to serve in the military until discrimination was ended in the armed services. "From coast to coast in my travels I shall call upon all Negro veterans to join this civil disobedience movement and to recruit their younger brothers in an organized refusal to register and be drafted," Randolph told the Senate Armed Services Committee. ". . . In the words of the spiritual, we will be buried in our graves before we will be slaves."

In launching the League for Non-Violent Civil Disobedience Against Military Segregation, Randolph galvanized the black community and turned up the heat on Truman. It would have been impossible for him to have won congressional approval for desegregation of the armed forces. But as commander in chief, Truman had the power to make policy with the stroke of a pen. Presidential aide Phileo Nash sought Gibson's advice in drafting an executive order ending discrimination in the military.[26]

Truman's favorite generals, Marshall and Eisenhower, defended the status quo. But Truman agreed with his Committee on Civil Rights that had condemned military segregation as repugnant. Clifford recalled, "He thought it was outrageous that men could be asked to die for their country but not allowed to fight in the same units because of their color."[27]

On July 26, 1948, Truman issued Executive Order 9981 that called for the desegregation of the armed forces. To implement this policy change, he formed the President's Committee on Equality of Treatment and Opportunity in the Armed Services. "It is hereby declared to be the policy of the President that there shall be equality of treatment and opportunity," he said, "for all persons in the armed services without regard to race, color, religion or national origin. This policy shall be put into effect as rapidly as possible, having due regard to the time required to effectuate any necessary changes without impairing efficiency or morale."

General Bradley, Eisenhower's successor as chief of staff, shared the viewpoint of Marshall and Eisenhower that the army wasn't ready for "instant integration" and shouldn't be used for social experiments. Like Eisenhower, Bradley was influenced by the army's southern prejudices. "A very high percentage of Army volunteers and career soldiers came from the Deep South," Bradley recalled in his memoirs. "Many of our large and important bases—such as Fort Benning—were located in the Deep South. To have desegregated the Army overnight as Truman wished would have caused utter chaos, not only within the Army ranks but also within the Deep South communities where our bases were located."

On the day Truman issued his order, Bradley was at Fort Knox on an inspection trip. At a meeting with officers, Bradley was asked how Truman's order would impact army life. Bradley expressed doubts whether the army could be fully desegregated "until it had been totally achieved by the American people." Unaware that several reporters were in the audience, Bradley was embarrassed when his comments were made public and quickly wrote Truman that the army would not resist the presidential directive.[28]

Truman faced considerable resistance. The army was the slowest of the armed services in responding. In January 1950, the army announced that African Americans would be "assigned to any unit without regard to race or color." Truman then pressed for the elimination of racial quotas. By April 1950, the quota had been dropped. In the Korean War, 90 percent of the army's units would be integrated.[29]

Half a century after Truman's executive order, the Pentagon conducted a comprehensive survey on racial attitudes. More than forty thousand members of the armed services were interviewed. The Defense Manpower Data Center reported that there is still a racial gap in the military. Nearly half of all African Americans in the armed services said that they had experienced a racially offensive encounter, compared with a third of whites. Only 17 percent of whites said that the military was inattentive to the problem of racial discrimination compared with 62 percent of African Americans. But there were indications that blacks and whites had good living and working relationships. The survey found that 82 percent of whites in the armed forces had a close friend who was African American, compared with only 59 percent of the general white population.

Truman would look back on the desegregation of the armed forces as "the greatest thing that ever happened to America." It was his most important accomplishment in domestic policy. Thirteen years after the decision, the Reverend Martin Luther King, Jr., said that Truman's executive order ranked with Lincoln's Emancipation Proclamation. General Colin Powell, the first African-American chairman of the Joint Chiefs of Staff, said that the Second Reconstruction began with Truman's desegregation of the armed forces. "I was able to rise to the top of the Armed Forces because of those who went ahead and proved we could do it," Powell said on the golden anniversary of Executive Order 9981, "and Harry Truman who gave me the opportunity to show I could do it."[31]

CHAPTER 10

Mutual Respect

"When Franklin Roosevelt died," Harry Truman recalled in his farewell address to the American people, "I felt there must be a million men better qualified than I, to take up the Presidential task."[1]

Truman had not wanted the job and went on the 1944 Democratic ticket with genuine reluctance. At a White House luncheon following the 1944 convention, Truman observed that FDR was in ill health. From that moment on, Truman sensed that he was destined to play a larger role. "I wake up every morning in a cold sweat dreading that it might be today," Truman confided to his family.[2]

"I shall attempt to meet your expectations," he told residents of his hometown, "but don't expect too much of me." There was nothing false about Truman's modesty. Though he had been a highly regarded senator, he was an accidental president. In succeeding FDR, he had a difficult if not impossible act to follow. More than anyone, he understood his limitations "Have you ever had a bull or a load of hay fall on you?" he asked reporters. "I don't know if you newspapermen ever pray, but if you do, please pray for me now."[3]

Truman's popularity surged in the early weeks of his presidency. In June 1945, 87 percent of the American public approved of his job performance, which was nearly a third higher than FDR's final poll rating and exceeded Roosevelt's highest point. But Truman didn't regard himself as an indispensable man and was already thinking of Roosevelt's most popular commander as a possible successor.[4]

Shortly after V-E Day, Truman said at a White House senior staff meeting that the nation couldn't afford to lose Eisenhower's services in peacetime. Stephen T. Early, FDR's press secretary and an Eisenhower confidant, told Truman that General Ike "wanted to come back and get away from things for a while, then write two or three books, and then possibly lead the preparedness movement in the United States." This favorably impressed Truman.[5]

On June 21, 1945, Truman was asked at a press conference about Eisenhower's future. "I have no plans except that General Eisenhower is going back to finish his job in Germany," Truman said. "General Eisenhower is entitled to most anything he wants, and I want to help him get it. He is a grand gentleman and an able leader and a diplomat as well. An unusual combination in a military man."[6]

Later that summer, he became more specific. At a breakfast on the White House veranda with FDR's alter ego Harry Hopkins and Ambassador Joseph E. Davies, Truman told them of his high regard for Eisenhower. The president had just returned from the Potsdam Conference. Davies urged Truman to limit Eisenhower's stay in occupied Germany so that he would not "be scarred up over there" for his "usefulness should be preserved for political service in the future here, when it might be desperately needed." Truman and Hopkins concurred.[7]

If Eisenhower would be willing to accept the presidency, Truman told FDR's men, he would not seek another term and would support General Ike in 1948. Truman also confided to Robert G. Nixon of International News Service during the Potsdam Conference, "I told Ike that if he wanted to be President, I'd help him to be."[8]

Eisenhower wasn't looking for a promotion. At his June 1945 homecoming in Abilene, Eisenhower was asked by reporters about the possibility of a political future. "There is no use [in] my denying that I'll fly to the moon because no one has suggested it and I couldn't if I wanted to," he replied. "The same goes for politics. I'm a soldier and I'm positive no one thinks of me as a politician. In the strongest language you can command you can state that I have no political ambitions at all. Make it even stronger than that if you can. I would like to go further even than Sherman in expressing myself on this subject."[9]

But the more Eisenhower disavowed a political career the more the public wanted him. As the nation's most popular soldier and a world figure, he struck many voters in both parties as a reassuring leader for the postwar era. On five previous occasions, Americans had elected generals to the presidency. The Richmond editor Douglas Southall Freeman, George Washington's biographer, suggested that it was the general's "duty to the nation" to seek the presidency. "Of course I valued his opinion," Eisenhower wrote in *At Ease.* "But I remained insistent in my belief that because a man had risen to high rank during war, and had been successful in a number of military campaigns, this alone was not important to the nation's peacetime progress."[10]

Truman believed in the ideal of the citizen soldier and saw in Eisenhower the attributes of Cincinnatus, the farmer and soldier who had returned to the plow. No other president appointed more military men to senior positions in his administration than Truman: Marshall as secretary of state and then defense; Walter Bedell Smith as ambassador to the Soviet Union and then director of the Central Intelligence Agency; Clay as governor of Germany; MacArthur as governor of Japan; Brigadier General Charles E. Saltzman as assistant secretary of state; Major General William H. Draper as undersecretary for the army; Admiral Alan G. Kirk as ambassador to Belgium; General Frank T. Hines as ambassador to Panama; and General Thomas Holcomb as ambassador to South Africa.

From their first meeting, Truman had liked and admired Eisenhower. Truman thought he had demonstrated exceptional leadership skills in World War II, occupied Germany, and in running the army. During Eisenhower's twenty-six months as chief of staff, Truman gained even more respect for him. Eisenhower, who had also worked with Roosevelt, found Truman more open and forthright. John S. D. Eisenhower recalled his father's relationship with Truman: "He certainly sympathized with and supported his superior—it was impossible, especially in Truman's earlier years, to dislike him—but Dad always referred to him, even in talking to me, simply as 'The President.' "[11]

As chief of staff, Eisenhower had a standing invitation to the Oval Office. In thanking Eisenhower for a gift of scotch, Truman wrote: "I can't tell you how much I appreciate your thoughtfulness in bringing it to me. I think I'll inhale it rather than pass it out to these 'thugs' who hang around here and drink my whiskey. Maybe you and I could think up an occasion when we could share it."[12]

After their break years later, Eisenhower recalled: "When I was Chief of Staff, President Truman always wanted me to come over at about 5:00 in the afternoon for a drink with him and a few of his friends in the White House. I never went, though; I always said I had too much to do."[13]

Yet Truman and Eisenhower spent much time together. Beyond their regular policy sessions at the White House, the commander in chief and his chief of staff also went on the road. In April of 1946 they journeyed to Chicago by overnight train and both addressed an Army Day rally at Soldier Field. "Our Army has written many glorious chapters in the Nation's history, but none so brilliant as the last," Truman declared in the open-air stadium. In June of 1947, Eisenhower flew with Truman aboard the

"Sacred Cow" and attended the reunion of the president's old outfit, the Thirty-fifth Division. "We are honored by the presence of our highest-ranking Army officer, General Eisenhower," Truman told his audience in Kansas City's Municipal Auditorium. Later that month, Truman and Eisenhower traveled to Princeton University and accepted honorary degrees along with Eleanor Roosevelt and former President Hoover.

Eisenhower was looking forward to stepping down as chief of staff, and sought Truman's advice on his next career move. It had been his ambition to take the presidency of a small college, write books, and speak out in behalf of internationalism. In the spring of 1947, he was approached by Thomas J. Watson, chief executive of IBM and a trustee of Columbia University, about accepting the presidency of New York City's oldest and most prestigious institution of higher education. Watson was a liberal Democrat once described by Hopkins as "the only business friend that Roosevelt has." Truman respected him and thought that Eisenhower would be a good choice to succeed the aging Nicholas Murray Butler as Columbia's president.

"I have discussed with the President the proposition you present to me," Eisenhower reported to Watson. "The President heartily concurs in your conviction that in the suggested post I could render a worthwhile public service. In fact he advised me to consider it favorably."[15]

Just a week after Truman and Eisenhower received their degrees from Princeton, Columbia University announced that General Ike would be its next president. In announcing his decision, Eisenhower told reporters at the Pentagon that his new job did not mean that he was leaving the army. "As long as I am above ground I am never going to leave the Army," he said. "Wherever I am, the interest of the Army and of the National Security will always be Number One with me."[16]

It would be another eight months before Eisenhower would end his service as chief of staff and nearly a year before he assumed the presidency of Columbia. In the meantime, he figured prominently in speculation about the 1948 presidential election.

Truman sensed that the Democratic party might need Eisenhower's popularity to retain the presidency in 1948. The Republican party had been gaining strength since 1938, and won both houses of Congress in 1946 for the first time in sixteen years. Senator J. William Fulbright of Arkansas, one of the Democratic party's emerging leaders, suggested that Truman ought to step down in favor of a Republican. Without Roosevelt's leadership, the New Deal coalition was splintering. Wallace, FDR's second vice president, challenged Truman from the left and made known his intentions to run for the presidency as a third-party candidate. On the right, southern conservatives were also unhappy with Truman.[17]

Eisenhower was embarrassed in the fall of 1947 when he was inaccurately linked to the Wallace insurgency. He was not unfriendly with the former vice president, and his brother Milton had been among Wallace's aides during his years as FDR's secretary of agriculture. But neither of the Eisenhower brothers supported Wallace's campaign against Truman. "Only this morning I noticed an account of a radio broadcast in which I was accused of having held a long and secret conference with Mr. Wallace and two of his colleagues, the alleged purpose of their visit being to persuade me to declare for the Democratic nomination with the purpose of ousting Mr. Truman," Eisenhower reported in a letter to Milton.

"Not only is the entire story fantastic—the only one of the individuals mentioned in the story that I personally knew was Mr. Wallace—but the implication that I had even countenanced people talking to me about a subject like this while I am still in the Army is very close to a challenge to a soldier's loyalty. The commentator did end his story with the conclusion that I had given Mr. Wallace no satisfaction because—according to him—I was personally hoping for the Republican nomination! The fact is that I have not even seen Mr. Wallace at a distance since he left the administration and I have never had a private talk with him in my life. Moreover, I have never mentioned the word 'politics' to him, nor he to me."[18]

But Eisenhower discussed politics with others. New York Governor Thomas E. Dewey, the 1944 Republican presidential nominee and the presumed front runner for 1948, discouraged Eisenhower from running for office. On his return after V-E Day, Eisenhower sat next to Dewey at a dinner in New York. Eisenhower later told others that Dewey spent much of the night attempting to convince him that a political career would be a mistake. Even though Eisenhower agreed with Dewey, the governor did not let up and "harped on [the] subject [the] entire evening."

Dewey continued to regard Eisenhower as a rival. When they chatted at a public function at which Eisenhower was to speak, he sought Dewey's advice. Eisenhower's performance left Dewey even more worried. "He gave the best speech I ever heard," Dewey told associates. In the fall of 1947, Dewey was still obsessed with Eisenhower. "He is obviously concerned about General Eisenhower's candidacy, and certain that he, Eisenhower, could dispose of it very quickly if he wanted to," Defense Secretary Forrestal wrote in his diary after sitting next to Dewey at a dinner. "He said Ike was obviously campaigning. He thought, however, that Eisenhower's boom had been launched too early and that the general did not realize how complicated his position would become the longer the boom is permitted to continue. Politics look very simple to the outsider whether he is a businessman or a soldier—it is only when you get into it that all the angles and hard work become apparent."[19]

Most Americans doubted that Eisenhower would give up his uniform to seek the presidency. When the Gallup poll asked in the winter of 1947 whether Eisenhower would run in 1948, 61 percent of respondents predicted that he wouldn't run, while 21 percent said that he would. He had been deliberately vague about his political affiliation, and the public was evenly divided about whether he was a Democrat or Republican.[20]

"I thought he was a Democrat," Truman recalled years later, "and he implied that he believed in everything that Roosevelt and I had been doing. And when he was 18 years old, he had campaigned for a Democratic governor of Kansas, George Hodges, before he went to West Point. I really don't think he knows what he is. I thought he could be a Democrat, and if he wanted to, could run on the Democratic ticket."[21]

Eisenhower had been more candid about his political views with FDR's Hopkins. "Amongst other things, Eisenhower told me that he and his family had always been Republicans and had voted against FDR every time up until 1944," Hopkins wrote in notes of their conversations in Frankfurt, "but that he did vote for Roosevelt this last time."[22]

In looking ahead to 1948, Eisenhower was not ready to declare his political allegiance. As chief of staff, he met frequently with politicians from both parties and conferred with political writers and syndicated columnists on a background basis. Eisenhower once told Walter Lippmann that he disliked excessive partisanship and said that he would seek to remain above the fray if he ever sought public office. "You don't suppose a man could ever be nominated by both parties, do you?" Eisenhower asked the noted columnist. Lippmann told Eisenhower that would be most unlikely.[23]

It was the Democratic party that courted Eisenhower for 1948. The resurgent Republicans were confident they could recapture the presidency without him. Less than a year after Truman first mentioned the presidency to Eisenhower during the Potsdam Conference, he casually returned to the subject when they lunched at the Pentagon. "General, if you ever want to run for President on the Democratic ticket," Truman said, "we'll support you."

Eisenhower responded in good humor that he had no such ambitions.[24]

Clark Clifford confirmed years later that Truman offered to step aside in Eisenhower's favor. "I believe that he [Truman] was concerned over the possibility that the Republican conservative, or even reactionary forces, could get control of the government," he recalled. "He thought that would be a calamity. And he was a very modest man. He had followed this great figure of FDR and I think he had the feeling if he could help the Democratic party find a man who could win, that President Truman would be rendering the greatest service that he could render to his country."[25]

In the fall of 1947, Secretary of the Army Kenneth C. Royall conferred with Truman about Eisenhower's candidacy. An August 1947 Gallup poll showed Eisenhower leading Truman for the first time in a trial heat. Truman held the edge over Dewey and MacArthur in the same poll. Royall, a towering North Carolinian and veteran of both world wars, was close to Truman and Eisenhower and hoped that he would not have to choose between friends in the '48 presidential race.

Though Royall vowed to support Truman, he told the president that working against Eisenhower would be an impossibility. Royall offered to resign from the administration to avoid this conflict. Truman assured Royall that this wouldn't be necessary. But he had an assignment for him.

Truman asked Royall to meet with Eisenhower and let him know that the Democratic presidential nomination was his if he wanted it. That was not all. In an offer of extraordinary generosity and without precedent, Truman said that he would be willing to go on the ticket as Eisenhower's vice-presidential running mate. Eisenhower later made an off-the-record confirmation of this offer to C. L. Sulzberger of *The New York Times*. In January 1955 Ike told Ohio's Democratic Senator Frank Lausche that Truman twice "personally asked me to run on the Democratic ticket for President with himself as the candidate for Vice President. I told him no both times." Cabell Phillips first reported Truman's offer in his 1966 book *The Truman Presidency*. Eisenhower declined to comment when Phillips asked him about this incident. Truman denied it in a letter to Phillips. But Royall told Phillips that his account was "substantially correct."

Eisenhower, though moved by Truman's message, told Royall that he hadn't changed his mind and wasn't interested in the presidency. "I do not know the details of his talk with General Eisenhower," Clifford said later of Truman's offer. "I think at that particular stage, he and President Truman were friends and they got along well. President Truman had a very real respect and regard for him. I do not know what General Eisenhower's opinion was of President Truman, but in any event, it is my information that those talks didn't lead anywhere."[26]

Once Truman was convinced that Eisenhower meant what he said about shunning politics, he decided to seek a full term. Truman felt that he had done a good job and that his programs were worth fighting for. Washington lawyer James H. Rowe, who had been among FDR's savviest advisers, began plotting a reelection strategy for Truman in the summer of 1947. Rowe drafted a thirty-three page memorandum for Truman at the suggestion of Budget Director James E. Webb. Clifford would later make slight revisions to Rowe's report and add a brief section on civil rights. Though Clifford later claimed excessive credit for shaping Truman's strategy, documents at the Truman Library indicate that the report was written by Rowe.

"The aim of this memorandum," Rowe began, "is to suggest a course of political conduct for the Administration to follow from September 1947 to the November 1948 elections."

Rowe made these observations:

> 1. Governor Dewey will be the nominee of the Republican Party. This tentative conclusion is of course based on the usual factors. Among these is the fact that, at least at the present time, a strong candidate is required to defeat President Truman.
>
> 2. President Truman will be elected if the Administration will successfully concentrate on the traditional Democratic alliance between the South and West.
>
> 3. Henry Wallace will be the candidate of a third party. As of September 1947 the majority of informed opinion does not favor this particular hypothesis. . . . For one thing the men around Wallace are motivated by the Communist Party line.
>
> 4. The independent and progressive voter will hold the balance of power in 1948; he will not actively support President Truman unless a great effort is made.

Rowe advised Truman that his reelection chances would be pegged to the farm vote, organized labor, liberals, African Americans, Jews, and Catholics.

> 5. The foreign policy issues of the 1948 campaign will be our relations with the USSR and the Administration's handling of foreign reconstruction and relief.
>
> 6. The domestic issues of the campaign will be high prices and housing.
>
> 7. The conflict between the President and the Congress will increase during the 1948 election.

Rowe then outlined how Truman could take advantage of his incumbency by forging alliances with labor and progressive independents, isolating

Wallace from mainstream liberalism, and drawing a sharp contrast between the Democratic and Republican parties:

> A crucial—but easy—step forward to November 1948 is to create in the public mind a vote-getting picture of President Truman. From as objective a perspective as possible, I submit that the present public attitude toward the President is about as follows: Both the original "honeymoon" and the later violently critical period of public opinion toward the President seem to be over. Emerging instead is the picture of a man the American people like. They know now that he is a sincere, courageous and able man, and, in the cliche so often heard, that he is a man "trying to do his best."[27]

That was Eisenhower's opinion. He did not know whether Truman could win reelection but thought he deserved a chance. Ike hoped that speculation about his 1948 political ambitions would end once he accepted the Columbia presidency. "I am taking a job that is, as far as I am concerned, removed from politics—personal politics," he told reporters at the Pentagon. But many people assumed that if he would take the presidency of a major university he couldn't refuse a presidential draft. Eisenhower in '48 clubs proliferated across the land.[28]

He was about to become a right-wing target. On December 5, 1947, he attended a dinner at the F Street Club hosted by the Bethlehem Steel Company executive John Gross and his wife Laura in celebration of Pennsylvania Republican Franklin H. Lichtenwalter's victory that fall in a special congressional election. Among the other guests were Senators Robert A. Taft, Eisenhower's future rival, and Arthur H. Vandenberg, the leader of the GOP's internationalist wing, Governor James H. Duff of Pennsylvania, Arthur Krock of *The New York Times*, and Frank Kent of the *Baltimore Sun*. A hush came over the room when Eisenhower began talking about how to deal with inflation. Sounding very much like Truman, he said that inflation could be brought under control only if all Americans were willing to make sacrifices. Taft pressed him for details.

Eisenhower responded that industry should lead the way, that organized labor is "political, and so is politics, which I don't know anything about and don't want to." He suggested that if Benjamin Fairless, president of United States Steel, announced that his company would hold the line on prices, saying "you can put us in the red if you want to, and you can ruin us," that other industries might follow this example. Taft told him that the issue was more complicated and that other groups like the farmers would never agree to a price freeze. Of the politicians and business executives listening to Eisenhower's thoughts, only Duff took his side.[29]

The right-wing commentator Fulton Lewis, Jr., who had made a career attacking Roosevelt and Truman, regarded Eisenhower as their political heir. One of the guests at the F Street Club dinner told Lewis about Eisenhower's comments. It is unclear whether the source distorted Eisenhower's words or Lewis twisted them. In a national radio commentary, Lewis snarled: "General Eisenhower, who has been mentioned as a possible presidential candidate, pronounced his views on how to cure the domestic inflation threat, and his proposal was that the government call in the big industrial leaders of the nation and put the pressure on them to agree to reduce all prices for a period of two or three years, so as to eliminate all profits whatsoever." Lewis claimed that Eisenhower had proposed a 100 percent tax on corporate profits, "and use the proceeds for a program of subsidies, to bring the prices down by force of government."

Eisenhower, already wary of politics and disdainful of many politicians, was offended but would not respond to the right-wing attacks. "On such occasions as the dinner the other night," he wrote Krock, "I normally succeed in keeping my mouth closed about matters concerning which soldiers are not expected to have opinions. It happened that something suddenly touched upon one of my deep-seated convictions and I was guilty of very warm advocacy of a particular idea. Possibly I was stupid in not realizing that the dinner was not the completely private social affair that I had supposed. Anyway, you have seen in the press how badly my simple little idea was distorted and misrepresented. But I still believe that some big man in the industrial world has an opportunity, or at least a chance, by sincere, even dramatic action, to help halt the inflationary spiral."

Vandenberg privately favored Eisenhower for the 1948 Republican presidential nomination and told him: "I would advise you, on the basis of many years of experience in politics, to take no notice whatsoever of the incident involving what you are supposed to have said at the Pennsylvania Dinner. Should you, however, decide to take public cognizance of that incident and clear up the matter, I would regard it as a real privilege if you would permit me to make a public statement, detailing not only what you did or did not say, but also who was responsible for the story."

Eisenhower, though, wanted the controversy to go away. As a young officer he had learned from Conner that ignoring unfair criticism was often the most effective rebuttal. But General Ike would never forget Vandenberg's thoughtful gesture nor the enmity of right-wing critics.[30]

Dewey worried about Eisenhower as a late-starting rival for the Republican nomination. According to Dewey's biographer, the New York governor went to see Eisenhower and made a point-by-point case why the general shouldn't run. Ike continued to insist that he was not interested in the White House.[31]

The American people had other ideas. When the Gallup poll included him as a Republican in January of 1948, he beat Truman in a trial heat while Dewey and Taft both trailed the Democratic president. He led Truman by 24 percentage points in New York State.[32] On January 10, he was endorsed for the GOP nomination by the Manchester *Union-Leader* in a front-page editorial and its publisher Leonard V. Finder announced that a slate of Eisenhower delegates would be entered in the March 9 New Hampshire primary. "General Eisenhower has not sought this office—but he is too good a soldier to refuse the command of the people he has served so long and well," the *Union-Leader* asserted. "He has not even been consulted in this instance, because the issue is what the people want, not what innate modesty compels him to prefer."

Finder had, in fact, shared his views about the '48 presidential race with Eisenhower. In mid-October, Eisenhower had given a speech in New Hampshire and stayed overnight at Finder's home. Partly because of this connection, Eisenhower couldn't very well ignore Finder's efforts in New Hampshire. If the general had remained silent, it would have appeared that Finder was acting with his tacit approval. "Someone will instantly jump to the conclusion that it is inspired—that it is merely additional evidence that I am conniving to get something that I publicly state I don't want," the general wrote wartime aide Harry C. Butcher.[33]

Eisenhower spent more than a week drafting a response to Finder. On January 22, 1948 he formally asked in a letter to the New Hampshire publisher to have his name withdrawn from consideration as a presidential contender. The general then made the letter public and it remains one of the more persuasive arguments why soldiers shouldn't become politicians.

Eisenhower told Finder:

> Months ago I thought that unqualified denial of political ambition would eliminate me from consideration in the coming campaign for the Presidency, because that office has, since the days of Washington, historically and properly fallen only to aspirants. . . . I have heretofore refrained from making the bald statement that I would not accept nomination, although this has been my intention since the subject was first mentioned to me. This omission seems to have been a mistake, since it has inadvertently misled sincere and disinterested Americans. But my reticence stemmed from cogent reasons. The first was that such an expression would smack of effrontery. . . . A second and even deeper reason was a persistent doubt that I could

> phrase a flat refusal without appearing to violate that concept of duty to country which calls upon every good citizen to place no limitations upon his readiness to serve in any designated capacity. On this point it is my conviction that, unless an individual feels some inner compulsion and special qualification to enter the political arena—which I do not—a refusal to do so involves no violation of the highest standards of devotion to duty.
>
> It is my conviction that the necessary and wise subordination of the military to civil power will be best sustained, and our people will have greater confidence that it is so sustained, when lifelong professional soldiers, in the absence of some obvious and overriding reasons, abstain from seeking high political office. This truth has a possible inverse application. I would regard it as an unalloyed tragedy for our country if ever should come the day when military commanders might be selected with an eye to their future potentialities in the political field rather than exclusively upon judgment as to their military abilities.
>
> Politics is a profession; a serious, complicated and, in its true sense, a noble one. In the American scene, I see no dearth of men fitted by training, talent, and integrity for national leadership. On the other hand, nothing in the international or domestic situation especially qualifies for the most important office in the world a man whose adult years have been spent in the country's military forces. At least this is true in my case.
>
> I am deeply regretful if a too simple faith in the effectiveness of a plain denial has misled any considerable number concerning my intentions and so allowed them to spend time and effort under erroneous impressions.[34]

As Eisenhower's office released the Finder letter, the chief of the army's Public Information Division told reporters that "General Eisenhower hopes through this means to inform every interested person or group that he is not in politics and that he would refuse the nomination even if offered."

Before making public the letter, Eisenhower showed it to Defense Secretary Forrestal. "He said he had come to a decision that he would not permit his name to be considered for the Presidency," Forrestal reported to Truman. ". . . I remarked to General Eisenhower that the language in his letter was conclusive, and meant that he was definitely out of politics. He agreed, and said that was his intention.

In his memo to the president, Forrestal wrote: "I told him that his letter would put him in a position of tremendous influence, above the battle, and that in this role he could still perform a great service to the country. There is no question in my mind as to his complete sincerity or that his letter reflects the outcome of a genuine moral struggle with himself."[35]

On the same day that Eisenhower removed his name from the presidential race, he sent Truman his resignation as chief of staff: "I scarcely need assure you again of the high sense of distinction and privilege I have felt in the opportunity to serve under you. Your encouragement, understanding, and, above all, your friendship, have been priceless to me. You are likewise aware that I shall always hold myself available for any military duty that the Government may require of me."

In a handwritten response, Truman warmly addressed Eisenhower as "Ike" and expressed the nation's appreciation and his own. "I am sorry you are leaving," Truman wrote. "But I know that eventually your retirement must come. You have my heartiest good wishes in whatever you may decide to do—and my friendship and admiration always."

Truman sent another handwritten note on January 24, telling Eisenhower that at the time he had written the previous letter he had been unaware of the general's formal withdrawal from the presidential race: "Nevertheless, my letter to you would have been just as it was had I seen your 'General Sherman' letter before it was published. I am sure that you and I understand what politicians are doing."[36]

CHAPTER 11

Loophole

Truman made Eisenhower a wealthy man. It was during the Potsdam Conference that Truman told him that he would do anything in his power to be helpful. In his final weeks as chief of staff, Eisenhower took full advantage of Truman's offer.[1]

Their mutual friend Joseph E. Davies, former ambassador to the Soviet Union and one of Washington's more prominent lawyers, persuaded Eisenhower to think about writing his memoirs of World War II. The son of Welsh immigrants and a native of Wisconsin, Davies became a player in national Democratic politics as Woodrow Wilson's western campaign manager and was among his advisers at the Paris Peace Conference. Davies had been FDR's link to Stalin, Truman's special envoy to Churchill, an organizer of the 1943 Teheran Conference and member of the U.S. delegation to the Potsdam summit. He jovially referred to himself as "the country's messenger boy." With FDR's encouragement, Davies had written a 1941 bestseller, *Mission to Moscow*, which predicted that the Soviet Union would play a critical role in defeating Nazi Germany. Stalin presented him with the Lenin Peace Prize and Truman gave him the Medal of Merit, which was then the nation's highest civilian honor. Davies, whose wife Marjorie Merriweather Post was the heiress to the General Foods fortune, had wealth before their marriage. Truman and Eisenhower enjoyed his company because Davies was charming without pretension.

Davies implored Eisenhower to write his own book. "In contemplating the whole business," the general told Davies, "I realize that except for your needling and pushing, I would never have had the courage to bring the matter to a definite conclusion. I think you, more than anyone else, convinced me that I might have something worth saying. Moreover, it was because you took the lead in 'negotiation' that I had the patience—possibly the ego—to talk to publishers at all."[2]

Eisenhower wasn't poor but wanted to improve his financial condition. Between 1942 and 1947 he had a total income of $59,976.67 and had paid $9,715.84 in taxes.[3] "This is the one chance in my lifetime to build security for my family," he said of a possible book deal. "The soldier leaves the Army as poor as he enters it." He would soon be earning $25,000 as president of Columbia along with his $15,000 military salary. His five-star rank and income were permanent. Though on active duty in name only, Eisenhower considered himself on call for special assignments. The median income in 1947 was $7,437 for lawyers and $10,700 for physicians.

There was intense competition among New York literary houses for General Ike's wartime memoirs. He turned down several offers of a $500,000 advance, which would be the equivalent of $5 million in the current market. Before signing a book contract, he wanted to minimize his taxes. If he paid straight income tax on his book earnings, Eisenhower would be in the 75 percent tax bracket, and he thought it unfair that he would keep only a fourth of his book earnings.

Then he learned of another possibility. Douglas M. Black, the president of Doubleday & Company, Inc. and a Columbia trustee, and William E. Robinson, vice president and business manager of the *New York Herald Tribune*, suggested how Eisenhower could pay a much lower tax rate. "They said that the Internal Revenue Service had always considered that any book written by a non-professional writer and sold by him in its entirety, together with rights of every kind, could be sold as a house and a lot can be sold," Eisenhower recalled. "Thus, they said, by disposing of the entire group of rights along with the book itself, there would be no reason for others to bother me on the subject, and the whole process could be handled on a capital gains basis as far as taxes were concerned."[4]

It was an uncommon loophole. Truman, though, could identify with Eisenhower's desire for financial security. Like Eisenhower, he had struggled to make ends meet for most of his life. As Eisenhower's tenure was ending as chief of staff, Truman had no qualms about helping him get a tax break. Truman believed that the general deserved special consideration for serving his country with such distinction. "I got Ike a settlement on his book," Truman confirmed in a 1954 interview.[5]

General Harry H. Vaughan, Truman's military aide, was in the room when Truman directed the Internal Revenue Service Commissioner George J. Schoenman to help Ike. "Eisenhower is not an author by profession, so this should be considered as a capital gain," Truman told the IRS commissioner, according to Vaughan.[6]

On December 20, 1947, Eisenhower conferred with Archibald Wiggins, undersecretary of the treasury, about his projected literary income. That same day, he formally asked for a ruling:

> Certain publishers have urged me to write a personal memoir of the war years. The proposal is that the publisher take, in one transaction, the complete "bundle of rights" that normally apply to a piece of writing. The sale would completely divorce me from any further influence or control over the manuscript or its exploitation in any field. There would be no further income of any kind accruing to me after the single transaction.
>
> I am not in any sense a professional writer. No income of any kind is derived from me from any writing, speaking or related activity. The question below is important to me, not only because I am anxious to comply with every requirement of law and of highest ethical standards, but because on its answer will largely depend decisions that I must now make.
>
> The question is whether, for tax purposes, the Treasury Department of the United States would regard the transaction above described as a capital gain or would it class the amount as income to be taxed under applicable income tax schedules. I appreciate your courtesy in undertaking to investigate this question and apologize for my intrusion on your time.[7]

Truman endorsed Eisenhower's proposal. Eisenhower met with Treasury Secretary John Snyder, Truman's fellow Missourian, and was advised on what conditions would have to be met for the book to be sold as a capital asset. "Under the facts stated," IRS Commissioner Schoenman replied to Eisenhower, "the literary work would be a capital asset in your hands. In accordance with Section 117 of the Internal Revenue Code, the sale of such asset would result in gain to you taxable as a long-term or short-term capital gain, depending upon the period of time the asset is held by you. If it is held for not more than six months, the gain would be short-term capital gain. If held for more than six months, the gain would be long-term capital gain. The basis to be used for computing such gain would be the cost to you of producing the manuscript. . . . The holding period for such literary property commences with the date that you complete the manuscript."[8]

Eisenhower got what he wanted. "The only question remaining to be resolved," the general wrote Davies, "is that of determining when we can call the script a finished one. The six months period of ownership begins on that date as you will see from the copy of the Treasury Department letter. However, I am happy to say that Mr. [Kenneth] McCormick of Doubleday stated that the time element was not of primary importance to them, and they seem perfectly ready to allow me whatever time is necessary to get the book done properly . . . since the next three or four months will be the only time available to me for intensive work, I do want to get my part of it finished as quickly as possible."[9]

Davies's partner Donald R. Richburg collaborated with the Treasury Department, Doubleday, and the *Herald Tribune* in working out final details of Eisenhower's contract so that his book income couldn't be taxed as a "contract for services." Eisenhower received $635,000 for his book and got to keep $476,250 after being taxed only 25 percent for the sale of a capital asset. If he had been taxed at the normal rate for this income, Eisenhower would have paid the government about $475,000. Because of the loophole allowed by the Truman administration, Eisenhower paid only $158,750 in taxes on the sale of his book.[10]

Eisenhower went right to the top in closing his settlement with the IRS. "This is to advise you," he wrote Schoenman, "that I completed the above manuscript entitled *Crusade in Europe* on March 24, 1948; that I held the manuscript and all rights incident thereto for a period in excess of six months after completion and that on Oct. 1, 1948 I sold, assigned, and transferred to Doubleday & Co., Inc., absolutely and forever, the above manuscript and all rights of every nature pertaining thereto for a lump sum consideration of $635,000. The full amount of the consideration was paid to me at the time of the sale." The general provided copies of his book contract and correspondence with Doubleday.[11]

Since Eisenhower had already been given preference at the highest levels and his tax break was a directive from the president, Schoenman promptly approved Eisenhower's terms. Though Eisenhower later asserted that the reduced tax rate "had been common practice" by the Treasury Department and IRS, the record clearly indicates that he got preferential treatment because of Truman's intervention and the efforts of Davies and Richburg. Several years later, Truman paid taxes at a 67 percent rate on his memoirs after expenses and made a net profit of $37,000 on an advance of $600,000. A provision requiring that literary works would be taxed as ordinary income was written into the Revenue Act of 1950. It would become known as the "Eisenhower amendment."

"Congratulations to you, Ike," Davies wrote after the book sale. "You have devoted your life to service to your country. You have never tried to make money. But nevertheless, you have made handsome provision for a secure future for Mamie and the grandchildren."[12]

Eisenhower wrote *Crusade in Europe* in less than two months, on a schedule that he described as a "blitz." His files contained most of the book's source material—his wartime correspondence and diaries. He dictated the narrative to secretaries and then edited the transcript in longhand. Each week he would spend a day working with two gifted editors, McCormick of Doubleday and Joseph Barnes, foreign editor of the *Herald Tribune.* Their draft would be revised into final form by Eisenhower's longtime aide Kevin McCann. It was a handsomely packaged book with photographs selected by Edward Steichen and maps drawn by the cartographer Rafael Palacio.[13]

Published in November of 1948, *Crusade in Europe* sold nearly 240,000 copies in two months and that total would reach 1.5 million. More than half a century later, Eisenhower's memoir ranks with those of Ulysses S. Grant and William T. Sherman on the short list of classic military studies by American soldiers. From the time of its publication, *Crusade in Europe* gained critical acclaim. "It is soldierly in the finest sense of that word," Robert E. Sherwood wrote in the *Herald Tribune Weekly Book Review.* "*Crusade in Europe* should be Textbook No. 1 in all military academies the world over for it provides basic lessons in the true meaning of that honorable term 'officer and gentleman.' For the rest of us, it provides a heartening demonstration of what we are pleased to call Americanism at its best."

Allan Nevins, the Civil War historian, wrote of Eisenhower's book: "It is a simple truth to say that this book is absorbing. Every intelligent citizen will find it so. The main reason for this is that General Eisenhower realizes that he has a great theme—the story of the most perfect alliance of nations in history, for the salvation and vindication of democracy in the greatest of world wars. . . . Above all, it expresses the personality of the author. Readers will feel that this is General Eisenhower speaking. That fact, indeed, is one of the chief merits of the work."[14]

In sending his book to Truman, Eisenhower wrote:

> I feel almost presumptuous in presenting to you this soldier's simple account of World War II. It makes no pretense to classification as history and it is certainly not literature. However, it represents, as accurately as I could make it, an account of the more important things than happened during the War with which I had any direct connection. Moreover, I am encouraged to send it on to you because of the kindly interest you have expressed to me concerning it on several occasions in the past.
>
> As explained in the fly leaf, this is the first volume that I have presented to anyone, except for those preserved for my immediate fam-

> ily. Although knowing that you are far too busy to attempt any complete reading, yet I do hope that you will find some of the maps and pictures effective in recalling to your mind events which involved the devoted efforts of millions of Americans.

Eisenhower closed his letter "with great respect."

Truman replied: "I can't tell you how much I appreciated your letter . . . and the book which came with it. You can rest assured that I'll spend the evenings from now on reading it with much pleasure. As you know, I am familiar with a great many of the things that went on behind the scenes during these campaigns and I will be particularly anxious to have your reaction and viewpoint on the subject. I feel highly complimented that you would send me the first volume."

In no small part because of Truman's intervention, Eisenhower now enjoyed financial security. On the flyleaf of the book he had sent to the president, General Ike wrote: "To Harry S. Truman—with lasting respect, admiration, and friendship, Dwight D. Eisenhower."[15]

CHAPTER 12

Shadow

In the months following his death, Franklin D. Roosevelt would become larger than life. Any successor would have suffered in comparison as Truman did. When Americans were asked early in 1948 to name the public figures that they most admired during the first half of the century, FDR led the poll with 43 percent, followed by Eisenhower with 17 percent. Theodore Roosevelt, MacArthur, and Hoover tied for third place with 7 percent, followed by Wilson and Dewey with 5 percent. Only 3 percent of the poll's respondents named Truman.[1]

Through the force of his personality and what he described as a "rendezvous with destiny," FDR changed the shape of American politics. Until the emergence of Roosevelt, the Democratic party had never won four consecutive presidential elections. But the New Deal coalition was coming apart. The 1946 midterm elections were a disaster for the Democrats and FDR's party was dealt another jolt in the winter of 1948 when an American Labor party candidate backed by Wallace won a special congressional election in the Bronx by trouncing the regular Democratic candidate. Even among Democrats, Truman was losing popularity. At the beginning of 1948, two-thirds of FDR's voters approved of Truman's job performance. By April, fewer than half gave him passing marks.[2]

"I didn't have the Roosevelt glamour and I never pretended to have it," Truman said in looking back on this phenomenon. Truman was viewed by many of FDR's allies as a political hack who had never outgrown his long association with Kansas City boss Tom Pendergast. FDR himself had opposed Truman's renomination for the U.S. Senate in the 1940 primary. Even after Truman became his vice president, Roosevelt treated him in a patronizing manner. "If you have any urgent messages you wish to get to me, I suggest you send them through the White House map room," FDR wrote Truman in January of 1945. "However, only *absolutely urgent* messages should be sent via the Map Room. May I ask that you make them as brief as possible in order not to tie up communications."[3]

In assuming the presidency, Truman vowed to support and defend his fallen leader's policies. "Tragic fate has thrust upon us grave responsibilities," he told the American people. "We must carry on." But he moved quickly to replace FDR's cabinet with a new team. Francis Biddle, Roosevelt's attorney general, was the first casualty. Two months into the Truman presidency, Biddle was given a day's notice to resign. The secretaries of state, treasury, labor, and agriculture joined the exodus of New Dealers. "Every President must have a cabinet of his own choosing," Truman wrote in *Year of Decisions*.[4]

"Truman didn't like the New Dealers very much, and said so," recalled James H. Rowe, the former Roosevelt aide. "I think it's only human nature that we weren't too fond of him."

Jonathan Daniels, FDR's press secretary, "had the feeling that the aristocracy of Democracy had passed away and the Pendergasts of politics were pouring in. . . . It was an amazing day to see the transition from the aristocrat of Hyde Park to what those of us who had been with Roosevelt, at that time, thought, was this little guy from Kansas City."[5]

Interior Secretary Harold L. Ickes, one of the more outspoken New Deal liberals, resigned in protest over Truman's nomination of California oil millionaire Edwin Pauley for undersecretary of the navy. Ickes alleged that Pauley had offered during the 1944 campaign to raise hundreds of thousands of dollars from oil interests if the federal government dropped its claims to offshore oil lands. Many of FDR's allies, including his widow Eleanor, sided with Ickes in this dispute with Truman. Pauley denied allegations of wrongdoing and Truman stood by him. But he asked Truman to withdraw his nomination.

Another prominent New Dealer, former Vice President Henry A. Wallace, who was serving as Truman's secretary of commerce, was asked to resign in September 1946 after he made a speech at Madison Square Garden attacking the administration's hardening attitude toward the Soviet Union. Wallace viewed himself as the true heir to the Roosevelt legacy and in late 1947 launched a third party to seek the presidency.

A Gallup poll in the spring of 1948 showed that only about a third of the American people approved of Truman's job performance. Raymond Moley, the former FDR brain truster, summed up Truman's dilemma in his *Newsweek* column: "On the 15th anniversary of its rise to power, the Democratic party is returning to the primeval chaos from which FDR lifted it. Minorities are not only drifting away; they are splitting up. Minority groupism as a political faith is at the end of its sandy rope. . . .

"Truman simply does not have what it takes to bring masses of city voters enthusiastically, almost fanatically, to vote Democratic. The vast majorities in the big northern cities were not voting Democratic in the past 15 years. They were voting Roosevelt."[6]

Ickes wrote Truman on March 27 with blunt advice: "You have the choice of retiring voluntarily and with dignity, or of being driven out of office by a disillusioned and indignant citizenry. Have you ever seen the ice on a pond suddenly break in every conceivable direction under the rays of the warming spring sun? That is what has happened to the Democratic party under you, except that your party has not responded to bright sunshine. It has broken up spontaneously."

The April 5 issue of *The New Republic* headlined its front-page editorial "Truman Should Quit." Publisher Michael Straight lamented that the Democratic party was dying under FDR's successor. "Truman has neither the vision nor the strength that leadership demands," he asserted.[7]

This view of Truman's plight was shared by the Americans for Democratic Action, the nation's most influential liberal political organization, which was founded in January of 1947. Even though the ADA agreed with many of Truman's policies, the group's leaders doubted that he could win a full term. "We honor President Truman for his unswerving support of the European Recovery Program, for his courageous advocacy of civil rights, and for his wise recommendations for domestic economic policy," the ADA's board declared in April of 1948. "But we cannot overlook the fact that poor appointments and faltering support of his aides have resulted in a failure to rally the people behind policies which in large measure we wholeheartedly support."

The liberal wing of the Democratic party hoped to draft Eisenhower as an alternative to the beleaguered Truman. "Recently the Democrats have taken the attitude that Mr. Truman cannot be re-elected," Eisenhower told Ambassador W. B. Smith, "therefore they do not want to renominate him. In this situation they are turning desperately to anyone that might give them a chance of winning, and they have the cockeyed notion that I might be tempted to make the effort. I don't know why they cannot accept the letter I wrote last January, but I think most of them know that my position was taken as a matter of conviction and that I expect to stand on it."[8]

Truman wasn't quite so sure about that. Forrestal wrote in his diary on March 26:

> Secretary of State Marshall called me this morning to say that he just had word from the White House that Franklin Roosevelt, Jr. was going to make a statement this afternoon to the effect that the Democratic party would have to draft General Eisenhower as its nominee for the presidency, and asked me for my suggestions. I said I would be glad to talk to young Roosevelt myself but doubted whether this could be effective and suggested that I inform General Eisenhower and see if he would care to talk to him.
>
> I called General Eisenhower and he was very reluctant to call [Roosevelt]. He said that if I called Roosevelt I could quote him [General Eisenhower] that he would be greatly distressed at any such move and public declaration. Senator McGrath told me that my calling would not affect young Roosevelt because he was very set in his ideas and was determined to go ahead.
>
> I called Eisenhower about 2:15, reported these facts to him, and he said that he would be willing to call. He called back in about ten minutes and said that he had got hold of Roosevelt and said that any action of this kind now, in the middle of very delicate situations in various countries abroad, could have the most dangerous consequences and might negate American policy. He said that he would personally urge in the strongest possible terms that any statement which might be interpreted abroad as implying failure to support the President at this most critical time or to indicate deep and serious splits of public opinion would be detrimental to the country. He said he was making this observation without reference to any political considerations, particularly as they affected himself; that he had tried to make himself clear on that point when he made his public statement some weeks ago. That he meant what he said then and was sorry that the people didn't believe him, but it still continues to be true.[9]

FDR, Jr., a vice chairman of ADA and member of Truman's Committee on Civil Rights, was undaunted by Eisenhower's reluctance. James Roosevelt, FDR's eldest son and California's Democratic national committeeman, and his brother Elliott joined FDR, Jr., in the effort to draft Eisenhower. James would be chairing California's delegation to the Democratic convention in Philadelphia. "I think in 1948, early, or late in 1947, I began to have the feeling that President Truman couldn't be re-elected," James Roosevelt said in a 1972 oral history, "and along with some other liberal Democrats who foresaw that Wallace was probably going to run as a third party candidate, we felt that the Democratic party needed a more popular figure to assure, or to have a real chance of, the Democratic ticket winning. . . . I was convinced that General Eisenhower was obviously a good executive and that he certainly was a national hero, and if he became a Democrat and subject to the influence of the Democratic party that he would be an effective president. And I still feel that perhaps he would have been an effective president, far more effective than he was as a Republican. So, we began to see whether the party would possibly draft him and accept him."[10]

Eleanor Roosevelt, who was named by Truman in December 1945 as a member of the U.S. delegation to the United Nations general assembly, declined to endorse him for renomination and worked behind the scenes to encourage an Eisenhower draft. "Eleanor Roosevelt herself had called several times to discuss it," Hubert H. Humphrey recalled. At the time, he was the young mayor of Minneapolis and Democratic-Farmer-Labor party nominee for the U.S. Senate. "Much of the pressure came from people associated with Franklin Roosevelt, old New Dealers, now new ADA'ers. They felt that their politics were purer and their ideas better than those of Truman's people."[11]

Mrs. Roosevelt, who offered her resignation from the UN delegation in the spring of 1948 (it was declined), wrote Truman in late March: "There is without any question among the younger Democrats a feeling that the party as at present constituted is going down to serious defeat and may not be able to survive as the liberal party. Whether they are right or wrong, I do not know. I made up my mind long ago that working in the United Nations meant, as far as possible, putting aside partisan political activity and I would not presume to dictate to my children or to anyone else what their actions should be. I have not and I do not intend to have any part in preconvention activities."[12]

Truman smoldered for weeks over the Roosevelt family's attempts to deny him renomination: "No professional liberal is intellectually honest," he wrote in another diary entry. "That's a real indictment—but as true as the Ten Commandments or the Sermon on the Mount. Most Roosevelts [aren't] either. Jimmy, Elliott and the mother used the White House for personal promotions, most of which cost the investors. Terrible."

Truman had a face-to-face meeting with James Roosevelt during the midst of his Draft Ike campaign. During a western swing, Truman addressed the Greater Los Angeles Press Club. Roosevelt later called on Truman in the presidential suite of the Ambassador Hotel. As he greeted the president, FDR's son was cheerful and smiling. Then Truman vented his rage: "Your father asked me to take this job. I didn't want it. I was happy in the Senate. But your father asked me to take it and I took it. And if your father knew what you are doing to me, he would turn over in his grave. But get this straight: whether you like it or not, I am going to be the next president of the United States."[13]

Truman and Eisenhower remained on cordial terms. On May 2, the Eisenhowers moved from Quarters Number One at Fort Myer into Columbia University's presidential mansion at 60 Morningside Drive. "Our stay in Washington was highlighted by our friendship with you and Mrs. Truman," Eisenhower wrote Truman from his new home.

"I hope everything is going well with you and that you are getting settled in your new undertaking," Truman responded. "As I told you once before, I think it is a wonderful one and one that will do the country as much good as any other one thing I can think of."[14]

More and more Americans were deciding that Ike could do more good in another role. In late spring, the Roper poll tested Eisenhower's strength as a possible Democratic and Republican nominee. He defeated Truman by two to one and beat Dewey by a clear but smaller margin. "It is hard to find another case in modern political history," pollster Elmo Roper observed, "where a man who had not lifted a finger to campaign for the presidency was so clearly the choice of the electorate."[15]

The Draft Eisenhower movement picked up the support of northern Democratic machine bosses, including Chicago's Democratic chairman Jacob M. Arvey, New York Mayor William O'Dwyer, and Jersey City's Frank Hague. Their opposition to Truman was on purely pragmatic grounds. "We were certain that Truman could not win," Arvey said.[16] In the weeks before the national conventions, Eisenhower kept talking to Democratic supporters. He conferred with ADA Chairman Leon Henderson, California's liberal Democratic Congresswoman Helen Gahagan Douglas, the Democratic national committeemen of Texas and New Hampshire, the assistant director of the CIO's political action committee, Virginia Senator A. Willis Robertson, and Chester Bowles, Connecticut's Democratic gubernatorial nominee and former director of the federal Office of Price Administration. Bowles was among the founders of ADA and was a leader of the Draft Eisenhower movement.

"No one knew Eisenhower's political views, and I felt it was quite possible that he did not have any," Bowles recalled. "I decided to find out. I called his office at Columbia University and an appointment was arranged for the following day. After a two-hour discussion I was convinced: 1) that he wanted to become president; 2) that this desire was qualified by his reluctance to participate in the turmoil of political life; 3) that his ideas on domestic policy were almost wholly unformed; and 4) that he was incredibly naive politically." Near the end of their discussion, Eisenhower asked Bowles if it might be possible for him to win the nominations of both parties. "I came away badly shaken," Bowles said.[17]

The '48 conventions were the first to be nationally televised and both Truman and Eisenhower followed the Republican gathering in Philadelphia with much interest. Truman told reporters that Senator Taft, "Mr. Republican," would have been the GOP's strongest nominee, though the polls indicated otherwise. Eisenhower was hoping for an internationalist GOP ticket of Vandenberg for president and Minnesota's former Governor Harold E. Stassen, a naval veteran of World War II, for the vice presidency. Ernest K. Lindley, the chief of *Newsweek*'s Washington bureau and its political columnist, twice wrote Eisenhower on the eve of the Republican convention, urging him to warn against choosing an isolationist nominee like Taft. Lindley suggested that the general could throw his support to Vandenberg, whose foreign policy views were also Eisenhower's. "I think that everything that it has been appropriate for me to say on the general issues of the day has been said," Eisenhower told Lindley, "and I must abstain from any attempt at influencing decisions of others, despite the critical nature of the times and of current problems."[18]

As the Republican front-runner, Dewey fell short of a majority on the first ballot, and liberal members of the Stop Dewey forces sought Eisenhower's permission to have his name placed in nomination. Eisenhower wouldn't talk to the GOP. "All Republicans thought they'd win easily," Eisenhower wrote in his diary. "So, no 'leaders' wanted me or bothered me. All the 'Republican' pressure on me was truly from the grass roots, because the bosses wanted the top man to be one they could control. The 'Democratic' pressures came from the bosses, all except Harry S. Truman and his personal crowd. They were desperate, and I was a possible port in a storm."[19]

Dewey won the nomination on the third ballot and chose California's liberal Governor Earl Warren as his running mate. If the Republicans had selected Taft or another isolationist, Eisenhower had discussed the possibility of speaking out and moving toward a more active political role. But Eisenhower had nothing against Dewey or Warren. The Republicans had chosen what appeared to be an unbeatable ticket.

That was why the Draft Eisenhower movement gained even more strength in the wake of the GOP convention. "I am not the least bit sorry about it," said Joseph L. Rauh, chairman of the ADA's executive committee. "I think if Eisenhower had been elected President in 1948, he probably would have been a liberal president on the Democratic side." Among the other young liberals for Eisenhower were Illinois gubernatorial nominee Adlai E. Stevenson, Arthur M. Schlesinger, Jr., and Joseph P. Lash.[20]

Shortly before the Democratic National Convention, Jimmy Roosevelt sent a telegram to all 1,234 delegates inviting them to a caucus in Philadelphia. It would be cosponsored by nineteen other prominent Democrats, including Arvey, O'Dwyer, Humphrey, Bowles, Senators Claude Pepper of Florida and Lister Hill of Alabama, and Governors Beauford H. Jester of Texas, Ben Laney of Arkansas, J. Strom Thurmond of South Carolina, and William J. Tuck of Virginia. Roosevelt said: "We are following the wishes of the huge majority of Americans who want the Democratic party to select a candidate of such stature that prosperity of our nation and a lasting peace for the world will become secure.

"It is our critical belief that no man in these critical times can refuse the call of duty and leadership implicit on the nomination and virtual election to the presidency of the United States. It is our duty to build a platform and conduct a convention which will justify our draft on such a candidate. Until this is accomplished we have no right to ask any prior pledges from any American."

Eisenhower's name wasn't mentioned in the telegram to delegates. But Roosevelt later acknowledged: "There was no one else outside of General Eisenhower who had any chance of opposing President Truman."[21]

The Draft Eisenhower movement threatened Truman's renomination. A *New York Times* survey of delegates on July 5 indicated that Eisenhower had substantial support in California, Illinois, New York, New Jersey, Pennsylvania, Texas, and growing support in the South. *Times* political analyst James A. Hagerty reported that "President Truman is facing a hard and possibly losing fight for the nomination."

Arvey said in a 1973 interview that Senator Millard Tydings of Maryland, the son-in-law of Eisenhower's friend Davies, met with Eisenhower at Morningside Heights and drafted a statement in which the general would say that while he hadn't sought the presidency, he had devoted his life to serving his country and could not refuse a call to duty if a political party drafted him for the presidency. According to Arvey, Eisenhower would make these comments in an interview with Krock of *The New York Times.* Arvey said that Tydings showed him Eisenhower's handwritten revisions in their proposed statement. "But," Arvey said, "the next morning at 8:15 Tydings called me. He said, 'It's all off.' He didn't explain why, but I have a feeling Tom Watson talked Eisenhower out of it."

Truman's allies controlled the convention machinery. A tribute to FDR had long been scheduled on the second night of the convention. But none of the Roosevelts were invited by the Democratic National Committee to address delegates because of a concern by Truman's men that Jimmy Roosevelt or FDR, Jr., might use the occasion to promote Eisenhower as their father's rightful heir. The craggy-faced actor Van Hefflin, a World War II veteran, delivered the FDR tribute.

As the convention neared, the Draft Eisenhower movement was taken seriously by Truman's camp. The affable George E. Allen, former secretary of the Democratic National Committee, was the liaison between Truman and Eisenhower. Allen played poker with Truman and golfed with Eisenhower. "There is a desire that Eisenhower make clear before the national convention that he will not take a Democratic nomination," Truman aide Eben Ayers wrote in his diary, ". . . and Allen may be the agent in trying to get this declaration out of Eisenhower."

At Truman's behest, Allen sought to get Eisenhower to make a statement about the Democratic presidential nomination. He had been a guest at Eisenhower's home when leading Democrats assured the General a first-ballot victory in Philadelphia and told him he could write his own platform. On the Fourth of July weekend, Allen stayed with the Eisenhowers as they celebrated their thirty-second wedding anniversary. Though Eisenhower was reluctant to comment on the Democratic Convention, Allen was persistent. "I was with him and sat down and helped when he wrote that under no circumstances would he accept, and he gave it the 'Sherman treatment,' and we gave that out to the press," Allen recalled. "I didn't work on it, he wrote it, but we all went over it together."[22]

Eisenhower declared, in a statement issued by the university's public information office, that "I shall continue, subject to the pleasure of the University Trustees, to perform the important duties I have undertaken as President of Columbia. I will not, at this time, identify myself with any political party, and could not accept nomination for any public office or participate in a partisan political contest.[23]

"This implies no intention of maintaining silence on any issue of importance to the country on which I may feel qualified to express an opinion."

By using the phrase "at this time," Eisenhower had not quite shut the door. It was also noted by supporters that he had said "could not" rather than "would not" accept the nomination. Connecticut Democratic Chairman John M. Bailey called for Eisenhower's name to be placed in nomination. A future chairman of the Democratic National Committee, Bailey noted that Eisenhower "never has said he will not serve if elected President." Senator Olin Johnston of South Carolina disclosed plans to offer a resolution asking Truman to withdraw in Eisenhower's favor. Pepper said that the Democrats could draft Eisenhower as a nonpartisan candidate.

Truman interpreted Eisenhower's statement the same way. "In my first talk with the President this morning," Ayers wrote in his diary, "when I discussed the Eisenhower statement briefly with him, the President showed some disgust with what Eisenhower had said, indicating it was weasel-worded, and he referred to the General as a s— a—."[24]

Just before the convention, Truman huddled with advisers and asked what would happen if Eisenhower's supporters placed his name in nomination. Most of this group told Truman that the draft movement was stopped and that his renomination was a sure thing. But Secretary of the Army Kenneth C. Royall said nothing. Truman then asked for his opinion. Royall warned that Eisenhower would be nominated by acclamation if delegates were given this option. As the meeting broke up, Truman asked Royall, Clifford, and Secretary of the Treasury John Snyder to join him in the upstairs study. "I agree with you about Ike," Truman told Royall. "What can we do to prevent this from happening?"[25]

With Truman's sanction, Royall phoned Eisenhower and got him to issue a statement that would end all speculation about his possible nomination. It would be a telegram to Senator Pepper. Clifford and Royall drafted the general's message. Eisenhower wired the senator: "No matter under what terms, conditions or premises a proposal might be couched, I would refuse to accept nomination."

Eisenhower also wrote Jimmy Roosevelt: "This is personal for you. The public press reports that you may be considering, in spite of my recent statement, the presentation of my name to the Democratic National Convention. . . . If these reports are correct, I respectfully but earnestly request and urge that you drop such intention because I assure you to carry it out would result in acute embarrassment to all concerned as well as confusion in the minds of many of our citizens. My decision which has twice been made public, is based upon my sincere conviction as to the best interests of our country. . . . I keenly realized that your reported statements not only do me high personal honor but imply the greatest possible confidence in me. I venture to invoke the aid of that confidence in asking you to accept my refusal as final and complete, which it most emphatically is."

This ended the Draft Ike movement and clinched Truman's renomination.

"The boom for Eisenhower never developed in 1948 because the General resisted the efforts of those who tried to change his mind," Truman wrote in *Years of Trial and Hope*. "Actually, it would be difficult to speculate on what would have been the outcome if Eisenhower had declared in 1948."[26]

CHAPTER 13

Miracle

Nobody gave him a chance. When Harry S. Truman finally won the 1948 Democratic presidential nomination, the odds against his reelection were twenty to one. Supreme Court Justice William O. Douglas embarrassed Truman by declining his offer of the vice-presidential nomination. Truman learned that Douglas had told others that he didn't want to be number two man to a number two man. During the debate over civil rights, southern delegates walked out of Philadelphia's convention hall and formed their own party.[1]

Political commentators were already looking back on the Truman years. During the '48 Democratic convention, Walter Lippmann wrote about the changing of the guard: "The country may say to the Democrats as they relinquish the power that they have held so long and the heavy responsibility they have borne through dangerous days: 'Hail and farewell. . . . We shall meet again.'" In watching the telecast of the convention, Truman noted in his diary that none of the speakers "seem to be for me wholeheartedly" with the notable exception of two African Americans. Even the keynote speaker, Senate Minority Leader Alben W. Barkley of Kentucky, stopped short of predicting a Democratic victory. It was the saddest convention in memory. "I found the most discouraged and downcast group I had ever seen," Barkley recalled. "You could cut the gloom with a corn knife. The very air smelled of defeat."[2]

But Truman never lost hope. "I had made up my mind long before the convention that I was going to be a candidate," he said years later, "because I knew if I backed out, it would look as if I felt I hadn't done the job as I thought it should be done, and I thought that if I could get out in the country and see and talk to the people, we would win."[3]

Truman chose Barkley as his running mate. One of the Democratic party's better campaigners and a skilled legislative leader, he was a popular choice. As a southerner, Barkley brought strength to the ticket in the region where Truman needed help.

In his acceptance speech, Truman brought the convention to life. He didn't begin speaking until after two in the morning. The Democratic party had always represented the underdog and Truman's fighting words rallied the faithful. "Senator Barkley and I will win this election and make these Republicans like it," he said. "Don't you forget that. We will do that because they are wrong and we are right."

Truman outlined the differences between the parties in black-and-white terms. "Victory has become a habit of our party," the president said. "It has been elected four times in succession and I am convinced that it will be elected a fifth time next November. The reason is that the people know the Democratic party is the people's party and the Republican party is the party of special interest and it always has been and always will be."

Reading from a black notepad, Truman noted the disparity between the liberal GOP platform and the performance of the Republican-controlled eightieth Congress. He made the surprise announcement that he was calling Congress into a special session to test the sincerity of the Republican commitment to affordable housing, expanded Social Security benefits, federal aid to education, an increase in the minimum wage, and civil rights laws. "Now, my friends, if there is any reality behind that Republican platform," Truman declared, "we ought to get some action out of the short session of the 80th Congress. They could do this job in 15 days if they wanted to do it, and still have time to go out and run for office."[4]

Richard L. Strout, covering the Democratic National Convention for the *Christian Science Monitor*, observed: "Harry Truman may not have given his party a victory in Philadelphia, but he gave it self-respect, and it was fun to see this scrappy little cuss come out of his corner fighting at 2:00 in the morning, not trying to use big words any longer, but being himself, and saying a lot of honest things that needed to be said. Unaccountably, we found ourselves on top of a pine bench cheering."[5]

By calling this special session, Truman put Dewey in a difficult spot. There were some moderate Republicans, including Vandenberg and Dewey's campaign manager Herbert Brownell, who favored enacting several of Truman's proposals. But the GOP congressional leaders were confident that Truman's days were numbered and gave him the brush-off.

"The Special Session is a nuisance but no more," Dewey wrote in a letter to his mother. His strategy was to ignore Truman.[6]

Dewey was mistaken. Truman would make the "do-nothing 80th Congress" the central issue of the fall campaign. In foreign policy, the Republican Congress had been generally supportive of the administration. Truman, though, had used his veto sixty-two times in thwarting conservative GOP legislation. Even before the Democratic National Convention, Truman had been attacking the eightieth Congress in his speeches. But the special session made it possible for Truman to turn the '48 election into a referendum on the Republican Congress.

The Soviet Union also tested Truman's resolve. The Marshall Plan to fund the economic recovery of Europe was just getting started and the Soviets prevented its satellite nations from accepting Truman's financial aid. In the summer of 1948, Soviet authorities in Germany announced a blockade of West Berlin, which was more than one hundred miles within Russian-occupied East Germany. "If we mean that we are to hold Europe against communism," General Lucius Clay declared, "we must not budge. I believe the future of democracy requires us to stay here until forced out." He recommended taking on the Russians with a military convoy. But Truman did not want to risk another war and instead supported an airlift that would provide the two million residents of the western-occupied areas of Berlin with more than 2.3 million tons of supplies by the spring of 1949. Though Dewey publicly went along with Truman's stand against the Soviets, he was less respectful of the president in off-the-record comments to reporters. "If that man will just keep his hands off foreign affairs," Dewey told Edward T. Folliard of the *Washington Post.*[7]

In August 1948, Truman and Eisenhower were both surprised by the testimony before the House Un-American Activities Committee of *Time* magazine's senior editor, Whittaker Chambers, in which he admitted his former membership in the Communist party and accused Alger Hiss, president of the Carnegie Endowment for International Peace, of having been a former agent of the Soviet Union. Hiss, who had been a senior official in the State Department during the Roosevelt and Truman administrations, had accompanied FDR to Yalta and served as the secretary-general of the United Nations at its creation. In 1947, Hiss left government and became president of the New York-based Carnegie Endowment. Eisenhower was chosen by Hiss as among the foundation's board members. "I am honored by the invitation to join your Board," the general wrote Hiss in May of 1948. Eisenhower asked Hiss in that same letter for background on the volatile Mideast situation. In the wake of the allegations, Hiss filed a lawsuit against Chambers for defamation of character. Eisenhower was concerned about fairness. "I have no means of knowing anything at all about the specific facts of this particular case," Eisenhower wrote to fellow Carnegie board member James Shotwell, "but it does strike me as curious, rather as incomprehensible, that there can be any recognized or legal procedure whereby the reputation of a man can be almost destroyed merely on the basis of another's startling accusations. In the circumstances, I am certain that Mr. Hiss will seek every possible avenue to establish the truth."[8]

Truman had a low opinion of HUAC and viewed the hearings as an attempt by isolationists to discredit liberal internationalism and embarrass his administration. At a press conference, Truman answered in the affirmative when a reporter asked whether he thought the committee's sensational charges were "a red herring." Truman agreed with Eisenhower that the committee's tactics were unfair. "They are slandering a lot of people that don't deserve it," the president said. Rep. Karl Mundt (R-South Dakota), a member of the HUAC panel, predicted that Truman would have to eat his statement word by word. When asked for comment on Mundt's remark, Truman replied, "General Eisenhower didn't think so. General Eisenhower didn't think so."[9]

Dewey might well have exploited the allegations about Hiss. But Wall Street lawyer John Foster Dulles, Dewey's adviser on foreign policy, was the chairman of the Carnegie Board and it had been on his recommendation that Hiss had been hired as the endowment's president. It would later become known that Truman had ignored an FBI report about Hiss in December 1945. Because the statute of limitations for his alleged spy activity had expired, Hiss couldn't be prosecuted for espionage. He was indicted by a federal grand jury in December of 1948 and convicted of perjury in 1950. The late Hugh Scott, who served as Republican national chairman in the '48 campaign, told Dewey's biographer Richard Norton Smith why Dewey refused to make an issue of the Hiss case. "He thought it degrading to suspect Truman personally of being soft on Communism," Scott said.[10]

Eisenhower, who liked both Truman and Dewey, had never made a political endorsement and stuck to this policy when asked about the '48 presidential race. "I have no intention of opening my mouth about the various candidates," he told reporters at a Chicago news conference. "I have no intention at this moment of taking any stand on partisan politics. I would like to be known just as an American. My name and whatever reputation I have was given me by three million soldiers who didn't ask if I was a Republican or a Democrat."[11]

In watching both of the major national conventions, Eisenhower was most impressed that summer with former Minnesota Governor Harold E. Stassen, who had made a serious bid for the Republican presidential nomination and seemed destined, at the age of forty-one, for a political future without limits. Stassen, who had two years of combat service and had received a bronze star as Admiral William Halsey's chief of staff in the Pacific, represented generational change and was the first World War II veteran to actively seek the presidency. "I trust that you will not allow yourself to become too discouraged by the disappointments encountered at Philadelphia," Eisenhower wrote Stassen in July of 1948.

> There is no room for doubt that your efforts of the past two years to awaken our younger peoples' deeper political consciousness and sense of responsibility and your insistence upon a liberal and enlightened approach to the problems of today have had a good effect. . . . The purpose of this note is to urge you to continue to devote your efforts and talents to the same basic purposes toward which they have been directed these past many months.
>
> I realize that you, like all the rest of us, have to face the problem of making a living. But even so, you will have an opportunity to continue as a leader in molding American thought. Already you have achieved a splendid and possibly a unique position in our country because of your experience in the political world, your war service, and your reputation for integrity and courage. You are most admirably equipped to continue the work you have started.
>
> Frankly, I regard it as a fine thing for our country that you made the fight that you did and merely want to remind you, as one veteran to another, that a lost battle does not necessarily mean the loss of a campaign.[12]

Eisenhower was avidly courted by Dewey. In late July the general and Mamie lunched with the Republican presidential nominee at Dapplemere, Dewey's 480-acre farm in Dutchess County. Dewey told reporters that they had discussed the Berlin crisis, unification of the armed services, and the Communist threat in France. On foreign policy, Dewey supported the Marshall Plan, Truman Doctrine, and the containment of Soviet expansionism. Eisenhower assumed that Dewey would win the presidency that fall and that a change in administrations would be good for the country. Though Eisenhower told mutual friends that he would make no endorsement, the general confided that Dewey was his preference.

"There is, among the people of all walks of life, a deep confidence that you are equipped to seek out solutions to problems of deep concern and worry in this country," Eisenhower wrote Dewey after a five-week vacation in the West. "These problems seem to be, by most people, simplified down to two words. They are 'Russia' and 'inflation.' If, by chance, the future should bring about some unforeseen meeting between you and me, I shall give you a more lengthy account of what I saw and heard."[13]

Dewey answered: "I certainly would like to get the rest of it but it looks as though I won't be around very much for the next six weeks. . . . The foreign situation seems to be continuously deteriorating and I hope I may have a very thorough discussion of our situation with you immediately after election."[14]

Eisenhower hedged his bets and kept on cordial terms with Truman. When Eisenhower was formally installed as Columbia's president in October, Truman sent this message: "The glory of our military system is that it is aimed at the maintenance of peace through adequate preparedness and eternal vigilance. The sense of moral and spiritual values which made you invincible in war will inspire and guide you as you assume the leadership in one of our great American institutions of learning. I know you will rise to the opportunity for continued public service which becomes yours today.[15]

"I am grateful indeed for the thoughtfulness of your recent messages of felicitations on my official installation here at Columbia and on my birthday," Eisenhower replied. "It is, of course, always heartwarming to be remembered by old friends, and when a friend is bearing such responsibilities and is so preoccupied with matters of moment as you are—the value of the remembrance is multiplied. One of the drawbacks to my present position is that I no longer have opportunity for the informal conversations I used to have with you that I enjoyed so much."[16]

Truman effectively used his incumbency to bolster his strength among Democratic constituencies. His opposition to the Taft-Hartley Act, which became law over his veto, brought organized labor into the '48 campaign in record numbers. Truman was the first presidential candidate formally supported by the American Federation of Labor. He gained support among Jewish Americans with his de facto recognition of Israel and pledged that fall to help make it "a strong, prosperous, free, and independent democratic state." Truman's executive orders in July of 1948 mandating an end of segregation in the armed services and the federal government were well received in the African-American community and would have major impact in the election's outcome.

The 1948 campaign was the last time that both major presidential nominees waged their campaigns on the railroads. Truman would make three hundred and fifty speeches and traveled more than thirty-one thousand miles. No presidential candidate before or since has ever gotten so close to the people. Dewey, sitting on his comfortable lead in the polls, started his campaign later than Truman's and made fewer appearances.

As a one-time farmer and the first Democratic president from the midwestern farm belt, Truman was effective in blaming Republicans for a sharp decline in grain prices. He alleged that the eightieth Congress had "stuck a pitchfork in the farmer's backs." What it had done was to slash federal grain-storage capacity by more than 80 percent. The farmers, who produced a record crop in 1948, had no place to store it and were forced to sell wheat and corn at below the cost to produce them. "Farmers all over the country are being forced to drop their grain or let it rot on the ground because the CCC no longer has the power to provide emergency storage space for a bumper crop," Truman declared. "While you sat here on a powder keg waiting for prices to blow up, they lit the fuse!"

When Republicans attacked Truman for shoring up farm prices through price supports, the president told farm audiences: "Only with a Democratic President and a Democratic Congress can you be sure that you will get a square deal on prices."[17]

Dewey, a gentleman farmer, underestimated voter anger in the farm belt, which was traditionally Republican. The urbane New Yorker, who seldom lost his cool in his public appearances, reacted harshly in rural Downstate Illinois when his "Victory Special" train accidentally backed up and narrowly missed the crowd in the little town of Beaucoup. "That's the first lunatic I've had for an engineer," Dewey said. "He should probably be shot at sunrise, but we'll let him off this time since no one was hurt."[18] Truman quipped that Dewey "objects to having engineers back up. He doesn't mention that under the great engineer Hoover, we backed up into the worst depression in history."

Until the end of the campaign, Truman kept on the offensive. "Now I have an old-fashioned notion that a candidate for public office has a duty to tell the voters where he stands on the issues in a campaign," he declared in his final campaign appearance. "But the Republican candidate refuses to tell the American people where he stands on any issue. The campaign is ending and you still don't know. All you have got is platitudes and double talk."

Despite his winning performance on the campaign trail, Truman's chances of achieving an upset were considered nonexistent. The Roper poll showed Dewey with a 15 percent edge in September and declared that the election was over. A *Newsweek* poll of fifty political experts was unanimous in predicting a Dewey victory. When this group was asked whose election would be in the national interest, Truman received seven votes. More than a third of those interviewed said that Truman couldn't overcome the Democratic party's three-way split and nearly two-thirds of the political analysts said that Truman wasn't big enough for the presidency. "I'm out slugging doing the best I can," Truman told his friend Irv Kupcinet of the *Chicago Sun-Times*. "No man can do more."[19]

The news media was certain that Truman's efforts weren't enough. In its pre-election issue, *Life* magazine ran a full-page photograph of the Deweys with this caption: "The next President travels by ferry boat over the broad waters of San Francisco Bay." The Alsop brothers wrote in their syndicated column: "Events will not wait patiently until Thomas E. Dewey officially replaces Harry S. Truman." Drew Pearson claimed to have the inside story about Dewey's cabinet in a column written on election day. The November edition of *Kiplinger's* magazine, with the front-page headline, "What Dewey Will Do," included a thirty-two page analysis of the new Republican administration. *The New York Times* projected that Dewey would carry twenty-nine states with 345 electoral votes, compared to Truman's eleven states and 105 electoral votes, with Thurmond getting four southern states with 38 electoral votes, and four states uncertain.

Then the people spoke.

On election night, the results were inconclusive. Dewey was doing well in the Northeast, Thurmond had indeed won four states in the Deep South, but Truman was exceeding all expectations. The radio commentator H. V. Kaltenborn told his audience at midnight: "Mr. Truman is still ahead but these are returns from a few cities. When the returns come in from the country the result will show Dewey winning overwhelmingly." Kaltenborn was misinformed. Truman came on strong in the farm belt and in the West and would win five states that Dewey had carried over FDR in '44. Dewey said after the election that the farm vote was decisive in '48. African Americans supported Truman by nine to one—providing the margin of victory in the key states of Illinois, Ohio, and California. Wallace failed to carry a single state and got less than 1.2 million votes. The undecided vote, which traditionally goes against the incumbent, broke in favor of Truman. When all the votes were counted, it turned out that Truman had achieved the greatest upset in American political history. He garnered 49.5 percent of the popular vote and carried twenty-eight states with 303 electoral votes. Of the states carried by Truman, FDR had won twenty-three in all four of his victories. Truman had salvaged Roosevelt's grand coalition and even won a majority in the South.

Graceful in defeat, Dewey wired Truman: "My heartiest congratulations to you on your election and every good wish for a successful administration. I urge all Americans to unite behind you in support of every effort to keep our nation strong and free and establish peace in the world."[20] The New York governor told reporters that he was "just as surprised as you are," but had no regrets and would not make another run for the presidency.

The most enduring image of the '48 election is the picture of Truman gleefully flaunting the "Dewey Defeats Truman" headline of the *Chicago Tribune*. "This is one for the books," Truman chortled. What made this so special for Truman is that the *Tribune* of that era was the voice of midwestern isolationism and a persistent critic of the Roosevelt and Truman administrations.

Truman was helped by an unusually strong group of Democratic candidates at the state and local levels that included Adlai E. Stevenson for governor of Illinois, G. Mennen Williams for governor of Michigan, Frank Lausche for governor of Ohio, U.S. Senate nominees Hubert H. Humphrey of Minnesota, Paul H. Douglas of Illinois, Lyndon B. Johnson of Texas, Clinton Anderson of New Mexico, Estes Kefauver of Tennessee, and Robert Kerr of Oklahoma. The Democrats recaptured both houses of Congress and a majority of the nation's governorships.

In an exchange with his favorite Englishman, Truman analyzed the great upset. From Chartwell, Churchill wrote: ". . . my hearty congratulations on your gallant fight and tremendous victory. I felt keenly the way you were treated by some of your party and in particular Wallace who seemed to us over here to be a greater danger than he proved. But all this has now become only the background of your personal triumph. Of course it is my business as a foreigner or half a foreigner [Churchill's mother was American] to keep out of American politics, but I am sure I can now say what a relief it has been to me and most of us here to feel that the long continued comradeship between us and also with the Democratic party in peace and war will not be interrupted. This is most necessary and gives us the best chance of preserving peace."[21]

Truman responded: "I had a terrific fight and had to carry it to the people almost lone handed but when they knew the facts they went along with me. It seemed to have been a terrific political upset when you read the papers here in this country. Really it was not—it was merely a continuation of the policies which had been in effect for the last sixteen years and the policies that the people wanted."[22]

Eisenhower, who had given Truman little chance, had voted for Dewey but admired the president's comeback. The general wrote Truman:

> The political history of the United States reveals many unusual developments, but certainly at no point does it record a greater accomplishment than yours that can be traced so clearly to the stark courage and fighting heart of a single man.
>
> It seems almost needless for me to reaffirm my loyalty to you as President; or to assure you again that I always stand ready to attempt the performance of any professional duty for which my constitutional superiors believe I might be specially suited. The simple purpose of this note is to bring you my sincere wishes for health, happiness, and success—to repeat my confidence that, in all of the grave responsibilities that you will continue to carry, in all the complex problems you must continue to solve, you will be motivated by one purpose only, the good of this great nation.
>
> My congratulations, my faith, and my sincere best wishes are yours always. With expressions of the utmost respect.[23]

In his "Dear Ike" reply, Truman wrote: "Of course, you didn't have to reaffirm your loyalty to me. I always know exactly where you stand.

"I hope the first time you are in the Capital City you will drop in and see me."[24]

Thus passed one of the most hectic periods in the life of President Truman, the year 1948, during which he faced up to his prospects for election to his high office and though written off by the pundits and subjected to unfair criticism and ridicule, he managed to win. To have made it through this near disaster—the loneliest campaign ever waged by a sitting president—would have been a superhuman task for anyone, but Truman carried it off, in large part because of his humble and rural background that had taught him to take each day's problems as they came and then do his very best. It was an ordeal, and yet he survived against all odds.

On Eisenhower's side there was a rather similar experience, if not nearly as dramatic. For an individual who had spent the better part of his life in the military, beginning with his arrival at West Point in June 1911, a bygone era, it was wrenching to leave the army and become a civilian, even if for General Ike the transition meant a move from Fort Myer to New York City and Columbia University's ornate presidential mansion on Morningside Heights. No sooner was he installed as president of a distinguished institution in the center virtually of the world's most impressive city when he found himself attempting to mediate the bitter differences between the armed services and making a special effort to sooth the hurt feelings of the navy's leading admirals who were certain that the newly organized U.S. Air Force and the rival U.S. Army were "out to get" their service. Eisenhower, who had passed up a chance to run for the presidency, admired Truman's brave comeback and looked forward to their next meeting.

CHAPTER 14

Pentagon

Following the great upset of '48, Eisenhower made his move to become a player in the second Truman administration. After just six months at Columbia University, he was becoming restless and bored. As a general of the army, he retained five-star rank and remained technically on active duty. In a letter to Secretary of Defense James V. Forrestal, Eisenhower wrote: "I can scarcely think of any chore that I would refuse to do wherever people in responsible positions feel that I might be able to help. I know you understand that you can call on me at anytime for anything."[1]

Forrestal went directly to Truman with Eisenhower's offer. "Specifically, what I had in mind was inviting him to come down, only with your approval, of course, to sit with us for a period of three or four weeks," Forrestal wrote the president. "I should like, if it were possible, to have him named by you for that interim period, and to preside over the Joint Chiefs, but if that were impossible an informal basis would be second best."[2]

Under any circumstances, Truman would have wanted Eisenhower on his team. But Eisenhower's overture was well timed. Truman's other favorite general, Marshall, was in ill health and had given notice of his resignation as secretary of state. Marshall underwent surgery for removal of a kidney on December 7, 1948. Dean Acheson was Truman's choice as Marshall's successor. But Truman, who had relied on Marshall for military advice, knew that Eisenhower could come closer than anyone else in filling this void.

Truman needed Eisenhower's help. The National Security Act of 1947 wasn't working. Under that law, the armed services were supposed to be unified as equal members of the National Security Establishment. Defense

Secretary Forrestal, who had thwarted Truman's original unification plan and shaped the '47 compromise, now admitted that it had been a failure. Each of the services were left intact as separate departments and their rivalries had gotten worse. The leadership of the navy and air force were practically at war. The navy sought to prevent the air force from building the B-36 bomber while the air force attempted to limit the role of naval aviation by opposing the proposed supercarrier *United States.* "I visited all three Chiefs of Staff and had with them most satisfactory talks," Eisenhower reported to Forrestal in late 1948, "I took occasion again to stress the importance of a united front on the part of the security establishment."

On learning from Forrestal that he could have a short-term or long-term role, Eisenhower asked whether he would have to give up the university presidency. "Naturally, if anything more than a very temporary assignment were contemplated," Eisenhower wrote Forrestal, "I think you and I would have to get together in advance and examine the whole thing very carefully and, of course, I should have as much advance warning as possible. If only a brief tour of service should be in sight, I could ordinarily make arrangements to report on short notice."[3]

Truman assured Eisenhower that his resignation from Columbia was not necessary. The general advised Truman from December of 1948 until July of 1949 and took a two-month leave from Columbia in February. "Idea is that I am to come here about January 21, 1949, to work as his [Forrestal's] military consultant for two to three months to iron out many of these difficulties," Eisenhower wrote in his diary. "Final approval of [armed forces unification] plan must be given by President, and then complete and loyal adherence to decision must be demanded and obtained. This means also that responsibility for major tasks as between the services must be fixed. Previous visits, on an occasional hit-or-miss basis, he no longer considers satisfactory."[4]

In early December, Truman and Eisenhower got together twice for discussions about the proposed budget for military expenditures and revision of the National Security Act. The three services had made budget requests of $30 billion and a report by the Joint Chiefs of Staff had recommended $23.6 billion. Truman had set a $14.4 billion ceiling for defense expenditures. Reporting to Forrestal on December 9, 1948, Eisenhower wrote: "I talked for half an hour with the President. Without pretending to quote him or to interpret accurately all that he said, I still got the following impressions: He seemed somewhat impatient that any of the Services should attempt to present a picture of being 'cut' when the total defense budget for 49–50 is $1.2 billion above 48–49. He feels that we should insist that our overall defense picture is growing brighter and should not use trick figures to give an opposite impression, either here or abroad."[5]

Forrestal told Eisenhower that he was uncertain about his own future at the Pentagon. He had disagreed with Truman's efforts to sharply reduce military spending and, on strategic grounds, the administration's recognition of Israel. Forrestal was among the few cabinet members declining to take an active role in Truman's 1948 reelection. It was his belief that the secretary of defense should be above politics. With Truman's knowledge and agreement, Forrestal had arranged for Republican presidential nominee Dewey to receive official briefings during the '48 campaign. When Dewey seemed headed for certain victory, there was speculation that Forrestal would be part of the new Republican administration. Dewey told reporters at an off-the-record briefing that he would probably retain Forrestal. Some of Truman's associates, including General Harry H. Vaughan, were seeking Forrestal's ouster on grounds of disloyalty. Those allegations were unfair. Forrestal had contributed $2,500 to Truman's campaign, the equivalent of $25,000 in today's currency. Truman, who had great respect for Forrestal's intellect and character, thought that he was showing signs of burnout and exhaustion after nine years at the highest level of government.[6]

Eisenhower was also worried about his friend. "Jim [Forrestal] is looking badly," Eisenhower wrote in his diary on January 8, 1949. "He has a conscience and a sense of duty. Those coupled with his feeling of urgency and his terrific, almost tragic disappointment in the failures of professional men to 'get together,' leads him to certain errors. Among these none is worse than the way he treats himself. He gives his mind no recess, and he works long hours that would kill a horse. Except for my liking, admiration, and respect for his great qualities, I'd not go near Washington, even if I had to resign my commission completely. To a certain extent these same feelings apply to HST, but he does not see the problems so clearly as does Jim, and he does not suffer so much due to the failure to solve the problems. I like them both."[7]

It was time, in Eisenhower's opinion, for Truman to take command and get tough with the uniformed leadership of the armed services. "I believe the President has to show the iron underneath the pretty glove," the general wrote in his diary. "Some of our seniors are forgetting that they have a commander in chief." When Eisenhower sat down with Truman in the Oval Office on February 9, he told the president that the services should be "put on sharp notice by the Commander in Chief that he demands: (a) Complete respect for the decisions of the Secretary of Defense. (b) That appointments, assignments, and relief will be on the recommendation of the Secretary of Defense. (c) That the Joint Chiefs of Staff must, as his own body of military advisers, act decisively—and must place Joint Chiefs of Staff work in first priority, even if it demands 90 percent of all their working time. Absences not tolerated except of unavoidable causes. (d) That every Presidential decision is a command that must compel complete and loyal support, or individual must ask for reassignment."[8]

At the same time, Eisenhower said that the secretary of defense "must follow up on all this and assert his authority so firmly that any defection brings instant action."

It was at this meeting that Truman asked Eisenhower to become presiding officer of the Joint Chiefs. "Long conversation with the President this afternoon," the general wrote in his diary.

> I agreed to act as chairman of joint chiefs of staff for a brief (I hope) period pending change in law or formal arrangements for getting 'unification' on the rails. The President agreed (1) to lay down law to secretaries of service departments and chiefs of staff; (2) to get an undersecretary for Mr. Forrestal; (3) either to get a chairman of chiefs of staff by law or by appointment of [General Joseph T.] McNarney as president of chiefs of staff; (4) to support strongest possible air force; (5) to back Mr. F. and me to hilt in forcing compliance with directives; (6) to cut certain of Navy's assumed missions in order to obtain more money for air; and (7) to get some help in modernizing Army's equipment.
>
> Talked for an hour. Most satisfactory. The only disturbing thing is that President and Mr. F apparently assume that I have some miraculous power to make some of these warring elements lie down in peace together.[9]

It was Truman's hope that Eisenhower could use his political skills to build consensus among the Joint Chiefs for budgets, reorganization of the armed services, and strategy. Eisenhower wrote in his diary February 19:

> There is clearly evident a realization on part of [the Joint Chiefs of Staff] . . . that they must work efficiently, intensively and cooperatively if they are to regain and preserve the prestige that properly belongs to them. They see the fallacy of exploiting—each on his own—whatever influence each might have in Congress for the moment, and in this way permit shrewd investigators and analysts to play one service against the other to the detriment of the whole. I

> personally and very earnestly believe that 15–16 billion dollars per year is all that this country need spend for security forces—if it is done every year (with some additional amounts to cover past deficits). I will have no part of any scheme for increasing the total until we've gotten this much and used it efficiently. All know this—consequently they are ready & eager to begin again, from the very bottom, the study of our strategic position, in the effort to obtain the best possible layout of defense forces. Unless they make progress in agreeing upon "must" tasks and, therefore, "must" appropriations, around which a desirable peace time structure can be built, I'll quit and begin criticizing! That will be the only way left to get action—but it would be repugnant—and out of character![10]

At a February 25 meeting of the Joint Chiefs, Eisenhower presented them with a new statement of war policy that defined the strategy of containment: "The security of the United States requires the pursuance of a definite policy to insure, at the earliest possible moment, the holding of a line containing the Western European complex preferably no farther to the west than the Rhine." Less than four years after Eisenhower's visit to the Soviet Union, he instructed the Joint Chiefs: "Develop a level of military readiness which can be maintained as long as necessary as a deterrent to Soviet aggression, as indispensable support to our political attitude toward the USSR, as a source of encouragement to nations resisting Soviet political aggression, and as an adequate basis for immediate military commitments and for rapid mobilization should war prove unavoidable."[11]

Truman gave his approval to amendments on armed services unification recommended by Forrestal, Eisenhower, and Clifford. On March 5, 1949, he called for the creation of a single Department of Defense and changing the three services from executive to military departments under the defense secretary. Truman, on Eisenhower's recommendation, called for the chairman of the Joint Chiefs of Staff to be nominated by the president, confirmed by the Senate, and to serve as the military adviser to the president and defense secretary. "We should seize this opportunity to strengthen our defense organization which is so vital to the security of this nation and the peace of the world," Truman declared in his message to Congress. These amendments to the National Security Act of 1947 would be enacted by the summer of 1949.[12]

On the night of March 21, Eisenhower had an attack of stomach cramps that was diagnosed as an inflammation of the intestinal tract. He was in bed for a week and on a liquid diet. Truman told Eisenhower that Florida sunshine would be the best medicine for a swift recovery. The president made available the Little White House at Key West and had Eisenhower flown south on the new presidential airplane *Independence.* "I am gradually getting to the point where my doctor allows a little activity," Eisenhower wrote Truman from the submarine base on April 6. "At least he cannot object to my attempting to thank you for the special attention you sent me. According to all laboratory reports my physical condition steadily improves, however, the endurance index is below par! Consequently, I am content to remain in my quarters reading, resting, and occasionally dabbing on canvas . . . I am grateful for your thoughtfulness in making all this possible—and thank you again for your personal prescription."[13]

Truman replied: "I can't tell you how much I appreciated your note of April sixth and I am just as happy as I can be that you are progressing to full physical recovery. I hope you will stay as long as it is necessary to accomplish that purpose. I am also happy that my prescription is having the desired effect."[14] Eisenhower stayed in Key West for fifteen days and presided over a meeting of the Joint Chiefs who visited the naval base.

In the meantime, Forrestal was breaking down. "Jim F is apparently highly discouraged," Eisenhower wrote in his diary. "He blames himself far too much for the unconscionable situation now existing. He is obviously most unhappy."[15] Two decades later, Eisenhower recalled in *At Ease* that in those early weeks of 1949 "it became obvious that the Secretary's physical and mental condition was deteriorating rapidly. When he would bring up the difficulties he was having and mention that if this sort of thing kept up he would have to resign, I never discouraged him. As much as I liked him, as much as I admired his good qualities, I came to believe that the best thing for Jim's sake and the Defense Department was for him to resign."[16]

On March 1, 1949, Truman summoned Forrestal to the White House and asked for his resignation. Forrestal would be replaced by Louis Johnson, a World War I infantry captain who went on to become national commander of the American Legion, then served in the Roosevelt administration as assistant secretary of war. As finance chairman of the Democratic National Committee during the '48 campaign, Johnson played a critical role in Truman's reelection. "Mr. President," Johnson said then, "if, after your election, you should have up for a Cabinet post two men otherwise equally qualified, one of whom believed in your victory, and if that man was I, I should ask you to take account of my loyalty."

Forrestal was appalled by Truman's choice. "Ike, I simply can't turn this job over to Louie Johnson," Forrestal told Eisenhower on the eve of Johnson's swearing-in ceremony. "He knows nothing about the problems involved and things will go to pot. I'll have to go to the President and withdraw my resignation immediately."

Eisenhower advised him otherwise. "I replied with all my strength, urging him not to do anything so foolish," he recalled. "I said to even attempt it would lay him open to criticism and, worse, it would have no effect in any event because the ceremony had been set up for that day and it was impossible to stop it."

Though Forrestal promised to take Eisenhower's advice, he then called Truman in the Oval Office. "Yes, Jim, that's the way I want it," Truman said. The president told his naval aide: "That was Forrestal. He wanted me to tell him whether I really wanted him to be relieved by Louis Johnson today."[17]

Forrestal was suffering from severe depression and was admitted on April 2 to Bethesda Naval Hospital for an "extended rest." On May 22, he plunged to his death from a sixteenth-floor window. Truman paid tribute to Forrestal "as truly a casualty of the war as if he had died on the firing line." Eisenhower noted in his diary that Forrestal was among the first American policymakers to urge caution in dealings with the Soviet Union.[18]

At Johnson's request, Eisenhower stayed on the job. "I agreed readily," the general wrote in *At Ease*, "not only because Mr. Johnson was a friend but because I was extremely anxious to see the Defense Department so organized that we could minimize the service rivalries that plagued it."[19]

When Johnson ordered construction cancelled for the supercarrier *United States* and reduced the carrier force by half, Secretary of the Navy John Sullivan quit in protest and the "revolt of the admirals" followed. Truman later fired Admiral Louis Denfield as chief of naval operations for encouraging political opposition to the administration's decision to build the B-36 bomber. Eisenhower supported Johnson's decision to cancel the supercarrier and favored cuts in "certain of [the] Navy's assumed missions to obtain more money for air."

Eisenhower considered himself a fiscal conservative but thought that Truman and Johnson were overzealous in their efforts to hold down defense spending. "One of our greatest troubles is inability to plan for a given amount of money," Eisenhower wrote in his diary. "Some new authority always intervenes to cut it down in spite of prior commitment by the President himself. Once [in January of 1947] he called me on the plane when I was in Coral Gables hospital to tell me he had to go back on a specific promise for $110 million for army equipment [tanks and trucks]. That was on advice of [budget director James] Webb, but generally the

President does not tell me himself, we just get the bad news. Right now, it comes through Secretary of Defense. We work like the devil on an agreement on a certain size budget, and then are told to reduce it. . . . We are repeating our own history of decades, we just don't believe we ever will get into a real jam."[20]

When offered a full term as chairman of the Joint Chiefs, Eisenhower turned it down. "Louis Johnson wants me to come to Washington as chairman of joint chiefs of staff, permanently, or at least, indefinitely," Eisenhower wrote in his diary in mid-July. "It is queer, but people in political life consider that anyone not in Washington is a lost soul, lost to ambition, to public regard, to any public usefulness. Of course I'll not do it—there are more able men available for that job than possibly any other in government. But he'll think I'm running out on him."[21]

On August 10, 1949, Truman signed the National Security Act amendments that created the new Department of Defense with the former executive departments of the army, navy, and air force as constituent members. The new law provided for a deputy defense secretary, three assistant secretaries, and for a chairman of the Joint Chiefs of Staff. "The best bet, of course, was Ike," Bradley wrote in his memoirs. It was on Eisenhower's recommendation that Truman nominated Bradley on August 12 as the first permanent chairman of the Joint Chiefs.[22]

Truman valued Eisenhower's contribution. The day after signing the law creating the Department of Defense, the president wrote Eisenhower:

> When I asked you, last February, to serve temporarily as presiding officer of the Joint Chiefs of Staff, you responded like the good soldier you are. I know how greatly this assignment disrupted your plans, and I want you to know how much I appreciate all that you have done, as well as all that you will do in the future as a consultant and adviser.
>
> The Chiefs have made outstanding progress since you became their presiding officer. This progress has come about because of two principal factors: the great effort you have put into the job, and the high regard for your objectivity and impartiality which all of the Chiefs have—a regard which all of them have mentioned to me on a number of occasions.
>
> The nation is extremely fortunate to have had the benefit of this most recent service by you. As President of the United States and as Commander-in-Chief, I want to thank you for a difficult job well done.[23]

Eisenhower replied: "I am more than grateful for your over-generous commendation of my recent work as Chairman of the Joint Chiefs. Had I been able to devote more time to the work more could undoubtedly have been done. Though I regret any errors of omission or commission I do assure you that it was, as always, a great personal honor and privilege to do what I could in the solving of important problems under your direction as Commander-in-Chief.

"You may be sure that I shall always respond to the best of my ability to any call responsible officials of our country feel they should make upon me."[24]

By this time, Eisenhower regarded Secretary Johnson as irresponsible in his zeal to cut spending for the armed services. The general, as Truman's military adviser, had argued within the administration for a minimum defense budget of between $15 billion and $16 billion. But when Johnson prevailed and shrunk the budget to $13 billion, Eisenhower asked to be relieved of his responsibilities as military adviser and considered resigning his commission. In Eisenhower's opinion, Johnson's budget cuts were politically motivated and reduced American military power below the safety point. Eisenhower was offended that Johnson frequently referred to the $13 billion program as "Eisenhower's budget" because of the general's participation in budget discussions. "I was the carpenter," he said in response to Johnson's comment. "Someone else was the architect."

In the spring of 1950, Eisenhower went public with his concerns, testifying before the Senate Appropriations Committee that the nation was at risk as the result of cuts in the defense budget. "We are fairly well on the proper line between economy and security," he told the senators. "But in certain details we've been a bit careless." The general warned that the Truman administration was "taking chances" by going "a bit too far" in the reduction of defense spending. Eisenhower urged an additional $500 million for defense spending.[25]

Truman attempted to minimize Eisenhower's criticism of the defense cuts. "The statements of General Eisenhower before the congressional committee were fundamentally in complete agreement with the policies we have pursued right along," Truman told reporters. "No fundamental differences between us."

The president said that he didn't think Eisenhower meant to imply that the nation's defenses were vulnerable. Truman was asked to comment on the general's assertion that the administration was "taking chances" in reducing the defense budget. "That is a natural feeling for any military man. If I didn't have in view the overall budget of the United States," the president said, "the military people would have more than half of it. They asked for $22 billion. You know they can't have that, and they know it, too."[26]

But Eisenhower was prophetic in his assessment of the defense cuts. Within three months of Eisenhower's testimony, the Communists would attack an ally halfway around the world without fear of reprisal.

CHAPTER 15

Trial Heat

In 1949, Truman and Eisenhower were the two most admired men in America in that order, followed by Winston Churchill. That summer, the general asked the president for a favor. In another five years, Eisenhower noted that Columbia University would be celebrating its bicentennial. Would it be possible, Eisenhower wondered, for Truman to authorize a stamp in recognition of this milestone? "I certainly do appreciate your belief that I'll be able to decide on the postage stamps for 1954," Truman replied good-naturedly. "As you know, that is two years beyond the end of this term and, of course I haven't made up my mind yet whether to quit or go ahead and be sure these stamps are gotten out for you." In a handwritten postscript, Truman told Ike: "Was glad to see you at the house the other evening. Hope we can do it again soon."[1]

Truman was eligible to seek reelection to a third term. But Republicans and conservative southern Democrats had passed a constitutional amendment denying this option to future presidents of the United States. As one of their first actions in 1947, the Republican-controlled Eightieth Congress approved a two-term limit for the presidency as the Twenty-second Amendment. Frustrated by a generation of defeat, Republicans were unanimous in their support for term limits. Democrats opposed the amendment by nearly three to one in the House and two to one in the Senate. As the sitting chief executive, Truman was exempted from the term limit. Even though the Twenty-second Amendment was in the process of being ratified by the states, Truman controlled his own destiny.

In looking ahead to the 1952 presidential election, there was much speculation about Truman and Eisenhower. Two-thirds of the respondents to the Gallup poll said in the fall of 1949 that Truman would seek reelection to a third term and only 23 percent predicted his retirement. A narrow plurality rated him as the favorite to win reelection.[2]

At his final press conference of 1949, held in the Oval Office on the Thursday afternoon before Christmas, Truman was asked if he thought that Eisenhower was vying for the presidency. "I do not," the president responded. "General Eisenhower and I are on the friendliest of terms, and always have been. I told you in 1948—when they [the Draft Eisenhower movement] were passing around all those remarks that there wasn't anything to them, and none of you believed me, but they happened to be the facts." Members of the White House press corps laughed at Truman's wry comments.

The president was then asked if he could remain friendly with Eisenhower even if he ran. "Why certainly I could. Certainly I could," Truman said.

"Mr. President, do you feel that you know what is in the general's mind?"

"I think I do," Truman answered.

Truman was asked if he felt certain that Eisenhower "is not a candidate for 1952, as he was not in 1948?"

"Yes, he said so; and that is as far as I care to go," was the president's rejoinder. "I think his word is good and it has always been with me."

But Truman acknowledged that something might be going on when asked if people were seeking to persuade Eisenhower to make a presidential bid: "I wouldn't be surprised about that. They have been trying to, ever since he got out of the Army."[3]

The second Eisenhower boom began not long after Truman's reelection in 1948. After snatching defeat from the jaws of victory, Dewey abandoned his own White House ambitions and began focusing on Eisenhower as the last best hope for a Republican restoration. "I felt that the Republican party was weak with the electorate, and that a new style of candidate was the only sure way to win," Dewey said years later, "and I was confident that General Eisenhower would win and I wasn't confident that anybody else would."

Eisenhower struck Dewey as a political natural. "In the first place, he was not handicapped with the label of a 'politician.' He had a personality which projected as far as he could be seen," Dewey said in an oral history interview. "He could be a mile away and you could see the enormous charm and attractiveness of that smile. He had equal capacity to charm people in private. His standing in the world was at the very pinnacle. The confidence of the American people in him was at the pinnacle."

Dewey, who had come close enough to the presidency to feel the burdens of the office, respected Eisenhower's leadership skills and experience. "I'd seen quite a little bit of him, and gotten to know him better," the former New York governor recalled in 1970, "and had decided that his capacity for selecting good people, his grasp of the world situation which so few people had, and his ability to delegate made him well-qualified for President. In addition to that, he had substantial political experience, because he'd presented the Army budget to Congress many times."[4]

While Eisenhower was staying at Truman's Little White House at the naval base in Key West, Dewey wrote him in April of 1949: "As soon as you have fully recovered there are one or two things of some importance that I would like to talk with you about at your convenience."[5]

This meeting took place on July 6, 1949 at the Columbia presidential mansion in Morningside Heights. "He stayed at my house for two hours. He says he is worried about the country's future and that I am the only one who can do anything about it," Eisenhower wrote in his diary.

> The Governor says that I am a public possession, that such standing as I have in the affections or respect of our citizenry is likewise public property. All of this, though, must be carefully guarded to use in the service of all the people. . . . He feels that New York State is vital to any Republican aspirant to the presidency. He assumes I am a Republican and would like to be president. When this last came out I was flabbergasted. I must have had a funny look on my face, because he said, "I know you disclaimed political ambition in a verbose, wordy document, but that was when you were just a soldier."
>
> This reaffirms a conviction I have formed, which is that no denial of political ambition will ever be believed by a politician, unless the disclaimer is so old he is tottering rapidly to the grave. In this case the refusal would not be a denial of ambition, merely an expression of regret.
>
> The Governor then gave me the reasons he believed that only I (if I should carefully preserve my assets) can save this country from going to hades in the handbasket of paternalism, socialism, dictatorship. He knows that I consider our greatest danger the unawareness of our majorities, while aggregated minorities work their hands into our pockets and their seats to the places of the mighty. So he dwelt at length on the preservation of freedom, my favorite subject.

Dewey even mapped out the strategy for Eisenhower's election. Eisenhower should declare his adherence to Republican principles, then run for the New York governorship in 1950 with Dewey's support. Like Dewey, Eisenhower could use that office as a springboard to the presidential nomination. Dewey offered to appoint Eisenhower to the U.S. Senate seat left vacant by the resignation of Democrat Robert F. Wagner, "but advised against my taking it. His reasons are far too long to set down here, but fundamentally they are: Get elected governor and New York State is yours without necessity of taking unequivocal stand on national issues. This will not be true in Washington. He refused to take final answer of no on governor business, I am to let him know in the fall."

It would be a mistake, Dewey said, for Eisenhower to go public with his views on more than a few issues. "His basic reasoning is as follows," Eisenhower wrote:

> All middle-class citizens of education have a common belief that tendencies toward centralization and paternalism must be halted and reversed. No one who voices those views can be elected. He quotes efforts of Hoover, Landon, Willkie, himself. Consequently, we must look around for someone of great popularity and who has not frittered away his political assets by taking positive stands against national planning, etc., etc. Elect such a man to the presidency, after which he must lead it back to safe channels and paths.
>
> As indicated, the talk was long. I wish I could merely say what Sherman said. But how can I know today what the situation of this country will be four years from now, and whether I'll believe I could do something about it better than most others could. It all seems unreal and forced to me, but I'm not egotistical enough to give it any kind of an irrevocable, arbitrary answer at this moment.

Eisenhower told Dewey that he didn't want to go into politics and would "never willingly seek a vote." As in 1948, the general said that he would never shirk his duty but had yet to be convinced "that I have a duty to seek political office."

Dewey argued that there was no time to be lost. "Governor said, unless I do something, by 1950, of political significance [elected to governorship], I'm through," Eisenhower wrote.

Flashing his trademark grin, Eisenhower told his guest: "You've given me the best of reasons for doing nothing."

Dewey shot back, "Not if you want to preserve democracy." The general and the two-time Republican presidential nominee agreed to resume their conversation in several months. On the day after this session, Dewey named Wall Street lawyer John Foster Dulles as the junior senator from New York to fill the seat that could have been Eisenhower's.[6]

Soon afterward, Eisenhower was offered the Democratic nomination for the U.S. Senate. It was through their mutual friend George E. Allen that Truman made it known to Eisenhower that he would have the support of the administration and the New York Democratic party. With the appointment of Dulles, the Republicans now held both of New York's U.S. Senate seats and the governorship. Eisenhower would have been a certain winner for the Democrats and an instant contender for the '52 Democratic presidential nomination. New York Democratic Chairman Paul Fitzpatrick told Allen that Eisenhower had to be a Democrat because "a man of his convictions cannot be a Republican."

"Of course I assured him of my appreciation," Eisenhower wrote of Allen's mission, "but I reiterated that 'Nothing has occurred to change my convictions from those I made public on the general subject of my participation in politics in 1948.' "[7]

There was still considerable doubt about Eisenhower's political affiliation. When he registered to vote in October 1949, he declined to sign up with either major political party. Eisenhower declined comment when asked through Columbia University's public affairs office about his refusal to choose a political party. *The New York Times* quoted sources as saying that Eisenhower preferred to remain an independent. The *Times* reported that Eisenhower had been entitled throughout his military career to vote in his native Kansas by absentee ballot but had never done so.

In the same month that Eisenhower registered as an independent, the Gallup poll asked the American people whether they viewed him as a Democrat or Republican. Democrats were evenly divided in their opinion while Republicans by four to one viewed Eisenhower as one of them. A plurality of voters said they didn't know Eisenhower's political affiliation.[8]

That was by design. "I stick to my determination not to appear with a definitely Republican or Democratic party," Eisenhower wrote in his diary at about the time he registered to vote.

As a professional soldier, Eisenhower considered himself above partisanship. He wrote in his diary on January 1, 1950:

> I do not want a political career. I do not want to be publicly associated with any political party, although I fervently believe in the two-party system and further believe that, normally, a citizen is by no means performing his civic duty unless he participates in all applicable activities of his party, to include participation in precinct caucuses.

> Regardless of all faults that can be searched out in the operation of the American system, I believe without reservation that in its fundamental purpose and in its basic structure, it is so far superior to any government elsewhere . . . that my greatest opportunity for service is to be found in supporting, in renewing public respect for, and in encouraging greater thinking about these fundamentals. Since I believe that all Americans, even though they do so unconsciously or subconsciously, actually support these basic tenets of Americanism, it follows that in the field in which I should work (that is, the bringing of these basis tenets to our conscious attention) there is no difference between the two great parties. Therefore I belong to neither. Their function is to bring before the people the chance to choose between two different methods in the application of the principles to specific problems and to allow the people to choose between two specific slates of candidates. It seems to me that there are cogent reasons why I should eschew this partisan field of citizenship effort.
>
> In the first place, I shall never lose my direct and intimate interest in the legitimate aspirations and the welfare of our veterans of World War II. They, I hope, have confidence that I shall try to discharge toward them every obvious obligation—and they compromise both Democrats and Republicans. Whatever name or reputation I have, they have made for me—I cannot conceive of their believing that I was showing proper appreciation of this fact if I should join a political party. (At least I am sure that those of the opposite party would look at me with a jaundiced eye.)

Another reason to shun both parties, Eisenhower noted, was that he "should like to be of help from time to time in that type of governmental problem for which I have been educated. That classification is military. If my counsel is ever desired in that kind of question, I would like to be available no matter what political party happens to be in power at the moment. In other words, I should like to remain just what I've always been, a military officer instantly responsive to civil government regardless of its political complexion."

Eisenhower also suggested that his identification with a political party could compromise his standing as Columbia's president. His predecessor, Nicholas Murray Butler, didn't share this view. While serving as president of Columbia, Butler was the 1912 Republican nominee for vice president and eight years later made an unsuccessful bid for the GOP presidential nomination. Eisenhower, though, wrote in his diary that "having assumed the responsibilities of this post [the university presidency] I do not believe

Harry and Ike first met at the White House, in June 1945. As he pinned an Oak Leaf Cluster on his guest, Truman whispered that he would rather have the medal than the presidency. Mamie Doud Eisenhower is on the left. (Truman Library)

Arriving in Europe for the Potsdam summit, Truman was greeted by a fellow midwesterner. It was the beginning of a friendship. (Truman Library)

With General George S. Patton, Jr., at the raising of the American flag over the U.S. Group Council Headquarters in Berlin, July 20, 1945. By openly questioning policy, Patton would soon test Ike's leadership. (Truman Library)

On several occasions Truman offered to support Ike for the presidency. Truman indicated that he would even be his friend's running mate. (Eisenhower Library/Army Photo)

Truman's Lieutenants: Secretary of the Navy James V. Forrestal (*left, seated*) and Secretary of War Robert P. Patterson discussing unification of the armed forces at a White House conference, January 1947. Standing are Major General Lauris Norstad, Admiral William D. Leahy, Eisenhower, Admiral Chester W. Nimitz, and Admiral Forrest Sherman. (Army Signal Corps)

Truman enjoyed the most famous blunder in the history of American journalism. This photograph would become our most enduring image of a triumphant underdog. (Mercantile Library Association of St. Louis)

Senator Joseph R. McCarthy, center, greeted by Oregon Republican leader Donald Van Boskirk, left, 1948. The Wisconsin legislator was not yet a household name. Truman and Ike were appalled by his wild excesses. Yet McCarthy would turn them against each other. (author's collection, courtesy Donald Van Boskirk)

Ike's reaction to the news that Truman had removed MacArthur from command. Eisenhower supported this controversial decision. "When you put on a uniform," he told an aide, "there are certain inhibitions you accept." (*Stars and Stripes*)

On his retirement from the Army, Ike reported to Truman, June 1952. With Secretary of Defense Robert A. Lovett, left, and Secretary of the Army Frank Pace. (Eisenhower Library/Army Photo)

The 1952 Republican presidential nominee criticized policies that he had influenced. (*Chicago Sun-Times*)

Though Adlai E. Stevenson was Truman's choice for the 1952 Democratic presidential nomination, their relationship was uneasy. Eisenhower would not have run if he had known that Stevenson would be the Democratic nominee. (Ralph Frost, *Chicago Sun-Times*)

At their post-election meeting, Ike made little effort to conceal his bitterness toward Truman. "He had a chip on his shoulder," Truman wrote in his diary. (Eisenhower Library)

House Speaker Sam Rayburn, left, Bess W. Truman, and former President Herbert C. Hoover joined HST for the dedication of his presidential library in July 1957. Ike was a no-show. (Truman Library)

Breaking the ice, Eisenhower called on Truman at his presidential library in November 1961. HST gave him a personal tour. (Truman Library)

At graveside services for House Speaker Sam Rayburn in Bonham, Texas. Harry and Ike sat next to President John F. Kennedy, Arizona Senator Carl Hayden, and Vice President Lyndon B. Johnson. (Truman Library/*Dallas Morning News*)

it appropriate for me to proclaim a loyalty to a particular political party. We have here men and women of all parties—our alumni and supporters, upon whom we are dependent for our existence, likewise come from all parties. My joining a specific party would certainly antagonize some. In my conviction, even partial adherence to a specific party or any partial entry into the political field would demand from me an instant resignation at Columbia."

In declining to run in 1948, Eisenhower had argued against military men in politics. This issue still troubled him. "There is an angle to this same subject that is important, though little noticed," he wrote in his diary. "It is the danger—once we become accustomed to thinking of our military leaders as potential political leaders—that their selection (which is done by the party in power at the time of the selection) will certainly be based as much upon political consideration as upon their demonstrated military capacity. Such a grave occurrence in time of war could defeat the nation. That this line of reasoning is not baseless is demonstrated by the history of France throughout the nineteenth and early twentieth centuries."[9]

Yet Eisenhower was still listening to politicians and friends who wanted him to run in 1952. "The situation is far different . . . from what it was in 1948," the general wrote in his diary. "Then, all Republicans thought they'd win easily. So, no 'leaders' wanted me or bothered me. All the 'Republican' pressure on me was truly from the grass roots because the bosses wanted the top man to be one they could control. The 'Democratic' pressures came from the bosses, all except Harry S. Truman and his personal crowd. . . . . Now—everything is reversed!"[10]

Dewey represented the consensus of the Eastern Establishment in promoting Eisenhower for '52. "I had another long talk with Governor Dewey," Eisenhower wrote in November 1949. "He remains of the opinion that I must soon enter politics or, as he says, be totally incapable of helping the country when it will need help most. He is most fearful (as are thousands of others including myself in varying degree) that we, as a nation, will fail to see the dangers into which we are drifting and, as a consequence, will approve governmental actions from which there can be no retreat." However, Ike wasn't ready to shut the door. Though declining to run for governor, he wanted to learn more about his possible options in 1952.[11]

On October 15, 1950, Dewey appeared on the NBC television program *Meet the Press* and was asked by Leo Egan of *The New York Times* whether he would run for the presidency in 1952. "No, that one is out. I am definitely and finally removed and that is beyond consideration," Dewey said.

In following up, Egan asked if Dewey had any other candidates in mind. "Well, it's a little early," Dewey said. "But we have in New York a great world figure, the president of Columbia University, one of the greatest soldiers of our history, a fine educator, a man who really understands the problems of the world, and if I should be re-elected governor and have influence with the New York delegation, I would recommend to them that they support General Eisenhower for president if he would accept the draft."

Egan continued this exchange: "Governor, have you asked General Eisenhower if he is willing?"

"I have not," Dewey answered, though he had been in contact with Eisenhower on a regular basis over the previous fifteen months. Both men had wanted these discussions to be confidential.

In ending this segment of *Meet the Press*, Egan asked if Dewey knew whether Eisenhower was a Republican. "Well, I have listened to some of his speeches," the New York governor replied, "and I certainly should think that his philosophy would be in accordance with my own."[12]

Dewey had given Eisenhower notice of this unusually early endorsement for a presidential election that was more than two years away. "Today Gov. D. called me (I suppose from Albany) saying that if questioned he is going to announce his hope that I would accept a Republican draft in 1952," Eisenhower wrote in his diary two days before Dewey made his appearance on NBC. "There seemed to be no double talking about the matter. I merely said I'd say 'No comment.' "[13]

In a response to Dewey's public endorsement, Eisenhower wrote out a brief disclaimer and gave it to Columbia University's Office of Public Information for immediate release: "Any American would be complimented by the knowledge that any other American considered him qualified to fill the most important post in our country. In this case the compliment comes from a man who is Governor of a great state and who has devoted many years of his life to public service. So, of course, I am grateful for Governor Dewey's good opinion of me."

Eisenhower told the student newspaper, the *Columbia Spectator*, that he was not interested in making a bid for the White House. "I put my hand to a job and am doing my best. I don't know why people are always nagging me to run for President," the general said. "I think I've gotten too old. I have no desire to go anywhere else if I can help do what I want here at Columbia. This is the place for me."[14]

In his 1950 State of the Union message, Truman looked ahead to the year 2000 with hope and optimism. "The first half of this century will be known as the most turbulent and eventful period in recorded history. The swift pace of events promises to make the next 50 years decisive in the history of man on this planet," he declared. "The scientific and industrial revolution which began two centuries ago has, in the last 50 years, caught up the peoples of the world in a common destiny. Two world-shattering wars have proved that no corner of the earth can be isolated from the affairs of mankind. The human race has reached a turning point. Man has opened the secrets of nature and mastered new powers. If he used them wisely, he can reach new heights of civilization. If he used them foolishly, they may destroy him."

Truman said that the state of the union was good at midcentury and added that long-term prospects were even more encouraging: "If our productive power continues to increase at the same rate as it has increased for the past 50 years . . . the real income of the average family in the year 2000 would be about three times what it is today."[15] That would have meant an average family income of $12,400 in the year 2000. Truman underestimated inflation and the power of a growth economy. In 1997, the average American salary was $28,200. *Time* magazine had referred to Truman's 1950 forecast as a "heady vision of sustained U.S. prosperity."

It was still presumed that Truman would seek a third term in 1952. Three-fourths of Democratic voters told a Gallup poll in April of 1950 that Truman would run for a third term and nearly that many Republicans also believed that he would run. Truman told members of his cabinet in January of 1950 that he hoped none of them would be leaving the administration to run for political office because it was important to keep his team intact for 1952. At this meeting, he hinted strongly that he would be a candidate for another term. It was to his political advantage to give this signal. Once Truman announced his withdrawal from the 1952 election, his political influence would be diminished.[16]

By the spring of 1950, Truman had made up his mind. On a Sunday in mid-April, the president wrote about this decision in his diary:

> I am not a candidate for nomination by the Democratic Convention. My first election to public office took place in November 1922. I served two years in the armed forces in World War I, ten years in the Senate, two months and 20 days as Vice President and President of the Senate. I have been in public service well over thirty years, having been President of the United States almost two complete terms.
>
> Washington, Jefferson, Monroe, Madison, Andrew Jackson and Woodrow Wilson as well as Calvin Coolidge stood by the precedent. Only Grant, Theodore Roosevelt, and F.D.R. made the attempt to break that precedent. F.D.R. succeeded.

> In my opinion eight years as President is enough and sometimes too much for any man to serve in that capacity. There is a lure in power. It can get into a man's blood just as gambling and lust for money have been known to do.
>
> This is a Republic. The greatest in the history of the world. I want this country to continue as a Republic. Cincinnatus and Washington pointed the way. When Rome forgot Cincinnatus its downfall began. When we forget the examples of such men as Washington, Jefferson, and Andrew Jackson, all of whom could have had a continuation in the office, then we will start down the road to dictatorship and ruin. I know I could be elected again and continue to break the old precedent as it was broken by F.D.R. It should not be done. That precedent should continue—not by a constitutional amendment but by custom based on the honor of the man in the office.
>
> Therefore to reestablish that custom, although by a quibble I could say I've only had one term, I am not a candidate and will not accept the nomination for another term.[17]

Truman would not make public this decision for nearly two years. When the Gallup poll asked Democratic voters in April of 1950 to choose among eight possible contenders for the 1952 nomination, Truman led the field by a wide margin. But Truman's popularity had dropped in the early months of 1950 and in an April 12 Gallup poll, only 37 percent of the American people said that they approved of the president's job performance.

In April of 1950, Eisenhower emerged for the first time as the popular favorite among Republicans. Only one out of five Republican voters had listed Eisenhower as their choice in the summer of 1949. But by the spring of 1950, 37 percent of Republicans liked Ike compared with 17 percent for Taft. By an even wider margin, Eisenhower was also the choice of independent voters. There was confusion among the electorate about Eisenhower's political views. The general was regarded as a liberal by 60 percent of the voters and a conservative by 40 percent. There was no doubt about where Taft stood. "Mr. Republican" was identified as a conservative by 84 percent of the voting public.

Eight days after Truman had privately written of his intention to withdraw from the 1952 Democratic race, Eisenhower was embarrassed when a Gallup poll showed him overwhelming the president. Gallup had asked voters of both parties whom they would choose if Truman was the 1952 Democratic nominee and Eisenhower was his Republican challenger. Eisenhower was favored by 60 percent and Truman 31 percent with 9 percent undecided. The same poll indicated that a majority of voters considered themselves Democrats and that a plurality favored a Democratic Congress in 1952.[18]

"Lately a couple of Gallup Polls have put me back into the political gossip columns, although there never has been a complete cessation of loose talk about me as a presidential possibility," Eisenhower wrote in his diary. "A few evenings ago Gallup reported running me against President Truman. Bad business. But nothing to do about it. I hope the President is too philosophical to take real note of the 60-to-30 report against him."[19]

CHAPTER 16

Scoundrel Time

In the winter of 1950, Senator Joseph R. McCarthy looked vulnerable. He would be up for reelection in two years and had a legislative record of meager accomplishment. Back home there were questions about his personal and campaign finances and dubious ethics. The Wisconsin state bar had censured him in 1949 for violations of its ethics code. When the year 1950 began, McCarthy was among the more obscure members of the U.S. Senate. But within a hundred days, his name would become a household word. McCarthy would gain such notoriety and influence in American society that the first half of the decade would be long remembered as the McCarthy era. One of McCarthy's biographers referred to this period as "the nightmare decade." Truman and Eisenhower loathed McCarthy as a menace to constitutional rights. But neither the president nor the general could ignore him and McCarthy would eventually drive a wedge between them.[1]

McCarthy cared more about headlines than power. By raising his profile, the senator was seeking to improve his reelection prospects in 1952. As part of this effort, he booked five "Lincoln Day" addresses before Republican audiences in February of 1950. His first stop was in Wheeling, West Virginia, an old mining town on the eastern bank of the Ohio River, which was also the home of country music's "Original Jamboree." On his arrival in Wheeling, McCarthy told several Republican officials at the airport that he had drafts of two speeches—one on federal housing programs and another on alleged Communist infiltration of the American government. A former Republican congressman, Francis J. Love, told McCarthy that his speech would be broadcast on a local radio station and recommended that he give the speech about Communists in the Truman administration.[2]

There was a growing fear of communism. Americans were jolted in 1949 by the triumph of Mao's Red Army in the Chinese civil war and the news that the Soviet Union had tested their first atomic bomb. Three weeks before McCarthy's Wheeling speech, the former diplomat Alger Hiss was convicted of perjury. Six days before McCarthy's speech, the British scientist Klaus Fuchs (who had worked with U.S. atomic scientists) was arrested on charges of espionage. The Gallup poll reported that 70 percent of Americans believed that the Soviet Union wanted to "rule the world." At the peak of McCarthy's influence, a third of the American public thought that churches should be investigated for possible Communist infiltration.

In his speech, McCarthy tapped into those anxieties and fears with allegations that the Soviet Union was winning the cold war because of treachery at the highest levels of the Truman administration. As he spoke before an audience of 275 people in the McClure Hotel, McCarthy declared: "While I cannot take the time to name all the men in the State Department who have been named as members of the Communist Party and members of a spy ring, I have here in my hand a list of 205 that were known to the secretary of state as being members of the Communist Party and who nevertheless are still working and shaping the policy of the State Department."

McCarthy, it turned out, had no list. He didn't know the name of a single Communist working in the State Department. McCarthy came up with the figure based on what he had been told about a four-year-old investigation of State Department employees by then Secretary Byrnes. More than three thousand employees had been investigated and 285 had been given evaluations as possible security risks by Byrnes's committee. Only seventy-nine had been forced out. After subtracting this figure, McCarthy erroneously came up with 205 instead of 206. It is probable that the individuals who weren't terminated were cleared. But McCarthy alleged that they were fifth columnists still working in the State Department.

On his next stop after Wheeling, McCarthy in Denver was asked by reporters for documentation supporting his charges. The senator claimed that he had left the list on the plane in the jacket of his other suit. McCarthy later backtracked and, relying on a three-year-old report by a Republican congressional staffer, said that he had evidence of fifty-seven "card-carrying Communists" in the State Department.

On his western trip, McCarthy sent Truman an insulting telegram demanding that the administration provide Congress with full reports on State Department officials who had been classified as security risks. "Failure on your part," McCarthy wired the president, "will label the Democratic party of being the bed-fellow of international communism."[3]

Truman responded in a February 11, 1950 letter that he did not send but should have, for it showed how he felt about the Red hunter: "I read your telegram of February eleventh from Reno, Nevada, with a great deal of interest and this is the first time in my experience, and I was ten years in the Senate, that I ever heard of a Senator trying to discredit his own Government before the world. You know that isn't done by honest public officials. Your telegram is not only not true and an insolent approach to a situation that should have been worked out between man and man but it shows conclusively that you are not even fit to have a hand in the operations of the Government of the United States.

"I am very sure that the people of Wisconsin are extremely sorry that they are represented by a person who has as little sense of responsibility as you have."[4]

Through a spokesman, Secretary of State Acheson vehemently denied McCarthy's allegations. "There was not a word of truth in what the Senator said," Truman told reporters at a February 16 news conference.

Eisenhower thought that Truman and Acheson were mistaken in responding to the wild charges. "Senator McCarthy had been a little-known junior senator from Wisconsin," Eisenhower later wrote, and "might well have been forgotten if the Truman administration had not challenged [him] demanding that he produce his source of information or quit talking."

If Truman had been silent, McCarthy would still have gained immediate notoriety. The more conservative newspaper chains would have given McCarthy a forum. "There was an effort on the part of a certain segment of the press to discredit the administration in any manner they could," Truman remembered. "The truth had no weight with Scripps-Howard, Hearst, or the McCormick-Patterson axis for the simple reason that their objective was to discredit the President in everything he did." McCarthy's charges, though reckless and sensational, were taken seriously enough that he was featured on the covers of *Time* and *Newsweek*. Herblock, the editorial cartoonist for the *Washington Post*, depicted McCarthy as a thug and coined the term "McCarthyism" to characterize his wild excesses, false allegations, and trampling of civil liberties.[6]

On February 20, 1950, McCarthy gave a longer version of his Wheeling speech on the Senate floor. Berating Truman, McCarthy then ridiculed Acheson as "this pompous diplomat in striped pants, with a phony British accent." McCarthy attributed what he termed a decline of American power to a vast conspiracy: "The reason we find ourselves in a position of impotency is not because our only powerful potential enemy has sent men to invade our shores, but rather because of the traitorous actions of those who have been treated so well by this nation. . . . In my opinion the State Department, which is one of the most important government departments, is thoroughly infested with Communists."[7]

Defending his friend, Truman said, "I think Dean Acheson will go down in history as one of the great Secretaries of State." As for his accuser, Truman asserted, "I think the greatest asset that the Kremlin has is Senator McCarthy." Truman blamed the Republican leadership for encouraging McCarthy to sabotage American foreign policy.

Truman and Eisenhower challenged McCarthy when he attacked Philip C. Jessup, U.S. ambassador at large, as "having an unusual affinity for Communist causes." McCarthy warned that Jessup, as an adviser to Acheson, was "now formulating top-flight policy in the Far East affecting half the civilized world." Truman responded to McCarthy's charge by describing Jessup "as able and distinguished a citizen as this country has ever produced."[8]

Jessup, a professor of international law at Columbia University, was offered the position of provost by Eisenhower in the summer of 1948 but declined when Truman nominated him as U.S. ambassador to the United Nations. "I cannot see my way clear to leaving the field of international affairs," Jessup wrote Eisenhower. "I am in this international business and it is in my bones." An army veteran of the First World War, Jessup began his career in the State Department in the middle 1920s and later wrote the authorized biography of former Secretary of State Elihu Root. Just months before McCarthy's charges, Jessup had ended the Berlin blockade through skillful negotiations with the Soviet Union.

When McCarthy recklessly impugned Jessup's character, Eisenhower was appalled. As president of Columbia, Eisenhower told Jessup: "I am writing to tell you how much your University deplores the association of your name with the current loyalty investigation in the United States Senate. Your long and distinguished record as a scholar and a public servant has won for you the respect of your colleagues and of the American people as well. No one who has known you can for a moment question the depth or sincerity of your devotion to the principles of Americanism. Your University associates and I are confident that any impression to the contrary will be quickly dispelled as the facts become known."

Eisenhower's letter defending Jessup was made public during Senate hearings about McCarthy's allegations. When a retired soldier criticized Eisenhower's defense of Jessup, the general replied:

> I am just as concerned as you are with the nefarious plottings of the Communists. Certainly, I would not for one moment tolerate about me or defend a man who might be in any way tainted by active support of sympathy for Communists' designs. In the case of Philip Jessup, I have known him personally quite a while now. Moreover here at the University are men in whose judgment I have complete faith; they—who have known him a great many years—are unanimous in their praise of him as outstanding in his loyalty to American principles and in his readiness to sacrifice personal interest in the country's service. Under the circumstances, I had absolutely no alternative—when he was publicly attacked—but to voice my personal views. As his superior officer here at Columbia, silence on my part very probably would have been considered against Phil Jessup by those attacking him.[9]

With Truman and Eisenhower refuting McCarthy's charges, Jessup survived the senator's attack. Other diplomats, scholars, and some artists would be less fortunate. In the politically charged atmosphere of McCarthy's era, more Americans than not believed the Wisconsin senator's charges about treachery in the State Department. Approximately 40 percent of the public believed or approved of McCarthy's charges, according to a Gallup poll in the spring of 1950.[10]

There are historians who blame Truman for McCarthy's rise. The Justice Department during Truman's administration prosecuted and gained convictions against eleven leaders of the American Communist party on conspiracy charges. After it was disclosed that Soviet espionage agents had infiltrated the Canadian government, Truman appointed a commission in late 1946 to make recommendations on national security. Truman got their report in February of 1947 and acted promptly. On March 21, 1947, he issued Executive Order 9835 that established the first loyalty program in American history. This executive order stated: "There shall be a loyalty investigation of every person entering the civilian employment of any department or agency of the federal government."[11] In firing employees or refusing employment, the burden of proof was on the government to prove that, "on all the evidence, reasonable grounds exist for belief that the person involved is disloyal to the Government of the United States."

"The Loyalty Program was one that caused us a great deal of worry and difficulty for the simple reason that the approach of the [House Un-American Activities Committee] on this subject was one of persecution of the employees of the government and not an investigation to find the facts. I called in the Attorney General and my counsel, Clark Clifford, and told them to work out a program for testing the loyalty of those people whose loyalty was in any way questioned," Truman recalled six years after he issued the executive order. "But they were to show the employee every consideration and use as fair an approach in carrying out the program as possible. No man was to be discharged on suspicion."

Three million federal employees were investigated between 1947 and 1951. Only 212 federal workers were dismissed as a result of the Loyalty and Security Program. Another two thousand quit their government jobs because of this process. "Some thought the program wasn't strong enough," Truman remembered in 1953. "They thought everybody should be fired and start all over. Others thought that even if people weren't loyal to the government, they still had the right to work for the government."[12]

But the loyalty program had an impact beyond the nation's capital. The attorney general's list of subversive and front organizations, which was originally intended to be a classified document, was made public in late 1947 with devastating consequences. Groups were listed with alleged links to Communist, Fascist, subversive, or totalitarian viewpoints. Making this list public gave McCarthy and the House Un-American Activities Committee the weapon of guilt by association that led to the blacklisting of private citizens.

Clark Clifford wrote in his memoirs that his failure to "make more of an effort to try to kill the loyalty program at its inception" was the "greatest regret" of his long public career. In looking back on the loyalty program, Clifford described it as a "misguided and pernicious effort to eliminate 'subversives' from the government."[13]

Truman believed in fair play, due process, and freedom of thought. From the start, he regarded HUAC as a star chamber and abhorred McCarthyism. At the same time, Truman took the Soviet threat seriously and signed the executive order to make it more difficult for Russian agents to infiltrate the U.S. government or influence policy. The president told an official at the Democratic National Committee that "one disloyal person is too many." But Truman had confidence in the loyalty and patriotism of most federal workers and very much resented allegations by political opponents that his administration was overpopulated with Communists and fellow travelers.

FBI Director J. Edgar Hoover sought total control over Truman's loyalty program. Truman preferred to give more responsibility to the Civil Service Commission. "Let's be sure that we hold the FBI down," Truman told Clifford. "If we leave them to their own devices and give them what they want they will become an American Gestapo."

Hoover struck back. Just a week after Truman issued his executive order, the FBI director aligned himself with Republican critics of the administration. In an appearance before HUAC, Hoover testified that their hearings could play an important role in exposing "the forces that menace America—Communist and Fascist." Hoover added: "This Committee renders a distinct service when it publicly reveals the diabolic machinations of sinister figures engaged in un-American activities."

The FBI director said that mere background checks were inadequate to determine the loyalty of federal employees. Hoover told HUAC that the Truman administration had been slow in its response to the enemy within, despite being alerted to the danger by the FBI. From this moment on, Hoover was often helpful to Republicans seeking to make an issue out of Communists in American government.

Truman would have been justified in firing Hoover for insubordination. But at the beginning of the cold war, Hoover was politically untouchable, with a 79 percent favorable rating from the American public. Truman understood that Hoover was a formidable adversary. In a note to Clifford, the president conceded: "J. Edgar will in all probability get this backward-looking Congress to give him what he wants. It's dangerous."[14]

In the end, Hoover got most of what he wanted. The FBI's powers were expanded when the Republican Eightieth Congress provided it with two-thirds of the funding for loyalty investigations and reduced Truman's request for the Civil Service Commission by 80 percent. Truman then publicly announced that the FBI would coordinate loyalty investigations.

But Truman wanted these records to be kept confidential and declined HUAC's requests for government files. "The preservation of the strictest confidence with respect to loyalty files is the single most important element in operating a loyalty program which provides effective security for the government and justice for the individual employee," Truman told the Federal Bar Association in the spring of 1950. ". . . Disclosure of the files would result in serious injustice to the reputation of many innocent persons. This is true because the FBI investigative files do not contain proven information only. They include unverified charges and statements, as well as mere suspicions, which, upon investigation, are found to be untrue."[15]

When speaking of HUAC, Truman made little effort to conceal his disdain for their methods. "I've said many a time," he told students at Columbia University in 1959, "that I think the Un-American Activities

Committee in the House of Representatives was in the most Un-American thing in America."

Eisenhower shared Truman's concern about the abuse of individual rights by politicians in the name of anticommunism. "I am not exactly sure what the Committee hopes to accomplish," he wrote a friend during HUAC's 1947 hearings on alleged communism in Hollywood. "I have not been able to follow the details of the matter. I am quite certain, however, that such matters have to be handled with great wisdom and delicacy. We must not, in our own country, establish practices that by their very nature would interfere with legitimate rights of individuals. On the other hand, where it can be proved that an individual has taken an oath or has become a member of a party which is openly dedicated to destruction of our own form of government by force, it would appear that some form of decent defense should be available to us."[16]

As president of Columbia, Eisenhower had several encounters with HUAC. When the committee sought a list of textbooks used in social sciences courses at Columbia, Eisenhower told HUAC Chairman John S. Wood "that any school that failed to give its students a proper analysis of 'Das Kapital' would be miserably failing in its duty to society." Eisenhower, who would speak out against the "book-burners" later in the McCarthy era, thought that HUAC was overzealous in requesting lists of textbooks. "I agree with the basic objective of all those who are determined to protect academic freedom," Eisenhower wrote historian Henry Steele Commager. "Certainly I hope always to be on the side of those who oppose every threat to academic freedom and shall, to the limit of my ability, support the search for truth in the social sciences."

In March of 1950, the month after McCarthy's Wheeling speech, Eisenhower was invited by Wood to appear before HUAC and share his views about legislative proposals to fight subversive activities. Eisenhower declined. In his reply to Wood, the general shared his strong reservations about the committee:

> We should make certain that there is adequate protection against Communist infiltration into American life and institutions. In devising laws for this purpose, it seems apparent that we might incur other dangers, against which we should also be on guard. Among these risks would be, certainly:
>
> a) The danger of placing restrictions upon the Constitutional rights and freedoms of the individual that would weaken the very system of free government we are attempting to protect.
>
> b) Giving to some bureau or agency of government an unwar-

> ranted combination of executive, judicial and quasi-legislative powers, thus again violating a basic concept of our federal government, even though the purpose is to preserve our system.
>
> c) Building up another and possibly useless bureau or agency of government, where existing agencies, with some slight addition in strength, might logically and properly carry out missions laid upon them by the Congress. I think we should carefully avoid the practice of creating new bureaus of boards and of incurring all the disadvantages and evils that result therefrom.
>
> There will, of course, always be argument as to the best method of combatting the various "isms" that from time to time threaten our institutions. Those who believe that restrictive legislation serves only to drive such forces underground also believe that these false ideas gather greater strength when they are spread clandestinely and in the dark than when preached in the open, subject to public scrutiny and exposure.
>
> On the other hand, the spectacle of democratic government, helpless to defend itself against the false propaganda and lies of an ideology that openly proclaim its readiness to destroy by force every kind of government based upon the dignity of man, *is, of course, intolerable.*
>
> To sum up, I should say that it is my impression, in spite of my ignorance of the existing law, that we probably need additional legislation to enable us effectively to combat misguided and vicious persons within our borders. But we must be exceedingly careful, even to the extent of leaning over backward, to avoid the enactment of legislation which, by its character, would in itself tend to place unwarranted restrictions upon our guaranteed freedoms or which would be adding unnecessarily to the bureaucratic power of government—in effect pushing us away from real democratic government.[17]

Stung by Eisenhower's blunt warning, Wood didn't include the letter in the published record of the committee's hearings. Fair play and constitutional rights weren't on HUAC's agenda.

Emboldened by the attention he was getting, McCarthy became even more reckless in his allegations. Marshall, who was regarded by Truman and Churchill as the greatest living American, was accused of treason by McCarthy in the most outrageous falsehood ever spoken on the Senate floor. "How can we account for our present situation unless we believe that men high in this government are concerting to deliver us to disaster?" McCarthy said in June of 1951. "This must be the product of a great conspiracy, a conspiracy on a scale so immense as to dwarf any previous such venture in the history of man."[18]

There is no evidence that McCarthy believed any of this nonsense. He vilified the secretary of state as the "Red Dean." When he bumped into Acheson in a Senate elevator, McCarthy greeted him with a friendly "Hello, Dean." McCarthy couldn't understand why Acheson responded with scornful silence.

Truman viewed McCarthy's Democratic and fellow Irish-American ally Patrick A. McCarran, senator from Nevada, as a more destructive force because of his legislative savvy. McCarthy had limited political skills and was more interested in getting headlines than in passing legislation. As the chairman of the Senate Judiciary Committee and a high-ranking member of the Appropriations Committee, McCarran was a power in the Senate. In 1950, he sponsored the Internal Security Act designed to "protect the United States against certain un-American and subversive activities by requiring registration of Communist organizations, and for other purposes." Under the McCarran Act, groups designated as Communist organizations would be required to label all publications and public broadcasts as sponsored by "a Communist organization." The act created a Subversive Activities Control Board and also included a provision calling for the emergency detention of suspected spies, saboteurs, or subversives when a president declared an "internal security emergency." The McCarran Act passed the Senate by a seventy to seven vote, and it was overwhelmingly approved in the House.

Even though many of Truman's Democratic allies voted for the McCarran Act and urged the president to sign it, he would have none of it. Nearly everything about the McCarran Act violated Truman's sense of fair play. In his veto message, Truman said: "We can and we will prevent espionage, sabotage, or other actions endangering our national security. But we would betray our finest traditions if we attempted, as this bill would attempt, to curb the simple expression of opinion. This we should never do, no matter how distasteful the opinion may be to the vast majority of our people. The course proposed by this bill would delight the communists, for it would make a mockery of the Bill of Rights and of our claims to stand for freedom in the world. . . . We need not fear the expression of ideas—we do need to fear their suppression."

In concluding his veto message, Truman cited Eisenhower's leadership in a campaign to raise money for radio programming that would be aired from Western Europe for audiences in Soviet bloc countries. "Earlier this month, we launched a great Crusade for Freedom designed, in the words of General Eisenhower, to fight the big lie with the big truth," Truman said. "I can think of no better way to make a mockery of that crusade and of the deep American belief in human freedom and dignity which underlie it than to put the provisions of [the McCarran Act] on our statute books. . . . Our country has been through dangerous times before, without losing our liberties to external attack or internal hysteria. Each of us, in government and out, has a share in guarding our liberties. Each of us must search his own conscience to find whether he is doing all that can be done to preserve and strengthen them."[19]

The McCarran Act was passed fifty-seven to ten over Truman's veto in the Senate and two hundred and ninety-six to forty-eight in the House. No Communist organizations ever registered under the Internal Security Act and the Supreme Court held in 1965 that party members could not be compelled to register because it could be used as evidence to prosecute them in violation of their Fifth Amendment rights. The detention camps were never used. Two decades after Truman's unsuccessful veto attempt, the detention camp provision was repealed.

Truman and Eisenhower both viewed McCarthy as a cheap demagogue and pathological liar. But in late 1952, the Wisconsin senator would turn them against each other.

CHAPTER 17

A Distant War

Korea, a peninsula known as the Land of the Morning Calm, is bordered on the north by China and Russia and on the east by the Sea of Japan. In the spring of 1950, most Americans were unfamiliar with this distant land that had closed its borders to foreigners for hundreds of years. From 1910 until the end of World War II, Korea was under the harsh rule of the Japanese. During this period, Koreans were forced to live under Japanese laws, speak the Japanese language, and abandon much of their heritage. Franklin D. Roosevelt, doubtful that Korea was ready for nationhood after thirty-five years of colonial status, worked out an arrangement with Stalin for a postwar trusteeship. Following Roosevelt's death, Truman carried out this policy. In what was to have been a temporary measure, Korea was divided into occupation zones along the thirty-eighth parallel with the Soviet Union on the northern side and the United States in the more populous south. There were nine million people in the north and twenty million in the south. Following the Japanese surrender, the U.S. occupational government in South Korea made a serious mistake in keeping in office the hated Japanese administrative officials. This blunder undermined confidence in the United States on both sides of the thirty-eighth parallel. But the Pentagon and State Department sought to repair the damage and work toward a united Korea.[1]

When negotiations for unification between North and South Korea broke down, the United Nations became involved at Truman's request. The UN scheduled 1948 elections for the selection of one government. But the Soviets and North Koreans declined to participate. The Harvard and Princeton-educated Syngman Rhee, president of the Provisional Korean Republic (in exile) from 1919 until 1941, was elected by South

Koreans in 1948 as the first president of the Republic of Korea. Kim Il Sung, a fighter in the Korean resistance to the Japanese in the 1930s and Soviet army officer in World War II, took charge as premier of North Korea in 1948.

Truman and his advisers, including Eisenhower, approved of plans to reduce and withdraw occupational forces from South Korea. The Joint Chiefs of Staff reported to Forrestal in September of 1947 that "from a standpoint of military security, the United States has little strategic interest in maintaining the present troops and bases in Korea." It was signed by Eisenhower. In the spring of 1948, Truman approved a policy statement on the recommendation of the Joint Chiefs that said: "The United States should not become so irrevocably involved in the Korean situation that an action taken by any faction in Korea or by any other power in Korea could be considered a casus belli for the United States."[2]

Soviet troops withdrew from the Korean peninsula by December of 1948 and American forces were gone by the summer of 1949 but for a small advisory group. There was no indication that the U.S. troops would ever return. From Theodore Roosevelt to Truman, American presidents had written off Korea. General Douglas MacArthur, commander of U.S. occupation forces in the Pacific, told a British journalist in 1949 that "our line of defense runs through the chain of islands fringing the coast of Asia. It starts in the Philippines and continues through the Ryukyu Archipelago, which includes its main bastion, Okinawa. Then it bends back through Japan and the Aleutian Island chain to Alaska." MacArthur said nothing about Korea. Secretary Acheson, in a speech before the National Press Club in January of 1950, defined the U.S. defense perimeter in the Pacific as running from the Aleutians to Japan through the Ryukyus to the Philippines. Acheson left out Taiwan and South Korea, which did not go unnoticed in North Korea and in Moscow.[3]

For months, Kim Il Sung had been pleading with Stalin for the authority to lead an all-out attack across the thirty-eighth parallel with the aim of uniting all Korea under his leadership. When Kim went to Moscow in March of 1949, Stalin turned him down. According to records in the Soviet archives, Stalin rejected numerous appeals from the North Korean leader. But in the wake of Mao's October 1949 triumph in the Chinese civil war and the successful blast in the summer of '49 of the Soviet nuclear test, Stalin changed his mind. When Kim made an official visit to the Kremlin in April of 1950, Stalin authorized the invasion of South Korea. Stalin was doubtful that Truman would become involved in an Asian land war. Mao predicted that the Americans would not intervene because "they would not start a third world war over such a small territory."

At 4:00 A.M., on June 25, 1950, the North Koreans began firing across the thirty-eighth parallel. On this rainy Sunday morning, seven combat divisions and a line of Russian tanks stormed into South Korea in four columns and headed for the capital city of Seoul. It would fall within two days. Two more divisions attacked the south in the central mountains and another division struck on the east coast. The South Koreans were caught by surprise and their army offered little resistance to the invasion force. Two South Korean divisions dropped their weapons and joined fleeing refugees. North Korea was threatening to wipe them out. "Considering the relative strength and combat readiness of the forces that faced each other . . . in June of 1950," General Matthew B. Ridgway wrote, "it was a marvel that the North Korean armies were delayed at all in their drive to overrun all of South Korea."[4]

Truman was in Independence that weekend when Acheson telephoned him. "Mr. President, I have serious news," Acheson reported. "The North Koreans are attacking across the 38th parallel."

Acheson recommended that Truman ask for an emergency meeting of the United Nations Security Council and Secretary-General Trygve Lie, who denounced North Korea's aggression, complied. The United Nations was so dominated by the United States at midcentury that the general assembly refused to seat a delegation from the new People's Republic of China. In protest, the Soviet Union boycotted all UN meetings. As a member of the Security Council, the Soviet Union could have vetoed any UN action on North Korea. But with the boycott still in effect, Truman won unanimous support for the Security Council resolution that condemned North Korea for breaching the peace, called for an immediate end to the hostilities, and withdrawal of North Korean troops from South Korea.

Truman faced the most difficult decision of his presidency. He had effectively contained Stalin in Europe and the Mideast without going to war. But the Korean problem was different. A Soviet ally had invaded a nation that had been created under the sponsorship of the United Nations. Bradley told Truman that the United States had to draw the line. Truman agreed. In making his decision, Truman recalled how Hitler, Mussolini, and leaders of Imperial Japan had used brute force in the 1930s to expand their empires. "I recalled some earlier instances: Manchuria, Ethiopia, Austria. I remembered how each time that the democracies failed to act it had encouraged the aggressors to go ahead," Truman recalled. "I felt certain that if South Korea was allowed to fall, Communist leaders would be emboldened to override nations closer to our own shores. . . . If this was allowed to go unchallenged, it would mean a third world war."[5]

Two days after the United Nations vote, Truman announced that he was sending air and naval forces to aid the South Koreans. "The attack upon Korea makes it plain beyond all doubt that communism has passed beyond the use of subversion to conquer independent nations and will now use armed invasion and war," the president declared. ". . . A return to the rule of force in international affairs would have far-reaching effects. The United States will continue to uphold the rule of law."

After conferring with advisers on the Korean situation, Truman served them cocktails. "I have hoped and prayed that I would never have to make a decision like the one I have just made today. But I saw nothing else that was possible for me to do except that," the President said. Then, turning to John D. Nickerson, the assistant secretary of state for the United Nations, Truman said: "Jack, there's something I want you to know. In the final analysis, I *did this* for the United Nations. I believed in the League of Nations. It failed. Lots of people thought that it failed because we weren't in it to back it up. Okay, now we started the United Nations. It was our idea, and in this first big test we just couldn't let them down. If a collective system under the UN can work, it must be made to work, and *now* is the time to call their bluff."[6]

Truman could have gained congressional approval for his decision to intervene. At least two-thirds of the American public supported his decision. So did the Republican opposition. Dewey wired him: "I wholeheartedly agree with and support the difficult decision you have made today to extend American assistance to the Republic of Korea in combatting armed communist aggression. Your action there . . . was necessary to the security of our country and the free world. It should be supported by a united America." With this bipartisan support, Truman had a mandate for congressional action. Under Article 1, Section 8 of the Constitution, it is the Congress and not the president that has the power to declare war. But Truman's advisers, including Acheson and Senate Foreign Relations Committee Chairman Tom Connally of Texas, warned that South Korea might fall if there would be a prolonged debate over a war resolution. Though Truman saved time in bypassing Congress, it would prove to be a costly mistake. As public opinion shifted, the Korean conflict would become known as "Truman's War."[7]

On the day that the Korean War began, Eisenhower returned to New York from a fishing vacation in Canada. When Truman announced his decision to intervene two days later, Eisenhower telephoned the president in support of his stand. "The best check for sustaining world peace was to take a firm stand," Eisenhower told *The New York Times*, "and when our government guaranteed the Government of South Korea, there was no recourse but to do what President Truman did."

Three days after the invasion, Eisenhower was in the Pentagon sharing his thoughts on the Korean conflict with Army Chief of Staff J. Lawton Collins and his deputies, Generals Wade H. Haislip, Matthew B. Ridgway, and Alfred M. Gruenther. Eisenhower thought that the Pentagon wasn't responding quickly enough. Eisenhower wrote in his diary:

> I went in expecting to find them all in a dither of effort—engaged in the positive business of getting the troops, supplies, etc. that will be needed to settle the Korean mess. They seemed indecisive—which was natural in view of indecisiveness of political statements. I have no business talking about the basic political decision [to support or not to support South Korea]. It happens that I believe we'll have a dozen Koreas if we don't take a firm stand—but it was not on that basis that I talked to my friends. My whole contention was that an appeal to force cannot, by its nature, be a partial one. This appeal having been made, for God's sake, get ready! Do everything possible under the law to get us going.
>
> Remember, in a fight we (our side) can never be too strong! I urged action in a dozen directions—and left a memo for Brad. We must study every angle to be prepared for whatever may happen—even if it finally comes to use of A-bomb (which God forbid).

The day after Eisenhower's visit, Collins asked Truman for the authority to send combat troops into Korea. Bradley wrote in his memoirs that Eisenhower may very well have influenced Collins to make this large decision that committed the United States to a ground war in Asia. Truman authorized the deployment of a regimental combat team but held back on General MacArthur's request for two divisions.[8]

Eisenhower suggested to a friend in the British Ministry of Defense that the Korean War started "out of complete miscalculations on the part of our potential enemies as to the determination of the free world to protect itself.

"It is because of such beliefs," the general went on, "that I believe the United Nations, in taking the stand it has now taken in Korea, must be absolutely firm and must, if necessary devote its full strength to hold and maintain the position that it has announced for itself. Failure to do this would be interpreted as nothing less than another kind of Munich, and it is clear what the result of that would be."

At a White House luncheon on July 5, Truman sought Eisenhower's views on Korea. "I told the President that under the circumstances with which we were faced at the moment I thought the decision to intervene was wise and necessary," Eisenhower recalled a decade later. "In this situation the United Nations would have a real test of its viability, I observed. As for the United States, the government now had to make certain of attaining its objective. (This was, according to my information, to assure the territorial integrity of South Korea.)"

Eisenhower stressed that there was no time to be lost. "Our nation has appealed to the use of force," Ike told Truman. "We must make sure of success. We should move quickly to the necessary level of mobilization and begin at once to concentrate and use whatever forces may be required, including American ground troops. This act in itself will remove any doubt of the seriousness of our intentions."[9]

There would be no doubt about America's resolve, Truman assured Eisenhower. In the most fateful decision of his presidency, Truman chose to fight a war halfway around the world to thwart aggression. The Soviet and Chinese Communist leadership had underestimated him. "Korea is the Greece of the Far East," Truman told associates after the North Korean attack. "If we are tough enough now, if we stand up to them like we did in Greece three years ago, they won't take any next steps. But if we just stand by, they'll move into Iran and they'll take over the whole Middle East. There is no telling what they'll do if we don't put up a fight now."[10]

On July 7, 1950, the United Nations voted to send an allied military force to Korea and asked Truman to select its unified command. MacArthur, supreme commander of Allied Occupation Forces in Japan, was Truman's choice on the recommendation of the Joint Chiefs of Staff, as commanding general of the United Nations forces. Tall and imperious, the seventy-year-old MacArthur was the most enduringly popular American military figure of the twentieth century. A hero in both world wars, MacArthur was renowned as a strategist, most notably for his successful campaigns in New Guinea and the Philippines. As the military governor of Japan, he built a modern nation from the ashes of defeat in World War II and opened up Japanese society with democratic reforms.

Truman did not like MacArthur. Dulles, Truman's Republican foreign policy adviser, had been in Tokyo when the North Koreans launched their invasion, and reported to Truman that MacArthur had been slow to respond to the news of the Korean attack. But when Dulles suggested removing MacArthur from his command, Truman responded that there would be too much political fallout. Before Truman announced his commander for the Korean War, Eisenhower had confided to associates at the Pentagon that MacArthur was the wrong man. "In commenting upon General MacArthur," Ridgway noted in his diary, "Ike expressed the wish that he would like to see a younger general out there, rather than, as he expressed it, 'an untouchable' whose actions you cannot predict, and who will himself decide what information he wants Washington to have and what he will withhold."[11]

In his first visit to the Korean front, MacArthur predicted that a couple of American divisions would stop the North Korean advance and asserted that the war would be of brief duration. But the first two American regiments, which were without effective antitank weapons, were shattered by the North Koreans and turned back in disarray. "We were, in short, in a state of shameful unreadiness," said Ridgway, who was then deputy chief of staff.[12]

Eisenhower believed that the Truman administration's cuts in U.S. military power were partly responsible for the war. "The Korean situation seems to be in something of a stalemate over the past several weeks," Eisenhower wrote a friend on September 12. "Most of us are puzzled by some of the developments and certainly all of us are experiencing a definite feeling of frustration. However, we should not fall into the slovenly and easily acquired habit of just blaming others for all our misfortunes. However, it seems quite clear that, in one particular, the civilian authorities of our government must take a very considerable share of blame. They have never been very seriously impressed by a professional insistence upon the permanent maintenance of a 'task force' or as it is sometimes called a 'striking force.' It has always been obvious that a democracy, even one as rich as ours, could not maintain in peace the force that could promptly and successfully meet any trouble that might arise in any portion of the globe, particularly if such trouble should occur simultaneously in two or three places."[13]

Truman ran out of patience with Johnson and fired him as defense secretary in September 1950. The dismissal wasn't because of Johnson's defense cuts, which Truman had supported. Johnson lost Truman's confidence by feuding with Acheson and aligning himself with the secretary of state's Republican critics. "Louis began to show an inordinate egotistical desire to run the whole government. He offended every member of the cabinet," Truman wrote in his diary. "We never had a cabinet meeting that he did not show plainly that he knew more about the problems of the Treasury, Commerce, Labor, Agriculture than did the secretaries of those departments." When Truman dumped him, Johnson acknowledged that he had made more enemies than friends as defense secretary. Truman called General George C. Marshall out of retirement and nominated him as Johnson's successor.[14]

In the first forty days of American involvement, the North Koreans drove allied forces into the southeastern corner of the peninsula around the port of Pusan. By August, nearly all of South Korea was controlled by Communist forces. General Walton Walker, commander of the Eighth Army, had fought with Patton in World War II. When confronted with the possibility that his men would be driven into the sea, the native Texan evoked images of the Alamo in giving this order: "There will be no more retreating, withdrawal, readjustment of lines or whatever else you call it. There are no lines behind which we can retreat. This is not going to be a Dunkirk or Bataan. A retreat to Pusan would result in one of the greatest butcheries in history. We must fight unto the end. We must fight as a team. If some of us die, we will die fighting together."[15]

In mid-September MacArthur launched a daring invasion of the port of Inchon, despite approaches that rose and fell with the tide. It was the boldest gamble of MacArthur's career, a full-scale amphibious assault one hundred fifty miles behind enemy lines. The success of MacArthur's attack force set the stage for the liberation of Seoul and Walker's rout of North Korean troops south of the thirty-eighth parallel. Eisenhower wrote MacArthur: "You have again given us a brilliant example of professional leadership."

Truman sent MacArthur this tribute: "I know that I speak for the entire American people when I send you my warmest congratulations on the victory which has been achieved under your leadership in Korea. Few operations in military history can match either the delaying action where you traded space for time in which to build up your forces, or the brilliant maneuver which has now resulted in the liberation of Seoul. . . . I salute you all, and say to all of you from all of us at home, 'Well and nobly done.'"

By the end of September, MacArthur had fulfilled his UN mandate: "To repel armed invasion and restore peace and stability in the area." But Rhee wanted to unify all Korea under his leadership and made it known to the Americans that he would settle for nothing less. MacArthur favored conquering the north. Dean Rusk, assistant secretary of state for Far Eastern affairs, supported that goal. Eisenhower called for the destruction of the North Korean military capability. There was growing public support for expanding the war. A Gallup poll indicated that 64 percent of Americans wanted the fighting to continue north of the thirty-eighth parallel. Truman allowed MacArthur to cross the parallel. Marshall, who had just been confirmed as defense secretary, radioed MacArthur: "We want you to feel unhampered tactically and strategically to proceed North of the 38th parallel."[16]

The Truman administration had been warned about the possible consequences of enlarging the war. Chinese Foreign Minister Chou En-lai had sent word through the Indian ambassador that China would go to war if the Americans and South Koreans moved north of the thirty-eighth parallel. But Truman and Acheson obtained UN authority for MacArthur's forces to cross the parallel.

Truman, who favored a limited war, was concerned about Chinese intervention when Americans moved north of the thirty-eighth parallel. In mid-October, Truman summoned MacArthur to Wake Island for a discussion of the war's next phase. "I believe that formal resistance will end throughout North and South Korea by Thanksgiving," MacArthur assured his commander in chief. "There is little resistance left in South Korea—only about 15,000 men—and those we do not destroy, the winter will. We now have about 60,000 prisoners in compounds. In North Korea, unfortunately, they are pursuing a forlorn hope. They have about 100,000 men who were trained as replacements. They are poorly trained, led and equipped, but they are obstinate and it goes against my grain to have to destroy them. They are only fighting to save face. Orientals prefer to die rather than to lose face."

MacArthur went on: "It is my hope to be able to withdraw the 8th Army to Japan by Christmas. That will leave the X Corps, which will be reconstituted, composed of the 2nd and 3rd Divisions and UN detachments. I hope the UN will hold elections by the first of the year. Nothing is gained by military occupation. All occupations are failures."

Truman nodded in agreement.

"After elections are held I expect to pull out all occupying troops," MacArthur said. "Korea should have about ten divisions with our equipment, supplemented by a small but competent air force and also by a small but competent navy. If we do that, I will not only secure Korea but it will be a tremendous deterrent to the Chinese Communists moving south . . . a threat that cannot be laughed off."

The president then addressed his major concern: "What are the chances for Chinese or Soviet interference?"

"Very little," MacArthur replied. "Had they interfered in the first or second months it would have been decisive. We are no longer fearful of their intervention."

MacArthur was dismissive of the Chinese threat: "This is the hour of our strength, not of our weakness. We no longer stand hat in hand. If the Chinese Communists cross the Yalu, I shall make of them the greatest slaughter in the history of mankind," the Far Eastern general told his commander in chief.[17]

Truman told MacArthur that he had never had a more satisfactory conference. On October 19, 1950, just four days after the Wake Island conference, the North Korean capital of Pyongyang fell to UN forces. "The war is very definitely coming to an end shortly," MacArthur told reporters at his headquarters in Tokyo.

For Truman, that kind of good news was a rarity in the fall of 1950. November of that year was the gloomiest month of his presidency. It opened with a shootout on Pennsylvania Avenue. The Trumans were living in temporary quarters at Blair House just down the street while the White House was being renovated. On the afternoon of November 1, Truman was the target of an attempted assassination. Two Puerto Rican nationalists, one armed with a German automatic pistol and the other firing a Lugar, sought to storm past the guard booths. Twenty-seven shots were fired in a two-minute exchange between the nationalists and White House guards. One of the assailants and a guard were killed. Two guards and the second assailant were wounded. "I was never in danger," Truman told reporters. "The thing I hate about it is the fact that these young men—one of them killed, and two of them badly wounded."

From Morningside Heights, Eisenhower wired his friend: "I am profoundly thankful that no harm came to you in the unfortunate and disgraceful incident of this afternoon."

"I am most appreciative of your solicitous concern in sending me that kind message," Truman responded. "The incident was so unnecessary, and I am deeply distressed than it was necessary for three of our valiant guards here to make such great sacrifices."[18]

Six days after the assault on Blair House, Truman got another jolt. Republican critics of the administration were the biggest winners in the 1950 midterm election. The Democrats lost twenty-eight seats in the U.S. House and five in the Senate in the 1950 midterm elections. Even though Democrats narrowly retained both houses, Truman's governing majority was gone. Senate Majority Leader Scott Lucas of Illinois and Majority Whip Francis J. Myers of Pennsylvania, Truman's most valued allies in the Senate, were among the casualties. Truman was displeased with Congressman Richard M. Nixon's election as the new Republican senator from California and Joseph McCarthy's role in the defeat of Maryland's Democratic Senator Millard Tydings. On an election night cruise on the *Williamsburg*, the president made little effort to hide his disappointment. A moderate social drinker, Truman sipped more bourbon than usual at this political wake.[19]

The worst was yet to come.

MacArthur split his forces in a two-pronged drive toward the Yalu River, and China moved closer to intervention in the Korean War. For months, the Chinese had warned that their forces would not allow Americans to reach their border. MacArthur had assured Truman at Wake Island that the Chinese would not enter the war unless UN forces invaded Manchuria. But while Truman was conferring with MacArthur, Chinese "volunteers" were already moving into North Korea. Crossing the Yalu River by night, the Chinese soldiers moved on foot and hid out during daylight. The Chinese attack wiped out MacArthur's forward South Korean divisions and exposed the Eighth Army's advance units. At Unsan, forty-five miles south of the Yalu, Chinese forces surrounded a U.S. regiment and attacked from all sides. Three battalions were shattered.

MacArthur ordered the air force to bomb the dozen bridges over the Yalu. When the Joint Chiefs reversed this order, MacArthur replied: "Men and material in large force are pouring across bridges over the Yalu from Manchuria. This movement not only jeopardizes but threatens the ultimate destruction of my command." Truman, overruling the Joint Chiefs, authorized MacArthur to bomb the Korean halves of the bridges. In a month of bombing raids, only a third of the bridges were knocked out. By then, the Yalu had frozen over and the Chinese could move into Korea without bridges. When Chinese forces suddenly quit fighting in early November, a newly confident MacArthur predicted that the war would be over by Christmas.

On November 24, MacArthur launched his "end-the-war" offensive, and for two days, his plan seemed to be working. The Eighth Army advanced toward the Yalu with little opposition. But more than one hundred and eighty thousand Chinese troops were waiting for them and attacked with overwhelming force. The entire Eighth Army was threatened and forced into retreat. On the east coast, with more than twenty thousand Chinese troops threatening the destruction of X Corps, MacArthur ordered withdrawal of the entire force. MacArthur wired the Joint Chiefs: "The Chinese military forces are committed in North Korea in great and ever-increasing strength. . . . We face an entirely new war. . . . My strategic plan for the immediate future is to pass from the offensive to the defensive with such local adjustments as may be required by a constantly fluid situation."[20]

The Chinese offensive shattered Truman's hopes. His plan had been to keep it a limited war. But the president's decisions to allow MacArthur to proceed north of the thirty-eighth parallel and to bomb the Yalu bridges had enlarged the conflict. In October, the Gallup poll reported that two-thirds of the American public believed that Truman had done the right thing in defending South Korea. But after China entered the war, a similar poll found that half of the American people thought Truman's intervention had been a mistake and only 39 percent approved.

Truman vowed to hang tough. "The Chinese attack was made in great force, and it still continues. It has resulted in the forced withdrawal of large parts of the United Nations command. The battlefield situation is uncertain at this time," a grim-faced president told a news conference. "We may suffer reverses as we have suffered them before. But the forces of the United Nations have no intention of abandoning their mission in Korea."[21]

Eisenhower, who agreed with Truman's decision to intervene, had doubts about his performance as a war leader. In early November of 1950, Eisenhower wrote in his diary: ". . . poor HST, a fine man who, in the middle of a stormy lake, knows nothing of swimming. Yet a lot of drowning people are forced to look to him as a lifeguard. If his wisdom could only equal his good intent."

After the Chinese rout of MacArthur's forces, Eisenhower commented in his diary: "The Korean situation is tragic, although I still believe that MacA. can stabilize the situation if he comes back far enough to stretch the hostile lines and expose their communications to incessant air attack."[22]

On December 15, 1950, Truman declared the Korean situation a national emergency. In a nationally televised address, Truman asserted, "What the free nations have done in Korea is right, and men all over the world know that it is right. Whatever temporary setbacks there may be, the right will prevail in the end. . . . No nation has ever had a greater responsibility than ours has at this moment. We must remember that we are the leaders of the free world. We must understand that we cannot achieve peace by ourselves, but only by cooperating with other free nations and with the men and women who love freedom everywhere."[23]

In this global struggle, Truman had a new task for Eisenhower

CHAPTER 18

Alliance

Truman wrote a "Dear Ike" note on October 19, 1950: "First time you're in town I wish you'd come and see me. If I send for you we'll start the 'speculators' to work." When Eisenhower, on an alumni tour for Columbia, arrived at Chicago's Blackstone Hotel on October 23, he received a message asking him to call Truman. "I placed the call immediately and was informed by the President that he should like to have me come to Washington, to talk in general terms about an assignment for me involving a command for the Atlantic Pact defensive forces."

The North Atlantic Treaty, which was signed by the United States and eleven nations in Washington, D.C., on April 4, 1949, marked an important and historic change in American foreign policy. For one hundred and fifty years, the United States had followed George Washington's policy of avoiding alliances with European powers. "The great rule of conduct for us in regard to foreign nations is to have with them as little political connection as possible," Washington declared in his farewell address. Truman and Eisenhower, in the early conflicts of the cold war, recognized the urgency of ending the U.S. tradition of noninvolvement. NATO was created in response to the 1948 Soviet coup in Czechoslovakia and the Soviet blockade of Berlin. The NATO pact committed member nations to "continuous and effective self-help and mutual aid." It also pledged that "an armed attack against one or more" of its allies "in Europe or North America shall be considered an attack against them all."[1]

Senator Taft of Ohio, leader of the Republican opposition, challenged Truman's wisdom in making this commitment. "I think the pact carries with it an obligation to assist in arming, at our expense, the nations of Western Europe, because with that obligation I believe it will promote war in the world rather than peace," Taft said in voting against the treaty. The Senate approved the NATO pact in July of 1949 by an eighty-two to thirteen vote, though the debate would continue for another two years.

On December 20, 1950, former President Hoover, in a national radio address, declared that the United States should retreat from Europe and become the "Gibraltar of Western Civilization." Hoover went on: "We are not blind to the need to preserve Western Civilization on the Continent of Europe or to our cultural and religious ties to it. But the prime obligations of defense of Western Continental Europe rests upon the nations of Europe."

"The country is not going back to isolationism. You can be sure of that," Truman said when asked for comment on Hoover's speech. In his 1951 State of the Union message, Truman eloquently defended his commitment to NATO: "The heart of our common defense effort is the North Atlantic community. The defense of Europe is the basis for the defense of the whole free world—ourselves included. . . . Strategically, economically, and morally, the defense of Europe is a part of our own defense."

Eisenhower, who admired Hoover, was appalled by his isolationism. "I am forced to believe he's getting senile," the general wrote in his diary. "God knows I'd personally like to get out of Europe and I'd like to see the United States able to sit at home and ignore the rest of the world. What a pleasing prospect, until you look at ultimate consequences, destruction."[2]

Most Americans were in agreement with Truman and Eisenhower about NATO's importance. Three out of four respondents to the Gallup poll approved of U.S. membership, according to the Gallup poll, with only 14 percent opposed. By more than five to one, Americans said that it was more important to "stop Russia" in Europe rather than Asia.

It was destined to become the most successful military alliance in history. The Soviet Union, with 175 divisions, loomed as a threat to the security of Western Europe. But once Truman committed the United States to the defense of its allies, Stalin understood that the Red Army would be starting a major war if it advanced into western territory. "It is a simple document," Truman said at the 1949 signing of the NATO treaty, "but if it had existed in 1914 and in 1939, supported by the nations who are represented here today, I believe it would have prevented the acts of aggression which led to two world wars."[3]

Truman never considered anyone but Eisenhower for the role of supreme commander. In offering the appointment, the president told him that he was the unanimous choice of the leadership of a dozen nations. Truman asked whether he would take command of the alliance. "Well, Mr.

President, as long as you ask it, I'm still on the active list of the Army and I've got to go," Eisenhower said.

"I don't want to issue an order," Truman replied. "If you say you won't do it, why, I'll make some excuses to these people."

Eisenhower wouldn't hear of it. "I see no possible excuse for keeping me on the active list as long as I live unless I consider it a duty to answer the call of my Commander-in-Chief," the general said. "Now, I just want to know this—do you think I could do it better than anybody else?"

"Absolutely," Truman answered. "There's no one else in sight."

"All right, then, I'll go," said Eisenhower.

Truman's selection was acclaimed on both sides of the Atlantic. Bradley wrote in his memoirs that Truman had wanted to hold off Eisenhower's appointment until after NATO had fielded air, sea, and land forces and had reached agreement on allowing Germany to participate. "But after the onset of the Korean war, we began to talk in terms of naming Ike much sooner so that he could bring his prestige to bear in the massive task of rearming Western Europe," Bradley recalled.[4]

Eisenhower, who had grown restless and frustrated at Columbia, wasn't unhappy to be back in uniform. He offered his resignation to the university's trustees but accepted an indefinite leave. When a friend suggested that Truman might be taking advantage of him, he wrote back:

> I am a little astonished at your use of the expression "talked into." As you know, I am an officer on the active list which I will always stay, by reason of a special Act of Congress, affecting a few of us, unless I voluntarily remove myself from it. It is clear that my official superiors don't have to do any talking if they actually want me to take any military assignment.
>
> But over and above such considerations and addressing myself to the merits of the case, I would conclude from your statement that you do not attach the same importance to the success of the Atlantic Defense Pact as I do. I rather look upon this effort as about the last remaining chance for the survival of Western civilization. Our efforts in the United Nations have been defeated by the vetoes of hostile groups—but in the Atlantic Pact we are not plagued by the hostile groups and are simply trying to work out a way that free countries may band together to protect themselves.
>
> . . . Of course if the authorities can find anyone else who will tackle the job, and who they believe can perform it, then I hasten to agree with you that man would probably do it far better than I could. . . .

> But I still would not agree that there is any job in the world today that is more important than getting Atlantic Union defensive forces and arrangements off to a good, practical, and speedy start.[5]

In a memorandum for Truman that outlined his views on the European situation, Eisenhower wrote: "Our struggle for survival against Soviet imperialism will continue until either we or the Soviets are destroyed or the other side has recognized the hopelessness of attempting to conquer the free world through force and will seek, with us, a reasonable and practicable basis for living together in the world. This they will never do except to gain time.

"Because the opponent is militant in the political world as well as in the field of force, he develops a many-sided and complex system of attack, using force, deceit, propaganda and subversion. . . . We must never lose light of the fact that Western Europe is the keystone of the defensive arch we are trying to build up. In this arch the United States is the foundation."

Eisenhower concluded: "We need to help encourage Europe in every possible way, but we should not over-emphasize the favorable consequences of assuming the responsibility for command. It is always possible that this act might create an even greater European tendency to sit back and wait, in a renewed confidence that the United States has assumed an inescapable and publicly stated responsibility."[6]

Truman, Marshall, and Acheson gave Eisenhower a big send-off as he departed for Europe on January 6, 1951. "Mr. President, I devoutly pray that the mission on which I am leaving this morning will result in nothing but peace, security, and tranquility for our various nations of the western Atlantic," the supreme commander declared.

"I agree with you, General," Truman responded, "and I know that's going to be the result. You have the wholehearted backing of the people of the United States and I know that you will have that same backing from eleven other nations who are in the Atlantic Treaty. Good bye and good luck."

Eisenhower saluted his commander in chief, then embarked on his journey.

On landing in Paris, he greeted the people of the alliance nations with this radio message : "I return to Europe as a military commander, but with no miraculous plans, no display of military force. I return with an unshakable faith in Europe—this land of our ancestors—in the underlying courage of its people, in their willingness to live and sacrifice for a secure peace and the continuance and the progress of civilization."[7]

Europe had changed a great deal in the five years since Eisenhower had stepped down as military governor of Germany's American zone. Since the United States began sending economic aid under the Marshall Plan in 1948, Western Europe had done much to improve industrial and agricultural production. By the time that Eisenhower took command of NATO, Western European nations were exceeding prewar production levels by a fourth. In 1949 Germany split into two states, the Federal Republic (West Germany) and the German Democratic Republic (East Germany). Truman and Eisenhower favored bringing West Germany into the alliance. Italy, which had been governed by fascism for more than a generation, established itself as a republic in 1946 and was among NATO's charter members.

World War II had changed Europe in other ways. Six of NATO's members had colonial empires: Britain, France, the Netherlands, Belgium, Portugal, and Italy. But their grip on the colonies had been weakened during the war and emerging nationalist movements were demanding independence. British Prime Minister Clement Attlee's Labour government led the way in dismantling its colonial holdings. India, the jewel in the crown of the British Empire, was given its independence in 1947, dividing into the countries of India and Pakistan. Burma and Ceylon were also granted nationhood. Other imperial powers were slower to retreat from their empires. The Netherlands, which lost the Dutch East Indies to the Japanese during World War II, fought a two-year conflict before recognizing Indonesia's independence in 1949. France, which had been humiliated by Germany in 1940 when it fell within six weeks, was in the midst of losing a war to revolutionary forces over control of its colonies in Indochina. Twenty thousand Frenchmen died in the first five years of the war in Indochina. Nationalist guerrillas led by Ho Chi Minh had driven the French out of the jungles of northern Vietnam in October of 1950 and gained control of the Mekong Delta in central Vietnam. General Jean-Marie de Lattre de Tassigny, who had commanded the First French Army under Eisenhower in World War II, was named in December of 1950 as the French high commissioner and commander in chief for Indochina.

Truman selected Eisenhower for his political as well as his military skills. In his 1951 State of the Union message, Truman talked about Ike's importance in launching NATO. "To put these plans into action," the president said, "we sent to Europe last week one of our greatest military commanders, General Dwight D. Eisenhower. General Eisenhower went to Europe to assume command of the united forces of the North Atlantic Treaty countries, including our own forces in Germany. The people of Europe have confidence in General Eisenhower. They know his ability to put together a fighting force of allies. His mission is vital to our security.

We should all stand behind him, and give him every bit of help we can."[8]

Eisenhower, who would be leading multinational forces from the Arctic to the Mediterranean, began with a three-week, thirteen thousand-mile tour of NATO countries. He was warmly received in the European capitals, though the crowds that greeted him were much smaller than the throngs that had hailed the Allied victory in 1945. His popularity was undiminished. Eisenhower was admired throughout Europe as a symbol of freedom and democracy.

On this whirlwind trip, he put it on the line in conversations with European leaders. If they wanted America's help, other members of the alliance would have to carry their share of the military burden. Eisenhower spoke with candor about how the isolationists were seeking to cut back America's role in defending Europe. He needed to know whether Europe was willing to pay the price for its long-term security.

Eisenhower's first meeting was with French Defense Minister Jules Moch, who pledged cooperation but vehemently opposed allowing West Germany into the alliance. Moch said that the French people were determined to avoid the fourth invasion of their country in less than a century. He lamented that the war in Indochina had drained resources and noted that the army was low on equipment. Eisenhower told Moch that in the North African campaign, "when things looked particularly bad and I was surrounded by the long faces on my staff, I reminded them with good effect that if it had been an easy task, such good people would not have been sent to do the job. Let us remember that."

French Prime Minister Rene Pleven, like Moch, was against letting Germany into the alliance. Pleven told Eisenhower that "German rearmament might be considered a provocation" by the Soviet Union and would be unwelcomed in France. The premier talked with Eisenhower about French Communists and neutralists. The Communists received more than five million votes in the 1946 national elections. Pleven told Eisenhower that the neutralists were a graver threat than the Communists. Many of the neutralists, Pleven alleged, had been "collaborators" during the Nazi occupation of France. Pleven estimated that 80 percent of those voting for Communist candidates could be won over to the democratic side. "One must remember," said Pleven, "that many Frenchmen have suffered during the wars of 1914–18 and 1939–45. For these people the idea of a new war is a terrible one. Nevertheless, they will be ready to do their duty if we are able to convince them that our purpose is to establish a solid and efficient defense against aggression."[9]

Eisenhower's next stop was Brussels, where he told the defense minister, Colonel Edouard de Greff, that Belgian troops were below their necessary strength. On the basis of Belgium's population and the armed services ratio in other NATO countries, he said that Belgium should have about two hundred thousand men in uniform. The Belgian military had barely half of that number. "If one country falls behind, someone else soon falls behind also," said Eisenhower. "Each country should be striving to do more than the others." Eisenhower said he didn't know the state of the Belgian economy but he urged that they make a military commitment "that a farmer in Kansas would understand." The Belgian official pledged to make every effort to give him what he needed.

In the Netherlands, Eisenhower was even more disappointed. General Hendrik Kruls, the Dutch army's chief of staff, told Eisenhower that Prime Minister William Drees, who was a pacifist, was reluctant to support a military buildup and wouldn't permit him to meet minimum requirements. The Dutch defense minister told Eisenhower that the Dutch army had difficulties but noted "Holland's old and proud maritime traditions and the traditional pride in the Dutch Navy." Eisenhower told the Dutch officials that he found a lack of urgency and felt "there was still a certain leisureliness apparent." Kruls, who agreed with Eisenhower and told him so, resigned soon afterward.[10]

Eisenhower then went to Denmark, where he struck a similar theme. In response to a question from NATO's commander, the foreign minister said that Denmark was spending "about three or four percent" of its national income for defense. Eisenhower, noting that the United States was spending a much greater share of its national product for defense, said that all members of the alliance should be paying their fair share.

In Norway, Eisenhower paid tribute to the valor of its resistance movement against Nazi Germany. The royal family went into exile during the German occupation and a puppet state was formed, headed by the traitor Vidkun Quisling. "Our experience has been a sad one," King Haakon VII told him, "and I am convinced that we must have help and that agreements must be made to supply Norway with necessary forces." Eisenhower replied that it was imperative for Norway to build a defense of such strength that no one would ever think of invading their country. The king assured Eisenhower that Norway would do its part.[11]

Eisenhower was then off to London, where he stayed for three nights at Claridge's Hotel. The supreme commander lunched at Number 10 Downing Street with Prime Minister Clement Attlee, whom he had known during the war as deputy prime minister in Churchill's war cabinet. "He was a real supporter of NATO which of course endeared him to me," Eisenhower later wrote. Also attending this luncheon was Foreign Minister Ernest Bevin, NATO's founding father. In January of 1948, Bevin had taken the initiative and started the process that led to the creation of the alliance. Bevin was the key figure in persuading the Truman administration to break with the Washingtonian tradition of avoiding entangling alliances. "The political figure I liked best in the British Labour government of the SHAPE [Supreme Headquarters Allied Powers Europe] period was the Foreign Minister, Mr. Ernest Bevin," Eisenhower recalled years later. "Ernie Bevin was a heavy-set, down-to-earth, unpretentious man, full of humor and fun. He was never hesitant in talking about his lack of early educational advantages, he was resolutely self-confident, and he relied upon his energy, natural adaptability, and native common sense to carry him through the mazes of international politics." Though he didn't know it at the time, the luncheon at Number 10 would be his final meeting with Bevin, who was gravely ill. Bevin would resign from the cabinet on March 9 and died within a month.[12]

In Lisbon, his next stop, Eisenhower conferred with Portugal's dictator, Antonio Salazar at São Bento Palace. A former professor of economics at Coimbra University and the descendant of fishermen, he had ruled for two decades and his regime would last for thirty-six years. Brought into power by the military, Salazar told Eisenhower that he had made order out of chaos. Though a right-wing dictator, he disliked Nazi Germany and kept Portugal neutral during World War II. He allowed the Allies air bases in the Azores in 1943 and was credited by the Allies with playing a role in encouraging Spain to remain neutral. Salazar led Portugal into the United Nations and NATO. Eisenhower told the Portuguese leader that if all NATO members worked together that war could be avoided. Salazar agreed with Eisenhower, but noted that there were major differences between the Latin and Nordic countries of Europe. The Portugese leader said that the Latin countries lacked the civic and moral discipline that would permit democracy to function. Salazar was concerned about Soviet support of revolutionary movements in Portugal, noting that many Americans had the misperception that communism only developed in countries suffering great hardship. He told Eisenhower that war could be avoided only by strength and suggested that a war between the great powers would "leave neither victor nor vanquished" but "a universal catastrophe in which there would be little difference between victory and defeat." Eisenhower replied that there was only one thing worse than war and that would be to have a war and lose.[13]

From Portugal, Eisenhower flew in his propeller-driven air force Constellation to Italy. There were few allied leaders that he admired more than Italian Prime Minister Alcide de Gasperi, who had led the underground resistance to Mussolini during World War II and would lead the Italian government from 1945 until 1953. He told the prime minister that Italy couldn't be expected to produce war materials like the United States but that it could make an important difference in the Mediterranean region. De Gasperi pledged full cooperation with NATO and thanked him for "taking up this heavy burden." Not all of his countrymen held similar views. The Italian Communists staged mass demonstrations against Eisenhower in Rome with posters denouncing him in four-letter English obscenities. In the violence between demonstrators and police, four persons were killed and a hundred wounded. Eisenhower said later that he hadn't seen a single Communist demonstrator during his visit.

In Luxembourg, the smallest nation in the alliance, Prime Minister Pierre Dupong told Eisenhower that he was making an effort to rally public opinion behind the alliance and away from neutrality. Dupong told the supreme commander that all men of military age would be called into military service without exemptions. Eisenhower replied that this effort could set an example for other NATO members. The U.S. ambassador, Perle Mesta, who had been the unofficial hostess of the Truman administration before her diplomatic appointment, held a festive party for Eisenhower at the embassy.[14]

Eisenhower's return to Germany, his next stop, was the most dramatic moment of the tour. For the alliance to succeed, he believed West Germany needed to participate. But he also recognized that this would not be possible without a consensus of member nations. The *Wall Street Journal* reported a poll that indicated nearly half of West Germans opposed NATO participation even if granted full membership. The *Journal* also reported that a majority of German men would decline to serve in such an army. Given these attitudes, the *Journal* questioned whether the German government would ever agree to aid NATO.

Eisenhower had nearly cancelled his German stop because of bitter division on this issue within the alliance and the exploitation of this controversy by European Communists. "I am becoming increasingly doubtful of the advisability of visiting Germany at this time," he wired Acheson after his meetings with French leaders. "My doubts are based on the adverse propaganda surrounding the question of German rearmament." Eisenhower sought guidance from Acheson and John J. McCloy, the U.S. high commissioner in West Germany.

Acheson and McCloy responded that the cancellation of this visit would have an adverse effect on morale in West Germany. There was another issue, McCloy said, that Eisenhower needed to resolve. The Communists were circulating propaganda that Eisenhower disliked the German people and refused to shake hands with German officers. In an earlier cable,

McCloy said that German officers were resentful of Eisenhower's comments in his memoirs about his disdain for German commanders and his refusal to accept them as "comrades in arms." McCloy said that Eisenhower shouldn't elaborate or explain the statements in his book but could indicate a willingness to work with democratic-minded soldiers in defense of the West.[15]

At Frankfurt's Rhine-Main airfield, the man who defeated Hitler extended an olive branch. "I think it is fitting that I should make one remark about Germany, specifically because as you people know, when I entered Germany before, I was at the head of an army and Germany, the German nation, was our enemy," Eisenhower said. "For my part, bygones are bygones. I bear no resentment whatsoever against Germany as a nation, and certainly I do not bear any against the German people. . . . Now, I would be entirely a liar if I should say that at the time of the conflict I didn't bear in my heart a very definite antagonism toward Germany and certainly a hatred for all that I thought the Nazis and the Hitlerites stood for."

Eisenhower left no doubt that he would welcome Germany's participation in the alliance. "Of course I shall hope some day that the great German people are lined up with the rest of the free world," the supreme commander declared, "because I believe in the essential freedom-loving quality of the Germany people. Now, I hope, therefore, that one day they are aligned right up squarely with the rest of us. If they are, they must be on exactly the same status as all the others. I would never consent to be in command of any unit whose soldiers were not there believing they were serving their country and civilization and freedom."[16]

During three days in West Germany, the general conferred with Chancellor Konrad Adenauer, who had twice been imprisoned by the Nazis, the second time for his connection with the July 1944 assassination attempt on Hitler. Adenauer said that Eisenhower's public comments did much to overcome German apathy about future participation in the alliance. The German chancellor expressed his "complete satisfaction" with Eisenhower's visit and said that view was shared by "all German participants regardless of party affiliation."[17]

From Germany, Eisenhower returned to France, where he chose the site for SHAPE near the village of Rocquencourt about ten miles from Paris. The French government immediately made the land available for NATO's supreme command. Until the new headquarters was built, Eisenhower would be based at the Astoria Hotel.

In winding up his inspection tour, he flew into Iceland, which had been occupied by the Allies during World War II as an air base and was of strategic importance to NATO. Eisenhower, whose air force plane landed at Keflavik airfield in near-blizzard conditions, told Prime Minister Steinthorsson that he had twice attempted to make stops in Iceland during the war but stormy weather had prevented him from doing so. The prime minister, who headed the only NATO government without armed services, said that Iceland was defenseless and placed its fate in the hands of other allied powers, most notably the United States. Eisenhower said that he fully understood the reason why Iceland must rely on others and added that the real defense of the free world was in the hearts of free people. Small countries could make as great a contribution as large countries in courage, he said. The foreign minister termed Eisenhower's visit "extraordinarily beneficial" to their government.[18]

Eisenhower's final stop before heading home was in Ottawa, where he met with Prime Minister Louis St. Laurent, who had been among the first to propose an Atlantic alliance. Eisenhower reported to the cabinet on his inspection tour of NATO countries and told reporters: "I have been greatly encouraged by the growing realization all over [Western] Europe that the issues of peace and freedom are at stake and that they are willing and determined to do more to save those things."

Heading to West Point for the weekend, he prepared for a round of meetings in Washington, D.C. On January 31, he flew to National Airport, where he was greeted by Truman. After they lunched at Blair House, Truman and Eisenhower went across the street to the White House for a meeting in the cabinet room with Vice President Barkley, House Speaker Sam Rayburn, Acheson, National Security Adviser W. Averell Harriman, Defense Mobilization Director Charles E. Wilson, National Security Resources Board Chairman Symington, and members of the cabinet.

Truman opened the meeting by saying that he had asked "Ike" to tell the cabinet what he had observed in Europe and to repeat some of the things they had discussed at lunch. Eisenhower began by asking why Western Europe, with a population of 350 million people and vast industrial capacity, viewed Russia as such a grave threat. The answer was simple, he asserted. Even if it was at the point of a bayonet, the Russians had unity. In contrast, the West was divided. The supreme commander said that it was his mission to help bring about unity and stability. "My first job was to go around these countries and find out what they had in their hearts," he said. "I wanted to see how they feel about these questions."

Eisenhower told Truman's men that he had gotten the western allies to agree that they could "tell Russia to go to hell if they only would get together, raise enough men, and produce enough equipment." He reported that communism was declining as a political force in Western

Europe, even in France and Italy where the party had demonstrated strength in the early postwar years. The real Communist danger was promoting "neutralism," the general said.

Allied leaders were in agreement on the importance of a unified defense, Eisenhower said, and he listed the Netherlands as his only disappointment. He was baffled by their interest in a navy when their vulnerability to attack was on land. Eisenhower said that the Dutch weren't trying hard enough.

On the German question, Eisenhower said too many Americans were getting into the debate. He, personally, would like to have German troops among NATO's forces. Eisenhower said that he had good reason to know what good fighters they were. But he didn't want to use NATO as a bargaining chip in their dealings with other countries. Eisenhower said that he didn't care about Germany's differences with France. That should be worked out between those nations. Eisenhower said that he had spoken bluntly with German leaders and that they seemed responsive.

Eisenhower said that he found growing confidence in Europe but that the allies had immediate needs. "What we need is a rapid conversion of our economy so that we can get the equipment to these people. We've got to get them the equipment to end this idea of neutralism. I don't know how fast Charlie Wilson is producing tanks, but I know it's not fast enough," he said. "What we need is speed, more speed, and more speed in production. They're being told by the communist press in every country that it's no use, that we can't get the stuff there in time.

"Gentlemen," he declared, "there is only one thing for us to do and that is get this combined spiral of strength going up. These people believe in the cause. Now, they have got to believe in themselves. They have got to have confidence that they can do the job. The way we can give them that confidence is by sending equipment and by sending some American units over there to help morale."

He then discussed the strategy of defending Europe. Describing the continent as a long bottleneck, the general said that Russia was the wide part of the bottle, Western Europe was the neck, which stretched down to Spain, which is like the end of the bottle. On either side of the neck are bodies of water controlled by the western allies. "I want to build a great combination of sea and air strength in the North Sea," he said. "I'd make Denmark and Holland a great 'hedgehog' and I'd put 500 or 600 fighters behind them and heavy naval support in the North Sea. I'd do the same sort of thing in the Mediterranean. I'd put a great fleet of air and sea power in the Mediterranean, and I'd give arms to Turkey and the 'Jugs.'

"Then," he concluded, "if the Russians tried to move ahead in the center, I'd hit them awfully hard from both flanks. I think if we built up the kind of force I want, the center will hold and they'll have to pull back."

When asked about the possibility of an immediate Russian attack, he spoke with candor. The Americans had only two divisions in Europe. If the Soviets attacked now, Eisenhower said that U.S. forces would be wiped out. But if the Americans had ten or twelve divisions and the Western Europeans had their forces at strength, the outcome would be much different. Eisenhower said that there would not be sizable casualties if the Russians attacked under these circumstances unless someone made a serious blunder. Even if Western Europe couldn't hold out, he said there would be adequate forces to make an orderly withdrawal. He did not think that would be the case.

Barkley asked Eisenhower about Stalin's intentions.

Eisenhower was doubtful that the Soviet Union wanted another world war. "I personally think those guys in the Kremlin like their jobs. They can't see their way through to winning a war now and I don't think they'll start one. They know they'll lose their jobs, or their necks, if they start something they can't win," he said. Eisenhower added that NATO's military buildup wouldn't provoke a Soviet attack. "If the Russians really think that sixty or seventy divisions in Western Europe are a threat to them, they are crazy," he contended. "They have no business going to war over that and I don't think they'll do it."

In closing, Eisenhower declared, "I believe that our civilization is in one hell of a hole. I believe that we have to work and work like hell. I believe that we have to go all out and produce just as though we were in a war and that we have to get this spiral of strength going up in Europe. Right now, it is going down." Without naming Hoover or Taft, he criticized "people who say that we ought to build up our own strength here at home and let Europe go. That's nonsense."

General Ike then turned to Truman and apologized, saying that he knew that the president and his advisers didn't hold those views. "I'm a soldier and I have to do whatever job is given to me," he said. "I'm doing this job because it was given to me but I'm also doing it because I believe in it. I believe very deeply in it."[19]

Indeed, he was so committed to this cause that Eisenhower was ready to remove himself from 1952 presidential politics. The debate on sending American troops to Europe would go on for nearly three months. Eisenhower was most concerned about Taft's opposition to U.S. involvement in the alliance. On January 5, the day before Eisenhower embarked for Europe, Taft asserted that Truman had no right under the Constitution to be sending American troops abroad in peacetime without congressional approval. Taft, who had voted against the NATO pact, also opposed the appointment of an American as supreme commander. Taft didn't think that NATO was necessary because he doubted that the Soviets would seek to control Western Europe. His opposition to Truman's foreign policy had wide backing among congressional Republicans. Throughout Eisenhower's inspection tour, European leaders spoke with concern about Taft's power and influence.

Eisenhower sought out Taft for a meeting. The Ohio senator told the general that he would be glad to confer with him and volunteered to come to the Pentagon for a private talk. "I thought it might be possible for me to kill two birds with one stone," Eisenhower recalled years later. "My first purpose was to be assured that when I got to Europe, the United States government's position would be solid in support of NATO. If such assurance were forthcoming, from the chief spokesman of what seemed to be the opposition, there was also a way to kill off any further speculation about me as a candidate for the presidency."

Taft was about to launch a bid for the 1952 Republican presidential nomination. He had twice sought and been denied his party's nomination but appeared to be in a stronger position this time. His old rival Dewey had withdrawn from contention and endorsed Eisenhower. Unless Eisenhower decided to make the race, it was doubtful whether Taft could be stopped. Eisenhower had just overtaken Taft by a narrow margin in national polls of Republican voters.

But if Taft would endorse the principle of collective security, Eisenhower wouldn't have a compelling reason to run. Enlisting Taft's support for NATO was regarded as that important.

Before their meeting, Eisenhower, with the help of two aides, drafted this statement: "I want to announce that my name may not be used by anyone as a candidate for President—and if they do I will repudiate such efforts."

The session with Taft was a disappointment. "I found my visitor concerned almost exclusively with the two specific questions of the number of American troops to be sent to Europe and the constitutional right of the President to send them," he later wrote. "I told him that these points were outside my immediate concern and insisted on an answer regarding support of the collective principle. I failed to get assurance. From the senator I gained the impression—possibly a mistaken one—that he and some of his colleagues were interested, primarily, in cutting the President, or the Presidency, down to size."

Eisenhower, who believed that Taft was "playing politics," tore up and discarded the statement of withdrawal from the presidential race. It was probably naive of Eisenhower to expect that the principled Taft would switch sides in the Great Debate. To maximize congressional support for NATO, Eisenhower decided "to keep some aura of mystery around my future personal plans."[20]

On April 4, 1951, the Senate approved Truman's decision to send four divisions to Europe by a sixty-nine to twenty-one vote. Under the resolution, Truman had to seek congressional approval for additional troops. "I agree with the basic thought expressed by the Senate," Eisenhower wrote in his diary. "If American public opinion does not support adequate reinforcement of Europe pending the development of adequate European force, and to inspire such development, then it is absurd for the President to send here a single soldier."[21]

CHAPTER 19

MacArthur

He was born to command. For more than half a century in three major wars and twenty campaigns, Douglas MacArthur led Americans into battle. More than just a military leader, he embodied the virtues of duty, honor, and country. With his corn-cob pipe, sunglasses, crushed hat, and faded khaki uniform, he exuded an epic grandeur. He spoke with eloquence and a sense of destiny. "Today the guns are silent. A great tragedy has ended. A great victory has been won," he told the American people in a radio address at the end of World War II. ". . . And so, my fellow countrymen, today I report to you that your sons and daughters have served you well and faithfully. . . . Their spiritual strength and power has brought us through to victory. They are homeward bound—take care of them."

From the start, it was a brilliant career. In 1903, he graduated first in his West Point class with the highest average any cadet had ever received. As the organizer of the legendary Rainbow Division, he was America's youngest division commander and most decorated officer of World War I. He would go on to become the U.S. Military Academy's youngest superintendent, the youngest chief of staff, and the youngest full general. From the trenches of the western front to the island fortress of Corregidor, he was fearless in the face of enemy fire. Of the twenty-two medals he received for combat, more than half were for bravery. As a student of military history, he regarded Alexander and Caesar as peers. In bringing a formal conclusion to history's bloodiest war, MacArthur spoke as a peacemaker when he accepted the Japanese surrender aboard the battleship *Missouri* in Tokyo Bay. "Let us pray that peace be now restored to the world, and that God will preserve it always," he declared at the simple ceremony. "These proceedings are closed."[1]

As supreme commander of the Allied Occupation Forces, he ruled Japan for six years with absolute authority. In recognition of this reality, the Emperor Hirohito told him: "I come to you, General MacArthur, to offer myself to the judgment of the powers you represent as the one to bear sole responsibility for every political and military decision made and action taken by my people in the conduct of war." The general showed compassion toward Hirohito. Though the victorious Allies prosecuted some Japanese militarists for their war crimes, MacArthur told the American government that he could find "no specific or tangible evidence" against Hirohito.

With regal bearing, MacArthur transformed Japan by presiding over social, economic, and political reforms. He promoted the growth of trade unions, introduced land reform, and women's rights. Of all accomplishments during the occupation, the old soldier was proudest of his role in drafting a constitution that outlawed war. "For years I have believed that war should be abolished as an outmoded means of resolving disputes between nations," he wrote in his memoirs. "Probably no living man has seen as much of war and its destruction as I had."[2]

MacArthur's flaws were as monumental as his virtues. He had an enormous ego, was politically ambitious, and was always on stage playing the role of Douglas MacArthur. He could be vain, arrogant, and petty. Throughout his career, he was incapable of admitting a mistake and was condescending toward superiors. He once confided that FDR was "a man of great vision once things were explained to him." Despite his fame, MacArthur was resentful of other commanders. While serving as MacArthur's aide in the 1930s, Eisenhower wrote in his diary that he had heard MacArthur's derisive comments "with respect to every prominent officer in the U.S. Army and officials in Washington. . . . I think that in his own mind, there is nothing ridiculous, absurd, or even unusual in his attitude. He was raised in the concept of Douglas MacArthur superiority. Actually he has become only pathetic."

In early 1942, when Eisenhower was serving as assistant head of war plans, he wrote in his diary about MacArthur's faltering response to the outbreak of war. On the day after bombing Pearl Harbor, the Japanese destroyed MacArthur's air force. "I still think he might have made a better showing at the beaches and passes," Eisenhower wrote, "and certainly he should have saved his planes on December 8, but he's still the hero!"

Eisenhower, who was involved in planning operations in the Far East while MacArthur was losing the Philippines, was harsh in his private assessment. "In many ways MacArthur is as big a baby as ever. But we've got to keep him fighting," Eisenhower wrote in January 1942. Later that month, Eisenhower added: "MacArthur has started a flood of communications that seem to indicate a refusal on his part to looks facts in the face, an old trait of his." On February 3, 1942, Eisenhower wrote: "Looks like MacArthur is losing his nerve. I'm hoping that his yelps are just his way of spurring us on, but he is always an uncertain factor." Several weeks later, Eisenhower wrote of MacArthur: "He is doing a good job where he is, but I'm doubtful that he'd do so well in more complicated situations. Bataan is made to order for him. It's in the public eye; it has made him a public hero; it has all the essentials of drama; and he is the acknowledged king on the spot. If brought out, public opinion will force him into a position where his love of the limelight may ruin him."[3]

For MacArthur's courage under fire in the Philippines, he was awarded the congressional Medal of Honor. Eisenhower objected when Marshall made the recommendation. "I saw little grounds for awarding this highest medal to him and told Marshall so," Eisenhower said years later. "Commanders of MacArthur's stature simply did not see that much combat or face extreme risks worthy of the Medal of Honor. But Marshall went ahead in the belief that we should do something and that MacArthur already held all the other medals the Army could give." Marshall would have presented the same medal to Eisenhower for his leadership in the successful 1942 Allied invasion of North Africa. "I told him that I would refuse to accept it," Eisenhower recalled years later, "and thought that all men in high command and headquarters jobs should be excluded from that honor."[4]

From the beginning of his presidency, Truman admired Eisenhower and disliked MacArthur. He referred to MacArthur in a June 1945 diary entry as "Mr. Prima Donna, Brass Hat, Five Star MacArthur. He's worse than the Cabots and the Lodges—they at least talked with one another before they told God what to do. Mac tells God right off." On the same day, Truman wrote: "Don't see how a country can produce such men as Robert E. Lee, John J. Pershing, Eisenhower & Bradley, and at the same time produce Custers, Pattons, and MacArthurs."[5]

After the Allied victories in their respective World War II theaters, Truman summoned home Eisenhower and MacArthur. Eisenhower promptly returned. MacArthur declined Truman's invitation. "I invited General MacArthur on several occasions," Truman recalled years later. "Something was always in the way."

Whatever his personal feelings, Truman trusted MacArthur as a military commander. It was Truman who selected him in 1945 as supreme commander for the Allied powers, in 1947 as commander in chief of the Far East command, and in 1950 as commander of United Nations forces in the Korean War.

During his term as chief of staff, Eisenhower was often frustrated in his dealings with MacArthur. The Far East general undercut the administration's policy on demobilization, reneged on a commitment to call publicly for an extension of the draft, and never delivered on a promise to issue a strong endorsement for the unification of the armed forces. Eisenhower wrote MacArthur that his silence on these issues had disappointed Truman. "He became so important in his own mind," Truman said of MacArthur, "that he was greater than the President of the United States. Time after time MacArthur went his own way."

In the first month of the Korean War, MacArthur called on Chiang Kai-shek in Formosa without consulting with Truman or Acheson. At the start of the war, Truman placed the Seventh Fleet in the Formosa Strait between the island and mainland China. Truman, who was seeking to prevent Chinese aggression against Formosa, declined Chiang's offer to join the Korean War on the allied side. By visiting Formosa, MacArthur announced that he considered Chiang an important ally. Truman sent Harriman across the globe to bring MacArthur into line on China policy. "He accepted the President's position and will act accordingly, but without full conviction," Harriman reported back.[6]

MacArthur openly disputed Truman's policy in a statement that was to be read August 28, 1950 at the Chicago convention of the Veterans of Foreign Wars. "In view of misconceptions currently being voiced concerning the relationship of Formosa to our strategic potential in the Pacific, I believe it in the public interest to avail myself of this opportunity to state my views thereon," he said in the written message. ". . . Nothing could be more fallacious than the threadbare argument by those who advocate appeasement and defeatism in the Pacific that if we defend Formosa we alienate continental Asia."

Truman, who learned of the general's comments from press reports, ordered MacArthur to withdraw the statement. In his memoirs, MacArthur said that he was "utterly astonished" by Truman's order. White House Press Secretary Charles G. Ross explained Truman's reason: "In the field of foreign relations there can be only one voice stating the position of the United States."

MacArthur had ignored other presidents. Hoover, whom the general admired, paid a political price for MacArthur's insubordination. In the summer of 1932, thousands of unemployed World War I veterans marched on Congress and asked for immediate payment of their bonus pensions. When Congress narrowly rejected the economic aid, the veterans camped out in the Anacostia flats. In late July, the veterans were ordered to evacuate. MacArthur, who was then army chief of staff, decided to take on this task. Hoover had given specific orders that Pennsylvania Avenue was to be cleared but that the federal troops were not authorized to cross the Eleventh Street Bridge into Anacostia.

As the bonus marchers peacefully headed back across the river, Hoover reiterated his order: "Don't allow any of our troops to go across the Anacostia Bridge." MacArthur, though, wanted to drive them from their camp. Eisenhower told MacArthur about Hoover's orders. "I don't want to hear them and I don't want to see them," the general replied. Then his troops stormed across the bridge, torched the encampment, and drove out the bonus marchers. The public blamed Hoover for this sorry episode. In his memoirs published two decades later, Hoover confirmed that his orders weren't followed. Franklin D. Roosevelt privately described MacArthur after this shameful episode as "one of the two most dangerous men in America." The other was Huey Long.[7]

MacArthur, whose heroes were Washington and Lincoln, had presidential ambitions. On the same day in the spring of 1948 that Truman announced that he would seek reelection, MacArthur issued a statement from Japan that he was available if called by the Republicans. "I am deeply grateful for this spontaneous display of friendly confidence. No man could fail to be profoundly stirred by such a public movement in this hour of momentous import," he said after his name was entered in the Wisconsin primary.

"I do not actively seek or covet any office and have no plans for leaving my post in Japan," he declared. "I can say and with due humility that I would be recreant to all my concept of good citizenship were I to shirk . . . any public duty to which I might be called by the American people."

MacArthur, who had roots in Wisconsin and was the grandson of a former governor, was so heavily favored in the March primary that *The New York Times* declared him the victor before a vote was cast. But another World War II veteran, Governor Stassen campaigned across Wisconsin and stunned MacArthur. Truman had no comment but chortled when asked about the general's setback. "Needless to say," Eisenhower wrote a friend after MacArthur's loss, "I shared your satisfaction in the Wisconsin results."

Eisenhower was blamed by MacArthur's camp for their chief's setback. Just weeks before MacArthur made known his interest in the White House, Eisenhower released his letter making the argument against a military man for the presidency. MacArthur was unmentioned in Eisenhower's letter to the New Hampshire editor. But in eliminating himself from the 1948 presidential race, Eisenhower openly questioned whether a military commander like MacArthur should become president. MacArthur would make bitter references to his former aide as "the best clerk I ever had" and "the apotheosis of mediocrity."

MacArthur, in Eisenhower's view, had little understanding of presidential politics. While working for MacArthur in 1932, Eisenhower recalled: "I shall never forget the time in Washington when receipt of instructions to report to the President [Hoover], led him to conclude, in the greatest seriousness, that he was to be invited to be the President's running mate in the succeeding election. It is this trait that seems to have destroyed his judgment and led him to surround himself with people...who simply bow down and worship." MacArthur wasn't on Hoover's vice-presidential list. During the 1936 presidential election, MacArthur was in the Philippines but predicted with certainty that Alf M. Landon would defeat FDR. When Eisenhower replied that Landon had virtually no chance and could not even carry his home state of Kansas, MacArthur flew into a rage and called Eisenhower stupid. Landon, who lost in one of history's biggest landslides, carried only Maine and Vermont. MacArthur never apologized for his tantrum.[8]

During his long service overseas, MacArthur lost touch with domestic politics. Between 1937 and the spring of 1951, he did not set foot in the continental United States. His long absence from the home front became part of MacArthur's legend. Between 1945 and the start of the Korean War in 1950, MacArthur left Tokyo on just two occasions, to Manila in 1946 and Seoul in 1948.

In an age when overseas presidential travel was rare, Roosevelt in 1944 and then Truman in 1950 journeyed across the Pacific to confer with MacArthur. "I thought that he ought to know his commander-in-chief and that I ought to know the senior field commander in the Far East," Truman said after flying to Wake Island in October 1950 for his first and only meeting with his Far East commander.

MacArthur was in all his glory. He had changed the course of the Korean War with what may have been his greatest triumph, the full-scale amphibious assault at Inchon. Seoul was recaptured and MacArthur had gotten a mandate from the United Nations to move across the thirty-eighth parallel for the purpose of uniting all Korea. By the time of their Wake Island meeting, Truman assumed that MacArthur's allied forces were on the verge of ending the war over a defeated enemy. "I'm glad you are here," Truman told the general. "I have been a long time in meeting you." MacArthur replied, "I hope it won't be so long next time, Mr. President."

As they opened their conference in a Quonset hut, the general asked for and got Truman's permission to smoke his pipe. "I've had more smoke blown in my face than any man alive," Truman wryly noted.

MacArthur apologized to Truman for the misunderstanding over Formosa. The general then delivered a progress report on the fighting, indicating that the war would be over by Thanksgiving. When Truman asked about the possibility of Chinese intervention, MacArthur responded that there was very little chance. Truman asked for MacArthur's thoughts on a Pacific alliance similar to NATO. "A Pacific pact would be tremendous, but due to the lack of homogeneity of the Pacific nations, it would be very difficult to put into effect," MacArthur said. "If the President would make an announcement like the Truman Doctrine, which would be a warning to the predatory nations, it would have a great effect. . . . The President should follow up this conference with a ringing pronouncement. I believe that at this time, after the military successes and the President's trip, it would have more success than a Pacific pact."

As MacArthur drove with Truman back to the airfield following their conference, they briefly talked politics. "Rather impertinently, I asked him if he intended to run for re-election," MacArthur recalled in his memoirs. "The Emperor had asked me about this in a recent visit in Tokyo." Truman, who avoided a direct answer, shifted the conversation by asking whether MacArthur might have presidential ambitions in 1952. "None whatsoever," MacArthur replied. "If you have any general running against you, his name will be Eisenhower, not MacArthur."

According to MacArthur, Truman professed friendship for Eisenhower but said he "doesn't know the first thing about politics." Truman, though, had offered to support Eisenhower for the presidency on several occasions and would make at least one more attempt before 1952. It is doubtful that Truman took MacArthur's disavowal of White House ambitions at face value. Truman's recollection of this conversation is that MacArthur regretted allowing Republican politicians to make a "chump" out of him in 1948.

In pinning a fourth oak leaf cluster to the Distinguished Service Medal on MacArthur's khaki shirt, Truman quipped, "They are pretty medals. I'd like to have them myself." MacArthur responded, "You give 'em, you don't take them."

Truman's citation said that MacArthur had "so inspired his command by his vision, his judgment, his indomitable will and his unshakable faith, that it has set a shining example of gallantry and tenacity in defense and audacity in attack matched by few operations in military history."

As Truman departed, MacArthur told him: "Good-bye, sir. Happy landings. It's been a real honor to talk to you." Truman told reporters: "I am very glad to have had this chance to talk . . . with one of America's great soldier-statesmen."[9]

On his return to Washington, Truman was asked at an October 19 news conference about his differences with MacArthur. "Let me tell you something that will be good for your soul," Truman replied. "It's a pity that you columnists and reporters that represent a certain press service can't understand the ideas of two intellectually honest men when they meet. General MacArthur is the commander in chief of the Far East. He is a member of the government of the United States. He is loyal to that government. He is loyal to the President. He is loyal to the President in his foreign policy, which I hope a lot of your papers were—wish a lot of your papers were. There is no disagreement between General MacArthur and myself."[10]

The war was still going well. Just a day after Truman's comments, MacArthur's men captured the North Korean capital of Pyongyang. But on the same day as Truman's news conference, MacArthur made the fateful mistake of splitting his forces by moving the X Corps to Korea's east coast. MacArthur, who ran the allied effort from Tokyo, was late to acknowledge warnings that China was about to enter the war. "MacArthur, like Custer at Little Big Horn," recalled General Matthew Ridgway, "had neither eyes nor ears for information that might deter him from the swift attainment of his objective—the destruction of the last remnants of the North Korean People's Army and the pacification of the entire peninsula."

When the Chinese struck in full force on November 25, MacArthur's troops were routed in the worst defeat that the United States had ever suffered. MacArthur cabled the Joint Chiefs of Staff: "We face an entirely new war." MacArthur, who had chosen his battles carefully in his long career, was unaccustomed to losing. Instead of accepting responsibility for his miscalculation that left allied forces more vulnerable to attack, MacArthur sought to blame the administration. Eisenhower recalled years later that MacArthur "had an obsession that a high commander must protect his public image and never admit his wrongs." When the Chinese sprang their trap and attacked across a three hundred-mile front, MacArthur shouldn't have been pointing fingers. "It should have been clear to anyone," Ridgway later wrote of MacArthur, "that his own refusal to accept the mounting evidence of massive Chinese intervention was largely responsible for the reckless scattering of our forces all over the map of Korea."

MacArthur called for more troops, the authority to strike Chinese sanctuaries across the Manchurian border, and the use of Nationalist Chinese forces in Korea. When Truman and the Joint Chiefs rejected these options, MacArthur told several editors of *U.S. News & World Report* that he was being forced to fight under "an enormous handicap, without precedent in military history." In a cable to Hugh Baillie of the United Press, MacArthur said that the allied setback "results largely from the acceptance of military odds without precedent in history—the odds of permitting offensive action without defensive retaliation."[11]

Truman and the Joint Chiefs were stunned by MacArthur's public dissent from their policies. Within two days of MacArthur's controversial interview, Truman issued this order: "No speech, press release, or other public statement concerning military policy should be released until it has received clearance from the Department of Defense."[12]

MacArthur ignored this directive. Eisenhower took it seriously. In his diary, the NATO commander wrote that "because people believe MacA. is trespassing on purely civilian functions, it becomes difficult for anyone in uniform" to discuss public issues. When Eisenhower told Harriman that he felt obliged under this order to be silent on political matters, Truman's foreign policy adviser replied: "I am very sorry to hear you say 'I will keep still in every language known to man.' You have the unique facility of being able to ring a bell every time you speak in any language. The trouble in the other situation was that the individual was not in sympathy with his government's policies, and in addition did not conform his public statements to those policies."[13]

The Korean situation improved when Ridgway took charge of the demoralized Eighth Army in December 1950 and restored its confidence. Under Ridgway's leadership, allied forces drove back the Chinese. By the end of March, Seoul was recaptured and enemy forces were pushed back across the thirty-eighth parallel. Ridgway, in response to what he termed a hypothetical question, asserted: "It would be a tremendous victory for the United Nations if the war ended with our forces in control of the 38th parallel."

Truman was looking to end the war. MacArthur's insubordination would end his career. In a March 20 message to MacArthur, the Joint Chiefs cabled: "Strong United Nations feeling persists that further diplomatic efforts should be made before any advance with forces north of the 38th parallel." MacArthur replied: "Recommend that no further military restrictions be imposed upon the United Nations Command in Korea. The inhibitions which already exist should not be increased." On March 24, MacArthur issued a communique which taunted the Chinese and undercut Truman's peace initiative. MacArthur asserted that China's attempt to conquer Korea had failed. "Within my authority as military commander," MacArthur declared, ". . . I stand ready at any time to confer with the commander in chief of the enemy forces in an earnest attempt to find any military means whereby the realizations of the political objectives of the United Nations in Korea . . . might be accomplished without further bloodshed."[14]

In his memoirs, Truman wrote of MacArthur's statement: "It was an act totally disregarding all directives to abstain from any declaration on foreign policy. It was an open defiance of my orders as President and Commander in Chief. This was a challenge to the authority of the President under the Constitution. It also flouted the policy of the United Nations. By this act MacArthur left me no choice—I could no longer tolerate his insubordination."

MacArthur aligned himself with Truman's critics. On April 5, 1951, House Minority Leader Joseph W. Martin made public a letter from MacArthur that said: "It seems strangely difficult for some to realize here in Asia is where the Communist conspirators have made their play for global conquest, and that we have joined the issue thus raised on the battlefield; that here we fight Europe's war with arms while the diplomats there still fight it with words; that if we lose this war to communism in Asia that the fall of Europe is inevitable; win it and Europe most probably would avoid war and yet preserve freedom. As you have pointed out, we must win. There is no substitute for victory."[15]

Truman knew what had to be done. "MacArthur shoots another political bomb through Joe Martin, leader of the Republican minority in the House," the president wrote in his diary on April 6. "This looks like the last straw. Rank insubordination . . . I've come to the conclusion that our Big General in the Far East must be recalled."

On April 11, 1951, Truman relieved MacArthur of his commands. "With deep regret I have concluded that General of the Army Douglas MacArthur is unable to give his wholehearted support to the policies of the United States government and of the United Nations in matters pertaining to his official duties," Truman said. "In view of the specific responsibilities imposed upon me by the Constitution of the United States and the added responsibility which has been entrusted to me by the United Nations, I have decided that I must make a change of command in the Far East."

MacArthur said that his firing was a vengeful reprisal. "No office boy, no charwoman, no servant of any sort would have been dismissed with such callous disregard for the ordinary decencies," he wrote in *Reminiscences*.

It was the most unpopular decision of Truman's presidency. Two-thirds of the American public disapproved of MacArthur's firing. But Eisenhower felt that Truman had done the right thing. "You know when you put on a uniform, you impose certain restrictions on yourself," Eisenhower told an aide. "MacArthur may have forgotten them."[16]

"I was sorry to have to reach a parting of the way with the big man in Asia," Truman wrote Eisenhower on April 12, "but he asked for it and I had to give it to him."

In a note to Harriman, Truman wrote of Eisenhower's work at NATO: "He seems to be on top of the situation and he also seems to understand the international situation better than another 5-star general I can name."[17]

U.S. News & World Report suggested that MacArthur and Eisenhower might be rivals for the presidency in 1952. "An idea making the rounds in Congress is that Republicans in 1952 may nominate MacArthur," the magazine reported, "and the Democrats nominate Eisenhower." A special Gallup poll showed Eisenhower would be favored by 51 percent to MacArthur's 27 percent.[18]

General Lucius Clay, who was familiar with Eisenhower's strong views about MacArthur, urged him not to get involved in the MacArthur controversy. "The MacArthur incident has caused the intense differences of opinion to burst into open flame and there are many who will fan the flame to realize political ambitions," Clay wrote Eisenhower. ". . . This we know. The Taft forces are definitely aligned with MacArthur who, because of his age, no longer seeks office but is determined to obtain vindication. Their official strategy (this is not hearsay) is to maneuver you into taking a position on the MacArthur issue, thus aligning you with the President and indirectly with his party and its inept conduct of government.

"I assure you that I am going to maintain silence," Eisenhower replied, ". . . not only because I see no other attitude for a soldier in uniform to take, but more importantly because I share your belief that some extreme partisans will do their best to use the incident to impede our effort to strengthen Europe. The job is tough enough as it is."

Eisenhower wrote MacArthur: "Sometimes I think that we shall never see the end of the persistent efforts of some sensation-seeking columnists to promote the falsehood that you and I are mortal enemies." MacArthur replied that he paid "absolutely no attention to scuttlebutts who would like to make sensational headlines."[19]

MacArthur returned home to a hero's welcome. His appearance before a special joint congressional session was his greatest performance: "I am closing my fifty-two years of military service. When I joined the Army, even before the turn of the century, it was the fulfillment of all my boyish hopes and dreams. The world has turned over many times since I took the oath on the Plain at West Point, and the hopes and dreams have long since vanished. But I still remember the refrain of one of the more popular barrack ballads of that day, which proclaimed, most proudly, that 'Old soldiers never die. They just fade away.'

"And like the old soldier of that ballad, I now close my military career and just fade away—an old soldier who tried to do his duty as God gave him the light to see that duty."

MacArthur, though, had no intention of fading away. In a prolonged national tour, he became more outspoken in his criticism of Truman's handling of the Korean War and the administration's policies. Eisenhower was disturbed by MacArthur's shrill and overblown rhetoric. Following MacArthur's appearance before the American Legion convention, Eisenhower told a friend that the old soldier "now, as always," was "an opportunist seeking to ride the crest of a wave."[20]

If MacArthur could not capture the White House, he was determined to prevent Ike from getting there. In the summer of 1951 he told Joseph P. Kennedy that Eisenhower could do great harm to the United States in the next five years because he lacked conviction. Just as during the war, MacArthur resented Ike's role as supreme commander in Europe. The old warhorse of the Pacific told Kennedy that NATO was a fraud and said that he would have demoted Eisenhower for testifying before Congress in favor of the Atlantic pact. MacArthur was doubtful that his former aide was ready for the rough and tumble of a political campaign. "He wondered how Eisenhower would stand up if they really turned their guns on him," Kennedy recalled, "and said that, knowing his temperament, he didn't think Eisenhower would stand up at all." MacArthur said that if Ike got elected, it would be an encore of General Grant's disastrous presidency.[21]

CHAPTER 20

Holding the Line

In the winter of 1951, NATO was a house divided. Britain was in an uproar over the selection of an American admiral as supreme commander of the Atlantic theater. France opposed the creation of a German army. Italy did not want Yugoslavia invited into the coalition. Portugal opposed the admission of Greece into the alliance unless Spain was also invited to join. Neither France nor Britain wanted Spain. "To produce Allied cooperation for World War II was far easier than developing a military defense for NATO and peace," Eisenhower acknowledged.

From Key West, Truman wrote Eisenhower in Paris: "Some of your problems began with the creation; others extend themselves into imponderables—those incalculable forces that project themselves into world affairs today, like pride of race and of blood and always national jealousies. I want you to know that I am fully mindful of the tremendous problems that are yours. It is because of my full appreciation of their gravity that I selected you to do the job."[1]

Stalin wanted more territory. The Soviet dictator controlled the largest military force in the history of the world. The Red Army had fifteen times more ground troops than the forces under Eisenhower's command in early 1951. To get what he wanted, Stalin had no hesitation about inflicting great suffering on his own people. Tens of millions of Russians were slain in the purges known as the Great Terror. Twenty million Soviet soldiers and civilians died in World War II. Western Europe had reason for fear.

What would happen if the Soviets attacked? "I refuse to consider the assignment an impossible one," Eisenhower wrote Churchill's former chief of staff in January of 1951. "I believe that if all of us can get in and do the kind of job that we should and can success will be ours. It is just not sensible to think that 190 million backward Eurasians can conquer the entire western civilization with its great history and its great economic, political, and material resources, if we are merely ready to forget all lesser considerations and get together on an intensive and cooperative program." Eisenhower also viewed American nuclear superiority as a deterrent to Soviet aggression.

It was a time of change on the continent. The Marshall Plan had sparked economic recovery and stopped the growth of communism in western Europe. "Without the Marshall plan," Eisenhower wrote that winter, "Europe would already be under the control of Moscow."[2]

In April of 1951, the same month that Eisenhower formally took command of Supreme Headquarters Allied Powers Europe (SHAPE), France and West Germany signed a treaty that created the European Coal and Steel Community. The plan, which was negotiated by French Foreign Minister Robert Schuman, promoted European unity and reduced the threat of war by placing Germany's military-industrial base under international control. It was France's boldest and most successful foreign-policy initiative of modern times.

As the flags of a dozen nations were unfurled, Eisenhower opened SHAPE headquarters in the summer of 1951. Built by the French government on sixty acres in a forest that was once the royal hunting preserve, the military complex was staffed with officers from all nations in the Atlantic pact. British Field Marshal Bernard Montgomery, Eisenhower's Allied land commander in the Normandy invasion, was deputy supreme commander. French General Alphonse Juin, who had fought with Eisenhower in the North African campaign, was NATO's commander in chief of ground forces in Central Europe. American General Alfred M. Gruenther, who had worked for Eisenhower in the Louisiana maneuvers and in North Africa, was reunited with his former boss as chief of staff.

Eisenhower brought new hope to the alliance. By 1952 there would be twenty-five allied divisions under his command and another twenty-five in reserve. Regional headquarters were established for northern Europe in Oslo, central Europe at Fontainebleau, and southern Europe in Naples. From the North Sea to the Mediterranean, the number of air bases was nearly doubled to seventy. Norway increased its defense budget 500 percent. The Netherlands and Norway doubled military spending. The French made five divisions available to Eisenhower and promised more. The British committed more than half of its army to NATO and pledged to increase productivity in defense plants.

Yet there were many frustrations. Seeking to build a more professional military force, Eisenhower urged leaders in each of the allied countries to extend the tour of military service under their draft. Citing Belgium's two-year requirement as the standard, Eisenhower was discouraged when none of the other nations followed their example. "Europe itself must have the will to defend itself," he told allied leaders.

The German question was unresolved. Truman and Eisenhower wanted a rearmed West Germany. The Soviets would be less likely to attack under these circumstances. The French did not want Germany's military power restored.

Eisenhower's wartime comrade Charles de Gaulle, a leader of the French political opposition in 1951, was a persistent NATO critic. Though de Gaulle liked Eisenhower, he viewed NATO as a surrender of French sovereignty.[3]

Through his friendship with the French economist Jean Monnet, Eisenhower became an advocate of European union. The short, wiry, round-faced Monnet, who was sixty-three in 1951, was the leading proponent of a federated Europe. Since the end of World War I, he had advanced the idea of European unity. Born into a wealthy family of cognac producers, Monnet went on to make a fortune of his own as an international banker. In his early thirties he served as deputy secretary-general of the League of Nations but quit disillusioned over the league's inability to get things done. A leader of the Free French during World War II, Monnet was put in charge of relief programs for liberated sections of France after the Normandy invasion. He was commissioned by de Gaulle to draft the postwar plan that was widely credited with the restoration of French economic power.

Among the qualities that made Monnet so politically effective was that he allowed others to take credit for his ideas. Although the plan for the European Coal and Steel Community was named for the postwar French foreign minister, it was devised by Monnet. The European Defense Community was also his idea. In the fall of 1950, he persuaded French Premier Pleven to propose a European army with a unified command structure. The Pleven Plan was designed to minimize the threat of a rearmed Germany by having all German soldiers under international command. Eisenhower was against it.

On June 21, 1951, Monnet lunched in Paris with Eisenhower, Harriman, and Gruenther. Monnet told Eisenhower that only through unity could Europe realize its potential. "Without unity," he went on, "everyone will go on seeking power for himself—and Germany will be tempted to seek it in an agreement with the East. Even at best, that would mean neutrality, which would be a blow to all Europe's morale. The strength of the West does not depend on how many divisions it has, but on its unity and common will. To rush into raising a few German divisions on a national basis, at the cost of reviving enmity between our peoples, would be catastrophic for the very security of Europe that such a step would be intended to ensure. If, on the other hand, you give France, Germany, and their neighbors common resources to exploit and defend, then Europe will recover the will to resist."

"To sum it up, what you're proposing is that the French and the Germans should wear the same uniform," Eisenhower said. "That's more a human problem than a military one."

"It's in that order that problems come up in Europe," Monnet replied. "What we have to do first of all is make people aware that they're facing the future together."[4]

Soon afterward, Eisenhower wrote Marshall that he had decided to support the Pleven Plan. "I have come to believe that at least most of the governments involved are sincere in their efforts to develop a so-called European Army. . . . The plan offers the only immediate hope that I can see of developing, on a basis acceptable to other European countries, the German strength that is vital to us.

"I am certain that there is going to be no real progress toward a great unification of Europe," he concluded, "except through the medium of specific programs of this kind."[5]

The Pleven Plan was taken seriously in the wake of Eisenhower's endorsement. Truman and Acheson joined Eisenhower in support of the European Defense Community. A treaty creating the force would be signed in 1952 by West Germany, France, Italy, Belgium, the Netherlands, and Luxembourg. But French opposition to the treaty led by de Gaulle stalled its ratification in the National Assembly.

In the most political speech of his tenure at NATO, Eisenhower struck the theme of European unity. Addressing the English Speaking Union in London before an audience that included Churchill, Eisenhower called for a federated Europe:

> It would be difficult indeed to overstate the benefits that would accrue to NATO if the free nations of Europe were truly a unit. But in that vital region, history, custom, language and prejudice have combined to hamper integration. Progress has been and is hobbled by a web of customs barriers interlaced with bilateral agreements, multilateral cartels, local shortages, and economic monstrosities. . . . Europe cannot attain the towering material stature possible to its peoples' skills and spirit so long as it is divided by patchwork territorial fences. They foster localized instead of common interest. They

> pyramid every cost with middlemen, tariffs, taxes, and overheads. Barred, absolutely, are the efficient division of labor and resources and the easy flow of trade. In the political field, these barriers promote distrust and suspicion. They serve vested interests at the expenses of peoples and prevent truly concerted action for Europe's own and obvious good.
>
> True security never rests upon the shoulders of men denied a decent present and the hope of a better future. But with unity achieved, Europe could build adequate security and, at the same time, continue the march of human betterment that has characterized western civilization.

Churchill confided to Eisenhower that he was "getting rather deaf" and could not hear the speech. But after reading it, the wartime prime minister wrote: "Let me say that I am sure this is one of the greatest speeches delivered by any American in my lifetime—which is a long one—and that it carries with it on strong wings the hope of the salvation of the world from its present perils and confusions."[6]

Eisenhower's dream of a United States of Europe would be unrealized. But the European Economic Community, another Monnet idea, would be established in 1958 by the treaty of Rome. NATO added two new members during Eisenhower's tenure as supreme commander, and Greece and Turkey entered the alliance in 1952. "With their resolute, hardy peoples, these nations are a significant addition to European defenses," Eisenhower said.[7]

As senior partners in the alliance, Truman and Eisenhower corresponded more frequently than at any period in their long association. "General Eisenhower was fully in accord with my policy in Europe. He worked for it diligently and devotedly from the day of his appointment as Supreme Commander until he returned to the United States," Truman wrote in *Years of Trial and Hope*. "He was always assured of my full support in everything he was doing in Europe."

In one of his earliest messages, Eisenhower advised Truman that his wife had joined him in France. "I am glad Mrs. Eisenhower is with you," the president replied. "I send her with my best wishes a special commission to insist that you take proper rest and to guard your health always." The Eisenhowers lived at first in the Trianon Palace Hotel at Versailles and then moved into a large house provided by the French government, the Villa St. Pierre in the Parc de Marnes near Marly Forest.

Truman was sympathetic when Eisenhower made reference to Churchill's criticism of NATO's command structure. "I read Winston

Churchill's critical remarks in the House of Commons," Truman responded. "In politics, the world over, even as in our own Congress, the opposition will not omit turning even the greatest of issues to partisan advantage."[8]

Eisenhower also kept in touch with Truman through W. Averell Harriman, who was then serving as special assistant to the president. Harriman and Eisenhower had been friendly since World War II when the railroad heir was FDR's envoy to Churchill and Stalin. Shortly before Eisenhower's NATO appointment, Harriman had donated his family's country estate to Columbia University as the site for a research and public affairs institution that Eisenhower had founded.

"Because of the somewhat involved position that I now occupy," Eisenhower wrote Truman, "it would appear that frequently my best point of American contact will be through Averell unless the subject should either be of such importance as to justify direct message to you."

In early 1951, Truman and Eisenhower were embarrassed when the commander of U.S. naval forces in the Atlantic and Mediterranean turned a routine meeting with a British admiral into an international incident by describing it as a conference. The French protested their exclusion. Pleven went directly to Truman with his complaint. After Truman assured him that this would not happen again, the American admiral held a second meeting with his British counterpart without inviting the French. "To create, unnecessarily, a feeling on the part of any government that it has been callously excluded," wrote Eisenhower, ". . . is well-nigh inexcusable." Truman was understanding. "Those things happen, as you know . . . when a fellow gets three stars on his shoulder he has to let people know that he wears them."

Eisenhower wrote back: "Thank you very much for your understanding letter, commenting on the Malta affair . . . I did not mean to exaggerate its importance—I merely was citing it as one type of difficulty that is always irritating because it is normally unnecessary."[9]

Eisenhower sought Truman's permission to delay any trips home. Once his headquarters at SHAPE was opened, the supreme commander almost never left the area. When Harriman left a message in mid-July 1951 that Truman wanted the general to return to Washington for a meeting, Eisenhower was under the misimpression that Truman wanted their meeting to be secret. "In my opinion any attempt to conduct a meeting on clandestine basis would inevitably become known and the results would be obviously undesirable and even unpleasant," Ike cabled. "I believe it to be distinctly undesirable for me to come to the United States before enactment by Congress of the military aid bill. To do so would almost certainly involve me in hearings of indefinite length before Congressional committees. In this event I would probably be drawn into numerous argumentative subjects largely unrelated to my own responsibilities."

What worried Eisenhower was getting caught in the political cross fire. He offered to come home after the hearings. As an alternative, Eisenhower suggested that Truman "might consider going on some appropriately planned maneuver with the Atlantic Fleet during the course of which you could anchor at some port to which I could easily be summoned. Examples would be Newfoundland, Iceland, and the Azores, depending entirely upon your time and inclinations . . . I repeat that if none of these ideas would appear to you to form the basis of a reasonable plan," Eisenhower concluded, "I will be quite ready to adjust my engagements and activities so as to come to Washington at any time you may designate."[10]

In a two-page handwritten response, Truman answered: "September or the first week in October will be an entirely satisfactory date for your return here. I had never expected to try to hold a secret meeting with you. Reports had come to me that you were not getting the proper support and cooperation from other departments and that you were handicapped by having to talk to NATO governments on a low level. I wanted to meet the situation in a manner to make your job easier and more satisfactory to you. That is all I wanted to talk about.

"Some progress has been made I can see by your message of yesterday.

"I didn't want you to get mixed up in the MacArthur affair or to be harassed by these nutty congressional committees. One man is enough for them to pick to pieces—and I'm accustomed to it. You come when you think conditions are right."[11]

Eisenhower preferred to wait. From SHAPE headquarters, he monitored developments at the mid-September NATO Council meeting in Ottawa. When Greece and Turkey were invited to join the alliance, Eisenhower wrote Truman: "The news thus far from the Ottawa meeting is very reassuring to us here." In the same letter, he reported that "it would be easier for me to visit Washington at the end of October rather than in the early part of the month when several maneuvers are scheduled. . . . Naturally, I stand ready to meet whatever desire you have."

"I am anxious that you come home and see me after this 82nd Congress has gone home," Truman replied. "There are many things I want to talk with you about. I am sure you and I understand each other. You are doing a grand job."[12]

On November 5, Eisenhower reported to his commander in chief. After Truman lunched with Eisenhower at Blair House, they went to the West Wing of the White House for a 3:15 meeting with cabinet members, senior presidential aides, and the Joint Chiefs of Staff. Truman opened this session by saying that Eisenhower should be kept fully informed by the State and Defense departments and intelligence agencies of all developments that affected his job. The president said that all branches of the armed services should also be cooperative and that Eisenhower's requests for weapons and equipment should be fulfilled. Truman said that he wanted Eisenhower to have this opportunity to present his views in person.

Eisenhower noted that it had been nine months since his previous visit to Washington. Truman interjected that he had not wanted to bring the general back during the "Great Debate."

In a reference to political speculation about his visit, Eisenhower wryly observed that another "great debate" seemed to be going on. The men around the table laughed at the general's comment. "I'm not interested in that," Truman jovially replied. "You can see anybody you want to and do anything you want to while you are here."

As the meeting went on, Eisenhower said that he was very satisfied with the cooperation he had received from Washington, but he voiced his disappointment that NATO had not been given enough weapons and material. In one case he had been blamed by one of the European governments for delays in the delivery of military equipment. "I am only going to get 103 tanks in the first half of 1952. Nineteen-hundred tanks in those same six months are going to be allocated for training purposes here in the United States. I can't do my job with 103 tanks!" Truman assured Eisenhower that he would get more tanks. Robert A. Lovett, who succeeded Marshall that fall as defense secretary, acknowledged that the Pentagon had been "slow in meeting some requirements" for "items that are not yet in production in this country." But Lovett said that the Defense Department had already delivered more than two thousand tanks.

Truman said that Eisenhower had mentioned at lunch that NATO should be informed about the tactical use of new weapons. Eisenhower's concern was for planning purposes. If there were new weapons, the supreme commander said it made no sense for his planning staff to be mapping strategy for an obsolete war. "We cannot think in terms of no atom bombs," Eisenhower said, "when atom bombs are on hand. Give me one of your boys from one of your scientific study groups who can give us the latest information."

The president then told Lovett: "I want this worked out."

There were difficulties within the alliance, Eisenhower reported. Just before leaving on this trip, Eisenhower said that the ranking Dutch officer on his staff had told him that the Netherlands government had doubts about staying in NATO. The argument for pulling out, Eisenhower said, was that the Netherlands got little benefit from membership and would be better off as a neutral. "I think," Eisenhower said, "if Holland ever dropped out of NATO or if any other small country did, the whole project would fail. It would be disastrous. We must not let it happen."

Truman commented that the Dutch had tried the same thing with Hitler and should have learned a lesson. Undersecretary of State James E. Webb asked Eisenhower if the Dutch were serious about dropping out. "The Hollanders," Eisenhower said, "are steering according to what they think their own self interest is. Our problem is to make the Hollanders—and everybody else in Europe—see that their self interest is best served by sticking together. I would like to repeat that I do not want to over-emphasize the danger of the Dutch pulling out."

Eisenhower said it did no good to pound the table with European leaders. "I can't do that," the general said. "I can only get other countries to do as much as they are willing to do, and no more. I can urge them, and explain to them, and try to convince them, but I can't force them."

After an hour, Truman declared the meeting adjourned. Eisenhower got nearly everything he wanted. But there was another reason why Truman had summoned Eisenhower home.[13]

CHAPTER 21

"*Between Us*"

As the 1952 election year approached, Truman was looking for a successor. The Korean War and the dismissal of MacArthur had taken a toll on his popularity. Though Truman had maintained his reputation for integrity, his administration was jolted by scandal in 1951. There were allegations of influence peddling at the Reconstruction Finance Corporation and the Internal Revenue Service. The Justice Department's reluctance to fight corruption had led to a crisis of confidence. Only a third of the American people approved of the way Truman was doing his job.

"I concluded that a great number of people in the country were rather fed up with twenty years of continuous Democratic rule," Truman said in a 1953 interview. "I began to think it would be better for the Democratic party and for the country if someone else would take over the responsibility so far as the Democratic party was concerned and if I myself got out of the picture as a candidate for President."

Truman also had personal concerns. His wife, Bess, who valued her privacy, was ready to give up her public role. She had also been concerned for her husband's safety since the 1950 assassination attempt at Blair House. "It made Mrs. Truman very ill. She had never seen anything like that before," Truman later recalled.

In deciding whether to run for a third term, Truman was thinking of his own mortality. If he stepped down at sixty-eight in January of 1953, he would be the nation's oldest chief executive in nearly a century. Truman believed that another term could shorten his life. Woodrow Wilson had died in retirement at sixty-seven. FDR had died in his fourth term at sixty-three. Truman told friends that Roosevelt would have lived for another decade if he had retired after his second term. In this same conversation, Truman said that he had no intention of dying at his desk. Not long after Truman won reelection in 1948, General Harry H. Vaughan asked whether he would run again in 1952. "Have you lost your mind?" was Truman's reply.[1]

By sending Eisenhower to NATO, Truman had given him a springboard to the presidency. As supreme commander of the western alliance, Eisenhower was a symbol of freedom and democracy. For the first time since Germany's surrender, Eisenhower had an international forum. A *Newsweek* cover story about Eisenhower taking command was headlined "Europe Finds a Leader." A U.S. Army colonel told *Newsweek*'s associate editor Harold Lavine that Ike wouldn't run for president. "Why should he?" the colonel asked. "He has a much more important job right now." Eisenhower had told his son, "I consider this to be the most important military job in the world."

But the presidency was a better job. When Eisenhower took formal command of SHAPE in April of 1951, his stock surged in 1952 presidential trial heats. The Gallup poll showed Eisenhower with decisive leads over the Democratic and Republican fields. He was also favored among independents. Democratic Senator Paul H. Douglas of Illinois called on both parties to draft Eisenhower in 1952. Of all American presidents, only George Washington had been elected without opposition. Eisenhower told friends it would be the ultimate honor to be nominated by both parties.

Truman sent Joseph E. Davies to Paris in June of 1951 to sound out Eisenhower on the possibility of running for the presidency as a Democrat. Eisenhower acknowledged to Davies that the chances were remote that he could be nominated by both parties. "There were things in both parties which appealed to him," Davies wrote in his diary. "Also in both, there were conditions and personalities which he could not tolerate. He named men in both parties he could not work with, and would not."

On the day of this meeting, Eisenhower wrote of Truman's Republican critics in his diary: "Taft, Wherry, et. al. (and especially [Republican Senator] Kem and McCarthy) are disciples of hate—hate and curse anything that belongs to the administration. Heaven knows there is plenty for which to criticize the administration legitimately and decently and strongly, but what they are doing is apt to make HST an underdog and backfire on them."

Like Truman, Eisenhower recognized that the American public wanted a change in administration. By not running for another term, Truman attempted to set the stage for the election of a new Democratic president. In looking back on this time, Eisenhower said that he could have run as a conservative Democrat in 1952 or as a moderate Republican. The Democratic nomination would have been his for the asking. But he thought the Democrats had been in power for too long.

"In many ways," Davies wrote of his visit with Eisenhower, " he felt that where a party had been in control for a long time, a change in party control would be beneficial to clean out dead wood; get rid of some bad growths; and preserve the two-party system, which otherwise might be jeopardized." In his first political speech delivered in 1909, Eisenhower had used similar arguments for voting out the Republicans after a generation of one-party rule.[2]

Truman had long viewed Eisenhower as a Democratic general. "It never occurred to the President that I might be a Republican," Eisenhower recalled. "He believed in Democrats so much that he assumed that anyone who had any sense would become a Democrat."

"I thought he was a Democrat, and he implied that he believed in everything Roosevelt and I had been doing," Truman said years later. "I really don't think he knows what he is. I thought he could be a Democrat, and if he wanted to, could run on the Democratic ticket."[3]

For the first time in his career, Eisenhower sought to distance himself from a presidential administration. During the debate over American participation in NATO, Republican Senators Kenneth S. Wherry of Nebraska and Taft had linked Eisenhower to the Truman administration. Eisenhower wrote investment banker Edward J. Bermingham: "I wanted you to know that my participation in this particular problem [NATO] carries no implication of my approval of governmental policies in other parts of the world, of any special political philosophy here at home, or of anything else that could stamp me as partisan or as member of any political or any other group. I am no more now a member of any Administration than I have been a member of any Administration during the 40 years since I first entered the military service."

Eisenhower took exception when a Hearst columnist depicted him as the Truman administration's 1952 presidential candidate. "You and I have often talked about some of the policies of the current Administration to which we both are violently opposed," Eisenhower wrote his friend William E. Robinson, a senior executive of the *New York Herald Tribune*. "So, you can see why I get just a bit irritated when I find anyone interpreting my readiness to respond to military orders, or the coincidence that, in a particular case, my views happen to coincide with those of the Administration, as meaning that I am part of any particular political or intellectual group. I certainly try to think for myself."

In an off-the-record session with C. L. Sulzberger of *The New York Times*, Eisenhower talked about Truman. The president, though a fine man in many ways, according to Eisenhower, only knew politics. Almost every move that Truman made was designed to win elections. As a result, Truman made too many appointments on the basis of politics instead of merit. Eisenhower said that his close friend George E. Allen, a Truman confidant, was honest but unqualified for his presidential appointment as a board member of the Reconstruction Finance Corporation. Sulzberger observed that Truman had shown good judgment in choosing Acheson as secretary of state and in standing by Acheson when polls showed him to be a liability. Eisenhower replied that if Truman dumped Acheson it would be an admission that Truman's own policies had been a failure.[4]

It was no accident that Eisenhower was viewed as a Truman man. He had lobbied Republicans, including Taft, to support Truman's commitment of American troops to Europe and had also spoken out against cuts in foreign aid. Eisenhower had tacitly backed Truman's firing of MacArthur. Eisenhower was closer to Taft than Truman on domestic policy. But it was Taft's opposition to Truman's foreign policy that compelled Eisenhower to explore a 1952 presidential bid. Like Truman, Eisenhower believed that the election of an isolationist president would have devastating consequences for the free world.

Throughout the summer of 1951, Truman was asked for comment about Eisenhower's potential candidacy. William H. Lawrence of *The New York Times* asked Truman at a press conference about Eisenhower's report in *Crusade in Europe* that the president had offered to support the general for the presidency. "Does that apply to '52 as in '48?" Lawrence asked.

"It certainly does," Truman answered. "I am just as fond of General Eisenhower as I can be. I think he is one of the great men produced by World War II, and I think I have shown that by giving him the most important job that is available for his ability."

Lawrence asked if that meant whether Truman was supporting Eisenhower as his successor. "You will have to translate that any way you can," Truman said. "I am very fond of General Eisenhower. I don't think he is a candidate for president on the Democratic ticket, and I couldn't very well help him to be a candidate on the Republican ticket because I don't think that would do him any good."

At another press conference, Edward T. Folliard of the *Washington Post* asked how long Eisenhower would stay on the job at NATO. "Well now,

Eddie," Truman replied. "Your guess is as good as mine. If you are referring to possibilities in 1952, I don't think that those duties will interfere with that, if the General is in that frame of mind. But I think General Eisenhower, under any conditions, would put duty to the country first."

Truman was loyal to Eisenhower. In the fall of 1951, the late Defense Secretary James V. Forrestal's diaries were published by the Viking Press. Forrestal had written in his diary that Truman sought to ease out Eisenhower as army chief of staff in late 1947 and replace him with General Omar Bradley. Eisenhower was astonished at the inaccuracy of Forrestal's diary. At a press conference in the Indian Treaty Room of the Executive Office Building, Truman was asked if he had sought Eisenhower's resignation as chief of staff.

"No indeed. No indeed," Truman replied. "General Eisenhower came to see me and asked me to appoint General Bradley. And I never wanted General Eisenhower to quit at all. Whenever I've been able to use him since I've always used him ever since."

A reporter then asked if Truman had told Forrestal that he hoped Eisenhower would take the hint and quit.

"I never had any such conversation that I can recollect," Truman said. "I am sure I didn't say that because I'm very fond of Eisenhower. He was an excellent Chief of Staff and General Bradley was too. And so was General Marshall. I haven't had a bad one."[5]

On the Sunday of October 14, 1951, Eisenhower celebrated his sixty-first birthday at a surprise party hosted by Gruenther. Earlier that same day, he took his first step toward the 1952 Republican presidential nomination. General Edwin D. Clark, an army friend and 1922 West Point graduate, had flown in for the weekend and had dinner at Eisenhower's home on Saturday night. On a 1948 fishing trip, Eisenhower confided to Clark that he might have future presidential ambitions. Even before Eisenhower was appointed to his NATO command, Clark had been promoting a movement to draft him for the 1952 GOP nomination. Clark lined up an important ally in Pennsylvania Senator (and former governor) James H. Duff, a liberal Republican and supporter of Truman's bipartisan foreign policy. Duff, who had been active in the 1948 effort to draft Arthur H. Vandenberg, was dismayed when Vandenberg declined to make any effort in his own behalf. The Pennsylvania Republican wanted to avoid getting burned again. Duff told Clark that he wanted nothing less than a written commitment from Eisenhower. Clark delivered.

In a five-page handwritten letter, Eisenhower told Duff: "You are one of only two or three people in the world to whom I have admitted and stated that by sentiment and by such skimpy voting record as I have been able to establish, I have been and am an adherent to the Republican Party and to liberal Republican principles.

"I am on a duty assigned to me by our Government," he went on. "No word or action of mine will, so far as I can control it, be allowed to damage performance of that duty. While on this job I shall make no political statement of any kind, because to do so would react adversely on American support of the free world's effort to establish collective security.

"In my conviction any American would have to regard nomination for the Presidency, by the political party to which he adheres, as constituting a duty to his country that would transcend any other duty. (In this particular case it would compel immediate resignation from the Army.)"

Eisenhower said his nomination would have to be a genuine draft since he would do nothing to advance the cause. "If under the conditions and circumstances described by the Republicans I would resign my commission and assume aggressive leadership of the party," the general wrote.[6]

Taft was the clear favorite of the Republican party's congressional wing and elected officials. A Gallup poll of Republican county chairmen indicated that 70 percent supported Taft and only 21 percent favored Eisenhower. In launching his presidential bid on October 16, 1951, Taft proclaimed that most Republicans "really desire me to be the candidate of their party." Soon afterward, Eisenhower wrote in his diary about how Republican money people were urging him to run against Taft. The steel executive Ernest T. Weir and Republican fund-raiser Harold E. Talbott, who visited Eisenhower in France, implored Eisenhower to become an active candidate.

"In the absence of some serious opposition," Eisenhower wrote, "Mr. Taft is going to capture the Republican nomination for president before the convention itself meets. In other words, when the convention convenes, there will be so many delegates pledged to him that opposition to him will be useless. . . . The proof is clear, according to these gentlemen, that Taft cannot be elected president of the United States...Mr. Truman, they believe, would beat Mr. Taft very easily. . . . They think that I would be easily elected because of what they call my appeal among independents and also among certain sections of the Democratic party."[7]

On October 25, 1951, the *New York Herald Tribune* endorsed Eisenhower for the presidency in a front-page editorial headlined "The Times and the Man." This was no ordinary endorsement. The *Herald Tribune* was the nation's most influential Republican newspaper. Horace Greeley, founding editor of the old *Tribune*, was involved in the creation of the Republican party and wrote powerful editorials against slavery. During the

1940 Republican convention in Philadelphia, the *Herald Tribune* played a decisive role in Wendell L. Willkie's nomination by endorsing him on the day of the balloting in the first front-page editorial in the newspaper's history. The *Herald Tribune* said of Eisenhower: "By deed and by word General Eisenhower has shown himself a keeper of the great liberties to which Republicanism is dedicated." The editorial said that Eisenhower had "the vision of the statesman, the skill of the diplomat, the supreme organizing talents of the administrator, and the humane sympathies of the representative of the people."

"I am overwhelmed by the overgenerous estimate the *Herald Tribune* makes of my qualifications and capabilities," Eisenhower wrote to Robinson, who was by this time a close friend. Robinson, who was concerned about Taft's fast start, had engineered the unusually early endorsement.[8]

Truman reacted favorably to the endorsement. "That newspaper has a right to do whatever it pleases, just as every other newspaper has," the president said when asked for comment. "And they certainly picked a fine man for their candidate."

On Monday, November 5, Truman and Eisenhower lunched alone for more than an hour at Blair House. Following this meeting, Eisenhower was asked by reporters if politics had been discussed. "Not a bit," was the general's reply.[9]

Two days later, Arthur Krock reported in *The New York Times* that Truman had offered Eisenhower the 1952 Democratic presidential nomination. "General Eisenhower did not accept the new offer," Krock wrote, ". . . but he strongly implied rejection by suggesting that great difficulties were presented by his fundamental disagreement with the Administration on labor policies, proposed amendments to the Taft-Hartley Act and other policies in the domestic field that have been sponsored by Mr. Truman."

Truman and Eisenhower denied Krock's report. "The story is completely without foundation," Eisenhower wrote *Times* publisher Arthur Hays Sulzberger in a letter that was never sent. "In fact, the President said nothing to me that could be so interpreted even by the most tortured and distorted type of reporting. . . . Of course, there is probably nothing hurt by the story except possibly the President's feelings."

At his next press conference, Truman was asked if he had talked politics with Eisenhower. "Did not," the president said. "He has made that statement, and so have I, and I think we both have reputations for telling the truth."

Krock's source for the Truman-Eisenhower article was Supreme Court Justice William O. Douglas. Later in the afternoon on the same day that he lunched with Eisenhower, Truman hosted a cocktail party at Blair

House for the Supreme Court. In a memorandum in Krock's papers, cosigned by Douglas, Krock wrote: "Truman said that he had a big day, that he had an interesting talk with Eisenhower; that he told Eisenhower his offer of 1948 held good for 1952; that Eisenhower said that would present a great problem to him, his differences with the Democratic [Truman] Party over the Wagner Act and labor policy alone being typical. Truman said that on this response 'we dropped the matter and left it there.'"[10]

In December 1951, the Gallup poll showed Eisenhower and Taft locked in a dead heat among Republican voters. But when Eisenhower was tested as a Democrat against Republican Taft in a 1952 general election matchup, it was a runaway. Eisenhower was favored by 62 percent to Taft's 31 percent. As a potential Democratic nominee, Eisenhower was favored over Taft by a fourth of Republican voters, more than two-thirds of independents, and nine out of ten Democrats.[11]

Before deciding on his own future, Truman was interested in Eisenhower's next move. "Dear Ike," the president wrote in longhand on December 18, 1951. "The columnists, the slick magazines and all the political people, who like to speculate, are saying many things about what is to happen in 1952. As I told you in 1948 and at our luncheon in 1951, do what you think best for the country. My own position is in the balance. If I do what I want to do, I'll go back to Missouri and maybe run for the Senate. If you decide to finish the European job (and I don't know who else can) I must keep the isolationists out of the White House. I wish you would let me know what you intend to do. It will be between us and no one else. I have the utmost confidence in your judgment and your patriotism."

Eisenhower replied in a handwritten letter:

> I am deeply touched by the confidence in me you express, even more by that implied in the writing of such a letter by the President of the United States. It breathes your anxious concern for our country's future.
>
> Part of my answer must almost paraphrase your own language where you say, 'If I do what I want to do . . .' There has never been any change in my personal desires and aspirations, publicly and privately expressed, over the past six years or so. I'd like to live a semi-retired life with my family, given over mainly to the study of, and a bit of writing on, present day trends and problems, with a little dirt farming thrown in on the side. But just as you have decided that circumstances may not permit you to do exactly as you please, so I've found that fervent desire may sometimes have to give way to a con-

viction of duty. For example—I'm again on military duty and in a foreign country!

Now, I do not feel that I have any duty to seek a political nomination, in spite of the fact that many have urged to the contrary. Because of this belief I shall not do so. Moreover, to engage in this kind of activity while on my present military assignment would encourage partisan thinking in our country toward a project of the utmost importance to the nation as a whole. (Incidentally it would be in direct violation of Army regulations.) So I shall keep still in all this struggle for personal position in a political party. Of course, a number of people know of my belief that any group of American citizens has a right to fight, politically, for any set of principles in which its members believe and to attempt to draft a leader to head that fight!

Because of these beliefs and because particularly of my determination to remain silent you know, far better than I, that the possibility that I will ever be drawn into political activity is so remote as to be negligible. This policy of complete abstention will be meticulously observed by me unless and until extraordinary circumstances would place a mandate upon me that, by common consent, would be deemed a duty of transcendent importance.

This answer is as full and frank as I am able to devise and I would be very regretful if you thought it otherwise. But when one attempts to discuss such important abstractions as a sense of duty applied to unforeseen circumstances of the future neither brevity nor arbitrary pronouncement seems wholly applicable.

This note brings to you and yours, from Mamie and me, our best wishes for a happy and prosperous 1952. To you personally, my continued esteem and regard.[12]

Eisenhower had been less than forthright in his response. Truman, who had always been candid with the general, deserved better.

CHAPTER 22

Decisions

On the first Sunday of 1952, Senator Henry Cabot Lodge, Jr., of Massachusetts declared at a press conference that Eisenhower was a Republican and that his name would be entered in the March 11 New Hampshire presidential primary. When asked whether this effort met with Eisenhower's approval, Lodge told reporters: "I will not be repudiated. Go ahead and ask the General."

From across the Atlantic, Eisenhower issued this statement:

> "Senator Lodge's announcement of yesterday as reported in the press gives an accurate account of the general tenor of my political convictions and of my Republican voting record. He was also correct in stating that I would not seek nomination to political office.
>
> "My convictions in this regard have been reinforced by the character and importance of the duty with which I was charged more than a year ago by our country and the other nations of the North Atlantic Treaty Organization. . . . Under no circumstances will I ask for relief from assignment in order to seek nomination to political office and I shall not participate in the pre-convention activities of others who may have such an intention with respect to me.
>
> Of course there is no question of the right of American citizens to organize in pursuit of their common convictions. I realize that Senator Lodge and his associates are exercising this right in an attempt to place before me next July a duty that would transcend my present responsibility. In the absence, however, of a clear-cut call to political duty, I shall continue to devote my full attention and energies to the performance of the vital task to which I am assigned.[1]

There was anxiety in Western Europe about Eisenhower's presidential fling. The Gallup poll asked residents of five NATO countries if the general could do the greater good as president or as allied commander. By more than four to one, the people of the NATO countries were hopeful that Eisenhower would remain on his post in Europe.[2]

Truman, who thought Eisenhower had chosen the wrong political party, said nothing to damage his candidacy. At his next press conference, Truman was asked if he was aware of Eisenhower's interest in the Republican nomination. "I read five or six newspapers every morning, and I am," Truman said with a dry chuckle.

"I always hoped he would turn out to be a Democrat," Truman admitted. "I had been told that he was a Democrat." His source, said Truman, was the brother of the late Kansas Governor George Hodges. Frank Hodges had sent Truman a copy of Eisenhower's 1909 speech before a Democratic group. "Thanks a lot for your further enlightenment on Ike," Truman wrote back. "I am very fond of him but I fear very much he is going to find himself in a very embarrassing position before he is through with this Republican propaganda move."

When asked for his thoughts on Eisenhower's first political move, Truman replied: "I don't want to stand in his way at all, because I think very highly of him, and if he wants to get out and have all the mud and rotten eggs and rotten tomatoes thrown at him, that is his business, and I won't stand in his way.

"My ideas and my position with regard to General Eisenhower haven't changed," Truman said. He still had confidence in the general and regarded him as "a grand man."

That did not mean Truman was ready to concede the 1952 election. His staff had given Truman the multivolume *Dictionary of American Biography* as his 1951 Christmas present. Truman was avidly reading the *DAB*'s profiles of historical figures. Truman was particularly fascinated with the life of General Winfield Scott. At the press conference after Ike's announcement, Truman noted that Scott had been nominated for the presidency in 1852 and suggested that there might be parallels in Eisenhower's situation. To learn more, the president urged the press corps to consult the *DAB*. "Read the biography of General Scott," said Truman. "That will give you the answer. You might also read the biography of the fellow that beat him. His name was Franklin Pierce."

Eisenhower's status at NATO would be unaffected by his political announcement, Truman said. "He will stay on as long as I can keep him there, because I want him to stay. I like him. And he is doing a good job," the president said. "I shall not ever relieve General Eisenhower except at his request."

If Truman was so fond of Eisenhower, did he think that the general's election would be the best alternative to a Democratic president? "I didn't say that," Truman said. "I don't think the country would be good under any Republican."

Truman was asked how he could run against someone he liked so well. "Easily," he replied. "I have done it before."[3]

Soon afterward, Truman wrote Eisenhower: "I had a press conference the other day in which many questions were asked me and I tried to answer straight from the shoulder. I have had a platter made of that press conference and I am sending it to you because I want you to know exactly what took place. As usual, the news hounds are trying to drive a wedge between us. As far as I am concerned that will never happen."

Eisenhower answered: "It is difficult to understand why any individual should want to produce irritation or mutual resentment between us. I suppose the hope is for an impulsive and possibly critical statement from one of us with respect to the other, thus making news. I deeply appreciate your determination to avoid any such thing—a purpose which does and will govern my own conduct."

Truman wrote back: "I certainly appreciated your good letter. . . . You can rest assured that no matter what the professionals liars and the pathological columnists may have to say, you and I understand each other."[4]

With Truman leaning toward retirement and Eisenhower aligning himself with the Republicans, the Democrats needed to fill the void. The president sounded out Chief Justice Frederick M. Vinson and offered him the presidential nomination. Vinson, though, told Truman that it would be inappropriate to use the high court as a stepping-stone to the White House. Truman then turned to Illinois Governor Adlai E. Stevenson, who said that he preferred to run for reelection. Vinson and Stevenson both urged Truman to go for another term. In early 1952, most Americans regarded Truman as a probable candidate.[5]

Meanwhile, the Eisenhower bandwagon was gaining steam. In the middle of February, more than fifteen thousand Eisenhower supporters attended a midnight rally in New York's Madison Square Garden. When Eisenhower watched a film of the cheering throng, he was moved. "Viewing it finally developed into a real emotional experience for Mamie and me. I've not been so upset in years," he wrote in his diary. "Clearly to be seen is the mass longing of America for some kind of reasonable solution for her nagging, persistent, and almost terrifying problems. It's a real experience to realize that one could become a symbol for many thousands of the hope they have."

Eisenhower wrote in his diary in late February: "Political people at home urge me to ask for relief. That strikes me as next to insane. Possibly my work here is not so important as the work devolving upon the president of the United States, but to my mind it is much more important than seeking the presidency. But if they will let me alone it is possible that I can soon (several months) turn the job over to another."[6]

"As you can well imagine," Eisenhower wrote Truman on the day of the New Hampshire primary, "my own life grows no easier. The complications of SHAPE responsibilities are enough to keep any man fully occupied throughout his waking hours. Add to this the many other kinds of personal and public questions that are constantly urged upon me, and I sometimes wonder how I keep my sense of humor."[7]

The race was on. Taft took advantage of Eisenhower's absence and spent three days campaigning in New Hampshire, making stops in twenty-eight villages and towns. Eisenhower won 1952's first primary decisively, sweeping every county in New Hampshire, and winning all fourteen delegates. On the Democratic side, Truman was upset in New Hampshire by populist Senator Estes Kefauver of Tennessee. Before the primary, the Associated Press had reported that Truman would win New Hampshire with between 65 and 75 percent of the vote.

Truman had not campaigned in the state and dismissed presidential primaries as "eyewash." But Eisenhower followed the results closely. One week after New Hampshire, Minnesota Republicans voted and cast more than 108,000 write-in ballots for Eisenhower. Former Minnesota Governor Stassen, who led Truman and Vinson in national polls, was almost defeated by the Eisenhower write-in. Stassen would never again be taken seriously as a presidential contender.

In the wake of Eisenhower's strong showing in the March primaries, the *Herald Tribune* columnist Walter Lippmann wrote that it was Truman's duty to call Eisenhower home. "My duty is to see that we attain our objective in Europe," Truman said when asked about Lippmann's suggestion. "General Eisenhower is the key man in attaining that objective, and he understands the situation, I think, very much better than Walter Lippmann or anybody else."

Truman was asked if Eisenhower, now that he was winning Republican delegates, had become more of a politician than a military man.

"In my book," the president answered, "he is a military man, and is doing a military job in a very able and efficient manner. I am not interested in his political career. He has a perfect right to do whatever he pleases in that line, and I told him that personally."

Would it be up to Truman or Eisenhower when the general quit NATO?

"General Eisenhower is in the midst of a very important job," Truman said. "He understands what the situation is in Europe much better than I do from this distance. I have told him that he can use his own judgment with regard to his return. Whenever he feels that it is proper and safe for him to return, he is at liberty to do so."[8]

For a brief time in the winter of 1952, Truman considered running again. In discussing this scenario with friends and advisers, Truman was cautioned. He went back and forth. On the final Saturday night of March, Truman addressed the party faithful at the Democratic National Committee's Jefferson-Jackson Day dinner. In ending his remarks, he made a dramatic announcement: "I shall not be a candidate for re-election. I have served my country, long, and I think efficiently and honestly. I shall not accept a renomination. I do not feel that it is my duty to spend another four years in the White House."

Tom L. Evans, Truman's close friend from Kansas City, was sitting in the audience and had been alerted by Truman that he would be making news. "I felt sure that the announcement was that he would seek re-election. That was my impression, and I think everybody felt that way. . . . I think he was trying to convey to me not to be too upset by the statement that he was going to give. . . . Frankly, I'm glad that his decision was not to. But it came as such a shock because knowing him as I did, and knowing him to be the politician that he is, I just couldn't conceive of him not running."

As Truman had confided to Eisenhower, he was interested in running for the U.S. Senate in Missouri. Republican incumbent James P. Kem was up for reelection in 1952 and if Truman had taken him on it would have been no contest. But on April 3, Truman took himself out of the running. "I shall not be a candidate for the United States Senate from Missouri," he said at a White House press conference. "That satisfies you, doesn't it?"

"President Truman would have liked very much to have been returned to the Senate of the United States," Evans recalled, "because that's where he enjoyed himself and enjoyed the work more than anything that he had ever done. It's my personal opinion that Mrs. Truman was opposed to it and that is probably why he didn't."[9]

Truman's withdrawal from the 1952 presidential race made Eisenhower's situation less complicated. Unlike 1948 when he refused to run against Truman, Eisenhower had not ruled out this option for 1952. But taking on the Democratic president would have been awkward, to say the least.

At an off-the-record lunch with reporters on March 20, Eisenhower said that in their dealings Truman had always been "decent and honest." In leaving NATO, Eisenhower wanted to show Truman the same level of respect. "I am of the opinion," Truman said in 1953, "that if I had announced early in 1950 or '51 that I intended to carry the fight to a conclusion, Eisenhower would not have been the candidate. Maybe I shouldn't say that. But I believe it sincerely."[10]

Just four days after Truman announced his retirement, Eisenhower served notice that he was quitting as allied commander. In a sealed letter to Truman delivered through Secretary Robert A. Lovett, Eisenhower asked to be relieved of his NATO command "on or about June 1st of this year.

"It would be unrealistic for me to ignore the influence of a number of American political incidents of the past winter upon the specific timing of this request," Eisenhower told Truman in the letter.

> Having maintained for years the position that I did not aspire to political office, I clearly miscalculated, last January, in assuming that by publicly reasserting that attitude, I could avoid the impingement upon my time and attention of political movements then in progress. This view is no longer tenable, and I deem it necessary to seek early termination of my military assignment so that any political activity centering about me cannot possibly affect the military service. My request contemplates transfer to inactive status on the date that I can make a final report to the proper officials in Washington. Moreover, in the event that I should be nominated for high political office, my resignation as an officer of the Army will be instantly submitted to you for your approval.
>
> With many others I share the conviction that America's interests and the peace of the world require that Western Europe be kept outside the Iron Curtain. Moreover, I believe this can be done, given a readiness to cooperate effectively among all nations of NATO. In spite of the great distance remaining between these nations and their goals, they have achieved, thus far, a marked degree of success in the task of building a viable defense structure in this critical region. For my part, I shall always be grateful to you for the staunch support and encouragement given to all here at SHAPE in a task that has constituted, for each of us, a most important duty to his own country, and to the peace of the world.[11]

Truman replied in longhand: "I received your letter about your retirement from the military service. It makes me rather sad. I feel as some of my friends have told me they felt when I took myself out of the political picture on Saturday, March 29. I shall handle the situation as you suggest . . . I hope you will be happy in your new role."

As an all-but-declared candidate, Eisenhower was learning about dirty politics. There was a whispering campaign in the spring, which Eisenhower's camp believed was started by Republican rivals, that the general was in failing health. Truman was asked at a May 2 press conference about rumors that Eisenhower "was a sick man."

"Oh, he's not anything of the kind," Truman responded. "He's in perfect health. He's as fine a man as ever walked. I have told you that time and again. He's just beginning to find out what happens to a candidate. That's mild to what he will have to face later on."

General Matthew B. Ridgway, who had succeeded MacArthur as supreme commander of United Nations forces in Korea and of the U.S. Far East Command, was selected by Truman as Eisenhower's successor at NATO. Eisenhower had recommended Gruenther, who would in turn replace Ridgway within a year.

Eisenhower asked Truman for retirement without pay. On Ike's June 1 return from Europe, he reported directly to Truman. Even after his break with Eisenhower, Truman would contrast Eisenhower's return with MacArthur's. Truman said in 1953 that MacArthur had violated military protocol in failing to report to his commander in chief. "Eisenhower did it when he was relieved of his command," Truman said. "The first person he reported to was the Commander in Chief."[12]

Truman, who wore a dark double-breasted suit, came outside to greet Eisenhower, who was wearing a light tan summer uniform. Instead of going to the Oval Office, Truman invited Eisenhower to the upstairs study. It had been seven years since their first meeting and their relationship had always been cordial. Eisenhower briefed Truman on the latest developments at NATO and then talked politics.

In the upstairs study, Eisenhower spoke with indignation about the right wing's vicious and personal attacks, not just on him but on other members of his family. Truman, who was also a target of hate groups, asked about the smears. Eisenhower went through a litany of the right wing's allegations. "If that's all it is, Ike," Truman told him, "then you can just figure you're lucky."

Truman recalled that Eisenhower said that he thought that promoting birth control in the underdeveloped nations of the Third World would be more effective than the administration's foreign aid programs in these areas. The president thought Ike was naive about the Catholic vote. "I asked him if he'd do me a favor," Truman recalled in his diary. "He said he would—if he could. I told him to make a speech on birth control in Boston, Brooklyn, Detroit, and Chicago. He did not get the point at all."

In looking ahead to the campaign, both men vowed that nothing would diminish their friendship. Truman's only regret was that Ike was running in the other party.

Eisenhower came back a day later and was decorated by Truman with a fourth oak leaf cluster in the Rose Garden. Mamie and Eisenhower's brother Milton were invited to the ceremony. Members of the Truman cabinet and representatives from NATO countries also attended the Eisenhower tribute. "In discharging his grave responsibilities," Truman said that Eisenhower "displayed great and consummate skill, inspirational military leadership, indomitable spirit, and the highest order of devotion to the causes of freedom. He symbolized his nation's unqualified determination to stand by its allies.

"General of the Army Eisenhower's extraordinary service merits the gratitude of not only the American people," Truman concluded, " but of free peoples everywhere."[13]

Then Eisenhower gave Truman a final salute.

CHAPTER 23

Abilene

Eisenhower, who was a resident of New York City, would run for the presidency as the man from Abilene. In launching the general's bid for the Republican nomination, his image makers wanted to remind the American public of his humble origins. The stage was set in Abilene for Eisenhower's transition from supreme commander to man of the people.

A crowd of fifty thousand people was expected for his first appearance as a Republican presidential candidate. In an era when live news coverage was rare, the New York-based radio and television networks made special arrangements to broadcast the campaign kickoff.[1] More than two hundred reporters from the nation's major news organizations made the long journey to the old cattle town. From all parts of the country, Ike supporters converged on Abilene for the year's biggest political event.

On the morning of June 4, 1952, Ike and Mamie were greeted by a cheering throng as they arrived in Abilene by special train. The general's first event was to help lay the cornerstone for a museum devoted to his career. The museum was being built by the Eisenhower Foundation in a cornfield just to the east of his boyhood home. Three brothers joined him for this ceremony.

"Forty-odd years ago, I left Abilene," he told the shirtsleeved crowd. "Since then I have seen demonstrated—in our own land and in far corners of the earth, on battlefields and around council tables, in schoolhouse and factory and farming communities—the indomitable spirit of Americans."

With genuine feeling, Eisenhower talked about lessons of his boyhood: "Our parents . . . believed the admonition the 'fear of God is the beginning of all wisdom.'. . . All would be well if man would take the cards that he had been dealt in this world and play them to the best of his ability."

"I found out in later years that we were very poor," he said, "but the glory of America is that we did not know it then."

As the general spoke, it began to rain.

At first, it was a drizzle. When the ceremony ended, it briefly cleared up. Then the skies darkened and the rain became a downpour. Throughout the afternoon, it kept falling. Eisenhower was scheduled to deliver his nationally televised address at 5:00 P.M. in an outdoor park. But the storm flooded the park and transformed it into a sea of mud. The rain and wind drove away most of the crowd. Eisenhower, who had learned in the military not to get upset about events beyond his control, borrowed a rain slicker, rolled his trousers up to his knees, and stepped up to the microphone.

Under dark clouds and lighting, he began his first political speech. Ike's immediate task was to establish that he was a Republican. His rival Robert A. Taft had been making the argument that the general was too closely identified with Democratic administrations to be a credible Republican candidate. Eisenhower, who made no reference in the speech to Truman, said that "a genuine two-party system is endangered if one party, by whatever means, becomes permanently or too-long entrenched in power. The almost inevitable consequence is graft and incompetence in remote and even in prominent places of government. Obviously, this is something that applies today: One party has been in power too long in this country."

Without specifically blaming the Truman administration, Ike said that the loss of China to communism in 1949 was "one of the great international disasters of our time." Eisenhower condemned corruption in the federal government, criticized the growth of the federal bureaucracy, and said that the federal tax burden was excessive. "I believe we can have peace with honor, reasonable security with national solvency," the general said. "I believe in the future of the United States of America."[2]

Eisenhower was never a great speaker and this was a subpar performance. The speech was overwritten and he may have had difficulty following the text in the stormy weather. "Only a fire and brimstone speech could have overcome the miserable conditions," Robinson recalled, "and Ike's speech was generally a disappointment."[3]

At his first political press conference, he was better. It was held before a capacity house in Abilene's Plaza Theatre, which had been the "opry house" in Eisenhower's youth. Leaning over a bank of microphones, Eisenhower deftly fielded a wide range of questions. He didn't say "no comment" once and came across as thoughtful, well-informed, and politically astute.

In his opening remarks, he sought to end speculation about his political history. "I have been asked specifically what is my voting record and why should I have ever stated I was a Republican," he began. "As you know, I have been in the uniformed services for a long, long time and there has been little if any voting record to speak about until after, in February 1948, I left active duty and felt that I had a right to participate as other citizens do in political activities."

Eisenhower disclosed that he had voted for Dewey in the 1948 presidential election, for Republican John Foster Dulles in a 1949 special election for the U.S. Senate from New York, and for Dewey's reelection as governor in 1950. "And that is my entire voting record," he said. "And to add another question that has risen in connection with this, I have never voted any Democratic ticket."

As for his political philosophy, Eisenhower said that he was in agreement with the Republican party's 1950 Statement of Principles and Objectives, which was used by GOP senatorial and congressional candidates in the midterm elections. Under this declaration, Republicans were committed to the reduction of federal spending and a balanced budget; tax reduction; foreign aid to countries resisting communism "if there is a program for progressive reduction"; an increase in Social Security benefits "with due regard to the tax burden on those who labor"; and opposition to secret international agreements "which have created new injustices and new dangers throughout the world."

Eisenhower said that he believed in free markets, opposed government controls of the economy, and favored a minimum of federal aid to education. He criticized proposals for national health insurance as "socialized medicine." In the field of civil rights, he supported "fairness and equality" for all citizens but opposed the creation of a Fair Employment Practices Commission. "I do not believe that we can cure all of the evils in men's hearts by law," he said.

Foreign policy was Eisenhower's strength. At the press conference, he said that peace and security were the most important issues of the 1952 campaign. Eisenhower did not mention that he would never have made the race if Taft had supported Truman's policies in Western Europe.

Eisenhower rewrote history when asked to assess Truman's foreign policy. "Of course, to start with, I have never been part of any administration," he said, though he had worked closely with Truman. "Therefore, I have not been either part of any organization that has helped to make up the total foreign policy of the United States. . . . The one thing that I have supported is this: The basic conception that if we allow Western Europe to fall within the Communist orbit . . . we will be in mortal danger."

A reporter from the *Detroit News* asked whether Eisenhower could wage a hard-hitting campaign against the Democrats, given his past association with two Democratic presidents. Eisenhower said that a group from Witchita had just presented him with a few campaign songs. "I've forgotten the words," he said, "but it recited some of the little successes that I've had in war and said that if I could do that, I could certainly whip the Democrats.

"I had many friends I've made through forty years," he went on. "I've never asked them whether they were Democrat or Republican, but, as far as any possible connection between me and a political administration of any kind, it's absolutely a shibboleth." Eisenhower was less than candid in claiming that he "did not know a so-called New Dealer." The late Harry L. Hopkins, the most important of the New Deal reformers, was among Eisenhower's friends.

Whom did he blame for the loss of China? "I am not going in any manner of means to indulge in personalities in anything I have to say," he said. "I do not know who is to blame for the loss of China. I do know that the diplomatic triumphs of that period, if any, were claimed by the party in power. The party in power therefore has to take some responsibility for any losses we have suffered."

Eisenhower was asked how to end the Korean War. "I would not think—from this distance—that it would be possible for our forces to carry through a decisive attack which we would call a tactical or strategic victory on the ground," he answered. "I believe we have got to stand firm and to take every possible stand we can to reduce our losses and try to get a decent armistice."

The general avoided a direct answer when asked whether he favored Senator McCarthy's reelection in Wisconsin. Though Eisenhower wanted to remove "any kind of communistic, subversive, or pinkish influence" from government, he believed the job "can be done without besmirching the reputations of any innocent man, or condemning by loose association or anything else."

What were his prospects of winning the Republican nomination?

"I haven't the slightest idea," he answered. "I came back because I found that in a position I had set up for myself I made one error: it was impossible for me to remain there and at the same time to carry on in the status that I had allowed to be set up for me in the United States. And having allowed it . . . I feel a great responsibility to a lot of people who, rightly or wrongly, believe that I can be of service to the United States in the political world. I'm not going to let those people down."

If he lost the nomination, could Eisenhower support Taft?

"First, I am not going to mention a personality," he replied. "I said that I will support any Republican ticket that is nominated by the Republican convention."[4]

Eisenhower faced an uphill battle for the nomination. Taft had at least one hundred more committed delegates than Eisenhower and appeared to be closing in on the nomination. In the first contested primary after Eisenhower's return, Taft won South Dakota by eight hundred votes out of more than sixty-eight thousand cast. But Eisenhower's strong showing surprised the Taft forces. General MacArthur, who made known his preference for Taft just before the primary, put him over the top.[5]

Taft was not letting up in his strategy of linking Eisenhower to Truman. As an answer to the "I Like Ike" button, Taft's camp distributed red-and-white buttons with the slogan "So Does Harry." In a national radio address that aired on the same afternoon that Truman honored Eisenhower at the White House, Taft declared: "In the Republican campaign of 1952 there must be no hesitation about attacking the foreign policy of Mr. Truman and Mr. Acheson. That policy has been the most disastrous period in the entire history of American foreign policy . . . I have been interested in the fact that my Republican opponents have spent their whole time attacking my position whenever I differed with administration policy—apparently they approve everything Mr. Acheson has done, and want to see a campaign run on a me-too basis. They seem to be afraid that a direct attack on the administration is an attack on General Eisenhower."[6]

At the White House, Truman was asked about Taft's criticism of Eisenhower. "I have no comment to make on the quarrels in the Republican party," Truman said. "They please me very much. But I don't want to get mixed up in them."

Truman was also asked for comment on Eisenhower's statement that the Democrats had been in power for too long. "I have no comment," said the president. "That is up to the people to decide."

What did Truman think of Eisenhower's transition to politics? "I would rather not comment on the opposition," he said. "When the time comes, I will have a lot of comment to make on all these things, but I am not ready to yet." Truman was asked if he still considered Eisenhower "a nice guy" after attacking the administration. "Yes, of course I do," Truman replied.[7]

CHAPTER 24

Showtime

For the third time in twenty years, Chicago was the stage for both major political conventions in the summer of 1952 and they would be watched by history's biggest audience, including Truman and Eisenhower. It was estimated that about seventy million Americans saw at least part of the Republican National Convention. For the first time, the television networks provided gavel-to-gavel coverage of both conventions. On the recommendation of the networks, the International Amphitheater on the Southwest Side was selected as the convention hall. The platform was placed in a corner of the auditorium and the delegates were seated diagonally because television producers said it would look better on the small screen. Television introduced minicameras, teleprompters, and the zoom lens for closeups at the 1952 conventions and it would have an enormous impact on the outcome of the Republican presidential race.[1]

If the Republican convention had been played under the old rules, Taft would have almost certainly won. The Ohio senator's allies controlled 60 percent of the Republican National Committee. In choosing the convention's officers, the national committee selected Taft allies Walter Hallanan as temporary chairman and Joseph W. Martin as permanent chairman. General MacArthur, also a Taftite, was named as the keynote speaker. MacArthur was actively working against Eisenhower's nomination. "It would be a tragic development indeed," MacArthur told a Michigan audience, "if this generation was forced to look to the rigidity of military dominance and discipline to redeem it from the tragic failure of a civilian administration."

On the convention's opening night, MacArthur was introduced by Hallanan as "the greatest military leader the United States has ever known."

In his address, MacArthur was sharply critical of Truman and Eisenhower without naming either. MacArthur accused the Truman administration of waste, corruption, and appeasement. In an unmistakable reference to Eisenhower, MacArthur attacked those who "foolishly permitted" Soviet forces to capture Berlin. MacArthur charged Truman with "discarding victory as the military objective" in Korea "and thereby condemning our forces to a stalemated struggle of attrition."[2]

On the second night of the convention, former President Herbert Hoover got a thirteen-minute ovation when he appeared on the rostrum. Like MacArthur, Hoover was for Taft. Hoover declared that NATO had been a failure because "the will is lacking" in European member nations. Without making specific reference to Eisenhower, Hoover suggested that the general had presided over a phantom force in Europe. It was Hoover's argument that the development of new weapons and technology would be "a far better defense for Europe." The former president suggested that NATO's attempt to build ground armies "is the road to militarism" and "a threat to all our freedoms."[3]

Taft was the favorite of the Republican party's officeholders. A majority of the GOP's senators, congressmen, national committeemen, and county chairmen were Taftites. Eisenhower, though, was more popular than Taft among Republican voters and the general public. In polls that were published just before the Chicago convention, Eisenhower led all Democratic contenders in general election matchups while Taft trailed them. *The New York Times* and *Chicago Sun-Times* published editorials during convention week that warned delegates that Taft couldn't win in November.

Truman gave Taft the edge over Eisenhower. On the eve of the Republican convention, the president wrote in his diary: "Taft has control of the organization and will no doubt seat enough delegates to have himself nominated."

As the convention opened, Taft claimed that he had at least 607 votes, three more than required for nomination. His count included disputed delegates from Texas, Georgia, and Louisiana. The Republican National Committee awarded Taft all of the Georgia and Louisiana delegates and more than 60 percent of the Texas delegates. In a blunder, Taft's allies voted down a proposal to allow television coverage of the deliberations. Henry Cabot Lodge, Jr., as Eisenhower's campaign manager, said that the closed hearings reflected a "public be damned attitude." Walter Cronkite, making his debut as the anchorman for CBS News, stood with a microphone outside the locked doors of the hearing room and made constant reference to the secrecy of the proceedings. "Let the people see and hear the evidence," demanded Dewey.

Television was unkind to Taft. On the Senate floor, the Ohio Republican was skillful in debate and respected for his intellect and thoughtful argument. But at the Chicago convention, Taft came across on the little screen as defensive and testy. With his engaging charm and smile, Eisenhower was more at ease on television. As the American public watched the convention, television transformed the Republican contest into a morality play.

Eisenhower's forces took their fight to the convention floor. Herbert Brownell, Eisenhower's strategist, proposed a "fair play amendment" that would prohibit any of the disputed delegates from voting on any of the credentials challenges. Led by Dewey, the twenty-five Republican governors endorsed this amendment. In recognition that a Taft victory in the credentials disputes would mean his nomination, delegates from the favorite son and uncommitted delegations backed Ike's amendment.[4]

The Taft forces unexpectedly offered their own amendment that would have allowed seven Louisiana delegates to have full voting privileges. On a roll call vote, Taft was defeated 658 to 548. Truman, who was watching these proceedings on television, understood the importance of this first roll call. "I am afraid," the president lamented, "that my favorite candidate is going to be beaten." Thereafter, the Eisenhower forces prevailed on all of the credentials votes.[5]

From then on, Eisenhower had control of the convention. There was speculation that Taft might throw his support to General MacArthur. But Taft, who was making his third and final bid for the presidency, later wrote: "Any such move was impossible before the first ballot. It would have been a surrender of principle and a betrayal of thousands of workers and millions of voters who supported me. Furthermore, these delegates were built up as Taft delegates, and I had no power to transfer them to anybody."

At the end of the first ballot, Eisenhower was nine delegates short of the nomination with 595 votes. Taft had five hundred votes. A switch by Minnesota's delegation from Stassen to Eisenhower put the general over the top. "It looks very much like my candidate for the Republican nomination has beaten himself," Truman wrote a cousin of Taft's defeat. "Of all the dumb bunnies—he is the worst."[6]

Eisenhower, who watched his nomination from his suite at the Blackstone Hotel, took the initiative and telephoned Senator Taft. In a graceful gesture, Eisenhower asked whether he could cross the street and visit Taft at his apartment in the Conrad Hilton Hotel. By tradition, the losing contender called on the victor. Taft, though surprised, was agreeable. "This is no time for conversation on matters of any substance. You're tired and so am I," the general told the senator. "I just want to say that I want to be your friend and hope you will be mine. I hope we can work together."

On his return to the Blackstone, Eisenhower had dinner in his suite with Herbert Brownell, who explained the procedure for selecting a running mate. Eisenhower had not known that the convention would automatically approve his selection. He wrote out a short list for Brownell that included Senator Nixon of California, House Minority Whip Charles A. Halleck of Indiana, Minnesota Congressman Walter Judd, New Jersey Governor Alfred E. Driscoll, Colorado Governor Dan Thornton, and Washington Governor Arthur B. Langlie. At Eisenhower's request, Brownell presided over a meeting of the general's more senior political allies for the purpose of recommending the vice-presidential nominee. For reasons of geography, youth, and his hard-hitting political style, Nixon was the consensus choice. Eisenhower, who readily accepted this recommendation, had not realized that Nixon was just thirty-nine years old. "I had been told that he was forty-two," Eisenhower would recall years later.[7]

After winning the nomination, Eisenhower wrote a telegram of resignation as General of the Army in his convention suite. Truman, who accepted Eisenhower's resignation, asked General Bradley to draft an order that would restore Eisenhower's rank, salary, and privileges. The president said that the order was to go into effect the day after the November 4 election in the event of an Eisenhower loss. Neither Truman nor Bradley informed Eisenhower of this action.[8]

Eisenhower had qualms about the six-thousand-word platform adopted by the Republican convention. In his hotel suite, the general told C. L. Sulzberger that the attacks on the Truman administration "were a bit savage." The platform committee was chaired by a Taft supporter, Colorado Senator Eugene Milliken. The 1952 Republican platform, which was adopted by a voice vote at the convention, was an indictment of the Roosevelt and Truman administrations. It accused the Truman administration of corruption and of even condoning treason. "We charge that they have shielded traitors to the Nation in high places," the platform stated, "and that they have created enemies abroad where we should have friends."[9]

In accepting the nomination, Eisenhower struck a more lofty tone. Millions of Americans had summoned him to lead a great crusade, he began. "I know something of the solemn responsibility of leading a crusade," he said. "I have led one. The aim of this crusade," he declared, was "to sweep from office an administration which has fastened on every one of us the wastefulness, the arrogance and corruption in high places, the heavy burdens and the anxieties which are the bitter fruit of a party too long in power."[10]

Truman understood partisanship and refused to take personally the criticism in Eisenhower's acceptance speech. After the general's nomination, George E. Allen called on Truman in the Oval Office. Allen, former secretary of the Democratic National Committee, enjoyed close friendships with Truman and Eisenhower. Before Truman had ruled out a 1952 reelection bid, Allen was worried that he would have to choose between friends. If that happened, Allen told Eisenhower that as a Mississippi Democrat he would support Truman "the way I always do." But with Truman out of the running, Allen switched his political loyalties. "Mr. President," Allen told Truman, "I want to tell you that I'm going to support General Eisenhower."

"I don't blame you a bit," Truman replied.[11]

Truman was unhappy about the state of the Democratic party. Senator Estes Kefauver, who had gained prominence for his fight against organized crime, was the nominal front runner for the Democratic nomination. Kefauver had scored a near sweep of the contested primaries and led the Democratic pack by a wide margin in national polls. Truman regarded Kefauver as a grandstander and loose cannon, whose hearings had damaged the regular Democratic organizations in some of the nation's largest cities. In his diary, Truman wrote of Kefauver: "What a President this demagogic dumb bell would make!"

The problem for Truman in finding a candidate to stop Kefauver was that all of the alternatives had serious flaws. If Eisenhower had run as a Democrat, he would have won the nomination without opposition. It is probable that Truman could have cleared the field for Vinson or Stevenson. As the Democrats convened in Chicago, Truman was prepared to support Barkley, although he privately regarded Barkley as too old and frail for the job. "He can't see. He shows his age," Truman wrote in his diary of the veep. "I wish he could be 64 instead of 74 at this date! It takes him five minutes to sign his name and, as President, he'd have to sign it 600 times a day—and no one can do it for him. . . . My good friend Alben would be dead in three months if he should inherit my job."

Leaders of organized labor had similar doubts about Barkley. At a breakfast meeting in Barkley's Chicago hotel suite, union leaders talked bluntly. "The job of President is too much for a man of your age," the CIO's political director Jack Kroll told Barkley. In response, Barkley said that he was four years younger than Churchill, who had just been returned to power. "I'm a very vigorous man. I'm like a man of forty," Barkley told the union officials. When Barkley failed to convince them that he was up to the physical demands of the presidency, he withdrew because "certain self-appointed political labor leaders" had vetoed his candidacy.

"If Barkley had stayed put, we would have nominated him," Truman recalled in 1953, "because no one can be nominated unless the head of the party—the President in the White House—wants him."

Senator Richard B. Russell of Georgia, who was a power on Capitol Hill, was the leader of the southern bloc in opposing Truman's civil rights agenda. "He has all the qualifications as to ability and brains," Truman wrote of Russell. "But he is poison to Northern Democrats and honest liberals. I doubt if he could carry a single state north of the Ohio river. . . . Too bad he had to be born in Georgia."

Another influential senator, Robert S. Kerr of Oklahoma, also sought the Democratic presidential nomination. An oil millionaire, Kerr was never more than a favorite son. "He has a gas record and a cloture record," Truman wrote of Kerr. "Labor, liberals and New Deal-Fair Deal Democrats won't support him."

Averell Harriman, who had started his campaign late, had been among the more notable public men of the Roosevelt and Truman eras. Franklin D. Roosevelt, Jr., would place Harriman's name in nomination at the Chicago convention. Truman liked and admired Harriman yet doubted his political appeal. "He is the ablest of them all," Truman wrote in his diary of Harriman. "Can we elect a Wall Street banker and a railroad tycoon President of the United States on the Democratic ticket? Ask someone else. I can't answer."[12]

Governor Adlai E. Stevenson had declined Truman's invitation to run and had spurned other efforts to get him into the presidential race. The witty and urbane Stevenson had won the governorship in 1948 by the largest margin in Illinois history. Born into one of the nation's great political families, Stevenson was the great-grandson of an early political ally and close friend of Abraham Lincoln, the grandson of Grover Cleveland's vice president, and the son of an Illinois secretary of state. The Princeton-educated Stevenson had been among the bright young men of the New Deal, a senior official in the Navy Department during World War II, and had been involved in the creation of the United Nations. But he was not eager to run for the presidency in 1952. "I have been in politics only three years," he wrote a friend in March, "and while I have learned a great deal, I have a great deal more to learn. My ambitious program in Illinois is well under way, but there is still much to be done."

Stevenson, who was newly renominated for a second term as governor, enjoyed the job and was very good at it. What he wanted was another four years in Springfield. Like Eisenhower, he thought that a change in national administrations might be good for the country in 1952. He also doubted whether Eisenhower could or should be defeated. Stevenson's hope was to run for the presidency in 1956. But the party's leaders had other ideas.

When Stevenson stepped up to the rostrum and delivered a fifteen-minute welcoming address, he charmed and captivated the convention. He spoke with humor of the Republican convention. "For almost a week," said Stevenson, "pompous phrases marched over this landscape in search of an idea, and the only idea they found was that the two great decades of progress in peace, and of victory in war, and of bold leadership in this anxious hour, were the misbegotten spawn of bungling, of corruption, of socialism, of mismanagement, of waste and of worse. . . . After listening to this everlasting procession of epithets about our misdeeds I was even surprised the next morning when the mail was delivered on time. I guess our Republican friends were out of patience, out of sorts, and need I add, out of office."

Stevenson paid tribute to the Democratic party's record of accomplishment, then spoke with candor about its troubles: "Where we have erred, let there be no denial; and where we have wronged the public trust, let there be no excuses. Self-criticism is the secret weapon of democracy, and candor and confession are good for the political soul. But we will never appease, we will never apologize for our leadership of the great events of this critical century all the way from Woodrow Wilson to Harry Truman. . . . But a great record of past achievement is not good enough. . . . We must look forward to great tomorrows.

"Who leads us is less important than what leads us," Stevenson declared. "A man doesn't save a century or a civilization, but a militant party wedded to a principle can."[13]

It was an extraordinary performance. The speech made Stevenson a national figure and established his reputation as the most eloquent speaker of his time. Even before this speech, Chicago Democratic boss Jacob M. Arvey was lining up Stevenson support in other delegations. Indiana Governor Henry F. Schricker made known his intention to place Stevenson's name in nomination with or without the reluctant candidate's approval. Pittsburgh Mayor David Lawrence, Arkansas Senator J. William Fulbright, and the young Massachusetts Congressman John F. Kennedy joined the Stevenson movement.

On the fourth day of the convention, Stevenson telephoned Truman. "He called me and asked me if the situation developed to the point where he would be put in nomination would it embarrass me," Truman wrote in his diary. "I told him it not only would not embarrass me but that it would please me in every way, that I have no commitments and if he is nominated I would put forth every effort possible to see that he is elected."

Truman instructed his alternate in the Missouri delegation, Thomas J. Gavin, to vote for Stevenson on the first ballot. "I didn't want Gavin to do anything until we knew who we wanted to support," Truman later recalled. "Gavin represented me as a vote for Stevenson in the convention."[14]

The 1952 Democratic convention was the last that went beyond the first ballot in the presidential voting. Kefauver led on the first ballot with 340 votes followed by Stevenson with 273, Russell with 268, and Harriman with 123 and a half. Stevenson gained fifty votes on the second ballot but Kefauver remained in front. On the third ballot, Stevenson clinched the nomination when Harriman withdrew in his favor. "This is the first time in my recollection that we have nominated a man for President on a real, honest-to-goodness draft," Truman said in presenting Stevenson to the convention at 2:00 A.M. on July 26. "He is able, capable, and will carry on the traditions of the Democratic party in the best way they can possibly be carried on."

Stevenson told the Democratic faithful: "I ask of you all you have; I will [give] you all I have, even as he who came here tonight and honored me, as he has honored you—the Democratic party—by a lifetime of service and bravery that will find him an imperishable page in the history of the Republic and of the Democratic party—President Harry S. Truman."

Eisenhower was favorably impressed with the Democratic party's choice. "I would have stayed in uniform," Eisenhower told his son, "if I had known the Democrats were going to run Stevenson."[15]

CHAPTER 25

First Break

In looking to the 1952 presidential election, Truman at first liked the choice. As a Democratic loyalist, his preference was for Stevenson. "There is no doubt that we are on the right track in the public interest," Truman wrote Stevenson in longhand after his acceptance speech. "You are a brave man. You are assuming the responsibilities of the most important office in the history of the world. You have the ancestral, political and the educational background to do a most wonderful job. If it is worth anything, you have my wholehearted support and cooperation."[1]

At the same time, Truman valued his friendship with Eisenhower and had done more than a little to build him into a presidential contender. Under the leadership of either presidential nominee, Truman was confident about the future direction of American foreign policy. Eisenhower had defeated the isolationists and the administration's most outspoken critics. If Taft had prevailed in Chicago, the bipartisan foreign policy consensus would have been disrupted. Truman hoped that the election of either Stevenson or Eisenhower would represent continuity to America's allies.

By the end of August, Truman would feel thoroughly betrayed by both men. During that month, Eisenhower and Stevenson competed to distance themselves from the Truman presidency. Each had different reasons for doing so. Eisenhower, who had no history in the Republican party, was portrayed by Taft as Truman's man. Some of Eisenhower's key supporters had played large roles during the Truman years. Former Secretary of State James F. Byrnes, former Secretary of the Army Kenneth C. Royall, former Ambassador to Great Britain Lewis W. Douglas, former Marshall Plan administrator Paul G. Hoffman, former atomic energy adviser Bernard Baruch, former Chairman of the Federal Reserve Board Marriner S. Eccles, former European special representative Milton Katz, and Reconstruction Finance Board member George E. Allen, who was in charge of fund-raising to build Truman's presidential library, were all supporting Eisenhower. General Lucius D. Clay, who had been a Truman Democrat and was military governor in occupied Germany during the Berlin airlift, was Eisenhower's closest political adviser. Eisenhower's refusal to personally attack Truman reinforced the perception among conservatives that Eisenhower was halfhearted in his criticism of the administration. As Eisenhower courted Taft's wing of the party, he sharpened his attacks on the administration.

In the political environment of 1952, Stevenson considered Truman's support a drawback. He had followed Truman's advice in selecting Senator John J. Sparkman of Alabama as his vice-presidential candidate. Though Stevenson admired much about Truman, he did not feel obligated to carry the administration's baggage. Stevenson established his national political headquarters in Springfield rather than Washington, D.C. When Truman asked him to retain Frank McKinney as Democratic national chairman, Stevenson chose Chicago lawyer Stephen Mitchell. "I don't think Adlai had anything particular against Frank McKinney," recalled Stevenson's aide Carl McGowan, "but to Adlai it seemed very bad politics. . . . The people would be saying, 'Why, this guy Stevenson can't even name his own national chairman. Truman has called all the shots. This isn't going to be any change. Stevenson is a Truman stooge and, if you really want change in Washington, you're only going to get it by voting Republican.'"[2]

On Tuesday, August 12, Truman hosted Stevenson and Sparkman for three hours at the White House. The Democratic ticket posed for pictures at Truman's desk, leaning over a paper that was the president's appointment list. Truman led Stevenson and his running mate into the Cabinet Room for a twenty-minute briefing on the international situation with Secretary of State Acheson, CIA Director Walter Bedell Smith, and chairman of the Joint Chiefs of Staff Bradley. Others at the meeting included Truman's aide John Steelman, Mutual Security Administrator Harriman, and Leon H. Keyserling, chairman of the President's Council of Economic Advisers. Truman then walked with Stevenson to the State Dining Room for a luncheon with the entire cabinet. The president took his guests on a guided tour of the newly refurbished White House, including the second-floor residential area. Truman then returned with Stevenson to the Cabinet Room for a private political discussion with strategists from both camps. At this meeting, Truman assigned two of his aides to work for Stevenson: Clayton Fritchey and David Bell. Both moved to Springfield for the duration of the campaign.

"I told the assemblage that our objective was to win the election, that I wanted to win as much as did the Governor," Truman wrote in his diary. "He said he thought I was more anxious, if that were possible, that he was to win. Then I told them that I wanted my staff to give the Governor every possible help and cooperation, that I was ready to take orders, that the nominee of the Democratic Party was its head and that all of us must obey orders."

Roger Tubby, Truman's press spokesman, said that Stevenson and his advisers were less than enthusiastic about Truman's offer. "I almost had the feeling that a Republican nominee had come into the house with his team to discuss the takeover," Tubby recalled. "It was not a really easy kind of session."[3]

Eisenhower wrote a confidential letter to the CIA's Smith, who had been his World War II chief of staff. "[For] the past two days my whole headquarters has been in a little bit of a steaming stew over an incident in which, according to the papers, you were at least briefly involved," Ike wrote. "It was the meeting that Governor Stevenson had with the President and the Cabinet. According to the reporters reached here, you were brought in to help brief the Governor on the world situation. . . . This meant—to the political mind—that the meeting was not only to show that the Illinois governor was one of the gang, but that the gang had met to canvass their entire resources in order to see what they could do to promote his election."

In a statement issued after Stevenson's White House visit, the general criticized Truman's briefing as "an unusual spectacle" that "implied a decision to involve responsible nonpolitical officers of our government who bear heavy responsibilities in our national defense organization into a political campaign in which they have no part."[4]

The next day, Truman cabled this invitation to Eisenhower: "I would be most happy if you would attend a cabinet luncheon next Tuesday the nineteenth. If you want to bring your press secretary and any other member of your staff I'll be glad to have them. If you can arrive at about 12:15, I'll have General Smith and the Central Intelligence Agency give you a complete briefing on the foreign situation. Then we will have luncheon with the cabinet and after that if you like I'll have my entire staff report to you on the situation in the White House and in that way you will be entirely briefed on what takes place. I've made arrangements with the Central

Intelligence Agency to furnish you once a week with the world situation as I also have for Governor Stevenson."

In their long association, Eisenhower had always responded in the affirmative when summoned by Truman. As a soldier, he showed deference and respect to his commander in chief. But in his new role as the Republican nominee, he was not about to accept the president's hospitality. Eisenhower respectfully declined Truman's invitation in this August 14 telegram:

> Thank you for your offer to have me brief[ed] by certain agencies of the government on the foreign situation. On the personal side I am also grateful for your luncheon invitation.
>
> In my current position as standard bearer of the Republican Party and of other Americans who want to bring about a change in the national government, it is my duty to remain free to analyze publicly the policies and acts of the present administration whenever it appears to me to be proper and in the country's interest.
>
> During the present period the people are deciding our country's leadership for the next four years. The decision rests between the Republican nominee and the candidate you and your cabinet are supporting and with whom you conferred before sending your message. In such circumstances and in such a period I believe our communications should be only those which are known to all the American people. Consequently I think it would be unwise and result in confusion in the public mind if I were to attend the meeting in the White House to which you have invited me.
>
> With respect to the weekly reports from the Central Intelligence Agency that you kindly offered to send me, I will welcome these reports. In line with my view, however, that the American people are entitled to all the facts in the International situation, save only in those cases where the Security of the United States is involved, I would want it understood that the possession of these reports will in no other way limit my freedom to discuss or analyze foreign programs as my judgment dictates.[5]

This telegram was immediately made public by the Republican nominee's Denver office. Eisenhower's campaign manager Brownell later wrote: "This declaration was greatly significant to the success of the campaign. Since Eisenhower had not been an enrolled Republican and had served in important capacities in Democratic administrations, many Republicans, especially in the conservative wing of the party, wondered whether Ike would act independently. They were greatly reassured by the letter."

The texts of the Truman and Eisenhower messages were distributed to reporters by White House Press Secretary Joseph H. Short. At a news conference, Truman said that he had no plans to meet privately with Eisenhower. "None whatever," Truman said. "Anything I say to him he is at liberty to quote. He has quoted a great many things already, some of it kind of garbled. But it's all right."[6]

Truman, who had done much to promote Eisenhower's career, was stunned by the coldness of the general's telegram. On a personal level, Truman was hurt and disappointed. Truman had always stood by his friends. Eisenhower had signaled that his friendship with Truman was expendable. On another level, Truman felt that Eisenhower had shown disrespect for the presidency of the United States. Truman would never again speak of Eisenhower with the warmth and friendliness that he had always shown in his correspondence and public comments. Before this incident, Truman said there had never been a break in his relationship with Eisenhower. "And I never thought there would be," Truman said, "even after he decided to be nominated for President. But the Republican inside boys, the fellows who wanted to get control of the government, got to him and made him believe that everything was wrong with me, and he believed it. . . . If he'd have stayed with his friends, even if he wanted to be elected President on a Republican ticket, he'd have been much better off, I think, because there are a lot of things I could have told him."

In a handwritten note, Truman wrote: "Dear Ike—I am sorry if I caused you embarrassment. What I've always had in mind was and is a continuing foreign policy. You know that is a fact, because you had a part in outlining it.

"Partisan politics should stop at the boundaries [of] the United States. I am extremely sorry that you have allowed a bunch of screwballs to come between us. You have made a bad mistake and I'm hoping it won't injure this great Republic. There has never been one like it and I want to see it continue regardless of the man who occupies the most important position in the history of the world.

"May God guide you and give you light.

"From a man who has always been your friend and who always wanted to be!"

Replying in longhand on his DDE letterhead, Eisenhower wrote: "Dear Mr. President: My sincere thanks for the courtesy of your note of the 16th. I assure you that your invitation caused me no personal embarrassment. My feeling merely was that, having entered this political campaign, I would have become involved in the necessity of making laborious explanations to the public, if I had met with the President and the Cabinet. Since there was no hint of National Emergency conveyed by the telegram of invitation, and since I belong, no longer, to any of the public services, I thought it wiser to decline.

"I repeat my gratefulness for the invitation and for the offer to send me weekly CIA reports. Through these I shall keep familiar with the foreign situation. Further, I assure you of my support of real bipartisanship in foreign problems.

"With renewed assurances of my respect and esteem."[7]

In reality, Eisenhower was as offended by Truman's note as the President had been by his refusal to come to the White House. "You should have seen the handwritten note I received after the event, from a high personage," Eisenhower wrote CIA Director Smith. "It breathed injured innocence, and warned me solemnly of the great error I was making in allowing 'screwballs' to come between us and to twist my thinking with respect to foreign relations. I answered courteously and respectfully."

On August 21, Eisenhower fielded questions from midwestern Republican leaders from Kansas City. "Will the voters know, as the campaign progresses," a Missouri Republican asked, "that this is a campaign against Trumanism?"

"I appreciate the sentiments you express and I know the implications of your question," Eisenhower said. "I personally do not like to express myself in terms of manufactured words. I believe we can be against maladministration. I believe we can be against the complacency, the arrogance, the complete indifference apparently to dishonesty in government that comes about through power long possessed. I believe that we can do it without trying to label it with any particular person's name. That is my own theory. If you are asking me, am I going to fight against this kind of thing with all of the power I have, the answer is a simple yes. If I am going to express it in the terms that you used, probably the answer would be no, but I am going to fight as hard as anybody else."[8]

Truman was astonished when Stevenson declared his independence of the administration. Tom Humphrey, the editorial page editor of the *Oregon Journal*, a Democratic newspaper that had supported Wilson and FDR but not Truman, had sent Stevenson a letter that asked: "Can Stevenson really clean up the mess in Washington." The governor responded: "As to whether I can clean up the mess in Washington, I would bespeak the careful scrutiny of what I inherited in Illinois and what has been accomplished in three years. . . . As evidence of my directions, I have established my headquarters here in Springfield with people of my own choosing rather than in Washington. The new national chairman instead of an old-line politician is a close personal friend."

Truman wrote two letters to the Illinois governor that were never sent but which show the extent of his anger at Stevenson. "I have come to the conclusion that you are embarrassed by having the President of the United States in your corner in this campaign," Truman wrote in the first letter. ". . . Since the convention you have treated the President as a liability . . . I have tried to make it plain to you that I want you elected—in fact, I want you to win this time more than I wanted to win in 1948. But—I can't stand snub after snub by you. . . . When the President, after much thought (from a political point of view, which may be beneath high-level consideration), asks the Democratic candidate to come to a strategy conference and is coldly turned down . . . it seems to me that the Democratic candidate is above associating with the lowly President of the United States."

In his second letter, Truman wrote Stevenson:

> Your letter to Oregon is a surprising document. It makes the campaign rather ridiculous. It seems to me that the Presidential nominee and his running mate are trying to beat the Democratic President instead of the Republicans and the General of the Army who heads their ticket.
>
> There is no mess in Washington except the sabotage press in the nature of Bertie McCormick's *Times-Herald* and the anemic Roy Howard's snotty little *News.*
>
> . . . I've come to the conclusion that if you want to run against your friends, they should retire from the scene and let you do it. When you say that you are indebted to no one for your nomination, that makes nice reading in the sabotage press, but gets you no votes because it isn't true.
>
> There are more votes on "skid row" than there are on the "North Shore" for the "Party of the People." New York, Illinois, Missouri, California, Ohio and the farm belt are worth more to you than Texas and the Dixiecrat states. You fired and balled up the Democratic Committee Organization that I've been creating over the last four years. I'm telling you to take your crackpots, your high socialites with their noses in the air, run your campaign, and win if you can. Cowfever [Senator Estes Kefauver] could not have treated me any more shabbily than have you.
>
> Had I not come to Chicago when I did, the squirrel-headed coonskin cap man from old man Crump's state, who has no sense of honor

> would have been the nominee. Best of luck to you from a bystander who has become disinterested.[9]

Truman was infuriated by Sparkman, who had made an unfavorable comment about the president's handling of the steel strike in an interview with *U.S. News & World Report.* "I've just been reading the reports of your spasm in the sheet run by that old counterfeit, Dave Lawrence," Truman wrote Sparkman in a letter that was unsent. "Why didn't you come to the man who knows for your facts? Why didn't you obtain those facts and state them from the Democratic platform instead of in an interview in a rotten Republican propaganda sheet?

"This is your second effort to offend the President of the United States by a bonehead approach. You and Adlai seem to be running against the President and the Administration instead of the Republicans and Eisenhower."[10]

At his August 21 press conference, Truman was asked about Stevenson's letter. "I have no comment because I know nothing about any mess," the president replied. Though Truman had soured on both candidates, he would not be ignored. "I am the key of the campaign and so of course I can't be a target on the Democratic side," the president said. "I will be a target for Eisenhower and his cohorts but not for the Democrats. . . . The Democratic party has to run on the record of the Roosevelt and Truman administrations, and that's all it can run on."[11]

Truman would not allow his party to run in any other direction. If Stevenson was reluctant to answer Eisenhower's attacks on the administration, Truman was ready and more than willing to fight back.

CHAPTER 26

Patriot Games

As the 1952 Republican standard bearer, Eisenhower wanted no part of Joseph R. McCarthy. Throughout his military career, Ike had shunned controversy and refused to engage in personalities. But once Eisenhower was nominated, McCarthy could not easily be ignored. Since McCarthy was up for reelection, Eisenhower had to either support or repudiate his least favorite political figure. Would he bow to the demands of party loyalty or follow his conscience?

McCarthy was at the peak of his influence. Eisenhower was unhappy when Taft's allies on the Republican National Committee gave McCarthy a prime speaking role at the Chicago convention. In this nationally televised speech, McCarthy ranted that Truman's foreign policy was "a combination of abysmal stupidity and treason." The Wisconsin senator had previously referred to General Marshall as the unwitting dupe of an immense Soviet conspiracy. He was also the author of the viciously distorted 1951 book, *America's Retreat from Victory: The Story of George Catlett Marshall.*

At an August 23 press conference in Denver, Eisenhower condemned McCarthy's methods without mentioning him by name when asked about the Wisconsin race for the U.S. Senate. "I am not going to support anything that is un-American in character, and that includes any kind of thing that looks to me like unjust damaging of reputation, where the man has not had the usual recourse to law," the general said. "Therefore, it is impossible for me to give what you might call blanket support to anyone who holds views of that kind; who holds views that would violate my conception of what is decent, right, just and fair."

McCarthy had not yet won renomination but was heavily favored in the

September 9 Wisconsin primary. In response to a McCarthy question, Eisenhower said that he believed in the two-party system and would support the nominees of his party. "If a man has been properly nominated by the Republicans in his state, I am going to state clearly that I want to see the Republican organization elected," he said.[1]

But did Eisenhower have to make that choice? Edward Meade Earle, a military historian at Princeton's Institute for Advanced Study, wrote Eisenhower that principles were more important than blind loyalty to his adopted political party. Earle, whom Eisenhower knew and admired, noted that presidents had to govern "with the support of members of his own party and a minority of the opposition." Since McCarthy and his ilk opposed everything that Eisenhower stood for and had made no commitments to support his programs, Earle argued that Ike should not reward them with an endorsement. Indeed, Earle warned that there could be "adverse political consequences" as a result of "your unconditional pledge to the most reactionary members of your party."

A week before the Wisconsin primary, Eisenhower replied to Earle that he understood "the mental pain" of the McCarthy issue. But the Republican presidential nominee said that it was his responsibility as party leader to support McCarthy if the senator won renomination. "I assume that none of us would, on the ground that an entire population was considered venal, oppose a decision reached by majority vote," he told Earle. "If a Wisconsin primary names an individual as its Republican candidate and I should oppose him on the ground that he is morally unfit for office, I would be indirectly accusing the Republican electorate of stupidity, at the least, and of immorality, at the most." In resolving this dilemma, Eisenhower concluded "that I could not ask for not the defeat of any duly nominated Republican, and this, stated backward, means that, politically, I want to see them elected."[2]

At the Denver press conference, Eisenhower was asked about the slurs against General Marshall by McCarthy and Indiana Senator William E. Jenner. "George Marshall is one of the patriots of this country," Eisenhower replied, "and anyone who has lived with him, has worked with him as I have, knows that he is a man of real selflessness—a man who has suffered with ill health. Maybe he has made mistakes. I do not know about that, but from the time I met him on December 14, 1941, until the war was over, if he was not a perfect example of patriotism and loyal servant of the United States, I never saw one. If I could say any more, I would say it, but I have no patience with anyone who can find in his record of service for this country anything to criticize."

Stevenson went before the American Legion's convention in Madison

Square Garden on August 27 and attacked McCarthy. "What can we say for the man who proclaims himself a patriot—and then for political or personal reasons attacks the patriotism of faithful public servants? I give you, as a shocking example," Stevenson declared, "the attacks which have been made on the loyalty and the motives of our great wartime Chief of Staff, General Marshall. To me this is the type of 'patriotism' which is, in Dr. Johnson's phrase, the last refuge of scoundrels."[3]

Less than two weeks later, a smiling Ike appeared with Marshall's most outspoken critic. Eisenhower was introduced by Jenner at an Indianapolis rally in the Butler University fieldhouse on September 9. Indiana Republicans had backed Taft at the convention and Eisenhower's strategists hoped to win their allegiance with a campaign appearance. The isolationist Jenner was trailing the state's Democratic governor in the Indiana senatorial race. Eisenhower, who detested Jenner, bowed to expediency and agreed to share the stage with McCarthy's sidekick. "The question came all the way back to us in New York," General Clay recalled. "And we felt that Eisenhower had to do it: that he had to appear with Jenner."

A thin-lipped hater, Jenner had denounced General Marshall as "a living lie" and a "front man for traitors." At the time of Eisenhower's visit, Jenner's political literature boasted of his vote against Marshall for defense secretary. Jenner had also voted against the North Atlantic Treaty. The senator made no reference to Marshall in Eisenhower's presence. Until Jenner needed Ike's coattails, the senator had been among the general's chief detractors. In a 1951 Chicago speech, he alleged that Eisenhower had gained his five-star military rank through Democratic political connections. "I never saw the New Deal pass out such favors to anyone unless he was one of their own," Jenner said.

In his remarks, Eisenhower made no reference to Jenner. Undaunted, the senator more than once clutched at the general's right arm and came close to embracing him. Eisenhower was enraged. At the conclusion of his address, Eisenhower turned to Congressman Charles A. Halleck and growled: "Charlie, get me out of here!" The general thought the whole episode was distasteful. "I felt dirty from the touch of the man," Eisenhower told speechwriter Emmet John Hughes.[4]

The photograph of Jenner lifting Eisenhower's arm would become among the more enduring images of the 1952 campaign. An editorial cartoon in the *St. Louis Post-Dispatch* depicted the flames of McCarthyism and Jennerism with a ladder next to an empty pedestal with Eisenhower's name on it and Marshall standing tall on his pedestal. It was captioned "Off on a Strange Crusade."

Truman was appalled that Eisenhower would allow himself to be used by Jenner. "Ike has taken up with McCarthy and Jenner, the proponents of the Big Lie," the president wrote his cousin Nellie Noland. "He has also discriminated against our Missouri senator. If he takes McCarthy and Jenner to his bosom along with Nixon he surely ought not to discriminate against our counterfeit. Kem is just a big liar and just as low down as McCarthy and Jenner, but not so clever. Ike ought not to mistreat him though, just because he's dumb."

Eisenhower was greatly embarrassed by his encounter with Jenner. Soon afterward, his aides put out the story that it took all of Ike's self-control not to take a swing at Jenner when he attempted to embrace him. Eisenhower himself never commented publicly about his rendezvous with the Indiana senator.[5]

On the same night Jenner was getting his picture taken with Eisenhower, McCarthy defeated former district attorney Leonard F. Schmitt by more than two to one in Wisconsin's senatorial primary. McCarthy carried sixty-nine of the state's seventy-one counties and received two and a half times the combined vote of the Democratic primary field. "I think the Wisconsin people are voting against Stalin," Schmitt said in the wake of McCarthy's triumph.

Eisenhower had been asked at his Denver press conference about whether he would appear on the same platform with McCarthy. "I haven't any idea," he replied. "You people expect me to know in detail what I am going to do. I certainly am not trying to conceal anything from you, but appearing on the same platform with somebody does not seem to me, in itself, to be such a heinous crime."

It was something that Eisenhower wanted to avoid. "I was determined to give no appearance of aligning my views with his," Eisenhower later wrote of McCarthy. "Consequently, I told my staff to make no plans for my visiting Wisconsin." But since Truman had carried Wisconsin in 1948 and Taft had won the 1952 Wisconsin presidential primary, Republican strategists argued that Eisenhower's presence in the state was critical to their party's chances. Republican National Chairman Arthur Summerfield argued that Eisenhower could not afford to write off Wisconsin. At a meeting of Eisenhower's senior advisers, Dewey pleaded to keep Wisconsin off the campaign schedule and warned that McCarthy would make trouble for Eisenhower. Dewey was voted down.

Eisenhower took the news glumly. After the Wisconsin campaign swing was booked, he made no attempt to cancel the trip. Instead he proposed making the best of an unpleasant situation. "Listen," Ike told Hughes, "couldn't we make this an occasion for me to pay a personal tribute to Marshall—right in McCarthy's backyard?"

Hughes, who wrote the general's Milwaukee speech, responded with enthusiasm to Eisenhower's suggestion. The text of Eisenhower's Milwaukee speech included this paragraph: "I know that charges of disloyalty have, in the past, been leveled against General George C. Marshall. I have been privileged for thirty-five years to know General Marshall personally. I know him as a man and as a soldier, to be dedicated with singular selflessness and the profoundest patriotism to the service of America. And this episode is a sobering lesson in the way freedom must not defend itself."[6]

On the night before Eisenhower's Wisconsin whistlestop tour, he stayed at the Pere Marquette Hotel in Peoria. Wisconsin Republican leaders had learned that Ike would be rebuking McCarthy in the Milwaukee speech. The Wisconsin senator and Governor Walter J. Kohler, who disliked McCarthy but was running for reelection on the same ticket, flew to Peoria and met separately with Eisenhower.

In a tense session with McCarthy, Eisenhower acknowledged that he would be speaking out in Marshall's defense. McCarthy protested that he had never called Marshall a traitor. "I told him," McCarthy later told William H. Lawrence of *The New York Times*, "that he would be better off choosing another state, another city, and another day for his defense of General Marshall." Eisenhower would not make that concession to McCarthy.

Governor Kohler, who made the same suggestion as McCarthy, got a more respectful hearing from Eisenhower. Kohler, a moderate Republican, had seriously considered running against McCarthy in 1952. Some of Ike's more influential political allies, including Helen Rogers Reid, the owner of the *New York Herald Tribune* and a Wisconsin native, had pledged their support if Kohler sought to oust McCarthy. But Wisconsin GOP leaders persuaded Kohler to run for another term as governor in the interest of party unity.

Like Eisenhower, Kohler was offended by McCarthy's reckless vilification of General Marshall. Yet Kohler suggested that the reference to Marshall should be dropped from the Milwaukee speech. "Although he agreed with the principle it expressed," Eisenhower's campaign manager Sherman Adams recalled, "Kohler felt strongly that the defense of Marshall stood out sharply from the rest of the speech, a discussion of domestic communism, as an unnecessarily abrupt rebuff to McCarthy. To him it looked as though Eisenhower was going out of his way to stir up an issue which did not call for an airing on that particular platform."[7]

It was uncertain what Eisenhower would do. His support for Marshall was measured. In a letter to his running mate two days before the Milwaukee speech, Eisenhower denied that he had ever made a 100 percent endorsement of Marshall's public record. "I have always defended General Marshall's patriotism and sense of duty," Eisenhower told Nixon. "In doing so I have not endorsed any errors of judgment he may have made while occupying posts in China or elsewhere subsequent to V-J Day in 1945. I saw him operate in the critical times of World War II and under conditions where only the highest sense of duty kept him performing as he did."[8]

As the Eisenhower train rolled through Wisconsin on Friday, October 3, McCarthy was aboard. At his opening stop in Green Bay, Eisenhower said that he "deeply appreciated" that Kohler and McCarthy had joined him in Peoria "to accompany me into your state. I particularly appreciated it because of the recent and very serious illness of Senator McCarthy." The senator had recently undergone surgery for a rupture of the diaphragm.

"The differences between me and Senator McCarthy are well known to others," Eisenhower said. "But what is more important, they are well known to him and to me, and we have discussed them. I want to make it very clear about one thing. The purpose that he and I have of ridding this government of the incompetent, the dishonest, and above all, the subversive and the disloyal are one and the same. Our differences have nothing to do with the end result that we are seeking. Our differences apply to method."

Eisenhower said that the executive branch of the government could get rid of subversives "with absolute assurance that American principles of trial by jury, of innocence until proof of guilt, are all observed, and I expect to do it."[9]

Meanwhile, Eisenhower's camp was divided over the Milwaukee speech. Senior aides at the New York headquarters were in favor of defending Marshall. On the campaign train, speechwriter Gabriel Hague thought it was important for Eisenhower to stand up for principle in the Milwaukee arena. But Hague was outnumbered. Kohler had won over Adams. When Adams conferred with Ike about the Milwaukee speech, he brought along Kohler and General Wilton B. Persons. Eisenhower asked if Adams wanted to omit the tribute to Marshall. "That's what I'm going to recommend," Adams replied.

"Take it out," Eisenhower said tersely.

It was a colossal blunder. *The New York Times* reported in its October 4 edition that Eisenhower had deleted a paragraph defending Marshall after McCarthy had suggested that the Republican presidential candidate should not make these comments in Wisconsin.[10]

Eisenhower's camp sought to contain the damage. The Associated Press quoted a senior source in the Eisenhower campaign denying that

McCarthy had a role in censoring the Milwaukee speech. Soon afterward, the general confirmed at an off-the-record press briefing that he had withdrawn the Marshall tribute after talking to McCarthy.

Marshall told reporters that he had no comment about the '52 campaign. "My father was a Democrat. My mother was a Republican. I'm an Episcopalian," he said. "I never voted and I'm not voting this time." The general's wife felt his pain. "George will not tell you but I will," Katherine Tupper Brown Marshall told the journalist Marquis Childs in 1953. "He sat in front of that radio night after night waiting for General Eisenhower to say a word in his defense."[11]

Truman, who had often referred to Marshall as "the greatest living American," now viewed Eisenhower as America's leading ingrate. "I can't have any use for a man who treats Marshall that way," Truman told aides. The president, who was often criticized for standing by his friends even when some were under ethical clouds, believed in loyalty. "You don't kick the man who made you," Truman said of Eisenhower's surrender to McCarthy. Under any circumstances, Truman would have been disappointed by Eisenhower's failure to defend Marshall. But Truman had been smoldering for weeks since Eisenhower had publicly spurned his invitation to the White House briefing. The Milwaukee incident gave Truman an opportunity to take off the gloves.

On the campaign trail, Truman became unforgiving in his attacks on Eisenhower. "The Republican candidate showed in Wisconsin what he has shown throughout this campaign," Truman declared in Colorado Springs, "that in his mind, the end of getting elected justifies the means. To him it appears to justify betrayal of principle and friends. That kind of moral blindness brands the Republican candidate as unfit to be President of the United States."

Truman kept pouring it on. "The Republican candidate knows, or he ought to know how completely dishonest Joe McCarthy is," Truman said from the rear platform of his campaign train in Utica, New York. "He ought to despise McCarthy, just as I expected him to—and just as I do. Now in his bid for votes, he has endorsed Joe McCarthy for re-election and humbly thanked him for riding on his train. I can't understand it. I had never thought the man who is now the Republican candidate would stoop so low. . . . But this much is clear to me. A man who betrays his friends in such a fashion is not to be trusted with the great office of President of the United States."

In Hartford, he accused Eisenhower of ingratitude and disloyalty. "He has compromised every principle of personal loyalty by abetting the scurrilous big-lie attack on General George C. Marshall," Truman declared. "I never heard of anything as awful as that in my life . . . I stand by my friends."[12]

Stung by Truman's accusations, Eisenhower responded to the criticism in Newark: "I have abandoned no part of my belief in any of the men whom I consider great American patriots. In this group stands General George C. Marshall."

For the rest of his life, Eisenhower would complain about the unfairness of Truman's attacks. "God, this man goes around saying that I let George Marshall be called a traitor in my presence and I never said a word," Ike lamented to an aide in 1958. "Why, I was never on any platform where any such thing took place in my presence."

Eisenhower regretted his surrender to McCarthy. A decade later, he wrote that he would never have withdrawn his comments about Marshall if he had known about the political storm that would follow. Truman, who was hurt when Eisenhower turned his back on him, understood ambition and political partisanship. But for the rest of his life, Truman would never understand how Eisenhower took a walk on General Marshall. Just as McCarthy had divided America, he turned Truman and Eisenhower against each other.[13]

CHAPTER 27

Days of Anger

As their friendship dissolved in the heat of the 1952 campaign, the Truman-Eisenhower rift changed from bitter words into mutual contempt. The president was hurt and disappointed that the general scorned policies that he had influenced. Eisenhower's alliance with the isolationist right offended Truman. "I nearly choked to hear him," Truman told an aide. Eisenhower was angered by Truman's personal attacks. "I believe the American people like to feel that their President is not as completely partisan as is a candidate," Eisenhower wrote Dewey. "There was nothing that Mr. Truman did that so shocked my sense of the fitting and the appropriate as did his barnstorming activities while he was actually the President of the United States."

Truman had several reasons for his involvement. The 1952 election would be a referendum on his administration and Truman proudly defended his record. As the Republicans stepped up their attacks, the president welcomed this fight. Another motivation was personal. Truman was angry with Eisenhower. In a letter to a cousin, Truman wrote that Eisenhower "has completely distorted the truth on Korea." The president was furious at Eisenhower's rough comments about Secretary of State Acheson and also by Ike's failure to defend General Marshall.[1]

In his first shots at the Republican presidential nominee, Truman was respectful. "I have known him for a long time," Truman said in Minot, North Dakota. "I have known him ever since he was a major in the Army. I have always been very fond of him. He was a great general. He did a wonderful service for the country in World War II. But he doesn't know the first principle about the program that is necessary to keep this country running."

Truman kept hitting the theme that Eisenhower was out of touch. "My advice to you is, don't take a chance on a fellow who doesn't known any more about the interior workings of the civil government of the United States than does that great General Eisenhower," Truman told an audience in Cut Bank, Montana. "And I am very fond of him. I like him as a general, but I am not sure I am going to like him for President of the United States."

On this same campaign swing, Truman said of Eisenhower: "He was an excellent general, but his mind is a military mind and the military mind can't understand civilian people. That's the reason they made the President commander in chief of the armed forces of the country. . . . Now I like Ike, and I like him fine as a commanding general. . . . If you like Ike as much as I do, you will vote with me to send him back to the Army where he belongs."

Truman portrayed Eisenhower as a tool of the interests. "He may not know it, but he has become the front man for the lobbies," Truman said. The former World War I artillery captain linked Eisenhower to the professional military brass and big business. "The Republicans have General Motors and General Electric and General Foods and General MacArthur and General Martin and General Wedemeyer," Truman said. "And they have their own five-star general who is running for president, and I understand he will carry some other generals with him to give him a hand in the political campaign. That's a lot of generals—every general I have mentioned in this list is in the general's column, except general welfare, and general welfare is with the corporals and privates in the Democratic party."[2]

In the late summer, Eisenhower was so tepid in his criticism of the Democrats that the Scripps-Howard newspaper group criticized him for "running like a dry creek." His problem, according to *Newsweek*, was to make a moderate message compelling enough to attract the votes of independents and ticket-splitting Democrats. By the middle of September, Eisenhower was making an all-out assault on the Truman administration.

In seizing the offensive, Eisenhower vowed to clean up what he referred to as the mess in Washington. "We are going to cast out the incompetent, the irresponsible, and the wasteful," the general asserted in Des Moines. ". . . We are going to cast out the crooks and their cronies." Eisenhower alleged that "bad judgment, loose associations, wretched morals, and disloyalty" had "appeared in our government" during Truman's administration.

Eisenhower was asking for nothing less than a no-confidence vote on the Truman government. "We are tired of this crowd," Eisenhower told a gathering of Republican precinct captains in Chicago's Orchestra Hall. "We want them out for the good of America. . . . When I say clean them out, I am not talking about a face-lifting job, or a repaint job. This is going to be the full treatment."

At the same time that he called for change, Eisenhower assured voters that the entitlement programs of the New Deal would be left intact. "Every social gain that was made and has been made for the American people we will vigorously maintain," Eisenhower said. "Social gains are no longer a political issue. Both parties have put the social laws on our books. Those things are there to make certain that American citizens can face a life in this country without fear."[3]

Eisenhower bore no rancor toward Stevenson, who gave state workers time off to attend the general's speech when he campaigned in Springfield and invited the Republican presidential nominee to lunch at the governor's mansion. In his remarks, Eisenhower acknowledged Stevenson's thoughtful gesture.

As the campaign went on, it seemed less a contest between the Republican and Democratic candidates than a Truman-Eisenhower grudge fight. Truman sought to pin responsibility on Eisenhower for the 1945 allied failure to obtain transit rights into Berlin. "This was completely unfair," Truman's White House aide George M. Elsey said years later. "General Eisenhower had no responsibility for deciding these matters on postwar occupancy of Germany."[4]

Truman argued that Eisenhower had endorsed a "reign of slander" by campaigning with McCarthy and Jenner. Eisenhower ripped into the "scandal-a-day" administration and "slander-a-day" Democratic campaign. When Truman criticized the general's 1948 opposition to the desegregation of the armed services, Eisenhower pointed out that Truman as a senator had voted to uphold poll taxes in southern states. Truman alleged that Eisenhower gave him bad advice about the Soviet Union after World War II. Eisenhower responded that the Free World had lost more than 100 million people to communism during each year of the Truman presidency.[5]

Truman, who had more than once offered to help Eisenhower become his successor, would later deny ever having done so. But in the fall of 1952, Truman publicly acknowledged these efforts. "I knew him. I trusted him. At one time, I thought he was qualified to be President," Truman told the Democratic faithful in St. Louis. "But since he has gone into politics, he does not seem to be the same man."

Eisenhower said that Truman was mistaken. "I am no different today than I was in those days when they wanted me to head their ticket and save their jobs," the general declared at a rally in Madison Square Garden. "They miscalculated if they thought that by offering me their party's support, I would never call upon them to answer to the American people for their failures, their futilities, and their lack of faith."[6]

As for the accusation that he had bowed to expediency, Eisenhower wrote a sympathetic Democrat: "Had I merely wanted to be President, there have been times in the past seven years when I certainly had far brighter prospects by identifying myself with the Fair Deal, than I have by deliberately choosing to enter the list against it."[7]

Truman alleged that the Republicans had turned to Eisenhower out of desperation. "The special interest fellows who run the Republican party are so anxious to get control of the government for their own purposes that they won't stop at anything," Truman declared. "They did not pick one of their own gang to be their candidate for president. They knew the people would see through that. They picked a man who has spent all his life in the Army and doesn't know much about what they have been doing or about what has been going on in the United States."

As Eisenhower pledged to support the entire Republican ticket, Truman took him to task for making alliances with senators of dubious reputations. "I know the Republican candidate must be sadly embarrassed by some of the people who are on the ticket with him this year. He is ashamed to endorse them, but he is not willing to come out against them. In fact, he's in a terrible fix," said Truman. "He is going to be in a worse fix than that before we get through with him."[8]

Truman was appalled that Eisenhower made appearances with Senators William E. Jenner and Joseph R. McCarthy. But it was the general's endorsement of a lesser-known political figure that provoked Truman's most vitriolic attack. Former Republican Senator Chapman Revercomb of West Virginia was attempting a comeback in 1952. The isolationist Revercomb had voted to weaken the armed services and abolish the draft. Revercomb also opposed the Marshall Plan and Truman Doctrine. As chairman of the committee that drafted the Displaced Persons Act of 1948, Revercomb set restrictive immigration quotas that discriminated against Catholic and Jewish refugees. The 1948 Republican presidential nominee Dewey had pleaded with Revercomb to lift these restrictions. Revercomb turned him down. Dewey then punished the West Virginia senator by withholding his endorsement. Revercomb lost his reelection bid. Eisenhower, who was trailing Stevenson in West Virginia, had no qualms about supporting Revercomb. "We want a Republican Senate," Eisenhower said in Point Pleasant, West Virginia, with Revercomb at his side. "We want Senator Revercomb back in that Senate."[9]

That was too much for Truman. In a message to the National Jewish Welfare Board, Truman denounced Revercomb as "the champion of the anti-Catholic, anti-Jewish provisions of the original DP bill." Then Truman went after Eisenhower: "The Republican candidate for the presidency cannot escape responsibility for his endorsements. He has had an attack of moral blindness, for today, he is willing to accept the very practices that identified the so-called 'master race,' although he took a leading part in liberating Europe from their domination.

"My friends," Truman went on, "the Republican candidate for president was asked about immigration, but he had no views on the subject. Yet it gave him no difficulty to appear on the platform with ex-Senator Revercomb and endorse him for election. This is a task which was too distasteful for the Republican candidate in 1948."

Truman was guilty of overkill. Alistair Cooke wrote in the Manchester *Guardian:* "If the election turns out to be very close some patient scholar years from now may discover that it was lost for Adlai Stevenson by a single ill-chosen, ill-timed sentence of Mr. Truman." Rabbi Abba Hillel Silver, former president of the Zionist Organization of America, issued this statement: "Much is permitted in a campaign, but the attempt by implication to identify a man like General Eisenhower—whose humanity and broad tolerance are known all over the world—with anti-Semitism and anti-Catholicism is just not permissible even in the heat of a campaign." New York's Francis Cardinal Spellman and Bernard Baruch, the Democratic elder statesman, condemned Truman's statement. Eisenhower was stunned by Truman's accusation. Republican National Chairman Summerfield referred to Truman's comment as the "most vicious utterance made in the history of American politics."[10]

Truman backtracked. "Certain Republican leaders have been deliberately distorting my statement," he said, ". . . as a charge that the Republican presidential candidate is anti-Catholic and anti-Jewish. I said no such thing, and indeed meant no such thing; and any fair person who reads what in fact I did say, must be as shocked as I am by the absurdities in the press of the last few days . . . I know that the Republican candidate for president is neither anti-Jewish nor anti-Catholic, but why does he give his endorsement to such men? That is what I condemned last Friday and this is what I condemn today."

Near the end of the campaign Eisenhower told a New York audience: "Our opponents in this election have reached a record low in mudslinging, distortion, vilification, and character assassination. One of the many examples of this was the charge, at first only whispered, but then openly spoken that I am anti-Catholic, anti-Semitic, and anti-Negro. That charge was made by the senior member of the partnership running against me."[11]

But the Republicans were playing just as rough. Speaking to a rally in Texarkana, Texas, Nixon referred to Truman, Acheson, and Stevenson as "traitors to the high principles in which many of the nation's Democrats believe." Nixon declared in the same speech that "real Democrats" were "outraged by the Truman-Acheson-Stevenson gang's toleration of and defense of Communism in high places." Truman would never forgive Nixon for this slur on his patriotism. "That's a word that shouldn't be used except in its connection with disloyalty to the government of the United States or any other country," Truman said in a 1959 interview. Nixon "can't get out of it in any other way. The statement that he made in Texarkana . . . was a plain statement that I was a traitor." Truman also said of Eisenhower: "I want to say that the man who could have stopped all that never opened his mouth."[12]

Eisenhower nearly dropped Nixon from the ticket after the *New York Post* disclosed on September 18 that the Republican vice-presidential nominee had been the beneficiary of a special political fund. "I don't think Eisenhower was morally outraged, but he saw it as a political problem that had to be solved," recalled campaign strategist Herbert Brownell, "and he didn't have enough background in politics or experience in campaigning to feel sure of himself. He was not sympathetic to Nixon's predicament." Nixon went on national television and salvaged his political future by making public his finances and challenging the other candidates to do the same. When it turned out that Stevenson also had a political expense fund, the Nixon controversy faded.[13]

The beleagured vice-presidential nominee was getting back at his running mate. In response to Nixon's challenge, Eisenhower released financial data, including copies of his correspondence with the Treasury Department regarding the tax break that he received for *Crusade in Europe*. Since Truman had personally approved of this special treatment, Eisenhower was immune from political attack on this issue.

Eisenhower's older brother Edgar wrote the Republican candidate, "I think you should ask Mr. Truman to reveal his income, and particularly any gifts of money which he may have received while President of the United States, other than that allotted to him." Edgar told Ike that Senator McCarthy could challenge Truman on his finances.

"You suggest that there might be some astounding information if Mr. Truman were to reveal his finances," Ike replied to his brother. "I am sure that is correct. We have considerable information about certain special funds and contributions, but may not inject this into the campaign unless the opposition continues to harp on that subject."[14]

It would have been foolish to have questioned Truman's finances. The president's salary had been increased to $100,000 in 1949. He did not have a pension or own a home of his own. In retirement, Truman would be forced to sell the family farm as a shopping mall.

By the fall of 1952, the American people were tired of the Korean War. Eisenhower gave the American people new hope for peace. When the Gallup poll asked which presidential candidate could better handle the Korean situation, Eisenhower was favored by more than seven to one. Even among Democratic voters, Ike held a three-to-one advantage.

Eisenhower, who had always defended Truman's decision to intervene in Korea, also believed that the war could have been prevented. As the campaign went on, Eisenhower became more outspoken in his criticism. Speaking in Cincinnati on September 22, Eisenhower alleged that the military action was necessary because of the Truman administration's blunders: "In January of 1950 our Secretary of State declared that America's so-called 'defensive perimeter' excluded areas on the Asiatic mainland such as Korea. He said in part: 'It must also be clear that [a guarantee against attack] is hardly sensible or necessary. . . . It is a mistake in considering Pacific problems to become obsessed with military considerations.' Five months later Communist tanks were rolling over the 38th parallel to assault South Korea. Twenty-seven months later the United States had suffered 120,000 casualties in a bloody, continuing conflict. Who made that mistake to which the Secretary of State referred? I leave the answers to you."

In his speech, Eisenhower neglected to mention that General MacArthur also had excluded Korea from the U.S. defense perimeter. So had the Joint Chiefs of Staff while Eisenhower was army chief of staff.

Truman fired back: "By attacking our efforts in Korea, and calling them a blunder, he has raised questions that strike a blow at the morale of the free nations fighting there. I never thought I would see a general, least of all this one, doing anything that could weaken the morale and faith of our country in the cause for which we are fighting—at the very time when our troops are locked in battle with the enemy.

"These and other developments," Truman said, "have led me to the firm conviction that the Republican candidate is not qualified. If he can't withstand the political pressures of a campaign any better than this, he will not be able to withstand the far greater pressures that bear down upon a president in office."

Eisenhower blamed Truman for American casualties in the distant war. "We are in a position where we are waging a war far from our shores, at great expense and great loss in terms of the blood of our young men," Eisenhower declared in Champaign, Illinois. "What we must do, first of all, is to make certain that those Southern Koreans, of whom there are twenty million, can be prepared to defend their own front lines. There is no sense in the United Nations, with America bearing the brunt of the thing, being constantly compelled to man those front lines. That is a job for the Korean. We do not want Asia to feel that the white man of the West is his enemy. If there must be a war there, let it be Asians against Asians, with our support on the side of freedom."

"I have never seen anything cheaper in politics," Truman replied. "We cannot do what he suggests—without appeasing communism in Korea—and he knows it. Of course, every one of us would like to be able to bring the boys back home. Nothing weighs more heavily on our minds and hearts than the sacrifices and casualties our forces are suffering there. If I could order them home without endangering our country, without imperiling our homes, I assure you, I would do it. But it cannot be done."

Speaking before an outdoor rally in Hartford, Truman issued this challenge to Eisenhower: "Now I want to say that he stated that he knows a panacea to cure the situation in Korea. . . . Now he has been my military adviser since I appointed him Chief of Staff. If he knows a remedy it's his duty to come and tell me what it is and save lives right now."

Eisenhower responded. In a nationally televised speech from Detroit, he vowed "to bring the Korean War to an early and honorable end." Eisenhower said that the Truman administration "cannot be expected to repair what it failed to prevent." A new administration would "forgo the diversions of politics" and "concentrate on the job of ending the Korean War."[15]

"That job requires a personal trip to Korea. I shall make that trip. Only in that way could I learn how best to serve the American people in the cause of peace," Eisenhower declared. "I shall go to Korea."

Truman derided Eisenhower's pledge as "an attempt to deceive the American people" and a "desperate attempt to get votes." In an effort to lessen the impact of Eisenhower's speech, Truman released documents on the U.S. decision to withdraw troops from Korea. Truman showed that the Joint Chiefs of Staff, including Eisenhower, had been participants in the decision. But Eisenhower's promise meant more to the American people than historical footnotes. In a political avalanche, Eisenhower carried thirty-nine of the forty-eight states with a plurality of six million votes over Stevenson. Eisenhower nearly swept the country outside of the once solidly Democratic South and split that region's popular vote. The Republicans recaptured the House and Senate by narrow margins.[16]

On the morning after the election, Truman sent the victor a telegram with a calculated insult. "Congratulations on your overwhelming victory," the president wired Eisenhower. "The *Independence* will be at your disposal if you still desire to go to Korea."

Eisenhower bristled at Truman's intimation that he might cancel the trip since he had won the presidency. "This dig hit Dad as tantamount to calling him a liar, implying that his statement was a mere political gambit rather than a pledge," John S. D. Eisenhower recalled two decades later. "From that time on the two were on cool terms."

In private, Eisenhower spoke of Truman with hostility and bitterness. "I remember him saying to me a while back, 'This politics is a dirty game, but nothing will affect us and our relationship,'" the president-elect told speechwriter Emmet John Hughes. Eisenhower now said that he wondered "if I can stand sitting next to him" at the inaugural ceremonies.

Eisenhower confided his bitterness about Truman to their friend Secretary of the Treasury John Snyder. "I tried to convince Ike that it was a politician fighting to win [who made those comments]," Snyder recalled. But Eisenhower was unforgiving. Another mutual friend, General Clay, attributed Eisenhower's anger to his political inexperience. "Of course, General Eisenhower couldn't understand President Truman's partisanship because he wasn't partisan himself," said Clay. "He took what Mr. Truman was doing for political reasons as a personal attack. I don't think President Truman ever intended it that way, but it certainly created a lot of unnecessary bad feeling."[17]

"His feelings were hurt in the campaign," Truman recalled in 1953. "He hadn't been in politics, and he didn't know anything about it. I took the hide off him for not protecting General Marshall. It was a case of Eisenhower being a military man who has been protected all his life from adverse criticism. In politics you can talk about God himself, and [everyone] can quarrel with you. And you have to be able to take it. If you don't, you don't last long. After it's all over, you don't pay any attention to it."

But Truman's feelings were also bruised. "It seems that the people think I have lost an election and have been discredited," he wrote in his diary. "I wonder." Six days after the election, Truman sent a memorandum to his special councel, Charles Murphy, asking for a complete set of the general's campaign speeches in booklet form with Murphy's analysis of Eisenhower's words. Truman also asked for the Republican platform and "its relation to Eisenhower's speeches." The president also wanted the general's comments about McCarthy, Jenner, and the Korean War. Truman also requested "an analysis of Nixon's talks. His attacks on the President. His soap opera speech. The facts about his income. Who the people are who support him." Ken Hechler, a White House aide, obtained this material for Truman with help from the Republican National Committee, news organizations, and Eisenhower's CIA Director Allen Dulles. Truman's "Ikelopedia" was six hundred pages long.[18]

Eisenhower meant much of what he said. "He could never forget the personal attacks that Truman had made on him during the campaign," recalled campaign manager Sherman Adams. "Because Eisenhower was never trained as a politician . . . he did not so easily shrug off campaign oratory after the election was over."

"I told him," Truman said of Eisenhower, "he would find out a lot of things he didn't know about himself once he got into a rough and tumble campaign, and he did."[19]

CHAPTER 28

Changing of the Guard

Truman looked forward to retirement. As Eisenhower prepared to take charge, the outgoing chief executive made every effort to assure a smooth transition. More than seven years earlier, Truman had been unprepared when he took on the weight of the world. Truman wanted his successor to be ready from day one and for the first time established a formal transition process. Eisenhower was reluctant to accept Truman's help. "The President-elect has been coy about cooperating for the turnover," Truman wrote in his diary. "All that the present incumbent wants is an orderly transfer of authority . . . I am very much afraid that Ike's advisers have convinced him that he is dealing with a man who wants to embarrass him. That is not true. All I want to do is to make an orderly turnover. It has never been done."

Truman wrote Eisenhower about the international situation: "There is a resolution pending on Korea in the United Nations. The Iran problem is an extremely dedicate one and affects our relations with Great Britain. The Tunisian problem is also in that same class and affects our relationship with France and South Africa. There is a National Security Council problem regarding the allocation of resources. . . . All these things are vital policy matters which can only be decided by the President of the United States but I would prefer not to make firm decisions on these matters without your concurrence, although the decisions will have to be made."

"Because I believe so firmly in true bi-partisan approach to our foreign problems, I am especially appreciative of your letter," Eisenhower replied. ". . . I shall give priority attention to the matter and I will communicate with you further no later than Monday next."[1]

Two weeks after his election, Eisenhower called on Truman at the

White House. In contrast with their past meetings, there was no warmth between the former comrades. Eisenhower was formal and correct in addressing Truman. "When he came into the President's office, he had a chip on his shoulder," Truman later wrote in his diary. "I told him . . . that all I had in mind was an orderly turnover to him. . . . I gave him the world globe that he used in World War II which he had given me at Frankfurt when I went to Potsdam. He accepted that—not very graciously."

In the second week of his presidency, Eisenhower would write Truman: "I have just noticed the inscribed plate you had attached to the globe in this office, and I remember that I failed to thank you for your courtesy in returning it to me. It was a friendly gesture that I much appreciate."

During their private meeting, Eisenhower asked Truman if he had a chief of staff. "I told him that there is an assistant to the President, Dr. John Steelman, who coordinates the differences between cabinet officers and between the president's secretaries, but that any member of the cabinet and any secretary or administrative assistant is at liberty to see the President at any time on any subject."

Steelman had been asked by Truman to help with the transition. "If Eisenhower's elected and I suspect he will be," Truman had told Steelman before the November 4 election, "he'll ask you to stay. You ought to stay and help him get started anyhow. He doesn't know a thing on earth about it, and somebody had better help him."

As Truman predicted, Eisenhower hired Steelman.

Truman advised Eisenhower on the structure of the White House staff. "I think all this went into one ear and out the other," Truman later wrote.[2]

The president then escorted Eisenhower into the Cabinet Room for a meeting with Secretary of State Acheson, Secretary of the Treasury Snyder, Defense Secretary Lovett, and Mutual Security Administrator Harriman. Eisenhower was accompanied by Senator Henry Cabot Lodge, Jr., and Joseph Dodge, who were serving as his liaisons with the Truman administration. Lodge would later be named as ambassador to the United Nations and Dodge would become Eisenhower's first budget director.

"I have invited you gentlemen to meet with me here to establish the framework for full understanding of our problems and our purposes in the interim until January 20th," Truman said in opening this session.

> So far as our relations with other countries are concerned, I think it is important during this period to avoid needless differences between this administration and its successor for several reasons. It will show the world national unity in foreign policy. . . . It will help to maintain respect abroad for the power and influence of the United States from

> its allies and friends, and it may help to keep the Kremlin from creating a crisis in the mistaken notion that we are divided or wavering in our purpose to preserve the unity of the free world.
>
> It is also my purpose to do what can be done by this administration to facilitate the orderly transfer of our duties to our successors. I think this is in the best interest of the country. I want to make available to General Eisenhower and his associates the information that will be helpful to them in taking over the operation of the government. It is not my purpose to try to shift responsibility for actions taken by the government between now and January 20th. I am going to follow the policies I believe to be right up until that time and I will take full responsibility for them.
>
> There are certain questions on which it might be very important to our foreign policy for General Eisenhower to express his views. We want to do all we can to help the incoming administration by filling in the background on current problems and by making available in advance information concerning the problems you will have to deal with.

Eisenhower asked whether the president could provide him with briefing papers from their private meeting and the session in the Cabinet Room. Truman replied that he would and handed Eisenhower a memorandum from Snyder about challenges facing the next treasury secretary. Acheson then talked about the Korean peace negotiations, the Iranian situation, the French war in Indochina, and the dispute between France and West Germany over the European Defense Community. In concluding his remarks, Acheson stressed the importance of American economic and military aid to members of the western alliance.[3]

Acheson sensed from Eisenhower's demeanor that the president-elect had little interest in working with Truman's men. "General Eisenhower's attitude perplexed me," Acheson later wrote. "The good nature and easy manner tending toward loquacity were gone. He seemed embarrassed and reluctant to be with us—wary, withdrawn, and taciturn to the point of surliness. Sunk back in a chair facing the President across the Cabinet table, he chewed the earpiece of his spectacles and occasionally asked for a memorandum on a matter that caught his attention."

Eisenhower did not want to spend any more time with Truman than he had to. Following Acheson's presentation, Eisenhower asked for a copy of his remarks and then cut short the meeting. Since he was headed for a meeting at the Pentagon with Lovett and the Joint Chiefs of Staff, Eisenhower indicated that he did not need to be briefed on defense and national security issues. Lovett agreed with the general. Harriman, who took Eisenhower's hint, waived his briefing time.

Truman attributed Eisenhower's somber mood to the burden that he was about to inherit. "General Eisenhower was overwhelmed when he found what he faced," Truman wrote in his diary.

Eisenhower was distant and reserved because of their broken friendship.

At the end of November, the general kept his pledge and went to Korea. "I sincerely wish he didn't have to make the trip," Truman wrote in his diary. "It is an awful risk. If he should fail to come back, I wonder what would happen. May God protect him."[4]

On his three-day tour, Eisenhower met with commanders Mark Clark and James Van Fleet, South Korean President Syngman Rhee, and troops at the front, including his son, Major John S. D. Eisenhower. "My conclusion as I left Korea," Eisenhower later wrote, "was that we could not stand forever on a static front and continue to accept casualties without any visible results."

Eisenhower was determined to end the bloodshed. When General MacArthur publicly suggested that he had a plan to end the war, Eisenhower sent a message asking for an "informal meeting in which my associates and I may obtain the full benefits of your thinking and experience." MacArthur agreed to share his views "concerning solution of the problems involved in the Korean War and the Far East."

An indignant Truman issued a statement on December 9 calling on MacArthur to report his plan to the proper authorities. Two days later at a press conference, the president said, "General MacArthur is in the Army, and on active duty, and if he has anything that is of use to the Defense Department, he ought to tell them so they can make use of it." Truman noted that MacArthur's previous recommendations had been rejected by the administration "because it was felt that his plan would have enlarged the war."

Truman was asked about the suggestion made during the campaign that he could have gone to Korea and hinted that the war would be over by Christmas. "It was suggested, and I decided that it wouldn't serve any good purpose, it would be just a piece of demagoguery; and that is what it turned out to be," he said.

Did that mean, a reporter asked, that Truman viewed Eisenhower's trip as "a piece of demagoguery."

"Yes," Truman replied. "The announcement of that trip was a piece of demagoguery, and then of course he had to take it after he had made the statement."

Press Secretary Roger Tubby then whispered to the president.

"Roger suggested that maybe some good might come out of the trip," Truman told reporters. "If it does, I will be the happiest man in the world. I hope some good can come out of it."[5]

Eisenhower was so resentful of Truman's comments that he would have nothing more to do with his predecessor during the transition period.

Nothing came out of Eisenhower's meeting with MacArthur. "He didn't have any formal peace program at all," Eisenhower recalled. "What he was talking about was the tactical methods by which the war could be ended." MacArthur called for the use of atomic weapons in North Korea and China. It was the last time that Eisenhower would solicit the old soldier's advice.[6]

In looking ahead to the inauguration, Eisenhower told planners that he would be wearing an oxford gray coat and black homburg instead of the traditional cutaway coat and silk top hat. "I am not attempting to change the styles for America," Ike wrote in a memorandum, "but I believe the above would be more practical and businesslike than to cling too closely to the styles of 1900. It would certainly be more convenient in getting in and out of modern automobiles."

Truman was irritated that Eisenhower made this decision without consulting him. Milton Eisenhower wrote his brother that his decision was "a mistake" because Truman was still in charge of protocol questions. "So far as the outgoing President is concerned," Ike wrote his brother, "he is entitled, of course, to wear whatever he pleases, and will, of course, do so. On the other hand, I have not had a single incoming Cabinet officer or any of the Senators or members of Congress disagree with the proposal, even by a lifted eyebrow, for simplifying man's formal dress."[7]

"I don't want to get into any hat controversy," Truman said with a chuckle when asked by Edward T. Folliard of the *Washington Post* about Eisenhower's break with tradition. "The objective of my turning the presidency over to my successor is to do it as expeditiously and as easily as it can be done, and I am not going to get into any controversy on what I am going to wear. I will wear anything that will conform to decency."

Though Truman went along with Eisenhower's choice, he disapproved. "The President should wear the most formal of formal clothes when he's going to the inauguration," Truman said years later.[8]

In a farewell address to the nation, Truman said, "As I empty the drawers of this desk, and as Mrs. Truman and I leave the White House, we have no regret. We feel we have done our best in the public service. I hope and believe we have contributed to the welfare of this nation and to the peace of the world." From the moment he took the job, Truman said he felt that there were many men with better qualifications. "But the work was mine to do, and I had to do it. And I have tried to give it everything that was in me."

He wished Eisenhower a most successful presidency. "He needs the understanding and the help of every citizen," Truman declared. "He can't do the job alone. Regardless of your politics, whether you are Republican or Democrat, your fate is tied up with what is done here in this room. The President is the President of the whole country. We must give him our support as citizens of the United States. He will have mine, and I want you to give him yours."[9]

After reading a news report that the Trumans planned to leave by train after the inaugural ceremonies, Eisenhower wired the president: "It occurs to me that it may be much more convenient for you and your family to make the trip in the *Independence* rather than the presidential Pullman. If you would prefer to use the plane, I would be more than glad to express my desire to the Air Force that they make the plane available to you."

"Thank you very much for the offer of the *Independence*," Truman replied. "Since we have decided to go home by train we will use the car instead. I wrote you a note yesterday telling you how much I appreciate your courtesy in making the car available."[10]

At a press conference, Truman was asked if he would be riding to the Capitol with the new president. "Of course," Truman replied. "You see, he is riding down the Avenue with me. I am the President until he is sworn in."

Both men had threatened to break this tradition. "I'll never ride down Pennsylvania Avenue with him," Eisenhower had grumbled to an aide in the final days of the 1952 campaign. "I'll meet him at the Capitol steps."

Truman turned livid when aides told him that Eisenhower would prefer to have Truman pick up him at the Statler Hotel for their ride to the Capitol. He sent a message to Eisenhower's camp that the president-elect could drive to the Capitol without Truman unless Eisenhower picked him up at the White House.

On the morning of his inauguration, Eisenhower followed protocol and was driven in the parade car from the Statler to the White House. The Trumans had invited the Eisenhowers inside for an informal luncheon. "Mrs. Truman had gone to a lot of trouble," Truman said years later. "We had things all ready for him. But he didn't come." When Eisenhower arrived at the White House portico, he declined to come inside. "He sent word in that he was ready to go," Truman recalled, "so I went out and got in the car with him."[11]

Truman and Eisenhower had little to say to each other. House Speaker Joseph W. Martin and Senator Styles Bridges of New Hampshire sat together in the middle seat of the open limousine. According to Truman, Eisenhower told him: "I did not attend your inauguration in 1949 out of consideration for you, because if I had been present I would have drawn attention from you." Truman said that he replied, "Ike, you'd have come if I'd ordered you, don't worry about that." Truman wrote in his diary that Bridges gasped and Martin changed the subject.

It is questionable whether Truman and Eisenhower had this exchange. Eisenhower rode in a parade car in Truman's 1949 inaugural parade and attended the inaugural ball where he visited with Truman.

Eisenhower asked Truman if he knew who had ordered his son back from Korea for the inauguration. "I did," Truman replied. Eisenhower was grateful for this thoughtful gesture. John Eisenhower had sent his father a "message of protest" out of concern that he might lose a new assignment as acting intelligence officer for the Third Infantry Division. "Just tell him that crotchety old man in the White House did it," Truman told his successor.

A throng of a hundred and forty thousand gathered on the Capitol's East Plaza for the ceremony. Truman took his seat in a leather chair at the center of the platform. Then, to the strains of "Hail to the Chief," Eisenhower walked down the marble steps. After Chief Justice Fred Vinson administered the oath of office, Eisenhower shook hands with Truman and then Nixon. A grinning Ike, acknowledging the crowd's roar, then raised his arms in the V for Victory sign that was his trademark. He put on his glasses and read a prayer that said in part: "Almighty God, as we stand here at this moment, my future associates in the executive branch of government, join me in beseeching that Thou will make full and complete our dedication to the service of the people in this throng and their fellow citizens everywhere."

Three days later, Eisenhower wrote Truman:

> This note is to express my appreciation for the very many courtesies you extended to me and mine during the final stages of your Administration. The efforts you made to assure the orderly transfer of government, from your Administration to this one, are largely a matter of public knowledge but I am personally aware of the fact that you went to far greater trouble to accomplish this than almost anyone else could have known.
>
> On the personal side, I especially want to thank you for your thoughtfulness in ordering my son home from Korea for the inauguration; and even more especially for not allowing either him or me to know that you had done so.

> I sincerely wish for you many years of happy and useful work; and of course, Mamie joins me in sending affectionate greetings to the ladies of your family.

In an handwritten response, Truman wrote: "I can't tell you how very much I appreciated your good letter of the 23rd. It was a pleasure to help all I could in the orderly transfer from my administration to yours. I would never have mentioned the incident of your son, had you not asked me about it."[12]

CHAPTER 29

The Big Chill

Eisenhower ended the Korean War six months into his administration and went on to become one of the most popular and successful American presidents. In presiding over eight years of peace and economic growth, Ike started the interstate highway system, expanded Social Security, and produced three balanced budgets in eight years. Some of his more important accomplishments were initiated by Truman, including the first Civil Rights Act since Reconstruction, the St. Lawrence Seaway, and statehood for Alaska and Hawaii. In the spring of 1955, he achieved Truman's goal of bringing West Germany into NATO. Truman created the National Security Council and Central Intelligence Agency, which Eisenhower made into instruments of his foreign policy. In holding the line against the Soviet Union, Eisenhower followed Truman's foreign policy of containment. "There are very few things about the Eisenhower administration more striking," Richard Rovere of *The New Yorker* wrote in 1956, "than the numerous ways in which it resembles the Truman administration."[1]

Yet Eisenhower moved quickly to cut all ties with his predecessor. Between 1945 and 1952, Truman and Eisenhower had exchanged letters on a regular basis. After the transfer of power, their correspondence stopped. Eisenhower never sought Truman's advice. Just as Eisenhower had served him, Truman would have responded to his call. "I think the ex-President can always be of service to his country," Truman said at his final White House press conference.[2] But when Eisenhower selected the only other living former president, Herbert Hoover, as the chairman of a federal commission on government reorganization, Truman was snubbed. Former Postmaster General James A. Farley was appointed by Eisenhower as the Hoover Commission's ranking Democrat. Truman was left out.

Truman would not set foot in the White House during Eisenhower's presidency. The Eisenhowers lived in a newly restored home because of Truman. From the late fall of 1948 through the spring of 1952, the Trumans had given up their residence in the executive mansion while it was being restored. In the fall of 1951, Truman went over the blueprints with Eisenhower. "It is in very good condition, and General Eisenhower will be able to take up his residence in the house and work right here," Truman said in his farewell address. "That will be much more convenient for him, and I'm very glad the renovation job was all completed before his term began."[3]

After his predecessor moved out, Eisenhower wasted little time in getting rid of any evidence that Truman had ever lived at 1600 Pennsylvania Avenue. Truman's portrait was removed from public display and his piano was also moved out of view. Truman's favorite chandelier was replaced. The bowling alleys, which were built for Truman by friends in Missouri, were dismantled and moved out of the building.

Eisenhower decommissioned the USS *Williamsburg*, Truman's presidential yacht, and also announced that he would not be using Truman's Little White House at the naval submarine station in Key West, Florida. "I agree with you as to the convenience represented in the *Williamsburg*," Eisenhower wrote a friend. ". . . But I am committed to an Administration of economy, bordering on or approaching austerity. So in spite of the fact that I felt she performed a desirable, if not almost an essential service, I felt that the very word 'yacht' created a symbol of luxury in the public mind that would tend to defeat some of the purposes I was trying to accomplish. For the same reason I gave up the Presidential quarters at Key West."

Their scorn was mutual. "Why this fellow," Truman said in early 1953, "doesn't know any more about politics than a pig knows about Sunday." That fall, Eisenhower told a senior official in his administration that "Truman didn't know any more about government than a dog knows about religion."[4]

During his first term, Eisenhower encountered Truman just once. On September 8, 1953, their mutual friend Chief Justice Vinson died of a heart attack. Eisenhower eulogized him as "a man of exemplary character . . . whose death is a loss to America." At Vinson's funeral in the Washington Cathedral, Truman was sitting in a front pew when Eisenhower arrived. As Eisenhower nodded, Truman stood up and shook his hand. It would be six years before they would meet again.[5]

A month after Vinson's funeral, Eisenhower made a two-day trip to

Kansas City, where he opened a livestock show, addressed the Future Farmers of America, and the American Royal Cattlemen's dinner. Eisenhower greeted local dignitaries in the penthouse suite at the Muehlebach Hotel. Among his guests were Kansas City publisher Roy Roberts, Missouri Governor Phil M. Donnelly, Kansas Governor Edward F. Arns, Kansas Senator Frank Carlson and his former colleague Harry Darby, and his brother Arthur Eisenhower.

Truman sought to make an appointment. "After he had gotten settled over at the Muehlebach Hotel, I called up over there and told whoever answered the phone that I'd like to come over and pay my respects," he recalled in 1959. "I was very curtly told that the President's time was all taken up and that there was no opportunity for that to happen."

Eisenhower said later that he was unaware of Truman's call.

Thomas E. Stephens, the former Dewey aide then serving as Eisenhower's appointments secretary, interviewed other members of the traveling presidential staff and said that none had spoken with Truman. Six years after this incident, Eisenhower told C. L. Sulzberger of *The New York Times* that he had made an investigation of all telephone calls on the hotel's switchboard during his visit and could not find any record of Truman's call. "It was a damn lie," Eisenhower alleged.

George E. Allen, a longtime friend of both presidents, believed Truman made the phone call but Eisenhower never got the message. "Eisenhower felt very badly about it," Allen said. "He checked with the Secret Service. They couldn't find the call that had come in."

Colonel Robert L. Schulz, Eisenhower's aide, said that when Truman called Eisenhower's suite and identified himself, the operator replied "and I'm Julius Caesar." Schulz recalled, "With due respect to President Truman, who was accustomed to doing things himself at this point, I think he made a mistake making a phone call. He should have had somebody else do it for him. But indeed it was Harry Truman and so he was miffed and I don't blame him. I guess I would be miffed too. But this didn't come to the attention of President Eisenhower until many months or years later. And when he found out, I mean he raised within the official family holy hell."

While it is probable that Eisenhower did not know that Truman called, he clearly slighted Truman in his hometown. Eisenhower had time for local political figures but not for the thirty-third president of the United States. This was no accident. "In all of the six years I was with Eisenhower in the White House," Chief of Staff Sherman Adams recalled, "he made it a point to have nothing whatever to do with Truman. . . . One of the few times I saw Eisenhower angry was when Eric Johnson and Nixon came to him in 1957 with a plan for a big rally in support of mutual security at which he would appear side by side with Truman. Although mutual security is a cause close to Eisenhower's heart, he put his foot down at appearing on the same program as his predecessor."[6]

Truman, who was still a political force, suspected that Eisenhower's men were plotting to discredit him. Two weeks after the incident in Kansas City, White House counsel Bernard Shanley wrote in a memorandum to Cabinet Secretary Maxwell Rabb that "rumors are that Harry Truman is going to take off on the Old Man" in an upcoming speech before a New York audience. Shanley suggested that Truman's speech could be blunted if Eisenhower released an executive order on the desegregation of Washington, D.C., at about the same time. "Your approach as to a good way to take the steam out of Harry Truman . . . is an excellent one," Rabb replied. "We can't quite follow the plan you have thought up, but it might be wise for us to cast around and see if there isn't another way along these lines to meet the Truman thrust."[7]

The Eisenhower administration's attack on Truman was without precedent. Attorney General Brownell, who had been Dewey's campaign manager in 1948, was looking to settle a score with Truman for his triumph over Dewey. Brownell got clearance from Eisenhower and Adams to go after Truman. On November 6, 1953, Brownell delivered a luncheon speech before the Executives Club of Chicago and accused Truman of promoting a known Soviet agent. Using FBI files for this speech, Brownell resurrected Harry Dexter White, assistant secretary of the Treasury Department in the Roosevelt and Truman administrations, appointed in 1946 as the first American executive director of the International Monetary Fund. White resigned in March 1947 and died in August 1948 after testifying before the House Un-American Activities Committee. "Harry Dexter White was known to be a Communist spy by the very people who appointed him to the most sensitive and important position he ever held in government," Brownell alleged. "It is a source of humiliation to every American that during the Truman administration the Communists were so strikingly successful in infiltrating the government of the United States."

Brownell neglected to mention that Truman learned about the allegations against White after his confirmation by the Senate. Truman allowed White to remain at the IMF.

Democratic leaders rallied to Truman's defense. "It is infamous that the man who has done more than anyone else to organize and fortify the free world against Communism should be subjected to such a malicious political attack," declared Adlai Stevenson. House Minority Leader Sam Rayburn was outraged. "I can stand charges of crime and corruption,"

Rayburn said on the House floor. "But charges implying treason are unforgivable." The attacks on the patriotism of Democrats were "mean, untrue and dastardly." Rayburn concluded, "They should be stopped by somebody, and there is one man in the United States that can stop that kind of talk."[8]

At a press conference, Eisenhower admitted that he had advance knowledge of Brownell's speech. According to the president, Brownell had given him advance notice that he intended to make public "certain facts" about internal security. "I told him that he had, as a responsible head of government, to make the decision," Eisenhower said, "if he felt it was his duty to make these things public."

Eisenhower, though, distanced himself from Brownell's charges. The president was asked if Truman had knowingly promoted a Soviet agent. "No, it is inconceivable," Eisenhower said. "I don't believe that . . . a man in that position knowingly damaged the United States."

The House Un-American Activities Committee issued a subpoena directing Truman to appear before the congressional panel. "I would not issue such a subpoena," Eisenhower said when asked about HUAC's attempt to interrogate Truman. "I'd think there would be other means of handling it than issuing a subpoena."

Truman refused to appear before the committee. "If the doctrine of separation of powers and the independence of the Presidency is to have any meaning at all," Truman wrote HUAC chairman Harold Velde, "it must be equally applicable to a President after his term of office has expired when he is sought to be examined with respect to any acts occurring while he is President. The doctrine would be shattered, and the President, contrary to our fundamental theory of Constitutional Government, would become a mere arm of the legislative branch of the government if he would feel during his term of office that his every act might be subject to official inquiry and possible distortion for political purposes."

In a nationally televised address on November 16, Truman defended his handling of the White case, explained his refusal to testify before HUAC, and alleged that Brownell's attack was politically motivated. The former president said that he had learned of the accusations against White in February of 1946 when an FBI report was brought to his attention. "This report showed that serious accusations had been made against White," he said, "but it pointed out that it would be practically impossible to prove those charges with the evidence at hand." Truman said that he then blocked White's promotion to the managing directorship of the IMF but left him as a board member and under surveillance until the FBI had concluded its probe. "I want the American people to understand that the course we took protected the public interest and security," he said. ". . . The whole history of our Republic does not reveal any other such attack as this by a new administration on an out-going President. Up to now, no administration has ever accused a former President of disloyalty. In communist countries, it is the practice when a new government comes to power to accuse outgoing officials of treason, to frame public trials for them, and to degrade and prosecute the key officials of the previous government. It is not the way Americans behave."[9]

NATO's Supreme Commander Alfred M. Gruenther wrote Eisenhower: "The White incident, unfortunately, has had a very bad reaction in Europe—from the standpoint of U.S. prestige. It will probably all come out in the wash, but I regret that it had to take place at this time."

"The White case was unquestionably distorted in the papers," Eisenhower wrote back, "and I am quite ready to admit that the manner of its presentation was probably not the best." Nevertheless, Eisenhower said that Brownell's charges were accurate.

More than four decades after Brownell made his allegations, the National Security Agency released copies of decrypted Soviet cables that confirmed that White passed information to the Soviet Union. Files released from the KGB archives have also confirmed that White lost influence after Truman became president and was frozen out before he was separated from government. Brownell's attack on Truman was among the more shameful episodes in the history of the U.S. Justice Department.[10]

Truman, who got thousands of supportive telegrams after his response to Brownell, was confident that the American people would be for fair play. But the Gallup poll indicated that the Republicans had gained political advantage from Brownell's attack. About half of the poll's respondents said that they agreed with Brownell, while 29 percent agreed with Truman and 23 percent were undecided. A plurality of all voters said that it was "a good idea" for the Eisenhower administration to "bring up other cases of Communists in the government under the Democrats."[11]

During the controversy, Eisenhower said piously that he hoped that domestic communism would not be an issue in the 1954 midterm elections. Truman enjoyed watching Eisenhower's uneasy relationship with the Republican Congress. GOP conservatives slashed Ike's foreign-aid budget in the summer of 1953. Because of this opposition from his own party, Eisenhower relied on the Democrats for bipartisan support of his programs. On fifty-eight key votes in 1953, Ike relied on Democrats to get his programs passed when Republicans deserted him. Eisenhower became so annoyed with the Republican right that he talked with associates about the possibility of organizing a new centrist political party. Among the Republicans he viewed as out of touch with their times were House Speaker Martin and Senate Majority Leader William F. Knowland of California. "In his case," Eisenhower wrote in his diary of Knowland, "there seems to be no final answer to the question, 'How stupid can you get?'"[12]

As chairman of the Senate's Committee on Government Operations, Joseph R. McCarthy accused the Eisenhower administration of concealing evidence of espionage activities. These wild charges led to the nationally televised Army-McCarthy hearings. Truman told Fletcher Knebel of *Look* magazine that Eisenhower "ought to get his back up" and put an end to the spectacle. "I'd do it," said Truman, "if I had to go up to the Senate personally and make a speech." Eisenhower's strategy was to give McCarthy enough rope to hang himself. It worked. After McCarthy's reckless conduct in the hearings, the Senate voted to censure him by a vote of sixty-seven to twenty-two.

In his major speech of the 1954 campaign, Truman called for the election of a Democratic Congress to rescue Eisenhower from his own party's right wing. "If these were normal times, and there were no serious threats to the peace of the world," the former president declared, "I would hesitate to ask the people to turn the Congress over to the Democratic party while a Republican president occupies the White House. . . . But in the past 20 months we have had the spectacle of the Republican majority itself acting as if it were a party in opposition to its own Republican President."[13]

Eisenhower told Republican leaders in Ohio that he would never run a "partisan" administration like Truman. When Dewey implored him to take a more active role in the 1954 election, Eisenhower said that he did not want to be viewed as another Truman. Even if he barnstormed for Republican candidates, Eisenhower said, "I think that history proves that no President, regardless of his popularity, can pass that popularity on to a party or an individual."

Across the nation, Democrats made a strong comeback in the 1954 midterm elections. Democrats recaptured the Senate and House and gained a majority of the governorships. Truman was elated and Eisenhower was philosophical. "The Republican party must be known as a progressive organization or it is sunk," Eisenhower wrote in his diary. "I believe this so emphatically that I think that far from appeasing or reasoning with the dyed-in-the-wool reactionary fringe, we should completely ignore it and when necessary, repudiate it."[14]

"Modern Republicanism" and "dynamic conservatism" were among the phrases that Eisenhower used in describing his political philosophy. Truman was dubious about these labels. "As far as middle of the road attitude is concerned," Truman said when asked about Eisenhower's political views, "when a Republican walks in the middle of the road, he walks backward. When a Democrat walks in the middle, he walks forward."

In the wake of the 1954 elections, Edgar Eisenhower wrote his brother that "there are a great many people in all walks of life with whom I have talked, who have made the statement that there is very little difference between the policy of your administration and that of the former administration."

The Republican president wrote back that while the country

> is following a dangerous trend when it permits too great a degree of centralization in governmental functions . . . it is quite clear that the federal government cannot avoid or escape responsibilities which the mass of the people firmly believe should be undertaken by it.
>
> Should any political party attempt to abolish social security, unemployment insurance, and eliminate labor laws and farm programs, you would not hear of that party again in our political history. To say, therefore, that in some instances the policies of this Administration have not been radically changed from those of the last is perfectly true. Both Administrations levied taxes, both maintained military establishments, customs officials, and so on.
>
> You say that the foreign policy of the two Administrations is the same. I suppose that even the most violent critic would agree that it is well for us to have friends in the world, to encourage them to oppose communism both in its external form and in its internal manifestations, to promote trade in the world that would be mutually profitable between us and our friends . . . and to attempt the promotion of peace in the world, negotiating from a position of moral, intellectual, economic, and military strength. No matter what the party is in power, it must perforce follow a program that is related to these general purposes and aspirations. But the great difference is how it is done and, in particularly in the results achieved.

In the letter to his brother, Eisenhower said that his foreign policy had been more successful than Truman's and cited the overthrow of the left-wing government in Iran headed by Mohammed Mosaddeq. Eisenhower directed the Central Intelligence Agency to overthrow Mosaddeq's elected government and restore the Shah to his throne. "A year ago last January we were in imminent danger of losing Iran, and sixty percent of the known oil reserves of the world," Ike wrote. "That threat has been largely, if not totally removed. I could name at least a half dozen trouble spots of the same character."[15]

As Truman noted in 1954, the foreign policies of the two administrations were fundamentally the same. Yet Truman noted it was no longer bipartisan. Eisenhower's Secretary of State John Foster Dulles had served in the Truman administration. Other Republicans with senior foreign policy roles during the Truman years had included Lovett, John J. McCloy, Robert Patterson, Paul Hoffman, and Warren Austin. "The Republican administration immediately shut out all Democrats and even the Republicans who had worked with the Democrats on foreign policy," Truman said.

It bothered Truman that Eisenhower had frozen him out. At the tenth anniversary of the United Nations in San Francisco, Truman was invited to speak by Secretary General Dag Hammarskjöld. "The program while I was in the White House," Truman said in 1955, "was to implement the United Nations and try to settle things without people shooting at each other."

When Truman had surgery in January 1954 for the removal of his appendix and gall bladder, Eisenhower sent him a telegram wishing the former president a speedy recovery. Bess Truman wrote Eisenhower a thank-you note. This exchange was Eisenhower's first correspondence with the Trumans in more than a year. It would be another three years before Eisenhower would write Truman again.[16]

Eisenhower's feud with the former president was gaining attention. After *Look* magazine published its lead feature on "The Inside Story of the Ike-Truman Feud," Senator Lodge wrote Eisenhower that the "tone" of Truman's speeches were "so violent as to make [them] almost unbelievable" and he urged the president to "ignore" Truman's comments. "We should also remember," Lodge concluded, that Truman is regarded by the public "as an old man who is probably not too healthy. He could thus become an object of sympathy if any sarcastic or belittling remarks came from our side."

During his 1956 reelection campaign, Eisenhower showed his contempt for Truman by ignoring the former president's campaign oratory. "Whenever Truman said anything that required a rejoinder from the White House," recalled *Chicago Daily News* political writer Edwin A. Lahey, "Mr. Eisenhower would have his press secretary Jim Hagerty do the job. It was a little like a general assigning a corporal to answer another general's quips."[17]

As the Democratic party's ranking elder statesman, Truman took an active role in the 1956 campaign and tore into Eisenhower's record with gusto. He did not overlook Eisenhower's running mate. "Remember this, and remember it well," the former president told a rally in Pittsburgh, "you cannot elect Ike without electing Tricky Dicky."

Eisenhower had asked Nixon to tone down his rhetoric for the '56 campaign. In remarks at a breakfast before Nixon departed on a national campaign tour, Eisenhower told him: "By no means do we need to claim perfection. We don't need to indulge in the exaggerations of partisan political talk." Eisenhower meant it. When the Republican National Committee issued a brochure that included a reference to Democratic wars, Eisenhower repudiated it. "I don't believe that when America gets into war," Eisenhower said, "we can afford to call it anything but our war."

Ike's reelection was never in doubt. In his second race against Adlai Stevenson, Eisenhower invented what would later become known as the Rose Garden strategy. In an unmistakable attempt to contrast himself with Truman, Eisenhower said that he would be making few political appearances.

After Eisenhower made brief campaign stops in Ohio and Kentucky, Truman was gleeful. "In the beginning of this campaign," Truman told a Democratic audience, "it seemed Ike was planning to sit the election out—up on Cloud No. 9. He was just going to smile amiably and make a few public appearances, and then, according to the script, everybody was going to vote for him. However, after the campaign got started, some things began to happen that weren't written into Ike's script. The Democratic attacks on the Republican record began to strike home."

Truman disagreed with one of these attacks. When Stevenson called for a ban on the testing of nuclear weapons, Eisenhower accused him of playing politics with national security. Truman issued a public statement saying that Stevenson was wrong. "It ought not to have been put in the campaign at all," Truman said in a 1959 interview.[18]

Eisenhower won a second term with what was then the largest popular vote in American history and a plurality of nine and a half million votes, carrying all but seven of the forty-eight states. Despite Eisenhower's landslide, the Democrats retained their Senate and House majorities.

Truman did not extend his congratulations. Instead the former president vented his anger in a sarcastic letter that would never be sent. "My dear Ike," Truman began,

> You are elected again and this time without a Congress of your own choosing. A record with only one precedent, back a hundred and eight years ago—1848 when old Zach Taylor, another professional

> general, was elected with Millard Fillmore, who was the Know Nothing Candidate in 1856. Your V.P. is not that far advanced.
>
> I sincerely hope you'll wear a homburg hat and a short coat as you did in 1953 at the inauguration. You'll no doubt have your son present, as you should, but you won't have to scold me for having him there. You can now order him to be present yourself.
>
> I am sincerely hoping you'll pray as loudly and as long as you did in 1953—January 20th. I also hope you'll go to Egypt and Palestine and perhaps to Hungary and Poland in order to surrender to the Kremlin as you did in Korea in 1953.
>
> With Eastland, Thurmond, Talmadge, Holland, Byrd, and McClellan, you should be able to really inaugurate your so-called New Republicanism. By all means consult Lausche of Ohio, Revercomb of W. Virginia and your two boys from old Kentuck. With that crew you should be able to wreck TVA, give away the balance of our national resources, completely ruin our foreign policy and set the country back to 1896 and 1929.
>
> Best of luck and may the honest Democrats and Liberal Republicans save you from disaster.

Eisenhower would not have appreciated Truman's barbs. But his analysis of the election's split decision was not much different than Truman's. "Frankly, I think if I had known that we were going to get a Democratic Congress," Eisenhower told Republican Senator Styles Bridges, "I probably would have refused to run on the theory that it would have been better to have a Democratic President and have the responsibility fixed."[19]

CHAPTER 30

Twilight

The Missouri heat was sweltering. On July 6, 1957, the Harry S. Truman Presidential Library was dedicated in Independence atop a thirteen-acre knoll at the edge of Slover Park. Seventeen thousand individuals and organizations donated $1.75 million for the construction of the limestone and marble complex, which was a mile from Truman's home. "This library will belong to the people of the United States," Truman had said at its groundbreaking ceremonies. "My papers will be the property of the people and be accessible to them. And this is as it should be. The papers of the Presidents are among the most valuable sources of material for history. They ought to be preserved, and they ought to be used."

Former President Hoover, Eleanor Roosevelt, House Speaker Rayburn, Senate Majority Leader Lyndon B. Johnson, former Secretary of State Acheson, New York Governor W. Averell Harriman, House Majority Leader John W. McCormack, and Minority Whip Halleck were among Truman's guests for the dedication. "This is an important event in the life of the nation," Chief Justice Earl Warren declared at the ceremony on the portico. "The library which we dedicate is destined to become a midwestern center of study and research, not only for the period of Mr. Truman's presidency, but also for the whole complex picture of events surrounding it. The impetus it provides for extending the research resources of this great section which has meant so much to the development of the nation as a whole, represents a milestone in American history."

Warren, a former California governor and the 1948 Republican vice-presidential nominee, noted the role that Independence had played in the opening of the American West. "Mr. Truman's presidency naturally reflected this daring spirit of pioneer days as well as his own character as a man of action: tireless, fearless, and decisive. . . . The Truman era is already recognized as one of the most momentous periods in the history of our country and of the world."[1]

Eisenhower was a no-show. In 1955, Eisenhower signed the Presidential Libraries Act that brought all libraries into the National Archives system. Truman's library was the first to be built under this act. "With the building and grounds, we are giving the government a gift of $21 million," Truman said before the dedication. "I hope that the present occupant of the White House will follow this precedent and set up a library at Abilene."

White House Press Secretary James C. Hagerty announced that Eisenhower would send a message to be read by General Services Administrator Franklin G. Floete. Hagerty stipulated that Floete would be attending the dedication in his official role and not as Eisenhower's representative. An early draft of Eisenhower's message said that the Truman Library "stands for a life of public service in a decisive period of our nation's history." Eisenhower deleted this and another sentence congratulating "everyone who has taken part in this enterprise." The first draft closed "with best wishes." This, too, was dropped.

The edited version of Ike's message was cold and impersonal: "To all who have joined in establishing and dedicating the Harry S. Truman Library, I extend greetings. This building, now being presented to and accepted by the people of the United States, safeguards a treasure of presidential papers and exhibits. In it, scholars and visitors will have ready access to a vast store of significant material. Built on property donated by the City of Independence and constructed with funds given by citizens across the land, the Harry S. Truman Library will provide a fund of knowledge pertaining to recent decades in our Nation's history."[2]

The library's namesake was appalled. "I hope you were impressed with Ike's telegram to the people!" Truman wrote Acheson. "What in hell makes some of us tick?"

Eisenhower's rebuff overshadowed the dedication. "President Eisenhower still harbors a fierce personal distaste for his once generous patron, Harry S. Truman," Edwin A. Lahey reported in the *Chicago Daily News*. ". . . Only if he had sent the GSA employee who is up for night watchman at the library could Mr. Eisenhower have expressed his cold detachment more pointedly."[3]

Though offended by this snub, Truman was glad to have Eisenhower as his landlord. As a condition of the agreement with the federal government, Truman had the lifetime use of a suite of offices at the presidential library.

Since leaving the presidency, Truman was straining to make ends meet. Publication of his two-volume memoirs had been a critical success but a financial disappointment. Truman lamented to friends that he had given Eisenhower a tax break but the author of *Crusade in Europe* had not returned the favor. To maintain a suite of offices in Kansas City, Truman had sold several hundred acres of the family farm near Grandview. Truman would not go on corporate boards or accept consulting fees. "I could never lend myself to any transaction, however respectable, that would commercialize on the prestige and dignity of the office of the presidency," Truman said.

A month after the dedication of his library, Truman worried that he might have to compromise these principles. "Do you think that the presidential retirement bill will pass the House," Truman asked Rayburn in a handwritten note. "Sam, I'm not lobbying for the bill," Truman added. But if it failed, Truman told Rayburn, "I must go ahead with some contracts to keep ahead of the hounds."[4]

Truman did not have to take those fees. His longtime friends Rayburn and Senate Majority Leader Lyndon B. Johnson pushed through the Former Presidents Act of 1958. The bill provided a $25,000 annual salary for former presidents. This enabled Truman to live in comfort. It was more than the average physician's salary and four times the median salary for teachers in 1957. Under the 1958 act, Truman was also given the franking privilege for his mail and a $50,000 annual budget for his office. In the event of his death, Mrs. Truman would receive a $10,000 annual pension. Eisenhower, who would also benefit from the presidential retirement bill, signed it into law in August of 1958. If Truman's tax break made Eisenhower wealthy, Ike's signature assured Truman's financial security.

In his retirement, Truman gained popularity and stature. "Since he left the White House," Time reported in a 1956 cover article, "Democrats have come to look on Truman as a character, sometimes amusing, always indomitable, certainly admirable, almost always lovable." In January of 1958, Truman was the third "most admired man" in the world, according to the Gallup poll. Only Eisenhower and Churchill were held in greater esteem by the poll's respondents. Truman could be testy when asked about his relationship with Eisenhower. A reporter in the winter of 1957 asked Truman if he had any plans to make peace with Eisenhower. "It's all on one side," Truman snapped. "It's not on my part. I just don't give a damn about the situation."[5]

Yet there were indications that both men were open to a truce. Truman responded quickly when Eisenhower suffered a stroke in November of 1957. "I am shocked and disturbed by the news of the President's illness,"

Truman said. "I hope and pray for his quick recovery. I know the American people feel as I do in wishing for him as President, and for him as a person, the speediest return to good health."

In February 1958, Eisenhower got some negative press coverage for using the presidential aircraft to take Mamie to Arizona where she stayed at Elizabeth Arden's health club and resort. Truman said that this criticism was unjustified and that it was most unfair to attack any president through another member of his family. Speaking from experience, Truman recalled that he was blasted by the *Chicago Tribune* for using the presidential plane to fly to the bedside of his dying mother. "Why shouldn't the President use the best means of transportation when he needs it?" Truman asked. "I'll cheer when he uses the fastest jet transport."

Eisenhower was accused by some critics of spending too much time on the golf course. In an article for *Look* magazine, Truman came to Ike's defense. "I am sure that the problems of the Presidency follow him around the golf course. They must follow him to Gettysburg and anywhere else he may go," Truman wrote.[6]

In his correspondence with Acheson, Truman could be scathing in his criticism of Eisenhower's foreign policy. But for the most part, the nation's only living Democratic president was publicly supportive of his Republican successor's foreign policy. "You will never hear me stand on the sidelines and tell the President of the United States what the foreign policy should be," Truman said in 1955. The former president said that all Americans should support Eisenhower on foreign policy because he "is the only man who has the information upon which to base policy."[7]

The Suez crisis of 1956 marked the end of Britain and France as great powers. When the NATO allies joined forces with Israel and attacked Egypt, Eisenhower moved promptly to stop this blatant colonialism. On November 2, 1956, the United Nations General Assembly voted for a cease-fire and within four days the French and British agreed. "It does seem to me," Truman wrote Lyndon B. Johnson, "that the foreign relations committees of the House and the Senate and their chairmen and the majority leaders of the House and Senate ought to investigate this thing thoroughly, and force the man at the other end of the street to come up with a program to prevent a third world war."[8]

With the Soviets seeking to fill the power vacuum in the Middle East, Eisenhower asked Congress in January 1957 for authority to use force "against armed aggression from any nation controlled by international communism." The military and economic aid resolution became known as the Eisenhower Doctrine. Senator Fulbright, chairman of the Foreign Relations Committee, opposed Eisenhower's resolution, which he regarded as a blank check for military intervention. Two weeks after Fulbright made known his opposition, Truman aligned himself with Eisenhower. "I would like to express my appreciation of the views about the Middle East Joint Resolution that you expressed in your syndicated column yesterday," Eisenhower wrote Truman. "I feel that your attitude is in the high tradition of nonpartisanship on foreign policy matters of grave national concern."

In the first letter that he sent to Eisenhower in four years, Truman replied, "I appreciated very much your letter of the 15th regarding the article on the Congressional Resolution. I sincerely hope it passes promptly." But in accepting Eisenhower's thanks, he made a subtle reference to their 1952 differences. "As you know," Truman concluded, "I have always been in favor of a bipartisan foreign policy and have never myself made any statements or actions which would make a partisan matter out of foreign policy."[9]

When in 1958 the pro-Western government of Lebanon was threatened by rebel forces, Eisenhower responded under the terms of the Eisenhower Doctrine. The Sixth Fleet was ordered into the eastern Mediterranean and Eisenhower sent fourteen thousand marines into Lebanon. It was the first time in the century that the Americans had intervened in the Mideast. "Under the circumstances," Truman declared, "the President had no other choice. The peace of the world is at stake."

"I deeply appreciate your forthright support of the action, so reminiscent of one you took in somewhat similar circumstances, in order to protect the freedom of an independent nation and to help keep the peace," Eisenhower wrote Truman. "Your statement should assist the world more fully to understand that in the purpose of opposing direct and indirect aggression against free democratic countries, America does not divide on partisan lines."[10]

During this period, Eisenhower arranged for Truman to be briefed by General Charles P. Cabell, the deputy director of the CIA. "I want you to always feel that you can get such briefings whenever you desire," Eisenhower wrote Truman, "and we may from time to time take the liberty of suggesting them, if there seems to be a situation of grave national importance, as to which you would presumably wish to be impartially and authoritatively informed."

"I appreciated your permitting him to give me the information he did," Truman answered, "which, of course, I regard as strictly confidential."[11]

Truman also backed Eisenhower's Formosa policy. In 1955, Eisenhower gained congressional approval for the Formosa Resolution that authorized the use of force to protect Formosa and the nearby Pescadore

Islands. To deter Chinese aggression, Eisenhower resumed Truman's policy of maintaining the Seventh Fleet in the Formosa Straits. "When the present administration in Washington took office, it reversed the American foreign policy in the Pacific," Truman wrote in his syndicated column. "Reality and experience, however, compelled the administration to realize that they had misjudged the situation and they did an about face."

As Chinese Communists shelled the offshore island groups of Quemoy and Matsu, Truman called for the Eisenhower administration to take a firm stand and criticized Democrats who regarded the islands as expendable. Eisenhower sent a task force from the Seventh Fleet that provided the umbrella for Chinese Nationalists to maintain control of the offshore islands. "Let me express appreciation for the statement which you made on the Quemoy and Matsu situation," Eisenhower wrote Truman.[12]

In the spring of 1959, Truman lobbied the House Foreign Affairs Committee to support Eisenhower's foreign aid program. "If you start skimping on this program, you are playing with dynamite," Truman warned. "You ought not to cut this program unless you feel the situation is so bad you first cut congressional salaries."

Truman still had the ability to get under Eisenhower's skin. Interviewed by television's Edward R. Murrow, Truman denied that he had ever offered Eisenhower the presidency. In a visit to New York, Truman told reporters that Eisenhower "was a great military commander in Europe and in NATO, when he had someone to tell him what to do." A reporter then asked Truman who gave Eisenhower his orders. "The commander in chief," Truman replied with a chuckle. The former president added that Secretary of State Dulles "did pretty well" as a consultant to Acheson. "Dulles needs a boss," said Truman. "He doesn't have one."

On December 8, 1958, the peppery Truman made harsh comments about Eisenhower at a luncheon meeting of the National Press Club. Truman criticized Eisenhower's Korean peace agreement. "I didn't go over there and surrender," Truman said. When asked about his relationship with Eisenhower, Truman was less than accurate. "I have never been in touch with the President since I left the White House." Truman added that it would be up to Eisenhower to make the first move. "There isn't anything personal between the President and myself," Truman insisted. "Of course, he's been mad at me ever since I raised hell with him because he didn't knock Bill Jenner off the platform for calling General Marshall a traitor."

Two days after Truman's remarks, Eisenhower responded at a press conference. Folliard of the *Washington Post* asked the president: "Have you been mad at Mr. Truman, as he put it?"

"You people have had a pretty good chance to cross-examine me for the last six years," Eisenhower replied, "and I think that most of you have found that I have a little bit too much sense to waste my time getting mad at anybody."

As for Truman's comments about General Marshall, Eisenhower said, "To say that I have ever stood still while any man, in my presence, was reviling General Marshall, is not true." Eisenhower was on solid ground in that comment but less than accurate in claiming that he had "throughout the political campaign of '52—made known publicly my admiration and my respect for General Marshall."[13]

Eisenhower made several efforts to reconcile with Truman. In May of 1958 he had invited the Trumans to a Memorial Day luncheon at the White House and official ceremonies at Arlington National Cemetery honoring the unknown soldiers of World War II and the Korean War. "It occurred to me that because, though in different capacities, we both bore heavy responsibilities during critical periods of those conflicts," Eisenhower wrote Truman, "it would be only fitting and proper for us, together, to attend these solemn ceremonies. I should feel honored by your participation."

It was the first time that Eisenhower had invited his predecessor to the White House. But the Trumans had already scheduled a European vacation. "I regret very much that Mrs. Truman and I cannot be there," Truman wired Ike. "Unfortunately we will be out of the country at that time."

Eisenhower invited Truman to attend the 1959 tenth anniversary meeting of NATO foreign ministers. "In view of your role in the creation of this treaty," Ike wrote, "we of the Administration would welcome your presence at the ceremony and would hope that you would be willing to make some brief remarks." Eisenhower gave Truman more than two months notice.

But once again, Truman declined. "I wish that it were possible for me to attend," Truman wrote back. "Unfortunately, and much to my regret, I have already accepted an invitation to be in California at that time."[14]

In late April 1959, Eisenhower invited Truman to a stag dinner for Winston Churchill. "Should you by any chance be free on the night of the sixth," wrote Eisenhower, "I would be delighted if you would come to the White House to renew your friendship with our wartime associate. . . . I am sure that Winston would join me in this invitation if he were here."

For the third time, Truman declined. "I am sorry as I can be that I can't be with you and Sir Winston," Truman replied in longhand. "It is necessary for me to be in New York that evening, much to my regret."[15]

Truman's refusal was an embarrassment. Robert Pierpoint of CBS News asked Eisenhower if Truman was "avoiding or evading some of your invitations to meet with you at the White House."

Eisenhower replied that when he made a personal invitation, "I always make it quite clear in the notes that I write, that anyone with any reason, or that finds it inconvenient coming to that meeting, has the right to do so without question, and that I understand. Now, with respect to any other connection or invitations of that sort of thing, I'd say now we're getting into the strictly personal field and that there is nothing to be said about it."

But Eisenhower changed his mind. In his toast to Churchill at the black-tie dinner in the State Dining Room, he took a jab at the man who stayed away. Eisenhower said that several of the guests had told him: "I have some very important engagements, but to see Sir Winston once again is one of the greatest things that could happen to me and I have broken the important engagement in order to do so."

Truman was asked by a political correspondent if he declined Eisenhower's invitation for reasons other than a conflicting engagement. The former president told his newspaper friend to draw his own conclusion. "It was not possible for me to be present at the White House," Truman told Acheson, "because the invitation came too late—as intended."[16]

Later in the year, the White House announced that Eisenhower would be spanning the globe in a three-week goodwill tour of eleven nations. Senator Thomas Dodd of Connecticut urged Eisenhower to include Truman as part of the delegation in recognition of his leadership in shaping the postwar world. David Brinkley of NBC News reported that the consensus of Washington opinion was that if the White House wasn't big enough for Eisenhower and Truman, "it is doubtful that a jet airliner will be big enough either."

Eisenhower told Dodd that it would be impractical to take Truman on the trip. "The practical arrangements for a mission such as I am undertaking," Ike wrote, ". . . require that the personnel accompanying me be limited to staff assistants with minimum State Department representation."

Truman had no comment about Eisenhower's rejection of Dodd's proposal. But for the second time in his political career, Truman chuckled over a *Chicago Tribune* headline. In a banner across the top of its front page, the *Tribune* proclaimed that "Ike 'Can't Take' Truman." As in 1948 when the Chicago newspaper declared Dewey the winner, Truman struck a jaunty pose for wire service photographers with the Eisenhower headline. "I never did hear from the President on that proposed trip to Europe," Truman replied to a Texas political supporter. "The whole operation took place in the newspapers, mostly on the front page. He finally did make a statement that he could not take Truman and that was in the Chicago Tribune."[17]

On October 16, 1959, General Marshall died after a long illness, at Walter Reed Hospital. Marshall's death would bring Truman and Eisenhower together for the second time in the latter's presidency. "General Marshall long ago earned a place as one of the distinguished military and civil leaders of our century, an example of devotion to service and duty, an outstanding American," said Eisenhower, who ordered flags to be flown at half mast on all government buildings.

Truman was among the first to arrive for Marshall's funeral in the chapel at Fort Myer. His military aide General Harry H. Vaughan accompanied him. Soon afterward, Eisenhower arrived with his aide Colonel Robert L. Schulz and sat down in the front pew next to Truman. "Good morning, Mr. President," Eisenhower said in extending his hand. Truman greeted him warmly.

Marshall's death marked the twilight of the generation that built America into a superpower. Churchill had hailed Marshall as "the true organizer of victory" in World War II. Eisenhower was Marshall's personal choice to lead history's greatest invasion. With Marshall, Truman saved freedom in postwar Europe. As NATO's supreme commander, Eisenhower protected that freedom and carried on Marshall's legacy. At the end of the service, Truman and Eisenhower stood as Marshall's coffin was moved out of the chapel and placed on a caisson. Eisenhower saluted Truman and said, "Good-bye, Mr. President." Truman returned the salute.[18]

CHAPTER 31

1960

Eisenhower was the first lame duck president. Until the Twenty-second Amendment went into effect in 1951, there were no term limits for American presidents. If Republicans had not pushed through an eight-year constitutional limitation, Truman believed that Eisenhower would have been reelected in 1960. John S. D. Eisenhower also thought that his father would have gone for a third term. Though in his seventieth year, Eisenhower looked a decade younger. In December of 1959, Ike greeted cheering throngs on three continents. More than two-thirds of the American people approved of his job performance. By denying Eisenhower the opportunity to run again, Truman chortled that Republicans had cut their own throats.[1]

After fifteen years of Truman and Ike, the torch passed to a new generation. For the first time, both major presidential nominees were born in the twentieth century. Senator John F. Kennedy of Massachusetts, a war hero who looked like a movie star, was the Democratic presidential nominee. The forty-three-year-old Kennedy was the first Roman Catholic nominated for the presidency since Alfred E. Smith in 1928. Vice President Richard M. Nixon, forty-seven years old, was the Republican candidate. Even though Kennedy and Nixon had intelligence and leadership skills to match their ambition, Eisenhower and Truman were uneasy about this generational change. Eisenhower would have preferred another Republican candidate. His relationship with Nixon was complicated. In 1952 he nearly dumped Nixon from the ticket when questions surfaced about his political fund. Four years later, Eisenhower wanted another running mate and offered to appoint Nixon as secretary of defense. Nixon would not give up the vice presidency. In an undated handwritten list of prospective 1960 Republican presidential candidates, Eisenhower rated six men above Nixon. If Ike could have chosen a successor, it would have been Treasury Secretary Robert B. Anderson or General Gruenther. Eisenhower sought unsuccessfully to persuade Anderson and then Gruenther to seek the 1960 Republican nomination. Truman encouraged Kennedy's rivals and thought the young senator could be stopped.[2]

In many ways, 1960 was the most frustrating year of Eisenhower's presidency. The economy was slow to recover from the 1958 recession. Many Americans were alarmed by Fidel Castro's 1959 rise to power in Cuba and his alliance with the Soviet Union. Truman later blamed Eisenhower for losing Cuba "because he didn't have enough guts to enforce the Monroe Doctrine." Eisenhower sought to boost U.S. prestige in Latin America by embarking on a goodwill tour of Puerto Rico, Brazil, Argentina, Chile, and Uruguay in February of 1960. In a major embarrassment, an American U-2 spy plane was shot down over central Russia on May 1, 1960. Soviet leader Nikita Khrushchev used this incident to break up a summit conference in Paris. Eisenhower at first issued a statement denying knowledge of any violation of Soviet airspace. "It seems to me that the President of the United States ought not to admit that he doesn't know what is going on," Truman wrote Acheson on May 9. "It looks as if we are in a very ridiculous position with our friends. We have always been known for honesty and fair dealing as a nation and I really don't know how we are going to recover from this last blow."

Eisenhower was dejected. "I would like to resign," he confided to an aide in a moment of despair. But on reflection, he went before the American people and took responsibility for the spy flights. "No one wants another Pearl Harbor," he declared. "This means that we must have knowledge of military forces and preparations around the world, especially those capable of massive surprise attacks."[3]

Failure of the Paris summit was the biggest disappointment of Eisenhower's presidency. Eisenhower cancelled a June trip to the Soviet Union after Khrushchev suggested a postponement. In another setback, Ike's visit to Japan was cancelled following widespread anti-American demonstrations.

On the eve of the Republican convention, Eisenhower was furious when Nixon conferred with New York Governor Nelson A. Rockefeller about the GOP platform and issued a joint statement that implied that Eisenhower had been less than attentive to the nation's security. Rockefeller's proposed defense plank called for a massive buildup in defense spending.

At Eisenhower's insistence, Nixon had the defense plank rewritten to conform with administration policy. "I don't think that he feels that he was appeasing," Eisenhower said when asked if Nixon had gone too far to accommodate Rockefeller.

At the Republican convention in Chicago, Eisenhower delivered a prime-time speech in which he talked about the administration's record without mentioning Nixon's name. Though Eisenhower did not refer to Kennedy by name, he suggested that Nixon's Democratic rival lacked the maturity for the presidency. Ike proclaimed that the American people "realize, as never before, that the stakes in today's world are too high to risk their futures to the hands of frivolous, irresponsible, or inexperienced government."[4]

Truman had voiced similar doubts about Kennedy. His first choice for the Democratic presidential nomination was Missouri's wealthy and urbane Senator Stuart Symington, who had served as air force secretary in the Truman administration. Truman's second choice was Senate Majority Leader Lyndon B. Johnson of Texas.

Another reason Truman opposed Kennedy was his religion. The Baptist Truman questioned whether a Roman Catholic should be elected to the presidency. "The main difficulty with that situation has been that the hierarchy of the Catholic Church always wants to control the political operation of a government," Truman said in an off-the-record interview in late 1959. "When the Catholic Church gets to a point where it's in control, the government is always against the little people . . . I don't think the church ought ever to control the government."

In the early summer of 1960, Truman expressed similar views to Illinois State Representative Paul Simon, who visited him at the Truman Library. Kennedy had learned from other Democratic sources that Truman opposed a Catholic nominee.

Shortly before the convention, Truman called on Kennedy to withdraw. In a nationally televised press conference, Truman said that he was resigning as a delegate "because I have no desire whatever to be a party to proceedings that are taking on the aspects of a pre-arranged affair." Truman listed ten Democratic leaders "who have earned the right to be thought of in connection with the presidency." Kennedy wasn't among them.

Addressing himself to Kennedy, Truman said, "Senator, are you certain that you are quite ready for the country, or that the country is quite ready for you in the role of President in January 1961? I have no doubt about the political heights to which you are destined to rise. But I am deeply concerned and troubled about the situation we are up against in the world now and in the immediate future. That is why I would hope that someone with the greatest possible maturity and experience would be available at this time. May I urge you to be patient?"

Unmoved by Truman's plea, Kennedy replied, "I do not intend to step aside at anyone's request." JFK noted that six presidents of the United States were elected in their forties and that Jefferson wrote the Declaration of Independence and Washington led the Continental Army when they were younger than Kennedy.

Kennedy said that he still hoped to get Truman's support. "I think it would be very important to have his help," the Massachusetts senator said of his party's only living former president.[5]

Following Truman's performance, Acheson wrote: "I listened to your press conference and regretted that you felt impelled to say anything, though what you said was better than what you first told me you intended to say. It seemed quite inevitable that Jack's nomination would occur."

Truman agreed with this criticism. "What I want to know is how much of a damn fool can a man be—and still think he might be right," Truman replied to Acheson.

The former president was impressed with Kennedy's selection of Johnson for the vice presidency. Before accepting Kennedy's offer, Johnson sought Truman's advice. "He definitely thought it was a thing I should do," Johnson said.

In late August, Kennedy headed for Independence. "Come on in here, young man," Truman told him. "I want to talk to you alone." At a joint press conference with Kennedy, Truman was asked about his preconvention doubts about the candidate. "The Democratic National Convention has nominated him for President," Truman said. "The convention is the law for the Democratic Party. I am a Democrat and I follow the law."[6]

Several days later, Eisenhower met the press and did Nixon more harm than good. "Experience Counts" was Nixon's campaign slogan. Republican strategists were promoting Nixon as the most influential vice president of modern times. Charles H. Mohr of *Time* asked Eisenhower whether Nixon had a role in decision making. Mohr wryly observed that "the Republicans to some extent almost want to claim that he has had a great deal of practice at being President."

"He was not a part of decision making," the president answered. "That has to be in the mind and heart of one man." Like the heads of other large organizations, Ike said that he consulted subordinates, including Nixon. But after these discussions, Eisenhower said, "Who is going to decide—I am."

Eisenhower was asked whether he had used any of Nixon's ideas. "If you give me a week, I might think of one. I don't remember," Ike replied in ending the press conference. Back in the Oval Office, Ike realized that he had wronged Nixon and telephoned to apologize. But the damage had been done. Democratic strategists were quick to take advantage of Eisenhower's flip comment.[7]

At seventy-six years of age, Truman would give more speeches than Eisenhower and would also stir more controversy. Addressing a Labor Day crowd in Indiana, Truman departed from his text and noted that he had tried to block Kennedy's nomination. "I am from Missouri, you know, and I have to be shown," Truman said. "Well, he showed me. He proved to my satisfaction that he had what it takes to be a winning candidate and a good President—a lot of honest, old-fashioned courage, for one thing, and the vital quality of forceful, forthright leadership for another."

On the religious issue, Kennedy made Truman an ally. Democratic National Chairman Henry M. Jackson, who controlled Truman's schedule, made extensive use of the Baptist Truman in the Bible Belt. Truman dealt with the Catholic issue by citing Kennedy's war record. "How much evidence must a man present in order to prove that he is a loyal American?" asked Truman. "If he gave his life for his country—if he rode a flaming bomber down to his own death as a soldier at war—would that be enough proof? That is exactly what happened to John Kennedy's brother during World War II. But even more directly—John Kennedy himself was commander of a PT boat that was shot in two in the Pacific. . . . Did anybody then ask either of the Kennedys what church he belonged to?"

Truman alleged that in his hometown of Independence "the Republicans are sending out all the dirty pamphlets on the religious issue." Republican National Chairman Thruston B. Morton vehemently denied Truman's charge.[8]

Eisenhower condemned religious bigotry. "I not only don't believe in voting prejudice," Ike said at a press conference, "I want to assure you that I feel none. And I am sure that Mr. Nixon feels the same way . . . I would hope that religion could be one of those subjects that could be laid on the shelf and forgotten until after the election is over." But Eisenhower regarded Kennedy's youth and inexperience as valid issues.[9]

In all of his 1960 appearances, Truman poured abuse on Nixon, referring to the Republican presidential nominee as "Tricky Dick." Truman attacked Nixon as an opportunist, political slickster, and double-crosser. Speaking in San Antonio, Truman accused Nixon of being against the small farmer, against labor, against small business, and against public housing. "Come to think of it," Truman said, "I don't know what the hell he is for. And that bird has the nerve to come to Texas and ask you to vote for him. And if you do, you ought to go to hell—that's all I have to say!"

In a televised debate with Nixon, Kennedy was asked about Truman's profane remark. "Well, I must say that Mr. Truman has his methods of expressing things," JFK began. "He's been in politics for fifty years. He's been President of the United States. Maybe it's not my style, but I really don't think there's anything I can say to President Truman that's going to cause him at the age of seventy-six, to change his particular speaking manner. Perhaps Mrs. Truman can, but I don't think I can."

Nixon was less graceful in fielding the same question. His own use of foul language and ethnic slurs would become known more than a decade later when transcripts of his Watergate conversations were made public. But in the debate with Kennedy, Nixon piously condemned Truman. "One thing I have noted as I have traveled around the country are the tremendous number of children who come out to see the presidential candidates," Nixon said. ". . . It makes you realize that whoever is President is going to be a man that all the children of America will either look up to or will look down to, and I can only say that I am very proud that President Eisenhower restored dignity and decency, and, frankly, good language to the conduct of the Presidency of the United States."[10]

Eisenhower thought that Nixon had squandered his advantage in name recognition by agreeing to the televised debates with a lesser-known opponent. Kennedy's winning performance in the first debate was the turning point in what would be the closest presidential election in more than forty years.

It was Kennedy's theme "to get this country moving again." Kennedy claimed that the United States had declined in military power, was losing the space race to the Soviet Union, and had lost prestige in the world. Without any hard evidence, the Democratic presidential nominee charged that Eisenhower had allowed a "missile gap." This allegation was unfounded, though Eisenhower would not release secret intelligence reports that would have proved otherwise.

Stung by Kennedy's criticism, Eisenhower told a cabinet member: "I am going to do everything possible to prevent that Kennedy fellow from occupying the chair that I now occupy."

In a televised speech for Nixon, Eisenhower accused the Democratic presidential nominee of "amazing irresponsibility" for claiming that the United States had lost prestige in the world. "We are simply listening to a debasement of the truth."

Eisenhower's intervention in the campaign's final eight days had dramatic impact. In Philadelphia, Ike said of Kennedy: "Anyone who seeks to grasp the reins of world leadership should not spend all his time wringing his hands." At a rally in the New York Coliseum, Eisenhower appeared with Nixon and declared: "A nation needs leaders who have been immersed in the hard facts of public affairs in a great variety of situations, men of character, who are able to take the long-range view and hold long-range goals, men who do not mistake minor setbacks for major disasters and leaders who by their own records have demonstrated a capacity to get on with the job. This is why I am so wholeheartedly in back of Richard Nixon and Cabot Lodge."[11]

On the night of November 2, Truman led a torchlight parade with James A. Farley in the former Democratic national chairman's hometown of Haverstraw, New York. "We've had great Presidents in this country and Franklin Roosevelt was one of the greatest of the great," he told a rally at the local high school. "I was associated with him for more than, well let's see, nearly 18 years and I became very well acquainted with him and he insisted that I take a job I didn't want and that was Vice President. Got myself into more trouble than any man in the United States." As the old campaigner paused, the crowd roared with laughter. "I want to say to you that while I was in all that trouble I was working at the job, trying to get it done and I don't know whether I did or not. You can't tell anything about whether a President is great or small or what he is until he's been dead about fifty years and then if he's been any account at all, they may name him a statesman. Well, I'm a living politician and that's what I want to stay. I have no desire to be a statesman." The crowd roared.

Truman was just getting started. "Boy, I wish I could live another fifty years and see what takes place," he said. "If we have the right leadership, my friends, we'll have the greatest age that the world has ever seen. If we have no leadership, no telling what'll happen to us. I ask you to vote for John F. Kennedy and Lyndon B. Johnson. These are men you can trust. These are men who will give us the leadership we so greatly need and I also urge you to vote the Democratic ticket from top to bottom, and you'll make no mistake for the country or for yourselves."[12]

On the Sunday night before the election, Nixon made an unusual proposal involving Truman and Eisenhower. If elected as the nation's next president, Nixon vowed to send Eisenhower and Truman on a goodwill tour of Soviet bloc nations. Nixon said that he had consulted with Eisenhower. "He has indicated that he would be willing to take a trip to the satellite countries under these circumstances," Nixon said. "But he made a suggestion which I have heartily endorsed. He suggested so that this would be a bipartisan effort that not only he, but that two other former

Presidents, President Hoover and President Truman, also be included among those to make such trips."

The proposal to include Truman was surprising. "I realize that some Republicans who are listening will not like the idea of my suggesting that Mr. Truman go on such trips," Nixon said. ". . . But let me say, based on my own travels to Europe, this one thing that we must not forget: We have our differences at home, but abroad . . . Mr. Truman is honored because of the Marshall Plan, which I supported and which resulted in the rebuilding of Europe."[13]

Truman had no advance knowledge of Nixon's proposal. In Eisenhower's second term, the former president had declined an invitation from Secretary of State Dulles to make a goodwill trip to Greece and Turkey on the tenth anniversary of the Truman Doctrine. It is doubtful that Truman would have been any more receptive to Nixon's idea.

Eisenhower was even more surprised than Truman by Nixon's speech. Though Nixon had consulted him, Eisenhower had not authorized the use of his name. Nor had he agreed to make the trip. According to presidential secretary Ann Whitman, Ike was "astonished, did not like the idea of 'auctioning off the Presidency' in this manner, spoke of the difficulty of his traveling once he is not President, and felt it was a last-ditch hysterical action." Though annoyed that the vice president had ignored his wishes, Eisenhower wired his congratulations to Nixon after the speech.

Despite this incident, Eisenhower still very much wanted Nixon to win. "I shall exercise my right tomorrow, as I hope you will, also," Ike said in his televised pitch for Nixon on election eve. "For myself and because of my firsthand knowledge of their capacity, dedication and character, I shall vote for Richard M. Nixon and Henry Cabot Lodge, as again I hope you will."

In a record turnout of nearly sixty-nine million voters, Kennedy edged Nixon by a plurality of 112,881 votes. Kennedy's winning margin was one-tenth of 1 percent. "This is the biggest defeat of my life," Ike told a friend. "All I've been trying to do for eight years," Eisenhower grumbled to his son John, "has gone down the drain. I might just as well have been having fun."

Truman had a different outlook. "The free world has every reason to take heart at the decision of the American people to choose John F. Kennedy as their new president," Truman wrote in his column syndicated by the North American Newspaper Alliance. "I believe that not only our own people but people everywhere can expect a new surge of dynamic, decisive and productive leadership from this country." As for his personal view, Truman added, "I think John F. Kennedy will make a good President. I would not have been for him if I had not thought so."[14]

CHAPTER 32

Bygones

On November 1, 1961, the Trumans stayed overnight at the White House as President John F. Kennedy's guests. "No one can refuse an invitation like that, especially if he has lived there and is fond of the President who now lives there," Truman wrote Kennedy. But during his visit, Truman made headlines for his comments about Eisenhower. In a November 2 luncheon speech at the National Press Club, Truman did not mention Ike's name but said that the previous administration was "one of the most unfortunate periods in the history of American government." Truman declared that the Eisenhower administration held the country back by "wrong and unwise policies at the top."

At the press club, Truman was asked about the possibility of a reconciliation. At Kennedy's January 1961 inauguration, they had sat in the same area but avoided speaking. Truman replied that he had already started a Former Presidents Club with Herbert Hoover. "He's the president and I'm the secretary," Truman said. "The other fellow hasn't been taken in."[1]

Eight days later, Eisenhower applied for membership. For the first time in nine years, he called on Truman. Their mutual friend Joyce Clyde Hall, the founder of Hallmark Cards, informed Truman that Eisenhower wished to see the Truman Library. His own presidential library in Abilene was nearing completion and Eisenhower wanted to get a firsthand look to see how Truman's library was set up and managed. Hall advised Truman that Eisenhower would soon be in the area for the dedication of the Liberty Memorial monument. It was through Hall that Truman invited Eisenhower.

On the Friday morning of November 10, Eisenhower arrived at Kansas City Airport and was met by Hall and *Kansas City Star* publisher Roy Roberts. They headed directly for Independence in Hall's black limousine.

There was no advance publicity about Eisenhower's visit. News organizations were alerted when the party departed from the airport.

As Eisenhower arrived at the library's back entrance, Truman greeted him warmly at the door. "Come in, come in," Truman said as they shook hands. "It's good to see you again," Ike replied.

Truman escorted Eisenhower into his private office. "I want to have some time with him," Truman told his lawyer Rufus Burrus. "And when he gets ready to leave, I'll probably get up and go with him."

Both men were smiling as they emerged following a fifteen-minute conversation. As Truman began the tour of the library, Eisenhower asked whether he should sign the guest book. "Definitely," Truman responded with a chuckle, "then if anything is missing, we'll know who to blame."

In the museum lobby, Truman beamed as he showed the new wall-size mural, *Independence and the Opening of the West*, by the renowned painter Thomas Hart Benton. The mural showed the old town of Independence, the Oregon Trail, the Rocky Mountains, and the Great Plains. Truman himself had chosen the theme for the mural and had stipulated that his own image would not be part of it.

The two former presidents then stepped into the reproduction of the Oval Office. "This is a very unusual thing," said Eisenhower, who was impressed by the quality and detail of Truman's Oval Office. They paused in front of the replica of the big desk with the large green blotter and the famous THE BUCK STOPS HERE sign. Eisenhower had used the same desk, which Kennedy replaced with a smaller one. "They took out the big desk and put it in the cellar," Truman explained. "I don't know why."

"I don't know either," Ike replied.

Above the mantel was Truman's favorite portrait of George Washington and, just to the right, was a painting of the South American liberator Simon Bolivar that Truman had offered to give Eisenhower in 1952. As a gesture of goodwill, Eisenhower would later donate the world globe that he had given Truman in 1945 and that his White House predecessor returned in 1952. The globe is still on display in Truman's Oval Office.

Near the entrance of the museum, Truman pointed out Eisenhower's portrait. "You know that fellow?" Truman asked with a smile. Truman's portrait was on the left side of the entrance and Eisenhower's was on the right. "You've got it on the preferred side," Ike observed.

"Yes sir, General, and I had it put there," Truman said.

At this point, Truman excused himself, noting that "there is too much of me" in other parts of the museum. Library director Philip C. Brooks conducted the rest of the tour. "I gave the President the last will of Hitler and his marriage certificate," Eisenhower told Brooks. The library director replied that the documents were in the National Archives. "Oh, I thought those papers would belong here," Eisenhower said. "I gave them to him."

After the tour, Eisenhower rejoined Truman for another private talk. Truman pulled out a special edition of *Crusade in Europe* and said, "There is somebody's handwriting you might recognize."

As their conversation ended, Truman walked his visitor out to the library's back entrance. Eisenhower saluted his former commander in chief and said, "Good-bye, sir." Truman returned the salute.[2]

Three days later, Eisenhower wrote Truman: "Thank you for your courtesy in inviting me to see your library in Independence. I enjoyed the opportunity to examine at first hand how the documents pertaining to your Administration are handled. I was much impressed by the splendid building itself. Again, my gratitude for your invitation."

The following spring, he invited Truman to the dedication of the Eisenhower Library in Abilene. Truman accepted but had to change his plans after a death in the family. "I was as sorry as I could be that I was not able to be present for the dedication of your library," Truman wrote Eisenhower. "I am hoping that sometime in the near future I will be able to pay a visit there and I know that I shall enjoy it very much."[3]

Just a week after Eisenhower called on Truman, the former presidents were together again at House Speaker Sam Rayburn's funeral in Bonham, Texas. In the front pew of the First Baptist Church, Kennedy and Vice President Lyndon B. Johnson sat next to Eisenhower and Truman. More than one hundred members of Congress also attended the services. For Truman, Rayburn would always have a special place in his memories. It was in Rayburn's private office that Truman learned of FDR's death. Because of Truman's high regard for Rayburn, he had pushed through a law putting the House Speaker second in line of presidential succession. At Truman's insistence, Rayburn would always address him as Harry. Eisenhower, who was born in Rayburn's congressional district, had affection for "Mr. Sam." Before the services, Truman and Eisenhower chatted amicably. After the funeral, Eisenhower sat between Truman and Kennedy at the graveside service in the Willow Wild cemetery. "You know, having met as we did at the Library before that," Truman later said of Eisenhower, "it made it less awkward to meet at the funeral service. I'm glad we had a chance to do that."[4]

In November 1962, there was another presidential reunion at Eleanor Roosevelt's funeral. As she was buried next to FDR in the rose garden at Hyde Park, Eisenhower stood next to Harry and Bess Truman. The Kennedys and Johnsons were in the same row. By naming Mrs. Roosevelt as a delegate to the United Nations, Truman had made her "First Lady of the World" and he cherished their friendship. But her death was a painful reminder of Truman's mortality. Mrs. Roosevelt was five months his junior.

On November 22, 1963, Truman and Eisenhower were jolted by John F. Kennedy's assassination. Eisenhower, who was in New York for a United Nations luncheon, heard about the shooting from a New York police officer. "I share the sense of shock and dismay that the entire nation must feel at the despicable act that took the life of the President," Eisenhower said. "On the personal side, Mrs. Eisenhower and I share the grief that Mrs. Kennedy must now feel. We send to her our prayerful thoughts and sympathetic sentiments in this hour."

Truman was told of the shooting while having lunch at the Muehlebach Hotel. During his drive home, he heard on the radio that Kennedy had died. "I was very much shocked and hurt when I heard of the President of the United States," Truman later told reporters. "He was a good man, an able President, and he did a good job. And it's too bad these things have to happen particularly by some good-for-nothing fella who didn't have anything else to do than to try to take the head of state away from us."[5]

Kennedy's death brought Truman and Eisenhower closer together. Truman and his daughter Margaret spent the weekend in Blair House, their home during the White House renovation. The Eisenhowers, who had driven down from Gettysburg, were staying nearby at the Statler Hotel. On the Sunday before the Monday funeral, Washington was overcrowded with kings, presidents, ministers, and princes. "There were so many people of different ranks in Washington that it was a real problem," Eisenhower later told the writer William Manchester. "They called me and said Harry Truman was there without a driver. I said, 'Hell, I'll have my car. He can ride with me.'"

Admiral Robert Dennison, Truman's former naval aide, got the message that Eisenhower was attempting to reach Truman. "I called the Statler and got through to General Eisenhower," he recalled.

"Thank God, I've got you on the phone," Eisenhower told Dennison. "I don't seem to be able to get through to anybody."

"What can I do for you?" asked the admiral.

"All I want to know," replied Ike, "is whether Mamie and I could stop by to pick up President Truman and Margaret to go to the cathedral."

"Well, General," said Dennison, "I'll call you back."

"That's no problem," said Eisenhower. "I'll hold the phone."

"Well, the President is right here," the admiral said. Dennison asked Truman who replied, "Certainly."

After further discussion, Truman and Eisenhower decided to make their way to St. Matthew's Cathedral in separate cars. But they would ride in Eisenhower's limousine to the graveside service at Arlington. Neither Eisenhower nor Truman was up to the eight-block walk from the White House to the cathedral. The Kennedy family led a procession of more than two hundred dignitaries that included French President Charles de Gaulle, West German Chancellor Ludwig Erhard, Emperor Haile Selassie of Ethiopia, Queen Frederika of Greece, and King Baudouin of Belgium. The Trumans and Eisenhowers sat in the same pew at the church.

Following the funeral mass, the Eisenhowers headed for Arlington with Truman and his daughter Margaret. During the drive to the cemetery, the former presidents speculated over whether Kennedy's assassination might have been a conspiracy. Both decided that Lee Harvey Oswald alone had slain Kennedy. The two then shared reminiscences. When the Trumans and Eisenhowers arrived at the cemetery, it was a mob scene. Kennedy's grave was on the slope below the Custis-Lee Mansion. Though seats were reserved at the grave site for the Trumans and Eisenhowers, Ike afterward told Manchester that they ended up "out in left field."

As the Eisenhowers took the Trumans back to Blair House, Truman noted that nobody had eaten lunch and invited the Eisenhowers in. "When I discovered that the Eisenhowers were not planning to stay in Washington," Margaret recalled, "I suggested that they have something to eat before they went back to Gettysburg."

It was an informal luncheon. Sandwiches and coffee were served in the drawing room. The Trumans and Eisenhowers talked about the four days during which JFK was killed in Dallas and then buried in Arlington. The former presidents talked of how well the funeral had gone and of Jacqueline Kennedy's special grace.

"I think I'll probably be buried in Abilene," Eisenhower told Truman. "I don't know whether I'll have a Washington funeral or not, and I'm really not concerned about that."

Truman was uncertain whether he would have a funeral in the capital; he knew that he would be buried in the courtyard of his library.

As the conversation went on, Truman and Ike were invited to the White House. Admiral Dennison had been called to the door by a Secret Service agent. An army colonel told Dennison, "Mrs. Kennedy sent me over here to make a statement to President Truman, and she understands President Eisenhower is here. She's upset and embarrassed because she forgot to invite these two gentlemen to come over to the White House."

With all the foreign dignitaries in town for the funeral, the former presidents had been overlooked. The admiral brought the colonel into the drawing room where he extended the invitation.

"Please tell Mrs. Kennedy that I understand completely," Ike told the young officer. "My wife and I understand it, and it was very kind of her to think of us. But we must get back to Gettysburg. So please present our apology."

"I feel very much the same way," Truman said. "I appreciate her thoughtfulness and I understand why we weren't thought of in the first place. She has so much on her mind. But I, too, am tired. And I've got to rest and I'm sure she'll understand."

Truman and Ike picked up their conversation where they had left off. "They just kept on having another drink and talking," recalled Dennison. "I thought it would never end, but it was really heartwarming because they completely buried the hatchet and you'd think there had never been any differences between them. They were right back where they came in when Eisenhower came back from Europe. And, in the end, when they really had to go, President Truman, as he would, much to the horror of the Secret Service, went out to the curb and started talking again while the car waited to take the Eisenhowers away. It was really wonderful."

Eisenhower told Truman, "I think the press accounts of our differences have been somewhat exaggerated." Truman laughed.

As the former presidents exchanged farewells, they shook hands. "It was a long, lingering, silent handshake, with both men looking into each other's eyes," reported political correspondent Warren Rogers. "Margaret kissed General Eisenhower. Mamie Eisenhower kissed Truman on both cheeks."

Clifton Daniel, Truman's son-in-law, who would become managing editor of *The New York Times* not long after Kennedy's death, said that Truman and Ike had mellowed. "They were both much older, and a lot of water had gone over the dam, and my impression is simply that they were polite and civil to each other," Daniel recalled. "There's no reason why they shouldn't be after all those years. They had been very closely associated, and on that day they shared something very much in common. They shared with Jack Kennedy the fact that all of them had been President, and this engenders a greatness of spirit in people sometimes they don't otherwise have."[6]

On Eisenhower's seventy-fifth birthday in October 1965, Truman wired: "Happy birthday Mr. President. Seventy-five years is a wonderful milestone. That is when things begin to fall into place. Hope to see you around for many more years." Ike responded that he deeply appreciated Truman's "kindly thoughtfulness."

They would meet just once more, at a United Nations luncheon in Kansas City on June 6, 1966. Truman and Eisenhower sat together. "I think all the old animosities were forgotten," said Ike's brother Milton, who sat with them. "They had quite a good time together."

Three days after this lunch, Truman accepted an invitation to serve as honorary chairman for the Eisenhower Golden Wedding Anniversary Committee. "The news has just reached me that you have accepted the honorary chairmanship," Ike wrote. "I am more than delighted." In his own hand, Eisenhower closed the letter "with warm regard and great respect."[7]

Both men were slowing down. Truman suffered multiple concussions, broke two ribs, and was knocked unconscious in a bathroom fall in October of 1964. He would never fully recover. Truman also had an arthritic hip that made it difficult for him to walk. When Eisenhower suffered a major heart attack in November of 1965, Truman wired him best wishes. "Thank you very much for your note on my illness," Ike replied. "It is a partial recurrence of the attack I had ten years ago, and the doctors seem to think that I am making satisfactory progress." Eisenhower would suffer four more heart attacks in his retirement years.

In January of 1967, Eisenhower wrote from aboard the Santa Fe Railroad: "Last evening I came through Kansas City by train but found that we arrived at such a late hour that I gave up my intention of telephoning you. Mamie and I are on our way to southern California for our annual winter sojourn there and both of us merely wanted to send you greetings and best wishes for the coming year."

"I would have been delighted to have received your telephone call," Truman replied, "and I hope to have a chat with you upon your return to Gettysburg in the spring."[8]

That spring, Eisenhower invited Truman to join him as honorary co-chairman for an Anglo-American fund-raising drive to build a cathedral in Portsmouth, England. "That area was the principal embarkation point for the British-American forces on D-Day," Eisenhower wrote Truman. "I have been invited to be one of two honorary co-chairmen of the committee to serve along with you in the same capacity, if you should so agree."

"In the interest of history and your own magnificent contribution to that exalted period in the life of the free world," Truman replied. "I am delighted to accept."[9]

Eisenhower listed Truman among "the towering governmental figures of the West" in the final chapter of *Waging Peace*, the second volume of his White House memoirs. Truman placed sixth on a list of twenty-one leaders that was topped by Churchill, Hoover, Dulles, Marshall, and Roosevelt. Truman was listed ahead of Adenauer, de Gaulle, Eden, Attlee, and Macmillan. Acheson, Forrestal, and MacArthur did not make Ike's list. William B. Ewald, the former White House speechwriter who collaborated on Ike's memoirs, said that Truman's name was missing in the first draft of the list. "I pointed out that the omission appeared to glare from the page," Ewald recalled. Eisenhower added Truman's name and put him high on the list.

During an oral history interview for the Eisenhower Library in June of 1967, Eisenhower talked about Truman's December 1951 handwritten letter "in which he said he would like to talk to me about my plans for the future, because he hoped that it wouldn't be necessary for him to run again in order to keep the isolationists out of the White House." Even though Eisenhower had referred to this letter in his White House memoirs, he placed a twenty-year restriction on this part of the interview. "There's no real reason for restriction," Ike said, "except the old gentleman's so old, and he's forgetful, and I wouldn't want to annoy him."[10]

In April of 1968, at Palm Desert, Eisenhower suffered his fourth major heart attack. A month later, he was flown to Washington where he would spend the last year of his life in Walter Reed Hospital. When his heart stopped for the last time on March 28, 1969, the world mourned.

Truman wired Mamie: "Mrs. Truman and I were deeply distressed today to learn of the passing of General Eisenhower. You and your family have our sincere sympathy in this sad hour. We know you will be sustained by the warm affection which the American people have always felt for you and the President."

In his public tribute, Truman was gracious: "General Eisenhower and I became political opponents but before that we were comrades in arms, and I will not forget his service to this country and to Western civilization. He led the great military crusade that freed Western Europe from Nazi bondage, and then commanded the allied forces that stood guard over the liberated lands until they regained their strength and self reliance. For these achievements, which brought him the highest office and highest honors in the land, he must be long and gratefully remembered."

Truman, the last of the giants from the generation that saved the West, outlived Eisenhower by three years. For fifteen years, they led the American nation and the western world. Truman is remembered for his boldness in saving Greek independence and resisting aggression in Korea. In forging history's most successful military alliance, he and Eisenhower saved freedom in Europe. "You, more than any other man," Churchill told Truman in 1951, "have saved western civilization."[11] The same could be said for Eisenhower. Harry and Ike were the partnership that saved the West.

Endnotes

1. COMING HOME

1. Harry C. Butcher, *My Three Years with Eisenhower*, 867; *Public Papers, 1945*, 120.
2. *The New York Times*, June 19, 1945.
3. HST to DDE, May 8, 1945, President's Secretary's Files, HSTL.
4. *Public Papers, 1950*, 307.
5. DDE, *At Ease*, 155.
6. DDE, *Crusade in Europe*, 409.
7. DDE to HST, May 8, 1946, PSF, HSTL.
8. Rudolph L. Treuenfels, *Eisenhower Speaks*, 46.
9. Ibid, Joint Session of Congress, June 18, 1945, 33, 35, 40.
10. Scott Hart, *Washington at War: 1941–1945*, 263.
11. Butcher, *My Three Years*, 871.
12. HST to Bess Wallace Truman, June 19, 1945; Robert H. Ferrell, *Dear Bess: The Letters from Harry to Bess Truman, 1910–1959*, 516.

2. FROM THE HEART OF AMERICA

1. Richard H. Rovere, *The Eisenhower Years*, 346–7.
2. Kenneth S. Davis, *Soldier of Democracy*, 548.
3. *Selected Speeches*, 8; and *Soldier of Democracy*, 550.
4. DDE, *At Ease*, 72–3; *TNYT*, June 5, 1952.
5. HST, *Memoirs, Volume 1, Year of Decisions*, 112–3.
6. "Harry Truman's Missouri," *Life*, June 25, 1945.
7. HST diary, June 17, 1945, in Robert H. Ferrell, *Off the Record*, 47; and DDE, *At Ease*, 40.
8. Charles G. Ross, "A Personal Impression of Truman by One Who Knew Him From Boyhood," *St. Louis Post-Dispatch*, April 15, 1945.
9. DDE, *At Ease*, 97.
10. Davis, *Soldier of Democracy*, 90.
11. DDE, *At Ease*, 39.
12. Ibid, 40; and William Hillman, *Mr. President*, 102.
13. Hillman, 81.
14. HST memorandum, July 12, 1960, *Off the Record*, 388.
15. DDE speech, Dickinson County Young Men's Democratic Club, November 18, 1909, in *Eisenhower: The Prewar Diaries and Selected Papers, 1905–1941*, edited by Daniel D. Holt and James W. Leyerzapf, 5–7.
16. HST, *Year of Decisions*, 122.
17. DDE to Bristow, August 20, 1910, *Prewar Diaries*, 8.

3. PARALLEL LIVES

1. Jonathan Daniels, *The Man of Independence*, 70.
2. *The Autobiography of Harry S. Truman*, edited by Robert H. Ferrell, 30; and Ferrell, *Harry S. Truman: His Life on the Family Farm*, 124.

3. DDE, *At Ease*, 12.
4. Ibid, 118.
5. Margaret Truman, *Bess W. Truman*, 20; and John S. D. Eisenhower, *Strictly Personal*, 329.
6. Stephen E. Ambrose, *Eisenhower: Soldier, General of the Army, President-Elect*, 65.
7. HST's "The Military Career of a Missourian," his thirty-four page handwritten account of his service from the National Guard into World War I, was published in 1982 by the Harry S. Truman Good Neighbor Award Foundation. See also HST's autobiography, Chapter IV, "The First World War."
8. HST to BWT, October 6, 1918, 272–3, *Dear Bess*.
9. DDE interview with Forrest C. Pogue, June 28, 1962, EL.
10. Ambrose, *Eisenhower*, 84.
11. Ibid, 96.
12. Drew Pearson, "Washington Merry-Go-Round," September 4, 1950, *Des Moines Register*.
13. HST, *Autobiography*, 59.
14. HST to BWT, June 6, 1945, *Dear Bess*, 514.
15. Alonzo L. Hamby, *Man of the People*, 177.
16. DDE, *Prewar Diaries*, November 30, 1932.
17. Ibid, October 29, 1933.
18. Margaret Truman, *Harry S. Truman*, 90.
19. HST to BWT, July 26, 1935, *Dear Bess*, 374.
20. DDE, *Prewar Diaries*, June 15, 1932, 224.
21. Ambrose, *Eisenhower*, 95.
22. DDE to Bradley, July 1, 1940, *Prewar Diaries*, 466.
23. DDE to Patton, September 17, 1940, *Prewar Diaries*, 491; and DDE to Clark, October 31, 1940, 496–8, Ibid.
24. Richard Lawrence Miller, *Truman: The Rise to Power*, 347.
25. HST, *Autobiography*, 78.
26. "Billion-Dollar Watchdog," *Time*, March 8, 1943; and Bruce Catton, *The War Lords of Washington*, 116.
27. DDE message to Allied Expeditionary Forces, June 6, 1944, *Papers of Dwight D. Eisenhower, The War Years, v. 3*, 1913.
28. Ambrose, *The Supreme Commander*, 418.
29. HST, *Year of Decisions*, 192–3.

4. POTSDAM

1. HST to BWT, July 3, 1945, *Dear Bess*, 516.
2. HST diary, July 7, 1945, *Off the Record*, 49.
3. DDE, *Crusade*, 441–2.
4. Robert Murphy, *Diplomat Among Warriors*, 265.
5. HST diary, July 16, 1945, *Off the Record*, 52.
6. HST diary, July 17, 1945, *Off the Record*, 53.
7. Godfrey Hodgson, *The Colonel*, 333; HST diary, July 25, 1945, *Off the Record*, 55.
8. DDE, *Crusade*, 443.
9. *Strictly Personal*, 97.
10. *Mr. President*, 248.
11. Omar N. Bradley and Clay Blair, *A General's Life*, 444.

12. Forrest C. Pogue, *George C. Marshall, Statesman 1945–1959*, 19, 23.
13. HST, *Year of Decisions*, 392.
14. HST to Irv Kupcinet, August 5, 1963, *Strictly Personal and Confidential: The Letters Harry Truman Never Mailed*, edited by Monte M. Poen, 35–36.
15. Winston Churchill, *Triumph and Tragedy*, 638.
16. HST diary, July 30, 1945, *Off the Record*, 57.
17. DDE, *Mandate for Change*, 5; and *Crusade*, 444; HST's CBS interview reported in *Kansas City Times*, February 3, 1958; Bradley and Blair, *A General's Life*, 444.
18. *Crusade*, 444.
19. HST speech, July 20, 1945, *Public Papers*, 174–5.
20. Lucius D. Clay, *Decision in Germany*, 44–5.
21. *Crusade*, 443.
22. HST to DDE, August 1, 1945, PSF, HSTL; DDE to Charles G. Ross, August 8, 1945, DDE *Papers, v. 6*, 253.

5. FORTUNES OF WAR

1. HST to Evangeline Booth, May 25, 1945, *Harry S. Truman Encylopedia*, edited by Richard S. Kirkendall, 386; and DDE, *Crusade*, 287.
2. *Crusade*, 431.
3. W.R. Smyser, *From Yalta to Berlin: The Cold War Struggle Over Germany*, 42–3.
4. *Diplomat Among Warriors*, 283–4.
5. John S. D. Eisenhower, 1976 interview with author.
6. DDE message to Commanders, May 14, 1945, *DDE Papers, v. 6*, 39–41.
7. George C. Patton to DDE, August 11, 1945; and DDE reply August 23, 1945, *DDE Papers, v. 6*, 307–8.
8. Carlo D'Este, *Patton: A Genius for War*, 766.
9. DDE to Mamie Doud Eisenhower, September 24, 1945; *Letters to Mamie*, edited by John S.D. Eisenhower, 272.
10. Kay Summersby, *Eisenhower Was My Boss*, 278.
11. DDE to George C. Marshall, June 4, 1945, *DDE Papers, v. 6*, 134–5.
12. DDE to MDE, June 4, 1945, *Letters to Mamie*, 257.
13. Marshall to DDE, June 8, 1945, *DDE Papers, v. 6*, 135.
14. Merle Miller, *Plain Speaking: An Oral Biography of Harry S. Truman*, 339–40; David Eisenhower, *Eisenhower at War*, 198; and Ambrose, *Eisenhower*, 417.
15. DDE to MDE, September 25, 1944, *Letters to Mamie*, 212.
16. *Eisenhower Speaks*, 29.
17. W. Averell Harriman and Elie Abel, Special Envoy to Churchill and Stalin, 503.
18. Harriman oral history interview, HSTL.
19. DDE to HST, August 8, 1945, PSF, HSTL.
20. DDE to Clay, November 8, 1945, *DDE Papers, v. 6*, 521.
21. HST, *Year of Decisions*, 235.
22. *Crusade*, 442–3.
23. *Year of Decisions*, 496–7.
24. Earl Harrison to HST, *Department of State Bulletin, v. 13*, 607.
25. HST to DDE, August 31, 1945, *Public Papers*, 355–6.
26. DDE to HST, September 14, 1945, *DDE Papers, v. 6*, 353–4.
27. DDE to HST, September 18, 1945, *DDE Papers, v. 6*, 357–61.
28. *HST Encylopedia*, 386; and Clay, *Decision in Germany*, 250–1.

29. DDE to HST, October 8, 1945, *DDE Papers, v. 6*, 414–8.
30. DDE to Marshall, October 13, 1945, DDE Papers, v. 6, 435–7.
31. *TNYT*, September 13, 1945.
32. DDE to HST, October 26, 1945, *DDE Papers, v. 6*, 479–80.
33. HST news conference, *Public Papers*, 450–2.
34. *At Ease*, 314; and DDE oral history, July 20, 1967, Columbia University.

6. WHAT CAN I DO TO HELP?

1. *Public Papers 1946*, 1–5.
2. War Department transcript, HST-DDE telephone conversation, HST File, EM.
3. DDE to Arthur William Tedder, June 13, 1946, *DDE Papers, v. 7*, 1121.
4. DDE to Edward E. Hazlett, November 27, 1945, *DDE Papers, v. 6*, 555; DDE diary, December 15, 1945, *The Eisenhower Diaries*, edited by Robert H. Ferrell, 136.
5. John C. Sparrow, *History of Personnel Demobilization in the United States Army*, 273.
6. *At Ease*, 318; and Steve Neal, *The Eisenhowers*, 228.
7. HST, *Public Papers 1946*, 75.
8. Sparrow, 169.
9. Ibid, 169–70.
10. Geoffrey Perret, *Eisenhower*, 362.
11. HST to DDE, January 16, 1945, *Off the Record*, 81.
12. DDE to HST, January 30, 1946, *DDE Papers, v.7*, 814–5.
13. *Public Papers 1948*, 328–9.
14. *Public Papers 1945*, 546–60.
15. DDE to Hazlett, November 27, 1945; Robert Griffith, *Ike's Letters to a Friend*, 27.
16. *Public Papers 1945*, 409.
17. DDE to Bernard Baruch, January 5, 1946, *DDE Papers, v. 7*, 735–6.
18. *The Gallup Poll, Volume 1 1935–1948*, George H. Gallup, 546, 549.
19. *Public Papers 1946*, 171.
20. DDE to Robert P. Patterson, April 27, 1946, *DDE Papers, v. 7*, 1045.
21. *Year of Decisions*, 553; DDE Oral History.
22. DDE oral history.
23. DDE to Marshall, May 28 and June 4, 1945, *DDE Papers, v. 7*, 1085, 1102.
24. Douglas MacArthur, *Reminiscences*, 315.
25. DDE to MacArthur, January 28, and May 28 1946, *DDE Papers, v. 7*, 797–800, 1086–7.
26. Joseph Alsop, *I've Seen the Best of It*, 337–8; DDE interview with James; and *Gallup Poll, v. 1*, 550.
27. *The Forrestal Diaries*, edited by Walter Millis, October 6, 1947; and *TNYT*, March 9, 1948.
28. *Gallup Poll, v. 1*, 580.
29. Robert J. Donovan, *Conflict and Crisis: The Presidency of Harry S. Truman, 1945–1948*, 212.
30. *Public Papers 1946*, 274–7.
31. DDE diary, May 26, 1946, *Diaries*, 136.
32. *Public Papers 1946*, 277–80.
33. *TNYT*, September 18, 1952.
34. *Public Papers 1952–3*, 581.

35. *Gallup Poll, v. 1*, 557, 594.
36. Ibid, 557, 604; and *Off the Record*, 102.
37. HST diary, December 11, 1946, *Off the Record*, 103.
38. HST to Eleanor Roosevelt, November 14, 1946, PSF.

7. AMERICA'S MISSION

1. Dean Acheson, *Present at the Creation*, 195–6.
2. Joseph Marion Jones, *The Fifteen Weeks*, 113.
3. Ibid, 64.
4. Robert Rhodes James, editor, *Complete Speeches of Winston S. Churchill, v.* 7, 7285–93.
5. HST to Byrnes, January 5, 1946, *Year of Decisions*, 551–2.
6. Arthur Krock, *Memoirs: Sixty Years on the Firing Line*, 48; and W. Averell Harriman, transcript of conversation about the Cold War, May 31, 1967, Harriman Papers, LC.
7. *American Relations with the Soviet Union: A Report to the President by the Special Counsel to the President*, 12, 73, 75, HST Papers, Naval Aide File.
8. George F. Kennan, *Memoirs, v. 1*, 557–8.
9. Jones, 141.
10. HST, *Memoirs, Volume 2, Years of Trial and Hope*, 103–4.
11. *Public Papers 1947*, 178–9.
12. Ronald Steel, *Walter Lippmann and the American Century*, 438–9; Arthur Krock, *In the Nation: 1932–1966*, 173.
13. *Gallup Poll*, v. 1, 639.
14. DDE to Patterson and Forrestal, March 13, 1947, *DDE Papers, v. 8*, 1592–6.
15. *Triumph and Tragedy*, 305.
16. Walter Bedell Smith to DDE, June 26, 1947, EM.
17. DDE Memorandum to Joint Chiefs, May 10, 1947, *DDE Papers, v. 8*, 1701.
18. Pogue, *Marshall, v. 4*, 200.
19. DDE diary, May 15, 1947, *Diaries*, 141.
20. Marshall's Harvard speech, Jones, 281–4.
21. DDE diary, September 16, 1947, *Diaries*, 144.
22. Jones, 256, and V. M. Molotov, *Molotov Remembers*, 61–2.
23. Thomas Bonner, *Our Recent Past*, 326.

8. COMMON CAUSE

1. HST, *Years of Trial and Hope*, 47.
2. Townsend Hoopes and Douglas Brinkley, *Driven Patriot: The Life and Times of James Forrestal*, 324.
3. *Public Papers 1945*, 559.
4. DDE memorandum to Joint Chiefs, March 15, 1946, *DDE Papers, v.* 7, 929; and David McCullough, *Truman*, 829.
5. Carl Vinson profile, *Encylopedia of the United States Congress, v. 4*, 2059–60.
6. Hoopes and Brinkley, 332–3.
7. *Forrestal Diaries*, May 13, 1946, 161.
8. Ibid, June 4, 1946, 166–7.
9. HST to Patterson and Forrestal, June 15, 1946, *Public Papers 1946*, 396–7.
10. Hoopes and Brinkley, 336.

11. *Forrestal Diaries*, September 10, 1946, 205.
12. Clark M. Clifford with Richard Holbrooke, *Counsel to the President*, 153.
13. Hoopes and Brinkley, 346.
14. DDE diary, July 24, 1947, *Diaries*, 142.
15. *DDE Papers, v. 9*, 1867.
16. DDE diary, July 24, 1947 and January 8, 1949, *Diaries*, 142 and 152.

9. JACOB'S LADDER

1. Gunnar Myrdal, *An American Dilemma: The Negro Problem and Modern Democracy*, 997.
2. John Egerton, *Speak Now Against the Day: The Generation Before the Civil Rights Movement in the South*, 362–3.
3. Walter F. White, *A Man Called White*, 330–1.
4. HST to Tom Clark, September 20, 1946, David Niles Papers, HSTL.
5. HST statement and Executive Order, December 5, 1946, is reprinted in *To Secure These Rights: The Report of the President's Committee on Civil Rights*, p. vii–ix.
6. HST to BWT, August 4 and October 2, 1939, *Dear Bess*, 417 and 421; DDE to John S. D. Eisenhower, February 26, 1943, *DDE Papers, v. 2*, 997.
7. Roy Wilkins, *Standing Fast*; HST address at Sedalia, Missouri, June 15, 1940, reprinted in *Congressional Record*, July 25, 1940, 4546.
8. HST address to National Colored Democratic Association, July 14, 1940, reprinted in *Congressional Record*, August 30, 1940, 5367–9.
9. DDE, *Waging Peace*, 139; and Ambrose, *Eisenhower*, 54–5.
10. Morris J. MacGregor, Jr., *Integration of the Armed Forces, 1940–1965*, 21–2.
11. Ibid, 51–2.
12. *Eisenhower Speaks*, 26–7.
13. Ibid, 157–8.
14. Theodore Bilbo to DDE, November 15, 1945, and DDE reply, December 21, 1945, *DDE Papers, v. 7*, 672–3.
15. MacGregor, 156.
16. White to DDE, March 28, 1946, *DDE Papers, v. 7*, 986.
17. DDE to Lawrence Dunbar Reddick, February 12, 1947, *DDE Papers, v. 8*, 1514.
18. C. L. Sulzberger, *A Long Row of Candles*, 616.
19. DDE testimony before Armed Services Committee, MacGregor, 228–9.
20. E. Frederick Morrow oral history interview, February 23, 1977, for Eisenhower Library.
21. HST address before NAACP, June 29, 1947, *Public Papers 1947*, 311–3.
22. White, 348.
23. HST civil rights address, February 2, 1948, *Public Papers 1948*, 121–6.
24. *Gallup Poll, v. 1*, 722–3; and Ralph McGill, "Will the South Ditch Truman?," *Saturday Evening Post*, May 22, 1948.
25. HST to Ernie Roberts, August 18, 1948, *Off the Record*, 146–7.
26. A. Philip Randolph testimony, MacGregor, 303.
27. *Counsel to the President*, 208.
28. Bradley and Blair, 485.
29. MacGregor, 430–1.
30. *TNYT*, November 23, 1999.

31. Martin Luther King, Jr., *A Testament of Hope*, 155. General Colin Powell, address at HSTL, July 24, 1998.

10. MUTUAL RESPECT

1. HST Farewell Address, *Public Papers 1952–3*, 1202.
2. HST interview with David M. Noyes, post-presidential files.
3. HST informal remarks, in auditorium of the Reorganized Church of Jesus Christ of Latter Day Saints, Independence, Missouri, June 27, 1945, HSTL Vertical Files; and the president's comments to reporters are reported in Time, April 23, 1945.
4. *Gallup Poll, v. 1*, 512.
5. Robert H. Ferrell, editor, *Truman in the White House: The Diary of Eben A. Ayers*, 26–7.
6. *Public Papers 1945*, 64.
7. Joseph E. Davies to DDE, July 9, 1948, EM.
8. Robert G. Nixon oral history by Jerry N. Hess, HSTL.
9. *Eisenhower Speaks*, 45.
10. *At Ease*, 334.
11. Fletcher Knebel, "The Inside Story of the Ike-Truman Feud," *Look*, September 6, 1955; and *Strictly Personal*, 156.
12. HST to DDE, October 30, 1946, EM.
13. William B. Ewald, Jr., *Eisenhower the President*, 33.
14. *Public Papers 1946*, 185–6; and *Public Papers 1947*, 268.
15. DDE to Milton S. Eisenhower, May 29, 1947, *DDE Papers, v. 8*, 1737–8; and DDE to Thomas J. Watson, June 14, 1947, Ibid, 1757.
16. *Eisenhower Speaks*, 238.
17. Irwin Ross, *The Loneliest Campaign*, 9–10.
18. DDE to MSE, October 16, 1947, *DDE Papers, v. 9*, 1986–7.
19. Richard Norton Smith, *Thomas E. Dewey and His Times*, 481, 556–7; and *Forrestal Diaries*, October 15, 1947, 326.
20. *Gallup Poll*, v. 1, 626.
21. HST interview for memoirs, post-presidential files.
22. Robert Sherwood, *Roosevelt and Hopkins*, 913.
23. Steel, *Lippmann*, 480–1.
24. Clifford and Holbrooke, *Counsel to the President*, 188; Knebel, "Inside Story"; and Harry H. Vaughan oral history by Charles T. Morrissey, HSTL.
25. Clark Clifford oral history by Jerry N. Hess, HSTL.
26. *Gallup Poll, v. 1*, 676; Cabell Phillips, *The Truman Presidency*, 196–7; Sulzberger, *Last of the Giants*, 578; and Robert H. Ferrell, editor, *The Diary of James C. Hagerty, 1954–55*, 177.
27. James H. Rowe memorandum on Truman's 1948 strategy, *Miscellaneous Historical Documents Collection*, HSTL.
28. *Eisenhower Speaks*, 242.
29. Marquis Childs, *Eisenhower: Captive Hero*, 103–05; Krock, *Memoirs*, 282–3.
30. DDE to Krock, December 10, 1947, *DDE Papers, v. 9*, 2132–3; Arthur H. Vandenberg, Jr., *The Private Papers of Senator Vandenberg*, 423–4.
31. Smith, *Dewey*, 481.

32. *Gallup Poll, v. 1*, 702–3.
33. DDE to Butcher, October 21, 1947, *DDE Papers, v. 9*, 1995.
34. DDE to Leonard V. Finder, January 22, 1948, *DDE Papers, v. 9*, 2191–3.
35. *Forrestal Diaries*, January 22, 1948, 365–6; Forrestal to HST, January 24, 1948, PSF.
36. DDE to HST, January 22, 1948, *DDE Papers, v. 9*, 2194; HST to DDE, January 23, 1948, EM; HST to DDE, January 23, 1948, EM.

11. LOOPHOLE

1. *Crusade*, 444.
2. Ibid, 480; and DDE to Davies, December 31, 1947, *DDE Papers, v. 9*, 2174.
3. *TNYT*, October 15, 1952.
4. *At Ease*, 325.
5. HST, interview for memoirs, PPF; and letter to John W. McCormack, January 10, 1957, *Off the Record*, 346.
6. Vaughan oral history, HSTL.
7. DDE to Archibald Wiggins, December 20, 1947, EM.
8. George J. Schoenman to DDE, December 22, 1947, EM.
9. DDE to Davies, December 23, 1947, *DDE Papers, v. 9*, 2159–60.
10. *TNYT*, October 15, 1952.
11. DDE to Schoenman, December 1, 1948, EM.
12. Davies to DDE, December 29, 1947, EM.
13. *At Ease*, 326.
14. Sherwood reviewed *Crusade* for *New York Herald Tribune Weekly Book Review*, November 21, 1948; Nevins made his comments in advance of the book's publication.
15. DDE to HST, November 19, 1948, *DDE Papers, v. 10*, 313; HST to DDE, November 24, 1948, EM; *Crusade*, autographed copy from DDE in HST's personal library.

12. SHADOW

1. Elmo Roper, *You and Your Leaders*, 22.
2. John M. Fenton, In Your Opinion, 68; William E. Leuchtenburg, *In the Shadow of FDR: From Harry Truman to Ronald Reagan*, 25.
3. HST interview for memoirs, August 25, 1953, post-presidential files; and FDR to HST, January 22, 1945, PSF: Longhand Notes File.
4. *Public Papers 1945*, 1; *Year of Decisions*, 323.
5. James H. Rowe oral history, HSTL; Jonathan Daniels oral history, HSTL.
6. *Gallup Poll*, 724; Raymond Moley column, *Newsweek*, March 8, 1948.
7. Harold L. Ickes to HST, March 27, 1948, Ickes Papers, LC; *The New Republic*, April 5, 1948.
8. DDE to Walter Bedell Smith, April 12, 1948, *DDE Papers, v. 10*, 41.
9. *Forrestal Diaries*, March 26, 1948, 404–5.
10. James Roosevelt oral history, Bancroft Library, University of California-Berkeley.
11. Hubert H. Humphrey, *The Education of a Public Man*, 110.
12. Eleanor Roosevelt to HST, March 26, 1948, PSF.
13. Donovan, *Conflict and Crisis*, 401.
14. DDE to HST, May 7, 1948, PSF; HST to DDE, May 10, 1948, EM.

15. Roper, *You and Your Leaders*, 238.
16. Jacob Arvey interview in Milton Rakove, *We Don't Want Nobody Sent*, 18.
17. Chester Bowles, *Promises to Keep*, 173–5.
18. DDE to Ernest K. Lindley, June 23, 1948, *DDE Papers, v. 10*, 121.
19. DDE diary, September 27, 1949, *Diaries*, 164.
20. Joseph Rauh oral history, HSTL.
21. James Roosevelt telegram to delegates, July 3, 1948; Roosevelt oral history.
22. Ayers diary, July 6, 1948, 264; George E. Allen oral history, HSTL.
23. DDE to Robert Herorn, July 5, 1948, *DDE Papers, v. 10*, 124.
24. Ayers diary, July 6, 1948, 264.
25. Krock, *Memoirs*, 243–4.
26. DDE to Claude Pepper, July 8, 1948, EM; DDE to James Roosevelt, July 8, 1948, *DDE Papers, v. 10*, 129; *Years of Trial and Hope*, 186.

13. MIRACLE

1. HST diary, July 12, 1948, *Off the Record*, 141–2.
2. Alben W. Barkley, *That Reminds Me*, 200.
3. HST interview for memoirs, August 25, 1953, PPF.
4. Acceptance speech, *Public Papers 1948*, 406–10.
5. Richard L. Strout oral history, HSTL.
6. Smith, *Thomas E. Dewey and His Times*, 505.
7. Clay, *Decision in Germany*, 361; and Bill Lawrence, *Six Presidents, Too Many Wars*, 165.
8. DDE to Alger Hiss, May 19, 1948, *DDE Papers, v. 10*, 76–7; and DDE to James Thomson Shotwell, September 21, 1948, *DDE Papers, v. 10*, 214.
9. *Public Papers 1948*, 433, 438.
10. Smith, *Dewey*, 507.
11. *TNYT*, May 22, 1948.
12. DDE to Harold E. Stassen, July 12, 1948, *DDE Papers, v. 10*, 41–2.
13. DDE to Thomas E. Dewey, September 10, 1948, *DDE Papers, v. 10*, 184.
14. Dewey to DDE, September 14, 1948, EM.
15. HST to DDE, October 12, 1948, EM.
16. DDE to HST, October 16, 1948, *DDE Papers, v. 10*, 249.
17. *Public Papers 1948*, 506.
18. Smith, *Dewey*, 532.
19. *Chicago Sun-Times*, November 4, 1948.
20. Dewey to HST, November 4, 1948, PSF.
21. Winston Churchill to HST, November 8, 1948, PSF.
22. HST to Churchill, November 18, 1948, PSF.
23. DDE to HST, November 18, 1948, *DDE Papers, v. 10*, 310.
24. HST to DDE, November 26, 1948, EM.

14. PENTAGON

1. DDE to Forrestal, November 4, 1948, *DDE Papers, v. 10*, 283.
2. Forrestal to HST, November 9, 1948, *DDE Papers, v. 10*, 283.
3. DDE to Forrestal, November 24, 1948, *DDE Papers, v. 10*, 322.
4. DDE diary, December 13, 1948, *Diaries*, 150–1.
5. DDE notes for meeting with Forrestal, December 9, 1948, EM.

6. Hoopes and Brinkley, *Driven Patriot*, 421–22, 428–30.
7. DDE diary, January 8, 1949, *Diaries*, 152–3.
8. DDE memorandum for meeting with HST, February 9, 1949, EM.
9. DDE diary, February 9, 1949, *Diaries*, 157.
10. DDE diary, February 19, 1949, *Diaries*, 157–8.
11. Memorandum to Joint Chiefs, *DDE Papers, v. 10*, 516.
12. *Public Papers 1949*, 165–6.
13. DDE to HST, April 6, 1949, PSF.
14. HST reply, April 9, 1949, EM.
15. DDE diary, February 2, 1949, *Diaries*, 156.
16. *At Ease*, 333.
17. Hoopes and Brinkley, *Driven Patriot*, 445.
18. DDE diary, June 11, 1949, *Diaries*, 160.
19. *At Ease*, 332.
20. DDE diary, June 4, 1949, *Diaries*, 159.
21. Ibid, July 17, 1949, *Diaries*, 162.
22. Bradley and Blair, 504.
23. HST to DDE, August 11, 1949, EM.
24. DDE to HST, August 17, 1949, *DDE Papers, v. 10*, 726.
25. *Washington Post*, March 30, 1950.
26. *Public Papers 1949*, 233.

15. TRIAL HEAT

1. *Gallup Poll, v. 1*, 744; DDE to HST, July 11, 1949, *DDE Papers, v. 10*, 774; and HST reply, August 18, 1949, EM.
2. *Gallup Poll, v. 2*, 864.
3. *Public Papers 1949*, 584–5.
4. Thomas E. Dewey oral history, Columbia University/DDE project.
5. Dewey to DDE, April 11, 1949, EM.
6. DDE diary, July 7, 1949, *Diaries*, 161.
7. Ibid, September 27, 1949, *Diaries*, 162–3.
8. *Gallup Poll, v. 2*, 856.
9. DDE diary, October 14, 1949 and January 1, 1950, *Diaries*, 164 and 168–70.
10. Ibid, September 27, 1949, *Diaries*, 164.
11. DDE diary, November 25, 1949, *Diaries*, 166.
12. Rick Ball and NBC News, *Meet the Press: Fifty Years of History in the Making*, 24.
13. DDE diary, October 13, 1950, *Diaries*, 177.
14. DDE to Robert Harron, October 16, 1950, and comment in *Columbia Spectator*, *DDE Papers, v. 11*, 1384–5.
15. *Public Papers 1950*, State of the Union message, 3.
16. *Gallup Poll, v. 2*, 902–3; and *Time*, January 16, 1950.
17. HST diary, April 16, 1950, *Off the Record*, 177–8.
18. *Gallup Poll, v. 2*, 834, 903–4.
19. DDE diary, April 27, 1950, *Diaries*, 174.

16. SCOUNDREL TIME

1. Richard H. Rovere, *Senator Joe McCarthy;* and Fred J. Cook, *The Nightmare Decade.*

2. Thomas C. Reeves, *The Life and Times of Joe McCarthy*, 225–7.
3. Robert J. Donovan, *Tumultuous Years: The Presidency of Harry S. Truman 1949–1953*, 162–3.
4. HST to Joseph R. McCarthy (unsent), February 11, 1950, *Off the Record*, 172.
5. *Public Papers 1950*, 163; and DDE, *Mandate*, 316.
6. HST to Mary Jane Truman, November 14, 1947, *Off the Record*, 119; and Herbert Block, *Herblock: A Cartoonist's Life*, 133–5.
7. Barton J. Bernstein and Allen J. Matusow, *The Truman Administration: A Documentary History*, 401–7.
8. *Public Papers 1950*, 236.
9. Philip C. Jessup to DDE, August 1, 1949, *DDE Papers, v. 10*, 713; DDE to Jessup, March 18, 1950, *DDE Papers, v. 11*, 1014; and DDE to Francis Joseph Toohey, March 27, 1950, *DDE Papers, v. 11*, 1033.
10. *Gallup Poll*, 911–2.
11. Bernstein and Matusow, 358.
12. HST interview for memoirs, August 10, 1953, PPF.
13. Clifford and Holbrooke, *Counsel to the President*, 175, 180.
14. Richard Gid Powers, *Not Without Honor: The History of American Anticommunism*, 216; *Gallup Poll, v. 2*, 891; and Clifford and Holbrooke, 181.
15. *Public Papers 1950*, 270–1.
16. *Truman Speaks*, 111; and DDE to Walter Bedell Smith, October 29, 1947, *DDE Papers*, v. 9, 2014.
17. DDE to Henry Steele Commager, June 16, 1949, DDE Papers, v. 10, 638; DDE to John S. Wood, June 23, 1950, *DDE Papers, v. 11*, 1029.
18. Cook, *Nightmare Decade*, 332–3.
19. *Public Papers 1950*, 650, 653.

17. A DISTANT WAR

1. Clay Blair, *The Forgotten War: America in Korea, 1950–1953*, 37.
2. Ibid, 40; and Matthew B. Ridgway, *The Korean War*, 7,12.
3. MacArthur comments, Robert H. Ferrell, *Harry S. Truman: A Life*, 318; and Acheson speech, Bernstein and Matusow, 435.
4. Ridgway, *Korean War*, 17.
5. HST, *Years of Trial and Hope*, 332–3.
6. *Public Papers 1950*, 492; and Ferrell, *Harry S. Truman*, 323.
7. *Gallup Poll, v. 2*, 943; Thomas E. Dewey to HST, June 27, 1950, *Public Papers 1950*, 496; and Donovan, *Tumultuous Years*, 222–3.
8. *TNYT*, June 29, 1950, and DDE diary, June 30, 1950, *Diaries*, 175; Bradley and Blair, *A General's Life*, 539.
9. DDE to Kenneth William Dobson Strong, June 29, 1950, *DDE Papers*, 1184; *Mandate*, 82–3.
10. Margaret Truman, *Harry S. Truman*, 461.
11. *Years of Trial and Hope*, 336; Ayers diary, July 1, 1950, *Truman in the White House*, 359–60; and Blair, *Forgotten War*, 78–9.
12. Robert J. Dvorchak, *Battle for Korea*, 16.
13. DDE to Hazlett, September 12, 1950, *DDE Papers, v. 11*, 1311.
14. HST diary, September 14, 1950, *Off the Record*, 192.
15. Blair, *Forgotten War*, 168.

16. DDE to MacArthur, October 28, 1950, *DDE Papers, v. 11*, 1393; HST to MacArthur, September 29, 1950, *Public Papers 1950*, 662; *Gallup Poll, v. 2*, 943; and D. Clayton James, *The Years of MacArthur: Triumph and Disaster*, 489.
17. Transcript of HST-MacArthur conference at Wake Island, *Foreign Relations of the United States 1950, v.* 7, 948–60; and Vernon Walters, *Silent Missions*, 206.
18. *Public Papers* 1950, 696; DDE to HST, November 1, 1950, PSF; and HST to DDE, November 4, 1950, EM.
19. Donovan, *Tumultuous Years*, 298.
20. James, *Triumph and Disaster*, 521; and 536.
21. *Public Papers 1950*, 295.
22. DDE diary, November 6 and December 15, 1950, *Diaries*, 151, 182.
23. *Public Papers 1950*, 746.

18. ALLIANCE

1. HST to DDE, October 19, 1950, EM; DDE diary, October 28, 1950, *Diaries*, 178; J. A. Carroll and M. W. Ashworth, *George Washington, v.* 7, *First in Peace*, by J. A. Carroll and M. W. Ashworth, 406; Don Cook, *Forging the Alliance: NATO 1945 to 1950*, 278.
2. James T. Patterson, *Mr. Republican: A Biography of Robert A. Taft*, 477; Richard Norton Smith, *An Uncommon Man: The Triumph of Herbert Hoover*, 390; *Public Papers 1950*, 761; and DDE diary, March 5, 1951, *Diaries*, 189.
3. *Gallup Poll, v. 2*, 912; *Public Papers 1949*, 196.
4. DDE oral history; Bradley and Blair, *A General's Life*, 542.
5. DDE to Hazlett, November 1, 1950, *DDE Papers, v. 11*, 1396.
6. DDE memorandum to HST, December 16, 1950, *DDE Papers, v. 11*, 1488–92.
7. HST and DDE remarks, transcribed from newsreel; *At Ease*, 366.
8. *Public Papers 1951*, 9.
9. Record of conversations, with Moch and Pleven, January 8, 1951, EM; Walters, *Silent Missions*, 214.
10. Memorandum of conversation with the Belgian Ministry of National Defense, January 10, and Dutch minister of defense, January 11, 1951, EM.
11. DDE's conference with the defense minister and chiefs of staff, Danish armed forces, January 12; and Memorandum of conversation with King Haakon VII of Norway, January 13, 1951, EM.
12. *At Ease*, 375.
13. Memorandum of conversation with Portugese Prime Minister Antonio Salazar, January 17, 1951, EM; and Walters, *Silent Missions*, 216.
14. Memorandum of conversations with Italian prime minister, January 18, and with Luxembourg prime minister, January 19, 1951, EM.
15. DDE to Acheson, January 9, 1951, Harriman Papers, LC; John J. McCloy to Acheson, January 9, 1951, Harriman Papers, LC.
16. DDE remarks at Rhein-Main Air Base, January 20, 1951, EM.
17. McCloy to Acheson, January 24, 1951, Harriman Papers, LC.
18. Walters, *Silent Missions*, 218; Memorandum of conversation with Icelandic cabinet, January 25, 1951, EM.
19. Meeting of DDE with HST and the Cabinet, January 31, 1951, notes dictated by George M. Elsey, PSF.

20. DDE oral history; *Mandate*, 13–14; *At Ease*, 370–2; Patterson, *Mr. Republican*,483–4.
21. DDE diary, April 9, 1951, *Diaries*, 190.

19. MACARTHUR

1. Statement on the cessation of hostilities, and remarks at the surrender ceremonies on the USS *Missouri* in Tokyo Bay, September 2, 1945; Major Vorin E. Whan, Jr., editor, *A Soldier Speaks: Public Papers and Speeches of General of the Army Douglas MacArthur*, 148–50.
2. MacArthur, *Reminiscences*, 288, 303.
3. HST interview with Ben Gradus, "The Truman Tapes"; DDE diary, October 8, 1937, *Prewar Diaries*, 363; DDE diary, January 19, 29 and February 3, 23, 1942, *Diaries*, 44, 46, 49.
4. DDE interview with D. Clayton James.
5. HST diary, June 17, 1945, *Off the Record*, 46–7.
6. Rudy Abramson, *Spanning the Century: The Life of W. Averell Harriman*, 453.
7. *A Soldier Speaks*, 218–22; MacArthur, *Reminiscences*, 341; Ayers diary, August 26, 1950, 368–9; DDE oral history for Herbert C. Hoover presidential library; William Manchester, *American Caesar: Douglas MacArthur 1880–1964*, 153.
8. *TNYT*, March 9, 1948; DDE to Butcher, April 12, 1948, *DDE Papers, v. 10*, 38; William F. Longwood, *Ike*, 86; Childs, *Captive Hero*, 43; DDE diary, September 26, 1936, October 8, 1937, *Prewar Diaries*, 328, 363.
9. *Public Papers 1950*, 673; *Years of Trial and Hope*, 365–7; MacArthur, *Reminiscences*, 360–4; Donovan, *Tumultuous Years*, 284–5; James, *Triumph and Disaster*, 506; Ayers diary, October 19, 1950, 377–8.
10. *Public Papers 1950*, 679.
11. Ridgway, *Korean War*, 63, 74–6; James, *Triumph and Disaster*, 536, 541.
12. Joint Chiefs of Staff to Commander-in-Chief, Far East, December 6, 1950, PSF.
13. DDE diary, April 9, 1951, *Diaries*, 191; DDE to Harriman, April 2, 1951, and Harriman reply, April 9, 1951, *DDE Papers, v. 12*, 179–82.
14. James, *Triumph and Disaster*, 585–7.
15. *Years of Trial and Hope*, 441–2; MacArthur to Joseph W. Martin, March 20, 1951, Bernstein and Matusow, 455.
16. HST diary, April 6, 1951, *Off the Record*, 210; *Public Papers 1951*, 222–3; MacArthur, *Reminiscences*, 395; *Gallup Poll, v. 2*, 981; Walters, *Silent Missions*, 225.
17. HST to DDE, April 12, 1951, EM; and HST to Harriman, April 24, 1951, Harriman Papers, LC.
18. *U.S. News & World Report*, April 20, 1951; *Gallup Poll, v. 2*, 982.
19. Clay to DDE, April 13, 1951, EM; DDE to Clay, April 16, 1951, *DDE Papers, v. 12*, 211; DDE to MacArthur, May 15, 1951, *DDE Papers, v. 12*, 288.
20. MacArthur address before joint congressional session, April 19, 1951, *A Soldier Speaks*, 242–53; and Sulzberger, *A Long Row of Candles*, 685.
21. Amanda Smith, *Hostage to Fortune*, 651, 654.

20. HOLDING THE LINE

1. *At Ease*, 332; HST to DDE, March 9, 1951, EM.
2. DDE to Hastings Lionel Ismay, January 3, 1951, *DDE Papers, v. 12*, 10; and to Edward John Birmingham, February 28, 1951, *DDE Papers, v. 12*, 76.

3. Walters, *Silent Missions*, 228.
4. Jean Monnet, *Memoirs*, 335–6; and Cook, *Forging the Alliance*, 248–9.
5. DDE to Marshall, August 3, 1951, *DDE Papers, v. 12*, 458–60.
6. Text of DDE's London address before English Speaking Union, July 3, 1951, EM; and *TNYT*, July 4, 1951; Churchill to DDE, July 5, 1951, EM.
7. First Annual Report of Supreme Allied Commander Europe, April 2, 1952, Harriman Papers, LC.
8. *Years of Trial and Hope*, 259; DDE to HST, February 24, 1951, *DDE Papers, v. 12*, 67; HST to DDE, March 9, 1951, EM.
9. DDE to Harriman, March 14, 1951, *DDE Papers, v. 12*, 127–9; HST to DDE, March 26, 1951, EM; DDE to HST, April 7, 1951, *DDE Papers, v. 12*, 198.
10. DDE to Marshall, July 17, 1951, *DDE Papers, v. 12*, 426–7.
11. HST to DDE, July 20, 1951, EM.
12. DDE to HST, September 22, 1951, *DDE Papers, v. 12*, 560; and HST to DDE, September 24, 1951, EM.
13. Notes dictated by George M. Elsey of HST's meeting with DDE in the Cabinet Room, November 5, 1951, Papers of Eben Ayers, HSTL.

21. BETWEEN US

1. HST interviews, October 19, 1953 and September 8, 1959, PPF; Harry Vaughan oral history, HSTL.
2. *Newsweek*, July 23, 1951; *Gallup Poll, v. 2*, 976–7; Joseph E. Davies, "The Eisenhower I Know," *The Diplomat*, February 1953; Davies diary, June 1951, Davies Papers, LC; DDE diary, June 14, 1951, *Diaries*, 195; DDE speech, "The Student in Politics," November 18, 1909, *Prewar Diaries*, 5–7.
3. DDE oral history; HST interview for memoirs, PPF.
4. DDE to Edward J. Birmingham, February 8, 1951, *DDE Papers, v. 12*, 37–9; and to William E. Robinson, March 6, 1951, *DDE Papers, v. 12*, 97–9; Sulzberger, *A Long Row of Candles*, 701–2.
5. *Public Papers 1951*, 456–7, 441; Forrestal, *Diary*, 343; and *Public Papers* 1951, 569.
6. DDE to James H. Duff, October 14, 1951, "Eisenhower's First Move" by William Bragg Ewald, Jr., *TNYT Magazine*, November 14, 1993.
7. *Gallup Poll, v. 2*, 1021; DDE diary, October 29, 1951, *Diaries*, 103.
8. *New York Herald Tribune*, October 25, 1951; DDE to Robinson, October 31, 1951, *DDE Papers, v. 12*, 670–3
9. *Public Papers 1951*, 603; *TNYT*, November 6, 1951.
10. *TNYT*, November 8, 1951; DDE to Arthur Hay Sulzberger, November 10, 1951, *DDE Papers, v. 12*, 701; *Public Papers 1951*, 629; Krock memorandum on HST-DDE meeting, Krock Papers, Mudd Manuscript Library, Princeton University; and Krock, *Memoirs*, 268–9.
11. *Gallup Poll, v. 2*, 1030–1.
12. HST to DDE, December 18, 1951, *Off the Record*, 220; and DDE to HST, January 1, 1952, *DDE Papers, v. 12*, 830–1.

22. DECISIONS

1. Henry Cabot Lodge, *The Storm Has Many Eyes*, 97; *TNYT*, January 8, 1952.
2. *Gallup Poll, v. 2*, 1048–9.
3. *Public Papers 1952–53*, 19–24; and HST to Frank Hodges, January 15, 1952, PSF.

4. HST to DDE, January 14, 1952, EM; DDE to HST, January 23, 1952, *DDE Papers, v. 13*, 907–8; and HST to DDE, January 31, 1952, EM.
5. *Years of Trial and Hope*, 489–91; Clifford and Holbrooke, *Counsel to the President*, 282–3; *Gallup Poll, v. 2*, 1038.
6. DDE diary, February 12 and 28, 1952, *Diaries*, 214–16.
7. DDE to HST, March 11, 1952, *DDE Papers, v. 13*, 1049–50.
8. *Public Papers 1952–53*, 207.
9. Ibid, 225; Tom L. Evans oral history, HSTL; *Public Papers 1952–53*, 233–4.
10. Theodore H. White, *In Search of History: A Personal Adventure*, 351; HST interview for memoirs, PPF.
11. DDE to HST, April 2, 1952; *DDE Papers, v. 13*, 1155–6.
12. HST to DDE, April 6, 1952, EM; *Public Papers 1952–53*, 309; HST interview for memoirs, PPF.
13. Childs, *Captive Hero*, 134; HST diary, August 19, 1952, *Off the Record*, 264; *Public Papers 1952–53*, 398.

23. ABILENE

1. David Halberstam, *The Powers That Be*, 231–2.
2. *Mandate for Change*, 32–6; *TNYT*, June 5, 1952; Richard L. Strout, "Ike in Abilene," June 16, 1952, *The New Republic*.
3. William Robinson, "Drafting Ike," in *Eisenhower: American Hero* by the editors of *American Heritage Magazine*, 94–96; and Lodge, *Storm*, 109.
4. *TNYT*, June 6, 1952.
5. *Newsweek*, June 23, 1952.
6. Text of Robert A. Taft's remarks on NBC Radio Network, June 1, 1952, Taft Papers, LC.
7. *Public Papers 1952–53*, 400–2.

24. SHOWTIME

1. Halberstam, *Powers That Be*, 232–4; and Richard H. Rovere, "Letter From Chicago," *The Eisenhower Years*, 34.
2. MacArthur keynote, *Official Proceedings of the Twenty-Fifth Republican National Convention*, 67–76; and James, *Triumph and Disaster*, 651.
3. *Chicago Sun-Times*, July 9, 1952.
4. HST diary, July 6, 1952, *Off the Record*, 260; and Walter Cronkite, *A Reporter's Life*, 71–2; and Brownell, *Advising Ike*, 111–6.
5. HST to Ethel Noland, July 11, 1952, *Off the Record*, 261–2.
6. Taft, Post-Convention Analysis, Taft Papers, LC; and HST letter to Noland.
7. *Mandate*, 44–7; James C. Hagerty oral history for Columbia University/DDE project.
8. Childs, *Captive Hero*, 134.
9. Sulzberger, *A Long Row of Candles*, 771; Donald Johnson, editor, *National Party Platforms, v. 1*, 496–7.
10. *TNYT*, July 12, 1952.
11. George E. Allen oral history, HSTL; and Knebel, "Ike-Truman Feud."
12. HST diary, July 6, 1952, *Off the Record*, 259–61; Barkley, *That Reminds Me*, 236–41; and HST interview for memoirs, October 19, 1953, PPF.

13. Adlai E. Stevenson to Charles S. Murphy, March 17, 1952, *Papers of Adlai E. Stevenson, v. 3*, 533; Adlai E. Stevenson, *Major Campaign Speeches*, 3–6.
14. HST diary, July 24, 1952, *Off the Record*, 262; *Years of Trial and Hope*, 496.
15. *Public Papers 1952–53*, 509; Stevenson, *Major Campaign Speeches*, 10; John S.D. Eisenhower interview with the author, 1973.

25. FIRST BREAK

1. HST to Stevenson, July 26, 1952, *Off the Record*, 263.
2. Carl McGowan oral history, HSTL.
3. HST diary, August 12, 1952, PPF; and Roger Tubby oral history, HSTL.
4. DDE to Walter Bedell Smith, August 14, 1952, *DDE Papers, v. 13*, 1323–4; and *TNYT*, August 13, 1952.
5. HST to DDE, August 13, 1952, and DDE reply, *Public Papers 1952–53*, 517–8.
6. Brownell, *Advising Ike*, 129; and *Public Papers 1952–53*, 518–9.
7. HST to DDE, August 16, 1952, *Off the Record*, 263–4; and DDE reply, *DDE Papers, v. 13*, 1327.
8. DDE to Smith, August 23, 1952, *DDE Papers, v. 13*, 1331; *TNYT*, August 22, 1952.
9. John Bartlow Martin, *Adlai Stevenson of Illinois*, 644; HST to Stevenson, early August and late August 1952 (both unsent), *Off the Record*, 267–9.
10. HST to John J. Sparkman, late August 1952, *Strictly Personal and Confidential: The Letters Harry Truman Never Mailed*, edited by Monte M. Poen, 122–3.
11. *Public Papers 1952–53*, 530.

26. PATRIOT GAMES

1. *Mandate*, 317; *TNYT*, August 24, 1952.
2. DDE to Edward Meade Earle, September 2, 1952, *DDE Papers, v. 13*, 1345–7.
3. Stevenson, *Major Campaign Speeches*, 20.
4. Smith, *Lucius Clay*, 603–4; Jenner's criticism of Eisenhower, *DDE Papers, v. 12*, 557; Herbert S. Parmet, *Eisenhower and the American Crusades*, 128; and Emmet John Hughes, *The Ordeal of Power*, 41.
5. HST to Nellie Noland, September 26, 1952, *Off the Record*, 272; DDE's threat to punch Jenner, *Newsweek*, November 10, 1952.
6. *Mandate*, 317; Hughes, *Ordeal*, 41–2.
7. Reeves, *McCarthy*, 437–9; Lawrence, *Six Presidents*, 311; Sherman Adams, *Firsthand Report*, 31.
8. DDE to Richard M. Nixon, October 1, 1952, *DDE Papers, v. 13*, 1366–7.
9. Text of DDE's Green Bay remarks, HSTL; and *Newsweek*, October 13, 1952.
10. Adams, *Firsthand Report*, 32; and *TNYT*, October 4, 1952.
11. Marshall's comment, *Time*, October 27, 1952; and Marquis Childs, *Witness to Power*, 68.
12. *Public Papers 1952–53*, 740, 784–5, 831–2.
13. DDE on Marshall, *Newsweek*, October 25, 1952; and Hughes, *Ordeal*, 277; and *Mandate*, 318.

27. DAYS OF ANGER

1. Donovan, *Tumultuous Years*, 398; and DDE to Dewey, October 8, 1954, *DDE Papers, v. 15*, 1337–8; and HST to Nellie Noland, September 26, 1952, *Off the Record*, 272.

2. *Public Papers 1952–53*, 612, 642, 651, 654.
3. DDE address in Des Moines, September 18, 1952; speech before Cook County Republican precinct captains, September 5, 1952, DDE speech file, HSTL.
4. George M. Elsey oral history, HSTL.
5. HST's "reign of slander" comment, *Public Papers 1952–53*, 858; and DDE, "slander-a-day," remarks in Harrisburg, Pennsylvania, October 27, 1952, speech file; HST's comments about DDE's racial conservatism, *Public Papers 1952–53*, 787–802, and 986; DDE's criticism of HST on poll tax, *Newsweek*, October 27, 1952.
6. *Public Papers 1952–53*, 1033; DDE speech, Madison Square Garden, *TNYT*, October 31, 1952.
7. Draft of DDE response to George Creel, *DDE Papers, v. 13*, 1370.
8. *Public Papers 1952–53*, 555,600.
9. Text of DDE speech, Point Pleasant, West Virginia, September 24, 1952, DDE Speech File, HSTL.
10. *Public Papers 1952–53*, 862–3; Alistair Cooke, Manchester *Guardian*, October 30, 1952; Rabbi Silver's comments in *TNYT*, October 19, 1952.
11. *Public Papers 1952–53*, 891; DDE response, *Washington Post*, October 29, 1952.
12. Associated Press report of Nixon's comments, October 6, 1952; and Ken Hechler, *Working with Truman*, 277; HST interviews, October 21 and 22, 1959, tapes 10 and 11, PPF.
13. Brownell, *Advising Ike*, 124.
14. *TNYT*, October 15, 1952; Edgar Eisenhower to DDE, October 15, 1952, and DDE reply, *DDE Papers, v. 13*, 1393.
15. *Gallup Poll, v. 2*, 1087–8; DDE's criticism of Truman on Korean War, *TNYT*, September 23 and October 3, 1952; HST's response, *Public Papers 1952–53*, 789–90, 850.
16. *Mandate*, 72–3; *TNYT*, October 25, 1952; *Public Papers 1952–53*, 945–50.
17. HST to DDE, November 5, 1952, EM; John S. D. Eisenhower, *Strictly Personal*, 158; Hughes, *Ordeal*, 54; Donovan, *Tumultuous Years*, 399; Smith, *Clay*, 603.
18. HST interview for memoirs, Eisenhower folder, HST diary, November 15, 1952, *Off the Record*, 273; Hechler, *Working with Truman*, 276–7.
19. Adams, *Firsthand Report*, 44; and HST interview, PPF.

28. CHANGING OF THE GUARD

1. HST diary, November 15, 1952, *Off the Record*, 273; HST to DDE, November 6, 1952, EM; DDE to HST, November 7, 1952, *DDE Papers, v. 13*, 1414.
2. HST diary, November 20, 1952, *Off the Record*, 274; DDE to HST, January 28, 1953, EM; John Steelman oral histories for HSTL and Columbia University/DDE project.
3. Memorandum of meeting between HST and DDE, November 18, 1952, HST papers, PSF.
4. Acheson, *Present at the Creation*, 706; HST diary, November 15 and 20, 1952, *Off the Record*, 273–5.
5. *Mandate*, 95; *Public Papers 1952–53*, 1073–6.
6. DDE oral history for John Foster Dulles project, Princeton University.
7. DDE memorandum on inaugural dress, December 30, 1952, *DDE Papers, v. 13*, 1465; DDE to MSE, December 30, 1952, Ibid, 1469–70.

8. *Public Papers 1952–53*, 1090; HST interview, PPF.
9. HST farewell address, January 15, 1953, *Public Papers 1952–53*, 1202.
10. DDE to HST, January 15, 1953, *DDE Papers, v. 13*, 1505; HST reply, January 16, 1953, PSF, HSTL.
11. *Public Papers 1952–53*, 1090; Ewald, *Eisenhower the President*, 32; Knebel, "Ike-Truman Feud;" and Gradus, "The Truman Tapes."
12. HST, *Mr. Citizen*, 19–20; DDE to HST, January 23, 1953, *DDE Papers, v. 14*, 9; and HST to DDE, January 28, 1953, EM.

29. THE BIG CHILL

1. Rovere, *The Eisenhower Years*, 346.
2. *Public Papers 1952–53*, 1196.
3. Ibid, 1198.
4. DDE to Hazlett, July 21, 1953, *DDE Papers, v. 14*, 406–7; Rovere, *Eisenhower Years*, 72; Ferrell, *Harry S. Truman*, 391
5. *DDE Public Papers 1953*, 585; HST interview, September 10, 1959, Tape No. 7, PPF.
6. HST interview, October 21, 1959, Tape No. 9, PPF; Knebel, "Ike-Truman Feud"; Sulzberger, *Last of the Giants*, 578; George E. Allen oral history, HSTL; Robert L. Schulz, oral history, Columbia University; Adams, *Firsthand Report*, 47.
7. Bernard Shanley to Maxwell Rabb, October 29, 1953; and Rabb reply, November 9, 1953, EM.
8. Brownell speech, Chicago *Daily News*, November 7, 1953; Martin, *Adlai E. Stevenson and the World*, 91–2; D. B. Hardeman and Donald C. Bacon, *Rayburn: A Biography*, 381–2.
9. *DDE Public Papers 1953*, 758–9; HST to Harold Velde, November 11, 1953; and HST nationally televised speech, November 16, 1953, PPF.
10. Alfred M. Gruenther to DDE, November 22, 1953; and DDE reply, *DDE Papers, v. 14*, 688–9; Allen Weinstein and Alexander Vassiliev, *The Haunted Wood: Soviet Espionage in America—The Stalin Era*, 168.
11. *Gallup Poll, v. 2*, 1188–9.
12. DDE diary, July 10, 1955, *Diaries*, 291.
13. HST midterm election speech, Kansas City, October 16, 1954, reprinted in *U.S. News & World Report*, October 29, 1954.
14. DDE to Dewey, October 8, 1954, *DDE Papers, v. 15*, 1337–9; DDE diary, November 20, 1954, *Diaries*, 288–9.
15. Edgar Eisenhower to DDE, November 1, 1954; and DDE reply, November 8, *DDE Papers, v. 15*, 1386–9.
16. *Independence Examiner*, January 20, 1955; DDE to HST, January 22, 1954, PPF; and BWT reply, January 24, 1953, EM.
17. Henry Cabot Lodge to DDE, September 7, 1955, *DDE Papers, v. 16*, 1849; *Chicago Daily News*, July 6, 1957.
18. HST speech at Carnegie Music Hall, Pittsburgh, October 8, 1956, PPF; *DDE Public Papers 1956*, 777, 811; HST interview with David Noyes and William Hillman, October 22, 1959, Tape 13, PPF.
19. HST to DDE, November 28, 1956 (unsent), *Off the Record*, 341; and Neal, *The Eisenhowers*, 381.

30. TWILIGHT

1. HST remarks, May 8, 1954, PPF; Chief Justice Earl Warren address at dedication ceremony, July 6, 1957, HSTL vertical file; *Kansas City Times*, July 4, 1957.
2. White House press secretary James C. Hagerty statement, June 4, 1957, HSTL vertical file; Three drafts of DDE message for HST Library dedication, EM; DDE's final version, HSTL.
3. HST to Acheson, July 10, 1957, PPF; *Chicago Daily News*, July 6, 1957.
4. *Mr. Citizen*, 57–8; Marie Hecht, *Beyond the Presidency*, 187.
5. *Time*, August 13, 1956; *Gallup Poll, v. 2*, 1536; *Kansas City Times*, March 20, 1957.
6. *Kansas City Times*, November 27, 1957; Childs, *Captive Hero*, 276; HST, "My View of the Presidency," *Look*, November 14, 1957.
7. *Kansas City Times*, June 5, 1955.
8. HST to Lyndon B. Johnson, December 11, 1956, *Off the Record*, 343–4.
9. DDE to HST, February 15, 1957, PPF; HST reply, February 19, 1957, EM.
10. *TNYT*, July 16, 1958; DDE to HST, July 17, 1958, PPF.
11. DDE to HST, September 27, 1958, PPF; HST reply, September 30, 1958, EM.
12. HST column, *TNYT*, September 14, 1958.
13. *Washington Post*, May 6, 1959; *Kansas City Times*, February 3, 1958; *Washington Post*, December 9, 1958; *DDE Public Papers 1958*, 855–6.
14. DDE to HST, May 20, 1958, PPF; HST reply May 23, 1958, EM; DDE to HST, January 30, 1959, PPF; HST reply, February 3, 1959, EM.
15. DDE to HST, April 30, 1959, PPF; HST reply May 5, 1959, EM.
16. *DDE Public Papers 1959*, 367, 371; HST's comment, *Washington Post*, May 6, 1959; HST to Acheson, 1959, PPF.
17. DDE's letter to Senator Thomas Dodd, quoted in *Kansas City Times*, November 20, 1959; HST to Joe Bailey Humphreys, November 24, 1959, PPF.
18. *DDE Public Papers 1959*, 728–9; HST interview with Noyes and Hillman, October 21, 1959, Tape No. 9, PPF.

31. 1960

1. *Truman Speaks*, 44–5; John S. D. Eisenhower 1973 interview with author; *Gallup Poll, v. 3*, 1651.
2. Ambrose, *Eisenhower, v. 2*, 560; Brownell, *Advising Ike*, 124; Ewald, *Eisenhower the President*, 184–7; Neal, *The Eisenhowers*, 412.
3. HST to Acheson, May 9, 1960, PPF; Ambrose, *Eisenhower, v. 2*, 575; *DDE Public Papers 1960–61*, 403.
4. Ibid, 623, 589–601.
5. HST interview with Noyes and Hillman, September 11, 1959, PPF; author interview with Senator Paul Simon, January 25, 2000; HST statement, July 2, 1960, vertical file, HSTL; JFK response, *TNYT*, July 5, 1960.
6. Acheson to HST, July 17, 1960 and HST reply, August 6, 1960, PPF; *Time*, August 29, 1960.
7. *DDE Public Papers 1960–61*, 657–8; Ambrose, *Eisenhower, v. 2*, 600.
8. Text of HST's Labor Day speech in Marion, Indiana and newspaper clippings about his campaign swing, David H. Stowe Papers, HSTL. Undated text of HST's comments about the religious issue in the 1960 election, PPF; HST-Morton exchange in *Time*, September 26, 1960.

9. *DDE Public Papers 1960–61*, 678.
10. HST's comments about Nixon, *Time*, October 24, 1960; *Joint Appearances of Senator John F. Kennedy and Vice President Richard M. Nixon, Presidential Campaign of 1960*, 210.
11. Ambrose, *Eisenhower, v. 2*, 601; Theodore C. Sorensen, "Election of 1960," 453, in *The Coming to Power: Critical Presidential Elections in American History*, edited by Arthur M. Schlesinger Jr.; *Newsweek*, October 10, 1960; *Time*, October 31 and November 7, 1960.
12. *DDE Public Papers 1960–61*, 819, 833; HST torchlight parade remarks, *Joint Appearances of Kennedy and Nixon*, 357.
13. *Speeches of Vice President Richard M. Nixon, Presidential Campaign of 1960*, 1057–8; Ambrose, *Eisenhower, v. 2*, 603; *DDE Public Papers 1960–61*, 856.
14. Ellis D. Slater, *The Ike I Knew*, 230; John S. D. Eisenhower, *Strictly Personal*, 285; HST column on Kennedy's election, *Kansas City Times*, November 15, 1960.

32. BYGONES

1. HST to JFK, September 12, 1961, PPF; *TNYT*, November 3, 1961.
2. Rufus B. Burrus, Robert P. Kennedy, and Samuel A. Montague oral histories, HSTL; *The New York Times*, *New York Herald Tribune*, *Kansas City Star*, and *Kansas City Times*, November 11, 1961 editions.
3. DDE to HST, November 13, 1961, PPF; HST to DDE, May 7, 1962, EM.
4. Burrus oral history.
5. DDE and HST comments about JFK's death reported by CBS News.
6. William Manchester, *The Death of a President*, 504, 596; Admiral Robert Dennison and Clifton Daniel oral histories, HSTL; Margaret Truman, *Harry S. Truman*, 575–6; Warren Rogers, "Truman-Ike Feud at End," *Los Angeles Herald-Examiner*, December 5, 1963.
7. HST to DDE, October 14, 1965, EM; Milton S. Eisenhower oral history; DDE to HST, June 9, 1966, PPF.
8. DDE to HST, November 18, 1965, and January 6, 1967, PPF; HST to DDE, January 18, 1967.
9. DDE to HST, June 1, 1967, and HST reply, June 12, PPF.
10. *Waging Peace*, 652; Ewald, *Eisenhower the President*, 37; DDE oral history.
11. HST to Mamie Doud Eisenhower, March 29, 1969, PPF; HST tribute on DDE's death, PPF; Churchill is quoted in Roger Tubby's journal, which is excerpted in his oral history, HSTL.

Bibliography

MANUSCRIPTS

Dean Acheson Papers, Harry S. Truman Library.
Joseph Alsop Papers, Library of Congress.
Eben A. Ayers Papers, Harry S. Truman Library.
Clark Clifford Papers, Harry S. Truman Library.
Joseph E. Davies Papers, Library of Congress.
Dwight D. Eisenhower Papers, Dwight D. Eisenhower Library.
James A. Farley Papers, Library of Congress.
W. Averell Harriman Papers, Library of Congress.
Paul G. Hoffman Papers, Harry S. Truman Library.
Harold L. Ickes Papers, Library of Congress.
Arthur Krock Papers, Mudd Manuscript Library, Princeton University.
Charles S. Murphy Papers, Harry S. Truman Library.
David Niles Papers, Harry S. Truman Library.
Charles G. Ross Papers, Harry S. Truman Library.
Robert A. Taft Papers, Library of Congress.
Harry S. Truman Papers, Harry S. Truman Library.

ORAL HISTORIES

Dean Acheson, HSTL.
Sherman Adams, COHP.
Konrad Adenauer, HSTL.
George E. Allen, HSTL.
Joseph Alsop, COHP.
Eben A. Ayers, HSTL.
Evan P. Aurand, COHP.
Lucius Battle, HSTL.
Jack L. Bell, HSTL and COHP.
Bernard Bernstein, HSTL.
Andrew J. Biemiller, HSTL.
Richard M. Bissell, HSTL.
William McCormick Blair, HSTL.
Charles Bohlen, COHP.
Herbert Brownell, COHP and EL.
David K. E. Bruce, HSTL.
Lawrence E. Bunker, HSTL.
Rufus B. Burrus, HSTL.
Prescott Bush, COHP.
Henry Byroade, HSTL.
Ralph H. Cake, COHP.
C. Craig Cannon, COHP.
Tom C. Clark, HSTL.

Lucius D. Clay, COHP and HSTL.
Clark M. Clifford, HSTL.
Jacqueline Cochran, EL.
Matthew J. Connelly, HSTL.
Clifton Daniel, HSTL.
Margaret Truman Daniel, HSTL.
Jonathan Daniels, HSTL.
Harry Darby, COHP.
C. Girard Davidson, HSTL.
Robert L. Dennison, HSTL.
Thomas E. Dewey, COHP.
William K. Divers, HSTL.
Robert J. Donovan, COHP.
Roscoe Drummond, COHP.
Dwight D. Eisenhower, COHP, Dulles Oral History Project, Hoover Oral History Project, interviews with D. Clayton James about Douglas MacArthur, with Forrest Pogue about George C. Marshall.
John S.D. Eisenhower, COHP and EL.
Milton S. Eisenhower, COHP and EL.
George M. Elsey, HSTL.
Tom L. Evans, HSTL.
William Ewald, EL.
Arthur S. Flemming, EL.
Edward T. Folliard, HSTL.
Sue Gentry, HSTL.
Andrew J. Goodpaster, COHP and EL.
Wallace Graham, HSTL.
James C. Hagerty, COHP.
W. Averell Harriman, HSTL.
Paul G. Hoffman, HSTL.
Walter Judd, COHP.
Milton Katz, HSTL.
Mary Paxton Keeley, HSTL.
James Loeb, HSTL.
Robert A. Lovett, HSTL.
John J. McCloy, COHP.
E. Frederic Morrow, COHP and EL.
Charles S. Murphy, HSTL.
Robert D. Murphy, COHP.
Philleo Nash, HSTL.
Paul H. Nitze, HSTL.
Robert G. Nixon, HSTL.
John H. Ohly, HSTL.
Frank Pace, Jr., HSTL.
Edwin Noel Plowden, HSTL.
Joseph L. Rauh, HSTL.
J. Leonard Reinsch, HSTL.
Robert L. Riggs, HSTL.

James Roosevelt, University of California-Berkeley, Earl Warren Project.
Samuel I. Rosenman, HSTL.
Richard H. Rovere, COHP.
James H. Rowe, Jr., HSTL.
James J. Rowley, HSTL.
Robert L. Schulz, COHP and EL.
Merriman Smith, COHP.
John W. Snyder, HSTL.
John R. Steelman, HSTL and EL.
Richard L. Strout, HSTL.
Stuart Symington, HSTL.
Theodore Tannewald, Jr.
Roger Tubby, HSTL.
Harry H. Vaughan, HSTL.
Vernon Walters, EL.
Earl Warren, HSTL.

BOOKS AND ARTICLES

Abramson, Rudy. *Spanning the Center: The Life of W. Averell Harriman, 1891-1986.* New York: Morrow, 1992.

Acheson, Dean. *Among Friends: Personal Letters of Dean Acheson*, edited by David S. McLellan and David C. Acheson. New York: Dodd, Mead, 1980.

——*Present at the Creation.* New York: Norton, 1969.

——*Sketches from Life of Men I Have Known.* New York: Harper, 1960.

Ambrose, Stephen E. *D-Day June 6, 1944: The Climactic Battle of World War II.* New York: Simon and Schuster, 1994.

——*Eisenhower: Soldier, General of the Army, President Elect.* New York: Simon and Schuster, 1983.

——*Eisenhower the President.* New York: Simon and Schuster, 1984.

——*The Supreme Commander: The War Years of General Dwight D. Eisenhower.* Garden City, N.Y.: Doubleday, 1970.

Allen, George E. *Presidents Who Have Known Me.* New York: Simon and Schuster, 1950.

Alsop, Joseph W. *I've Seen the Best of It.* New York: Norton, 1992.

Barkley, Alben W. *That Reminds Me.* Garden City, N.Y.: Doubleday, 1954.

Bernstein, Barton J. and Allen J. Matusow, editors. *The Truman Administration: A Documentary History.* New York: Harper and Row, 1966.

Blair, Clay. *The Forgotten War: America in Korea, 1950-53.* New York: Times Books, 1987.

Block, Herbert. *Herblock: A Cartoonist's Life.* New York: MacMillan/A Lisa Drew Book, 1993.

Blum, John Morton, editor. *The Price of Vision: The Diary of Henry A. Wallace, 1942-1946.* Boston: Houghton Mifflin, 1973.

Bowles, Chester. *Promises to Keep: My Years in Public Life.* New York: Harper and Row, 1971.

Bradley, Omar N. and Clay Blair. *A General's Life.* New York: Simon and Schuster, 1983.

Branch, Taylor. *Parting the Waters: America in the King Years 1954-63.* New York: Simon and Schuster, 1988.

Brinkley, Douglas. *Dean Acheson: The Cold War Years, 1953-1971.* New Haven: Yale University Press, 1992.

Burns, James MacGregor. *Roosevelt: The Soldier of Freedom.* New York: Harcourt, Brace, 1970.

Butcher, Harry C. *My Three Years with Eisenhower.* New York: Simon and Schuster, 1946.

Byrnes, James F. *All in One Lifetime.* New York: Harper, 1958.

Catton, Bruce. *The War Lords of Washington.* New York: Harcourt, Brace, 1948.

Chace, James. *Acheson.* New York: Simon and Schuster, 1998.

Childs, Marquis W. *Eisenhower: Captive Hero.* New York: Harcourt, Brace, 1958.

——*Witness to Power.* New York: McGraw-Hill, 1975.

Churchill, Winston S. *The Second World War, Volume VI, Triumph and Tragedy.* Boston: Houghton Mifflin, 1953.

Clay, Lucius D. *Decision in Germany.* Garden City, N.Y.: Doubleday, 1950.

Clifford, Clark M. with Richard Holbrooke, *Counsel to the President.* New York: Random House, 1991.

Cook, Don. *Forging the Alliance: NATO 1945 to 1950.* London: Secker & Warburg, 1989.

Cook, Fred J. *The Nightmare Decade: The Life and Times of Senator Joe McCarthy.* New York: Random House, 1971.

Cronkite, Walter. *A Reporter's Life.* New York: Knopf, 1996.

Dalfiume, Richard M. *Desegregation of the U.S. Armed Forces.* Columbia: University of Missouri Press, 1969.

Daniels, Jonathan. *The Man of Independence.* Philadelphia: Lippincott, 1950.

Davis, Kenneth S. *Soldier of Democracy.* Garden City, N.Y.: Doubleday, 1945.

D'Este Carlo. *Patton: A Genius for War.* New York: HarperCollins, 1995.

Donovan, Robert J. *Conflict and Crisis: The Presidency of Harry S. Truman, 1945-1948.* New York: Norton, 1977.

——*Eisenhower: The Inside Story.* New York: Harper, 1956.

——*Tumultuous Years: The Presidency of Harry S. Truman, 1949-1953.* New York: Norton, 1982.

Dunar, Andrew J. *The Truman Scandals and the Politics of Morality.* Columbia: University of Missouri Press.

Dvorchak, Robert J. *Battle for Korea: The Associated Press History of the Korean Conflict.* Conshocken, Pa.: Combined Books, 1993.

Egerton, John. *Speak Now Against the Day: The Generation Before the Civil Rights Movement in the South.* New York: Knopf, 1994.

Eisenhower, David. *Eisenhower at War 1943-1945.* New York: Random House, 1986.

Eisenhower, Dwight D. *At Ease: Stories I Tell to Friends.* Garden City, N.Y.: Doubleday, 1967.

——*Crusade in Europe.* Garden City, N.Y.: Doubleday, 1948.

——*The Papers of Dwight D. Eisenhower,* 17 volumes, edited by Alfred D. Chandler, Jr., and Louis Galumbos. Baltimore: Johns Hopkins Press, 1970-1996.

——*Public Papers of the Presidents, 1953-1961,* in eight volumes. Washington, D.C.: Government Printing Office, 1954-1962.

——*The White House Years: Mandate for Change, 1953-1956.* Garden City, N.Y.: Doubleday, 1963.

——*The White House Years: Waging Peace, 1956-1961.* Garden City, N.Y.: Doubleday, 1965.

Eisenhower, John S. D., editor, *Letters to Mamie*. Garden City, N.Y.: Doubleday, 1978.
——*Strictly Personal*. Garden City, N.Y.: Doubleday, 1974.
Eisenhower, Milton S. *The President is Calling*. Garden City, N.Y.: Doubleday, 1974.
Ewald, William Bragg, Jr. *Eisenhower the President*. Englewood Cliffs, N.J.: Prentice Hall, 1981.
Fenton, John M. *In Your Opinion*. Boston: Little, Brown, 1960.
Ferrell, Robert H. *The Autobiography of Harry S. Truman*. Boulder: Colorado Associated University Press, 1980.
——*Choosing Truman: The Democratic Convention of 1944*. Columbia: University of Missouri Press, 1994.
——*Dear Bess: The Letters from Harry to Bess Truman, 1910–1959*. New York: Norton, 1983
——*The Diary of James C. Hagerty*. Bloomington: Indiana University Press, 1983.
——editor: *The Eisenhower Diaries*. New York: Norton, 1981.
——*Harry S. Truman: A Life*. Columbia: University of Missouri Press, 1994.
——*Harry S. Truman: His Life on the Family Farm*. Worland, Wyo.: High Plains, 1991.
——*Ill-Advised: Presidential Health and Public Trust*. Columbia: University of Missouri Press, 1992.
——*Off the Record: The Private Papers of Harry S. Truman*. New York: Harper and Row, 1980.
——*Truman: A Centenary Remembrance*. New York: Viking, 1984.
——*Truman & Pendergast*. Columbia: University of Missouri Press, 1999.
——*Truman in the White House: The Diary of Eben A. Ayers*. Columbia: University of Missouri Press, 1991.
Frank, Richard B. *Downfall: The End of the Imperial Japanese Empire*. New York: Random House, 1999.
Freeland, Richard M. *The Truman Doctrine and the Origins of McCarthyism*. New York: Knopf, 1972.
Fromkin, David. *In the Time of the Americans*. New York: Knopf, 1995.
Gaddis, John Lewis. *The United States and the Origins of the Cold War*. New York: Columbia University Press, 1972.
——*We Now Know: Rethinking Cold War History*. New York: Oxford University Press, 1997.
Gallup, George H. *The Gallup Poll: Public Opinion Index, 1935-1971*, in three volumes. New York: Random House, 1972.
Gardner, Lloyd C. *Architects of Illusion: Men and Ideas in American Foreign Policy, 1941-1949*. Chicago: Quadrangle Books, 1970.
Goodwin, Doris Kearns. *No Ordinary Time: Franklin and Eleanor Roosevelt: The Home Front in World War II*. New York: Simon and Schuster, 1994.
Goulden, Joseph G. *The Best Years, 1945-1950*. New York: Atheneum, 1976.
Greenstein, Fred I. *The Hidden-Hand Presidency: Eisenhower as Leader*. New York: Basic Books, 1982.
Gress, David. *From Plato to NATO: The Idea of the West and Its Opponents*. New York: The Free Press, 1998.
Griffith, Robert W. *Ike's Letters to a Friend*. Lawrence: University Press of Kansas, 1984.
——*The Politics of Fear: Joseph R. McCarthy and the Senate*. Lexington: University of Kentucky Press, 1970.

Grosser, Alfred. *The Western Alliance.* New York: Vintage Books, 1982.
Halberstam, David. *The Fifties.* New York: Villard Books, 1993.
——*The Powers that Be.* New York: Knopf, 1979.
Hamby, Alonzo L. *Beyond the New Deal: Harry S. Truman and American Liberalism.* New York: Columbia University Press, 1973.
——*Man of the People: A Life of Harry S. Truman.* New York: Oxford University Press, 1995.
Hardeman, D.B. and Donald C. Bacon. *Rayburn: A Biography.* Austin: Texas Monthly Press, 1987.
Harriman, W. Averell with Elie Abel. *Special Envoy to Churchill and Stalin.* New York: Random House, 1975.
Hart, Scott. *Washington at War: 1941-1945.* Englewood Cliffs, N.J.: Prentice Hall, 1970.
Hecht, Marie. *Beyond the Presidency.* New York: Macmillan, 1976.
Hersey, John. *Aspects of the Presidency.* New York: Ticknor and Fields, 1980.
——*Hiroshima.* New York: Knopf, 1946.
Hillman, William. *Mr. President.* New York: Farrar, Straus and Young, 1952.
Hodgson, Godfrey. *The Colonel: The Life and Wars of Henry Stimson.* New York: Knopf 1990.
Holt, Daniel D. and James W. Leyerzapf. *Eisenhower: The Prewar Diaries and Selected Papers, 1905-1941.* Baltimore: Johns Hopkins University Press, 1998.
Hoopes, Townsend and Douglas Brinkley. *Driven Patriot: The Life and Times of James V. Forrestal.* New York: Knopf, 1982.
Hughes, Emmet John. *The Ordeal of Power: A Political Memoir of the Eisenhower Years.* New York: Atheneum, 1963.
Humphrey, Hubert H. *The Education of a Public Man.* Garden City, N.Y.: Doubleday,1976.
James, D. Clayton. *The Years of MacArthur: Triumph & Disaster, 1945-1964.* Boston: Houghton Mifflin, 1985.
Johnson, Walter. *How We Drafted Stevenson.* New York: Knopf, 1955.
——editor, *The Papers of Adlai E. Stevenson,* eight volumes. Boston: Little, Brown, 1972-79.
Jones, Joseph M. *The Fifteen Weeks (February 21-June 5, 1947).* New York: Viking, 1955.
Karabell, Zachary. *The Last Campaign.* New York: Knopf, 2000.
Kennan, George F. *Memoirs: 1925-1950.* Boston: Atlantic Little Brown, 1967.
King, Martin Luther, Jr. *A Testament of Hope: The Essential Writings and Speeches.* New York: HarperCollins, 1986.
Kirkendall, Richard S. *The Harry S. Truman Encylopedia.* Boston: G.K. Hall, 1989.
Knebel, Fletcher. "The Inside Story of the Ike-Truman Feud." *Look, v. 19, Number 18.* September 6, 1955.
Krock, Arthur. *The Consent of the Governed and Other Deceits.* Boston: Little, Brown, 1971.
——*In the Nation: 1932-1966.* New York: McGraw Hill, 1966.
——*Memoirs: Sixty Years on the Firing Line.* New York: Funk & Wagnalls, 1968.
Lacey, Michael J., editor. *The Truman Presidency.* New York and Cambridge: Cambridge University Press, 1989.
Larson, Arthur. *Eisenhower: The President Nobody Knew.* New York: Scribner's, 1968.

Lawrence, Bill. *Six Presidents, Too Many Wars*. New York: Saturday Review Press, 1972.
Lodge, Henry Cabot. *The Storm Has Many Eyes*. New York: Norton, 1973.
MacArthur, Douglas. *Reminiscences*. New York: McGraw-Hill, 1964.
——*A Soldier Speaks: Public Papers and Speeches*. New York: Praeger, 1965.
Manchester, William. *American Caesar: Douglas MacArthur 1880-1964*. Boston: Little, Brown, 1978.
——*The Death of a President*. New York: Harper and Row, 1967.
Leuchtenburg, William E. *In the Shadow of FDR: From Harry Truman to Ronald Reagan*. Ithaca: Cornell University Press, 1983.
Lyon, Peter. *Eisenhower: Portrait of the Hero*. Boston: Little, Brown, 1974.
MacGregor, Morris J., Jr. *Integration of the Armed Forces, 1940-1965*. Washington: Center of Military History, United States Army, 1981.
Martin, John Bartlow. *Adlai Stevenson and the World*. Garden City, N.Y.: Doubleday, 1977.
——*Adlai Stevenson of Illinois*. Garden City, N.Y.: Doubleday, 1976.
McClellan, David S. *Dean Acheson: The State Department Years*. New York: Dodd, Mead, 1976.
McCoy, Donald. *The Presidency of Harry S. Truman*. Lawrence: University Press of Kansas, 1984.
McCoy, Donald and Richard T. Reutten. *Quest and Response: Minority Rights and the Truman Administration*. Lawrence: University Press of Kansas, 1983.
McCullough, David. *Truman*. New York: Simon and Schuster, 1992.
Mee, Charles L. *The Marshall Plan*. New York: Simon and Schuster, 1984.
——*Meeting at Potsdam*. New York: Evans, 1975.
Merry, Robert W. *Taking on the World: Joseph and Stewart Alsop—Guardians of the American Century*. New York: Viking, 1996.
Miller, Richard Lawrence. *Truman: The Rise to Power*. New York: McGraw-Hill, 1986.
Millis, Walter, editor. *The Forrestal Diaries*. New York: Viking, 1951.
Monnet, Jean. *Memoirs*. Garden City, N.Y: Doubleday, 1978.
Morrow, E. Frederic. *Black Man in the White House*. New York: Coward, McCann, 1963.
Moskin, J. Robert. *Mr. Truman's War*. New York: Random House, 1996.
Murphy, Robert. *Diplomat Among Warriors*. Garden City, N.Y.: Doubleday, 1964.
Myrdal, Gunnar. *An American Dilemma*. New York: Harper and Row, 1944.
Neal, Steve. *The Eisenhowers: Reluctant Dynasty*. Garden City, N.Y.: Doubleday, 1978.
Parmet, Herbert S. *Eisenhower and the American Crusades*. New York: Macmillan, 1972.
Parrish, Thomas. *Berlin in the Balance*. Reading, Mass. : Addison-Wesley, 1998.
Patterson, James T. *Grand Expectations: The United States, 1945-1974*. New York: Oxford University Press, 1996.
——*Mr. Republican: A Biography of Robert A. Taft*. Boston: Houghton Mifflin, 1972.
Perret, Geoffrey. *A Dream of Greatness: The American People 1945-1963*. New York: Coward, McCann, 1979.
——*Eisenhower*. New York: Random House, 1999.
Phillips, Cabell. *The Truman Presidency*. New York: Macmillan, 1966.
Pogue, Forrest C. *George C. Marshall: Statesman*. New York: Viking, 1987.
Poen, Monte M. *Letters Home by Harry Truman*. New York: Putnam, 1984.
——*Strictly Personal and Confidential: The Letters Harry Truman Never Mailed*. Boston: Little, Brown, 1982.

Powers, Richard Gid. *Not Without Honor.* New York: The Free Press, 1995.

Reeves, Thomas C. *The Life and Times of Joe McCarthy.* New York: Stein and Day, 1982.

Ridgway, Matthew B. *The Korean War.* Garden City, N.Y.: Doubleday, 1967.

Robertson, David. *Sly and Able: A Political Biography of James F. Byrnes.* New York: Norton, 1994.

Roper, Elmo. *You and Your Leader.* New York: Morrow, 1957.

Ross, Irwin. *The Loneliest Campaign: The Truman Victory of 1948.* New York: New American Library, 1968.

Rovere, Richard H. *The Eisenhower Years.* New York: Farrar, Straus, 1956.

——with Arthur Schlesinger, Jr. *The MacArthur Controversy and American Foreign Policy.* Revised edition. New York: Noonday Press, 1965.

——*Senator Joe McCarthy.* New York: Harcourt, Brace, 1959.

Schlesinger, Arthur M., Jr. editor, *The Coming to Power: Critical Elections in American History.* New York: Chelsea House/McGraw-Hill, 1972.

——*The Vital Center.* Boston: Houghton Mifflin, 1949.

Slater, Ellis D. *The Ike I Knew*, privately printed, 1980.

Smith, Amanda. *Hostage to Fortune: The Letters of Joseph P. Kennedy.* New York: Viking, 2001.

Smith, Jean Edward. *Lucius D. Clay: An American Life.* New York: Henry Holt, 1990.

Smith, Richard Norton. *Thomas E. Dewey and His Times.* New York: Simon and Schuster, 1982.

Smith, Walter Bedell. *Eisenhower's Six Great Decisions.* New York: Longmans, Green, 1956.

Smyser, W.R. *From Yalta to Berlin: The Cold War Struggle Over Germany.* New York: St. Martin's Press, 1999.

Spanier, John W. *The Truman-MacArthur Controversy.* Cambridge: Harvard University Press, 1959.

Sparrow, John C. *History of Personnel Demobilization in the United States Army.* Washington: Department of the Army, 1952.

Steel, Ronald. *Walter Lippmann and the American Century.* Boston: Little, Brown, 1980.

Stevenson, Adlai. *Major Campaign Speeches of 1952.* New York: Random House, 1953.

Strout, Richard L. *TRB: Views and Perspectives on the Presidency.* New York: Macmillan, 1979.

Sulzberger, C. L. *The Last of the Giants.* New York: Macmillan, 1970.

——*A Long Row of Candles: Memoirs and Diaries, 1934-1954.* New York: Macmillan, 1969.

Summersby, Kay. *Eisenhower Was My Boss.* New York: Prentice-Hall, 1948.

Truenfels, Rudolph L. *Eisenhower Speaks: A Selection of His Speeches and Messages.* New York: Farrar Straus, 1948.

Truman, Harry S. *Memoirs: Year of Decisions.* Garden City, N.Y.: Doubleday, 1955.

——*Memoirs: Years of Trial and Hope.* Garden City, N.Y.: Doubleday, 1956.

——*Mr. Citizen.* New York: Bernard Geis, 1960.

——*Public Papers of the Presidents, 1945-1953*, eight volumes. Washington: Government Printing Office, 1961-66.

——*Truman Speaks.* New York: Columbia University Press, 1960.

Truman, Margaret. *Bess W. Truman.* New York: Macmillan, 1986

——*Harry S. Truman.* New York: Morrow, 1972.

Vandenberg, Arthur H., Jr. *The Private Papers of Senator Vandenberg*. Boston: Houghton Mifflin, 1952.

Walters, Vernon A. *Silent Missions*. Garden City, N.Y: Doubleday, 1978.

Weinstein, Allen. *Perjury: The Hiss-Chambers Case*. New York: Random House, revised edition, 1997.

——with Alexander Vassiliev. *The Haunted Wood: Soviet Espionage in America—The Stalin Era*. New York: Modern Library, 1999.

West, J. B. *Upstairs at the White House*. New York: Coward, McCann, 1973.

White, Theodore H. *In Search of History*. New York: Harper and Row, 1978.

——*The Making of the President 1960*. New York: Atheneum, 1962.

White, Walter. *A Man Called White*. New York: Viking, 1948.

Wilkins, Roy. *Standing Fast: The Autobiography of Roy Wilkins*. New York: Viking, 1982.

Woodward, C. Vann, *The Strange Case of Jim Crow*. New York: Oxford University Press, revised edition, 1974.

Yergin, Daniel. *Shattered Peace: The Origins of the Cold War and the National Security State*. Boston: Houghton Mifflin, 1977.

Index